Evidence in European Asylum Procedures

Immigration and Asylum Law and Policy in Europe

Edited by

Jan Niessen
Elspeth Guild

VOLUME 25

The titles published in this series are listed at brill.nl/ialp

Evidence in European Asylum Procedures

By
By
Ida Staffans

MARTINUS
NIJHOFF
PUBLISHERS

LEIDEN • BOSTON
2012

Library of Congress Cataloging-in-Publication Data

Staffans, Ida.
  Evidence in European asylum procedures / by Ida Staffans.
     p. cm. -- (Immigration and asylum law and policy in Europe ; v. 25)
  Includes bibliographical references and index.
  ISBN 978-90-04-21996-0 (hardback : alk. paper)
  1. Asylum, Right of--European Union countries. 2. Emigration and immigration law--
European Union countries. 3. Appellate procedure--European Union countries. 4. Evidence
(Law)--European Union countries.
I. Title.
  KJE5202.S73 2012
  342.408'3--dc23

                                                        2012005694

ISSN 1568-2749
ISBN 978 90 04 21996 0 (hardback)
ISBN 978 90 04 21999 1 (e-book)

Printed by Printforce, the Netherlands

Contents

Abbreviations

AIT	Asylum and Immigration Tribunal
APD	Council Directive 2005/85/EC of 1 December 2005 on minimum standards on procedures in Member States for granting and withdrawing refugee status
BAMF	Bundesamt für Migration und Flüchtlinge
CEAP	Common European Asylum Policy
CEAS	Common European Asylum System
CFR	Charter of Fundamental Rights of the European Union
COI	Country of Origin Information
EAC	European Asylum Curriculum
EASO	European Asylum Support Office
ECJ	European Court of Justice
EU	European Union
EURODAC	European Dactaloscopy
FIS	Finnish Immigration Service
FTT	First-Tier Tribunal
GDISC	General Directors' Immigration Services Conference
GFG	Gerichtsverfassungsgesetz
GG	Grundgesetz
HO	Home Office
IAA	Immigration Appeals Authority
IAT	Immigration Appeals Tribunal
JHA	Justice and Home Affairs
KHO	Korkein hallinto-oikeus (Supreme Administrative Court)
MS	Member State
QD	Council Directive 2004/83/EC of 29 April 2004 on minimum standards for the qualification and status of third country nationals or stateless persons as refugees or as persons who otherwise need international protection and the content of the protection granted
RSD	Refugee Status Determination
SIAC	Special Immigration Appeals Commission
UT	Upper Tribunal

Acknowledgements

The research for this book was mainly carried out at the Centre of Excellence in Foundations of European Law and Polity Research, funded by the Academy of Finland and situated at the Faculty of Law, University of Helsinki, Finland. The book is based on the doctoral dissertation with the same name, which I defended at the University of Helsinki in October 2011.

The research project has received funding also from Suomalainen Lakimiesyhdistys, Oskar Öflunds stiftelse, Emil Aaltosen Säätiö, Finnish Academy of Science and Letters – Emil Öhmann Foundation, Eugen Schaumans fond and Lakimiesliitto.

During the research for this book, many persons offered support and advice. My supervisors professor Dan Frände and professor Olli Mäenpää have been of outmost importance throughout the project. Professor Outi Suviranta and professor Gregor Noll kindly offered their remarks and comments as pre-examiners appointed by the Faculty of Law, and professor Gregor Noll additionally took on the task of opponent at the public defence ceremony. Professor Pia Letto-Vanamo, vice-dean of the Faculty of Law and director of the Centre for International Economic Law at the University of Helsinki, has provided great support throughout the project.

Also my fellow doctorate students at the Centre of Excellence and the Faculty of Law have provided invaluable help and inspiration.

For all support I remain grateful.

Ida Staffans
Helsinki, December 1, 2011

Chapter I

Introduction

1. *To Begin With*

1.1. *To Grasp Realities*

When reading novels or stories the information in the book allows us to form our own picture of relevant events and circumstances. Likewise, in our everyday routines we form pictures and understandings of events around us that are of importance, to a greater or lesser degree, to our perception and understanding of the world. We perceive reality as it presents itself to us.

In dealings with evidence, the question is precisely about perception of realities. Evidence can be presented in a vast amount of different contexts. In the legal context, the presentation and assessment of evidence strives to give an outsider the possibility to understand reality, as this is relevant for the legal system and its norms. In most legal procedures, the aim is to present evidence of actual circumstances and events, so that the outsider can strive to gain a perception of the material reality. In some procedures, however, those who present evidence are allowed to choose the reality they want to reflect with the evidence, so that the reality presented becomes procedural rather than material.

Evidence thus forms bits and pieces of a puzzle, which reflects realities around us. Nevertheless, any picture and any puzzle is interpreted and understood in relation to the interpreter. Events, circumstances and information are inevitably interpreted and reflected with an outset in the experiences, preferences and knowledge of the interpreter.

This is what fascinates with evidence, especially when issues of evidence and perception of realities are placed in the legal environment. The idea of that judges and decision-makers are required, with the aid of evidence, to form a perception of the reality relevant to the case before them, to place this perception in relation to legal norms and furthermore to go about this assessment and perception in a manner affording their subjects legal certainty and foreseeable decision-making, seems to me challenging. That is, the notion of legal certainty in relation to evidence would imply that perception and assessment must be controlled and that the impact of external factors on assessment must be ruled out. How do we control perceptions of reality? How are norms and practices relating to the perception of reality construed? How does perception of reality fit into a normative frame?

1.2. Frameworks

Asylum procedure involves assessing applications for international protection. The procedure encompasses assessing claims for refugee status presented by foreign applicants before host state authorities and courts. Examining an application involves evaluations and considerations regarding a claim for refugee status presented as a ground for a need for protection. The outcome of the procedure is affected by factual matters relating to the individual case, including what can be established in evidentiary assessment, and by legal prerequisites imposed for assessment of the application.

The European Union (EU) has long striven to unify the outcomes of European national asylum procedures through approximation of the prerequisites for assessing asylum applications lodged in Member States, the ultimate goal being a "common procedure". The incentive for this development lies partly in a striving to hinder secondary movements between Member States but also, no doubt, partly in a striving to raise the standards of Member State asylum procedures. Included in the efforts towards a unified procedure is also procedural approximation of national asylum procedures.

Inherent to any judicial procedure, issues of proof and evidence also have their given place in asylum procedure. However, while evidentiary issues hold a central position in any judicial procedure, their position in asylum procedure is enhanced. This enhanced position stems firstly from the fact that the perception of reality in the asylum environment is a practically challenging task, as asylum procedure includes a prognostic theme of proof, vast cultural and lingual differences and often very small quantities of actual information. Secondly, the position of evidentiary issues is enhanced in asylum procedure because questions of proof are traditionally only loosely regulated in administrative procedures. Asylum procedure thus presents the decision-maker in the national environment with a difficult practical and theoretical situation in combination with comparably broad margins of appreciation.

Hence, solutions in terms of evidence in the asylum procedure have much to say about the environment in which they are made. Freedom is given in forming these solutions, and the solutions found are products of the legal environments in which they are formulated. However, the solutions found are also of vast importance for the procedure – by altering standards, requirements or expectations in terms of proof, the end result of the procedures is inevitably altered as well.

2. The Question at Hand

2.1. Evidence in European Asylum Procedures and Aims for the Study

The European Union decided early on to create common responses to issues relating to immigration and asylum.[1] These intentions were affirmed and turned into practice at the Tampere Summit in 1999, with an end protocol stating the goal of convergence as a "Common European Asylum System, including a common procedure and a uniform status" for refugees across Europe.[2] The strivings towards a common procedure has led EU to impose on its Member States also rules with the aim of procedural approximation, including some rules on evidentiary issues.

Clearly, immigration and asylum have been important areas of interest for the Union for many reasons. There are economic reasons for having joint procedures, as practical issues exist that easily benefit from common standards and procedures. Further, both the internal and external images of the Union benefit from integrated procedures as common procedures enforce the meaning behind 'us and them' as 'Europeans and others'.[3] The Union has nevertheless had to realise that the road towards a common procedure and uniform status was somewhat more bumpy than expected. The enactment of central pieces of legislation has been struggling and their harmonised transposition and implementation has been far from optimal from the point of view of convergence.

Pierre Legrand stated in 1996 that European legal systems were not converging.[4] Also in the asylum discussion voices have been raised arguing that European asylum procedures are not converging. Both measured in hard numbers, recognition rates and other factors and through the lenses of various organisations within and outside the Union, it is clear that European asylum procedures, despite all efforts towards harmonisation and integration, have not melted into one in the manner expected by those who masterminded

---

[1] For comments on the background legal framework see Peter Boeles, Maarten den Heijer, Gerrie Lodder & Kees Wouters, *European Migration Law* Ius Communitatis III (Antwerp – Oxford – Portland 2009) 315 ff and Neil Walker, "In Search of the Area of Freedom, Security and Justice: A Constitutional Odyssey", in *Europe's Area of Freedom, Justice and Security*, ed. Neil Walker (Oxford 2004) 3–37.

[2] Presidentiary Conclusions, Tampere European Council 15–16.10.1999.

[3] Anna Triandafyllidou, *Immigrants and National Identity in Europe* (London 2001) 55–76.

[4] Pierre Legrand, "European Legal Systems are Not Converging" (1996/1) *International and Comparative Law Quarterly*, 52–81.

developments.[5] Nevertheless, Union efforts towards the common are not end-
ing, and new legislation with the aim of procedural approximation is continuously presented.

Hence in Europe today there is a situation of comparably divergent national
asylum procedures despite efforts and a strong will of the European legislator to harmonize. The idea of this book is to study the use of evidence in
European appellate asylum procedures as an isolated part of asylum adjudication within the frame of harmonized and harmonizing national procedures
of the Common European Asylum System and to come to conclusions regarding national practice in evidentiary assessment in appellate asylum procedure
and the sources for and interaction of these practices. Through establishing
knowledge about this precise section of national decision-making, a deeper
understanding of the nature of European national asylum procedures is
gained.

The aim of this book is to explore the particular framework of evidentiary
standards of three selected appellate national asylum procedures in Europe
and to discuss the relationship between national procedures themselves and
between national procedures and other legal systems, including the EU legal
order and international law, in terms of evidentiary standards in appellate
asylum procedure.

Hence, on the one hand, the book studies evidentiary standards in German,
Finnish and English appellate asylum procedures. The book will present evidentiary practice and solutions for each appellate asylum procedure and also
study the background frameworks impacting on the evidentiary practices.
Evidentiary standards of national appellate procedures will be comparatively
explored, in order to come to conclusions on similarities and differences. The
central question thus concerns the evidentiary standards used in national
procedures.

On the other hand, the book sets out to study reasons and sources for evidentiary standards in above mentioned national procedures, their similarities

---

[5] Jean-Francois Durieux goes as far as to stating that "European States have [...] developed
their own doctrines..." in relation to the interpretation of refugee status. Jean-Francois
Durieux. *Salah Sheekh is a Refugee New insights into Primary and Subsidiary Forms of
Protection* Refugee Studies Centre Working Paper Series No. 49 (Oxford 2008). ECRE states
that the Common European Asylum System is a "myth rather than a reality" and that "a solid
EU legal framework is a necessary precondition if a CEAS is ever to function properly." ECRE:
*Comments from the European Council on Refugees and Exiles on the European Commission
Proposal to recast the Asylum Procedures Directive* (2010) 3. Developments in the EU have, on
a broader level of administrative law, been seen as also leading to approximation and "globali-
sation" of procedural administrative law. See Giacinto della Cananea, "Beyond the State: the
Europeanisation and Globalisation of Procedural Administrative Law" (2003/4) *European
Public Law*, 563–578.

and differences, with a starting point in EU requirements, the frameworks of international law and also in influences from the national level. In the analysis also influences on EU legislation will be observed. The central question concerns the sources and reasons for national evidentiary standards and the position of national evidentiary standards in regional legislative framework.

Thus firstly the study aims at an evidentiary analysis of asylum procedure as a particular procedure of administrative justice, from both the view of requirements imposed for evidentiary solutions in this procedure and from a pragmatic point of view with three European national appellate procedures in focus. Secondly, the study aims to answer questions relating to the position of as well international as regional norms and practice in the national procedures of Member States.

The book leans on comparative method, where the compared system is that of evidentiary standards in national appellate asylum procedures and where keys of comparison are evidentiary concepts. The choice of evidentiary standards as focus for the study is not self-evident, nor is it free from value-based assumptions. Evidence has been chosen as the object for the study on two grounds: Firstly, evidence is often a procedural element in the administrative environment that is fairly loosely regulated by national norms.[6] Thus, practice in terms of evidence has much to tell about background frameworks to procedure and can reveal interesting and important aspects of the legal framework in which asylum procedure operates. Secondly, evidence is part of the common European asylum procedure that has not been focused on explicitly, but which this book nevertheless argues is of crucial importance if common standards and procedures are to be achieved.

The aim for the study is *not* to undertake a survey of the implementation of relevant EU norms or norms from international law in selected Member States. This is not the purpose for the study and EU law includes only very few norms on evidence. Through the use of evidentiary keys of comparison, the evidentiary practices of different legal systems and their interaction will be studied. However, the outset for the study does not lie in any particular legal

---

[6] Olli Ryynänen states in his dissertation, focusing on evidence in taxation procedures, that evidentiary matters cannot be regulated precisely in law and that general principles of law, thus, are of particular importance when evidentiary frameworks are studied. Olli Ryynänen, *Proof in income tax assessment and litigation* (Helsinki 2000) 8. Susana Galera, again, states that procedural administrative law is a field that in the European context is "particularly influenced by 'national peculiarities'". Susana Galera, "European legal tradition and the EU legal system: understandings and premises about the rule of law's requirements" in *Judicial review A comparative analysis inside the European legal system*, ed. Susana Galera (Council of Europe 2010) 277–299 at 278.

system, national or regional, but in the keys of comparison and in the questions relating to the use of evidence posed in front of selected legal systems. Thus, question is not of an implementation-study but of a study of the evidentiary practices and their roots in selected legal systems.

2.2. *Frames*

This book concerns use of evidence in European appellate asylum procedures. The book is written from a comparative procedural standpoint, implying that many discussions regarding both aliens' and refugee law, also when these concern evidentiary matters and specifically regarding asylum procedure have been omitted or only noted. The aim of the book has not been to account for or engage in discussions outside the fairly strict frame of evidentiary asylum law, unless they have been of direct importance for solutions in terms of evidence. Even then, the study does not engage in discussions on interpretative issues but focus on the impact in national asylum procedures.

The book focuses on appellate asylum procedures, and of these, on procedures in the first appellate body competent to review decisions on applications for asylum taken by national authorities. The study has not taken account of evidentiary solutions in first instance authorities nor has it to any greater extent studied use of evidence in higher instances than the first appellate body. The reason for this framing is, on the one hand, that only procedures in the first appellate body have been considered similar enough to facilitate a fruitful in-depth, procedural comparison on a European level, and, on the other hand, that these procedures nevertheless represent a numerically significant segment of decision-making in European asylum procedures.

Further, this book concerns use of evidence in asylum procedure, but takes note only of use of evidence in determining refugee status. Thus, particular issues and questions linked to subsidiary or humanitarian protection, or in relation to considerations concerning residence permits on compassionate grounds, have not been included in the analysis. The main reason for sidestepping subsidiary and other forms of protection is linked to the scope of the study. Nevertheless, at least some of the concerns and results presented in the book are also valid for other forms of international protection and it should be noted that decisions on subsidiary or other forms of protection are often taken in the same procedure as decisions on asylum.[7]

---

[7] The EU also strives as far as possible to unify the procedure as to status in relation to asylum and subsidiary protection. In the re-negotiations on key directives undertaken in 2009 and 2010, asylum and subsidiary protection are referred to as "international protection".

National legislative changes in national have been incorporated as they stand as of 31.5.2011. EU legislation has been followed until 30.10.2011. Several key legislative acts of the European Union are at the time of writing open for negotiations. Proposed amendments and negotiations have been duly noted in the study.

This book focuses exclusively on evidentiary solutions and use of evidence, which implies that asylum procedure is explored from an evidentiary point of view, with its outsets primarily in procedural and evidentiary law. The evidentiary focus entails two important limitations to the study: Firstly, credibility is not dealt with separately as is often the case in asylum law, but is referred to as a question of evidentiary assessment. Thus, this study pre-supposes that assessment of credibility is taken within evidentiary assessment.[8] Secondly, the benefit of the doubt, which is an important procedural principle and rule in international refugee law, is also referred to exclusively within the evidentiary framework and is not considered separately as a material question of asylum law nor as a separate key of comparison.

2.3. Context

This book can be positioned at least in the national and the regional context.[9] Nationally, very little has been written on the particular matter of procedural asylum law. In the 1980s and early 1990s some text-books were printed on general Finnish refugee law, but these received comparably little attention.[10]

See Proposal for a Directive of the European Parliament and of the Council on minimum standards for the qualification and status of third country nationals or stateless persons as beneficiaries of international protection and the content of the protection granted, COM (2009) 551. The Asylum Procedures Directive is also open for negotiations following recasts in October 2009 and June 2011. See Proposal for a Directive of the European Parliament and of the Council on minimum standards of procedures in Member States for the granting and withdrawing of international protection, COM (2009) 554/4 and Amended proposal for a Directive of the European Parliament and of the Council on common procedures for granting and withdrawing international protection status (Recast), COM(2011) 319 final.

[8] For discussion on the role of credibility assessment inside and outside evidentiary assessment, see Chapter I.V 5.5.

[9] An international context could also be created for the book. See for instance Brian Gorlick, "Common Burdens and Standards: Legal Elements in Assessing Claims to Refugee Status" (2003/3) *International Journal of Refugee Law*, 357–376 and UNHCR, *Note on Burden and Standard of Proof in Refugee Claims* (Geneva 1998).

[10] Johanna Niemi-Kiesiläinen, *Pakolaisoikeus* (Helsinki 1988); Tapio Kuosma, *Legal Conditions of Refugees in Finland,* (Helsinki 1993). However, it was Matti Pellonpää who in the 1970s introduced the subject to Finnish legal scholarly debate. See Matti Pellonpää, *Turvapaikkaoikeuden myöntäminen* (Helsinki 1974) and Matti Pellonpää, *Alueellisen turvapaikkaoikeuden myöntäminen* (Helsinki 1976).

Rather, during the past few decades, Finns that have published in the area of immigration and asylum law have done so outside the national scholarly context.[11] However, a break in this trend is noted in 2011 when at least one thesis on the specific theme of international refugee law was defended at the University of Turku.[12] In relation to procedural aspects of asylum procedure most publications of relevance are found in the genre of administrative law.[13] It is nevertheless noteworthy that more generally in the field of administrative law, publications on procedural aspects of administrative judicial procedures have also been rare.[14]

While national debate has been silent on immigration and asylum law, it has clearly been more vivid on the subject of evidentiary law, as a result of close links between Finnish legal proceduralists and Scandinavian scholarly debates on theoretical evidentiary law. In Finland most famously Hannu Tapani Klami and his students have formulated evidentiary theories and pragmatic approaches to evidentiary law.[15] The impact of these theories of evidence on this study will be further discussed below in Chapter IV. 1.

On the European level procedural asylum law has been a topic given some academic attention during recent years. Whereas most debates concentrate on substantive issues of asylum law, recently, and perhaps fuelled by Union legislative action, books have also been written particularly regarding procedural aspects of refugee status determination (RSD).[16] Further, some research has

---

[11] For instance Pirkko Kourula, *Broadening the Edges: Refugee definition and international protection revisited* (The Hague 1997).

[12] Eeva Nykänen, *Fragmented State Power and Forced Migration: Study on Non-State Actors in Refugee Law* (Turku 2011).

[13] Olli Mäenpää, *Julkisuuslaki* (Helsinki 2008c) can offer insights into communication; Olli Ryynänen (2000) again deals with evidence in administrative setting.

[14] With the exception of a few books, such as Olli Mäenpää, *Hallintoprosessioikeus* (Helsinki 2007a); Olli Mäenpää, *Oikeudenkäynnin julkisuus hallintotuomioistuimessa* (Helsinki 2007b); Leena Halila, *Hallintolainkäyttömenettelyn oikeusturvatakeista* (Helsinki 2003); Pekka Hallberg, Pirkko Ignatius & Heikki Kanninen, *Hallintolainkäyttölaki* (Helsinki 1997).

[15] Hannu Tapani Klami, Minna Gräns & Johanna Sorvettula, *Law and Truth: A theory of evidence* (Helsinki 2000); Hannu Tapani Klami, *Todistusratkaisu* (Helsinki 2000a). Also Pasi Pölönen, *Henkilötodistelu rikosprosessissa* (Helsinki 2003) and Jaakko Jonkka, *Todistusharkinnasta* (Helsinki 1993) and, most recently, Timo Saranpää, *Näyttöenemmyysperiaate riita-asioissa* (Helsinki 2010), where empirical evidentiary law is studied.

[16] Pierre Boeles (*et al.*) (2009) 347 ff; Karin Zwaan (ed.), *The Procedures Directive: Central Themes, Problem Issues and Implementation in Selected Member States* (Nijmegen 2008); Gregor Noll (ed.), *Proof, evidentiary assessment and credibility in asylum procedures* (Leiden – Boston 2005a).

also been carried out on the specific issue of comparative procedural asylum law.[17]

2.4. *Definitions and Meanings*

At the interface between national, regional and international law, as well as between procedural, administrative and comparative law, a number of concepts require clarification. Definitions of key concepts will be provided throughout the study and no attempt to provide exhaustive explanations and definitions of all concepts will be made here. Nevertheless, some of the most fundamental concepts and expressions used must already at this stage briefly be explained.

When referring to asylum procedure, this study implies the entire procedure of refugee status determination in Member States, starting from the stages of application to the final instances of appeal. The concepts 'appellate asylum procedure' or 'review procedure' have been used to indicate the particular stage of asylum procedure in which the first appellate organ reviews or reconsiders a decision taken by a national authority, and which is the focus of attention for this study. In context, 'appellate asylum procedure' may also refer to the entire national review procedure, also beyond the first appellate instance.

The applicant is a third-country person applying for asylum in one of the EU Member States. The appellant refers to the same person, but as he or she represents him-or herself after an appeal, before the appellate organs in national asylum procedure.

The concept of evidence will be studied in detail throughout the book and the concept will gradually gain more specific meaning. But evidence at the outset refers to knowledge and information brought into a judicial procedure where it is given a particular procedural status. Thus, evidence is a procedural notion, whereas knowledge and information can also be used outside the procedural domain.

When referring to institutions in asylum procedure the choice has been made in context to subsume tribunals under the concept of courts.

---

[17] Guy S. Goodwin-Gill & Helene Lambert (eds.), *The Limits of Transnational Law: Refugee Law, Policy Harmonisation and Judicial Dialogue in the European Union* (Cambridge 2010); Sylvia Da Lomba, *The Right to Seek Asylum in the European Union* (Antwerp – Oxford – Portland 2004). In Hemme Battjes, *European Asylum Law and International Law* (Leiden 2006), the author undertakes a vertical comparison between European asylum norms and international refugee law.

In discussions where the difference between courts and tribunals is imperative, the concepts have been divided.

3. *Means and Methods*

3.1. *Methodological Choices*

The choice of method for legal research cannot be made in isolation as there always are reasons for the method chosen. It is indeed achievable to decide on questions of method in separation from questions of substance, if the interest of the researcher lies in the method itself and its possibilities as a tool for knowledge. However, in research with a focus on material questions of law, on legal dogmatics and on questions relating to the content of law, the choice of method must be fitted against the material context and *vice versa*. Explication of methodological outsets and choices thus forms an integrated part in the self-understanding of the researcher not only in terms of method for the research, but also in relation to the understanding of the subject of the research.

In this book, legal norms are analysed and systematized and legal constructions are explored in order to give them content and context. The framework is that of evidentiary asylum law in the European context. The book takes its outset in an understanding of that the aim also for legal research on evidence and asylum is to determine the contents of valid law through analysis and systematization of legal norms. The outset for the methodology of the study is thus taken in legal dogmatics.[18]

Legal dogmatics undertake interpretation and systematization of legal norms with the aid of legal sources.[19] The scope of legal sources to influence dogmatics is not self-evident, as traditional theories today may stand in conflict with the multileveled legal reality that norms exist in.[20] Further, the scope of legal sources may be dependent on the object of interpretation and systematization. As evidentiary issues traditionally are vaguely defined in legal

---

[18] Raimo Siltala, *Oikeustieteen tieteenteoria* (Helsinki 2003) 493–505, provides views on the contents of legal dogmatics and the requirements on research carried out with this method.

[19] Aulis Aarnio, *The Rational as Reasonable. A tratise on Legal Justification* (Dordrecht 1987), 89 ff, Aulis Aarnio, *Laintulkinnan teoria* (Juva 1988) 222–247 and Aleksander Peczenik, *Vad är rätt? Om demokrati, rättsskerhet, etik och juridisk argumentation* (Gothemburg 1995) 212–273 all present traditional principles of legal sources. See also Hannu Tolonen, *Oikeuslähdeoppi* (Helsinki 2003) 103–167.

[20] As also Anna Nylund realized in her dissertation, changes to the legal environment has led old and traditional teaching on legal sources to become invalid and partly obsolete. Anna Nylund *Tillgången till den andra instansen i tvistemål* (Helsinki 2006) 28–29.

norms, especially when entering the domain of administrative law and justice, a strict traditional normative dogmatic approach cannot be applied.[21] For the same reasons a traditionalist and strict legal positivism is not applied. As evidence is studied not only in theory, but also in relation to practice and the content of the theoretical norms on evidence, the dogmatics applied to the analysis is supported by practical analysis.[22] The aim for the book is not only to come to terms with the contents of legal norms and the requirements of law, but also to study the use and practical functioning of the norms, giving them content by practice.[23] Taking into consideration the place and the environment in which the research for this book has taken place, it is inevitable that the understanding of law has been influenced by the debate on critical legal positivism.[24] As in critical legal positivism the surface layer of law is here understood as a layer dependent on deeper structures of law, such as legal culture and tradition. In the practical analysis supporting the legal dogmatics of this book, weight is placed also with the influence of the deeper structures of law and the rational understanding of law and legal effects.

Distinction has been made between two forms of legal dogmatics: practical legal dogmatics and scientific dogmatics.[25] Practical legal dogmatics concern research on judicial decision-making with the primary aim to find reasons for decisions. Scientific dogmatics, on the other hand, involves also a theoretical-hypothetical frame and is critical to its outsets. It also presupposes scientific parameters for the research findings.[26] If using this distinction, this book is positioned within the field of scientific dogmatics and indeed is critical to its

---

[21] *Supra* at 6 and Hannu Tapani Klami, *Empirical Studies on Finnish Evaluation of Evidence* A research plan (Turku 1986) 11, where the author states that "There are not many explicit legal norms about evaluation of evidence. This seems to reflect the attitude of the legislator that evaluation of evidence is free [...] and that the holistic appraisal of all relevant facts, which is the essence of evaluation of evidence, cannot be regulated by legal norms."

[22] Mårten Knuts states in his dissertation that adequate interpretation and systematization also in line with traditional dogmatics require contacts and interrelations to context and application of law. Mårten Knuts, *Kursmanipulation på värdepappersmarknaden* (Helsinki 2010) 49.

[23] Anna Nylund uses a similar approach in her dissertation. Nylund (2006).

[24] Kaarlo Tuori who developed the critical legal positivism is also the co-director of the Centre of Excellence in European Law and Polity at the University of Helsinki. Kaarlo Tuori, *Critical Legal Positivism* (Cornwall 2002).

[25] Aarnio (1987) and Aarnio (1988). For an overview see Jaakko Husa, *Julkisoikeudellinen tutkimus* Acta Universitatis Lapponensis N:o 4 (Jyväskylä 1995) 196–206.

[26] The debate on the relationship between legal research and science has been vivid in Finland, and Tuori has presented the double citizenship of law. Tuori (2002) 297 ff. Further, Hupli sees the methodological emphasis (as opposite of normative emphasis) placed with jurisprudance as a sign of separation from the double citizenship. Tuomas Hupli, *Täytäntöönpanointressi yrityssaneerauksessa* (Helsinki 2004) 8. In Siltala (2003) 167 ff legal research is placed in the context of empiric science.

outsets. Nevertheless, it must be added that the influences of practical legal dogmatics, in the manner that this concept is presented in jurisprudence, are clearly notable in the practical support for the research.

Legal dogmatics as a starting point for the analysis of this book is given detail by two other approaches: Legal comparison and analysis *de lege ferenda*.[27] Of these, the comparative method is given a clear priority. Analysis *de lege ferenda* nevertheless form a given part of the critical environment of the book as solutions are presented to problems perceived.[28] The comparative approach will be presented in the next chapter but in relation to the dogmatic frame it must be said that the studies of countries involved in the comparative analysis are primarily descriptive whereas the general framework, the interrelationship and the interdependence of EU level legal norms and other systems of law, are studied according to a more critical approach.

3.2. *Use of Comparative Method*

This book relies to a great extent on comparative methodology.[29] Use of comparative method is not self-explanatory nor self-evident, but has been chosen as this particular method achieves the aims of the study. Comparative law can compare legal frameworks in order either to gain an understanding of 'foreign' systems, to understand one's 'own' legal framework better or to facilitate import or export of legal concepts and ideas.[30] For this study, comparative method has been chosen in order to gain knowledge of the evidentiary standards used in three selected appellate asylum procedures in Europe and to facilitate an analysis of the relationship and interaction between the national procedures themselves, on the one hand, and other legal systems and the national appellate procedures, on the other.[31] Thus, the aim is not to take a

---

[27] Relationship between legal dogmatics and comparative law, Husa (1998) 49–50.

[28] Hupli (2004) 9–10 and 16–18, refers to the melting down of traditional borders between legal research *de lege lata* and research *de lege ferenda*. Hupli argues that the inclusion of *de lege ferenda* aspects in legal research is a prerequisite posed by the rapid changes in law.

[29] See H. Patrick Glenn, "Com-Paring" in *Comparative Law A Handbook*, eds. Esin Öröcö & David Nelken (Oxford – Portland 2007) 91–108, where the author discusses comparative law as a discipline. For an outline of the comparative method see also John C. Reitz, "How to Do Comparative Law" (1998/4) *American Journal of Comparative Law*, 617–636.

[30] Antero Jyränki, "In fremden Spiegel" – Tankar om jämförande rättsforskning", in *Jämförande juridik: Vad, varför, hur?* Meddelande från ekonomisk-statsvetenskapliga fakulteten vid Åbo Akademi Ser A: 468, ed. Markku Suksi (Turku 1996) 9–24 at 12.

[31] For discussion on use of comparative law in European studies see David Nelken, "Comparatist and Transferability" in *Comparative Legal Studies: Traditions and transitions*, eds. Pierre Legrand & Roderick Munday (Cambridge 2003) 437–466, where the author points out that

clear outset in any national procedure, but a horizontal comparison between national legal systems. Also in the vertical comparison, between national, regional and international legal systems, the aim is to study the interaction between different levels without prejudice.[32]

Comparative method is lush. It holds within various options and possibilities also for innovative use.[33] The basic requirement for use of this method is that legal systems are compared, not only described.[34] In functional comparison on micro level functional equivalences in different legal systems are studied and analysed.[35]

In this book, functional equivalences studied are the evidentiary standards of appellate asylum procedures in three EU Member States.[36] The comparison strives to compare responses of these three legal systems to challenges of evidence in the asylum procedure and to study the relationship between these responses and other legal systems, primarily the EU legal order. As the field of evidentiary solutions for asylum appellate procedures is dependent on influences from as well a multilevel legal system as from several legal fields, such as administrative law, procedural law and evidentiary theory, the functional approach provides adequate tools for generic analysis of evidentiary practices.[37]

In order for the functional approach to be fruitful, the dogmatic approach must be adequately adapted. Thus, practical analytics and legal sources outside the strict positivist understanding are employed, to facilitate a functional understanding of law.

Pierre Legrand's statements regarding the non-conformity between European legal systems have been an inspiration for this book.[38] Imbedded in his statement lies however fundamental critique of comparative law.

---

comparative law must also be sensitive to the degree of approximation or harmonization in the studied systems. See also Heikki Kulla, Oikeusvertailu ja eurooppalainen hallinto-oikeus in Suksi (1996) 39–51.

[32] On verticality and horizontality in legal comparative studies see Husa (1998) 66–67.

[33] Jaakko Husa, *Johdatus oikeusvertailuun* (Helsinki 1998) 11. See also Nylund (2006) 29 ff on how comparative method can be used.

[34] Comparison, in turn, requires analysis beyond the descriptive. Konrad Zweigert & Hein Kötz, *Einführung in die Rechtsvergleichung* (Tübingen 1996) 6.

[35] Husa (1998) 13–14 and on micro- versus macro-comparisons also 60–62.

[36] *Ibid* at 70–71, regarding the choices of functional equivalences in comparative law.

[37] The functional approach to comparative law has been vividly criticised during past years. In Jaakko Husa, "Valkoista yksisarvista pyydystämässä vai mörköä paoessa – 'oikeaa oikeusvertailua'" in (2010/5) *Lakimies* 700–718 at 705–707, account is given and answers are provided for the criticism presented amongst others by Pierre Legrand and Gunter Frankenberg.

[38] *Supra* at 4.

According to Legrand, comparisons between legal systems often lead to wrong or at least inadequate results as it is close to impossible for an outsider to gain the 'insides' of another legal system.[39] Particularly troublesome to Legrand is the inclusion in comparative studies of systems from different sides of the gap between common and civil law.

Despite the challenges involved in comparison, especially when the comparison includes as well civil- as common law countries, the criticism presented by Legrand is not fully embraced by this study. Rather, his criticism serves as inspiration and as a point of reference also for the comparative study. The comparison undertaken may be challenging, but is certainly not irrelevant, as the integration of European asylum systems is today's reality. As changes indeed are taking place, it is of importance to understand the background frameworks and the position of different legal systems. Ulla Liukkonen goes as far as to stating that one of the tasks of comparative law today at the European level is to analyse the possibilities and boundaries for convergence of European legal systems.[40]

Jaakko Husa in a recent article also takes a stand for the present relevance of comparative law.[41] Husa writes that the a challenge for legal comparativists today is to take a step back from rigid requirements on theoretical support from either one pole or the other – Husa uses the example of Legrand versus Zweigert-Kötz – and to allow for integrated approaches to comparative law in order to put the method to use. Also for this study, the aim has been to in the forefront place the knowledge interest, which partly indeed is inspired from Legrand's criticism, together with a functional legal comparison.

Nevertheless, the study recognizes that comparative law is challenging and that optimality in comparative research does not imply absolute correctness. Anna Nylund states in her dissertation that the aim for comparative research is not to produce information completely free from mistakes, but to diminish the impact of possible mistakes on the outcomes of the research.[42]

The objects for comparison in the present study are three national appellate asylum procedures. As is natural for comparative methodology these procedures are not studied and compared in isolation, but the frameworks in which

---

[39] Pierre Legrand, "Uniformity, Legal Tradition, and Law's Limits" in (1996–1997/2) *Juridisk Tidskrift*, 307–322 at 308.

[40] Ulla Liukkonen, "Oikeuden yhdentäminen ja kansallinen diversitetti – näkökulma eurooppalaiseen kansainväliseen yksityisoikeuteen ja oikeusvertailuun" in (2010/5) *Lakimies*, 739–755 at 739.

[41] Husa (2010) 711.

[42] Nylynd (2006) 35.

they exist are duly taken into account.[43] Jakko Husa writes that comparative law researches societies, with the law as the objective – a view that is embraced by this study.[44]

The keys of comparison, *tertium comparationis*, for the comparative study are found in the evidentiary elements of appellate asylum procedure, as the solutions in respect of evidentiary issues in national procedures are compared.[45] The keys are defined as the burden of proof, evidentiary robustness, methods of evidentiary assessment and the standard of proof. These concepts are, firstly, defined in the appellate asylum context, taking into account relevant regional and international requirements and, secondly, positioned in the national appellate procedure used as keys of comparison with the aim of coming to conclusions regarding evidentiary standards used in three selected appellate asylum procedures to facilitate an analysis of the relationship and interaction between legal systems.

The use of abstract concepts as *tertium comparationis* clearly is challenging. The concepts do not necessarily have automatic semantic equivalents in the national appellate asylum procedures. Nevertheless, the keys of comparison all represent stages of the decision-making that form natural and integrated parts of any material appellate asylum procedure. Thus, it is imperative to understand the functioning of the concepts and their practical definitions, as the comparison aims at their functional equivalents in the different systems studied.

The keys of comparison mentioned above are general concepts of evidentiary law and therefore not particular for the asylum procedure. The choice to use general concepts instead of more asylum-sensitive concepts, such as for instance the benefit of the doubt, as keys of comparison was made in order to secure a close tie to general evidentiary law and in order to better benefit from research on general procedural and evidentiary law.

---

[43] David Nelken, "Defining and Using the Concept of Legal Culture" in Öröcö (*et al.*) (2007) 109–132. Also Roger Cotterell, "The Concept of Legal Culture" in *Comparing Legal Cultures*, ed. David Nelken (Dartmouth 1997) 13–31. See further, John Bell, "Administrative Law in a Comparative Perspective" in Öröcö (*et al.*) (2007) 287–311, where comparative methods in relation to administrative law are discussed. See also Nylund (2006) 34, where the need for understanding of deeper structures of law, influencing for instance the use of legal sources, is accentuated.

[44] Husa (1998) 12.

[45] In Hannu Tapani Klami, *Oikeusvertailun erityiskysymyksiä* Publications of the Institute for Jurisprudence (Helsinki 2000b) 30–38 the author discusses comparative law from the point of view of procedural and evidentiary law, and concludes that these are central and revealing elements of any legal system.

National procedures selected for comparison are Finnish, German and English appellate asylum procedures. The choice of countries to involve in the study has been mainly influenced by the following concerns: Firstly, Finland was chosen as a part of the study partly because of closeness to the procedure, as the author is Finnish. Partly, Finland is included in the study also on grounds of access to information, as Finnish asylum procedure is a closed procedure and information about the standards used in the procedure can only be obtained through scientific or research-oriented means. Secondly, England and Germany were chosen on grounds of their position in the regional, European framework. England and Germany are both powerful actors on the European asylum scene and vastly influence regional legislation. England and Germany also represent important asylum procedures in Europe in terms of numbers. Further, England and Germany represent countries with widely different procedural outsets: common law versus civil law, traditional inquisitorial procedure versus traditional adversarial procedure, and thus reflect some of the most challenging environments for regional impact.[46]

Further, pragmatic concerns such as the language skills of the author and access to procedures have also influenced the choice of countries.

3.3. *Materials*

This study has been undertaken with a wide material base. The material used for the study encompasses traditional materials for dogmatic legal research, such as law, its preparatory works, doctrine and case-law. To this extent, the material base is wide due to the comparative method used requiring legal sources from several legal systems to be studied. However, and as has been pointed out in the discussion on methodology, legal sources are employed also outside the strictly traditional understanding of source hierarchy.[47] The multilevel legal order impacting on asylum procedures makes it impossible to deny the impact of frameworks outside the traditionally national. Further, the subject of evidentiary standards and a practical analysis calls for empirical sources to a certain extent. These encompass case-law, interviews and observations of proceedings before appellate courts in three countries.

Oral hearings in appellate asylum procedure have been studied in three countries in order to provide the author with an understanding of the position

---

[46] See Csaba Varga, "Common Law and Civil Law: Encounters" in *Comparative Legal Cultures*, ed. Csaba Varga (Dartmouth 1992) 101–172 and also Xavier Lewis, "The Europeanisation of the Common Law", in *Transfrontier Mobility of Law*, Robert W. Jagtenberg, Esin Örükü & Annie J. de Roo, (The Hague 1995) 47–61.

[47] *Supra* at 19.

of oral evidence and the role of the oral hearing in asylum procedure. The choice of oral hearings to observe has not been determined by material concerns but rather by concerns of feasibility. In England and Germany, the author has observed hearings to the extent possible during visits to these countries. In Germany efforts were also made to observe hearings at different courts. In Finland oral hearings were observed to the extent allowed by the Helsinki District Administrative Court within the framework of the research permission granted for the research for this study. In connection to all observations, discussions have been undertaken with judges involved and other stakeholders.

Interviews with stakeholders were carried out in three countries. The choice of interviewees was made with a view to representing different stakeholders in the procedure in all countries. As most of the persons interviewed expressed a wish not to have their names revealed, a list of interviewees identified with their names has been given only to the academic reviewers of this thesis. The interviews have not been conducted according to a strict scientific method and are therefore not used as direct sources. Rather, the interviews serve as a basis for the understanding of the research subject for the author.

Lastly, case-law makes up an important part of the material base for this study. It should be noted that not all case-law reviewed has explicitly been referred to in the text. Rather, the study makes use in this respect, of purposive sampling as the criterion for selection of case-law.[48] Thus, decisions and case-files identified as being of particular importance for the study were selected and referred to explicitly as they dealt with questions of evidence in one manner or the other.

---

[48] This approach has also been used in, for instance, Noreen Burrows & Rosa Greaves, *The Advocate General and EC Law* (Oxford 2007) 8–9.

Chapter II

Substantive Framework for the Study

1. *Refugee Status Determination*

Before analysing how evidence works in appellate asylum procedures in Europe it is necessary to look at the legal environment of refugee status determination (RSD). This is called for because RSD is by nature a procedure of special demands and solutions, which does not neatly fit into traditional categories of judicial decision-making. The aim for this chapter is to explicate the background frameworks of the procedures for RSD in Europe.

1.1. *Definitions of Refugeehood*

In the context of international law a refugee is a person to whom the refugee definition of the 1951 Convention relating to the Status of Refugees (Geneva convention or [1951] Convention) applies.[1] In the context of the 1951 Convention, a number of rights attach to the status of refugee.[2] Furthermore, the Convention includes obligations for signatory states in respect of plausible refugees, such as asylum seekers. However, the Convention does not include an obligation to grant refugees asylum, but refers to the obligation not to refoule or return refugees to areas where their life or freedom would be endangered.[3] Nevertheless, the practice among European states has long been to grant the specific form of protection offered by asylum only and exclusively to recognised refugees, and further not to grant any other status than asylum to persons that have been recognised as refugees (and to whom exclusion is not applicable).[4]

---

[1] Convention relating to the Status of Refugees, Adopted on 28 July 1951 by the United Nations Conference of Plenipotentiaries on the Status of Refugees and Stateless Persons convened under General Assembly resolution 429 V of 14 December 1950, entry into force 22 April 1954, 189 UNTS 150. All EU Member States have signed the Convention.

[2] *Ibid* at Chapters II to IV.

[3] *Ibid* at Art 33(2).

[4] During a few years in the 1970s and 1980s Sweden granted asylum to persons they acknowledged not as refugees but rather as war deserters or draft evaders. This practice came to an

According to Article 1 A of the 1951 Convention a refugee is a person, who

> owing to well-founded fear of being persecuted for reasons of race, religion, nationality, membership of a particular social group or political opinion, is outside the country of his nationality and is unable, or owing to such fear, is unwilling to avail himself of the protection of that country; or who, not having a nationality and being outside the country of his former habitual residence as a result of such events, is unable or, owing to such fear, is unwilling to return to it.

and to whom certain criteria specified in the 1951 Convention for exclusion from or cessation of refugee status do not apply.[5]

Understandably, scholarly debate on interpretation of this definition has been lively, much due to the relatively vague expressions of the definition and debates are ongoing today on many of the elements of the definition.[6] However, since the 1951 Convention itself recognises the leading role of the UNHCR in interpreting the Convention, the guidelines issued by this organisation, for instance in the Handbook for interpretation of the Convention issued by the organisation in 1979 (and reedited in 1992)[7] can be seen as authoritative.[8]

The definition of the concept of refugee according to the 1951 Convention includes five core requirements:

- the applicant is outside his country of origin;
- the applicant belongs to a certain group in his home country and this is due to the applicant's religion, race, nationality, social group or political opinion;

---

end after it had been established that only refugees can be granted asylum. Speech by Anna Bengtsson, *The Common European Asylum System: Future Challenges and Opportunities*, Red Cross and UNHCR seminar, Stockholm, 4.11.2009.

5 *Supra* at 1, Art 1 A (2). For comments see Guy S. Goodwin-Gill & Jane McAdam, *The Refugee in International Law* (Oxford 2007) 63 ff., James C. Hathaway, *The Law of Refugee Status* (Toronto 1991) 29–188, Satvinder Singh Juss, *International Migration and Global Justice* (Cornwall 2006) 187–210 and Reinhard Marx, *Aufenthalts-, Asyl- und Flüchtlingsrecht* (Frankfurt a M 2005a) chapter 4, paras 15 to 20. For a comparative approach to the criteria for refugee status see Da Lomba (2004).

6 See for instance the discussion regarding subjectivity of fear in James C. Hathaway & William S. Hicks, "Is there a Subjective element in the Refugee Convention's Requirement of 'Well-Founded Fear'?" (2005/2) *Michigan Journal of International Law*, 505–562 and The Michigan Guidelines on Well-Founded Fear as presented at the Third Colloquium on Challenges in International Refugee Law, University of Michigan Law School, 26–28.3.2004.

7 UNHCR, *Handbook on Procedures and Criteria for Determining Refugee Status under the 1951 Convention and the 1967 Protocol relating to the Status of Refugees* (Geneva 1992).

8 The preamble to the 1951 Convention, *supra* at 7 states: "...the United Nations High Commissioner for Refugees is charged with the task of supervising an international convention providing for the protection of refugees...". See also same, Art 35 on cooperation between states and the UNHCR.

- there is a well-founded fear that the applicant will be persecuted in his or her home country;
- this well-founded fear for persecution is linked to the group belonging; and that
- the applicant due to the well-founded fear does not wish to or cannot avail himself or herself of the protection of the home country.[9]

A person who fulfils the criteria laid down in the refugee definition is *prima facie* a refugee. A person meeting the criteria is, however, not a refugee if the Convention's articles regarding exclusion apply. Grounds for exclusion from refugee status state that refugee status cannot be invoked by persons "with respect to whom there are serious reasons for considering that:

- he has committed a crime against peace, a war crime, or a crime against humanity, as defined in the international instruments drawn up to make provision in respect of such crimes;
- he has committed a serious non-political crime outside the country of refuge prior to his admission to that country as a refugee;
- he has been guilty of acts contrary to the purposes and principles of the United Nations."[10]

Additionally, persons receiving aid from UN agencies other than the UNHCR are excluded from refugee status.[11]

1.2. *Asylum*

Disregarding which source or definition is used, the essential core of refugee-hood stems from the refugee being a person not able or willing to avail him- or herself of the protection of the home country. By protection one here refers to the responsibility of the state to protect its citizens from persecution in the shape of systematised violations of basic human rights directed against the

---

[9] This presentation perhaps emphasises the bond between the applicant and the host state/ authorities. For a different manner in which to split up the definition and, thus, for a different emphasis see Aleksandra Popovic, "Evidentiary Assessment and Non-Refoulement: Insights from Criminal Procedure" in Noll (2005a) 27–56.

[10] On exclusion from refugee status under the 1951 Convention see Hathaway (1991) 189–230, Goodwin-Gill (*et al.*) (2007) 162 ff, Atle Grahl-Madsen, *The Status of Refugees in International Law Vol I* (Leiden 1966) 262–304 and Brian Gorlick, "Who needs and deserves protection?" (1997/4) *The Indian Journal of International Law*, 677–689. Also Geoff Gilbert, "Exclusion and Evidentiary Assessment", in Noll (2005a) 161–170.

[11] 1951 Convention, *supra* at 1, Art 1 D. Also UNHCR, *Note on the Applicability of Article 1 D of the 1951 Convention relating to the Status of Refugees and Palestine Refugees* 2.10.2002.

individual person.[12] This right to protection (or put otherwise, the state's responsibility to protect) has in the refugee regime been seen as more important than the bond between the home state and its citizen so that refugee law thus allows states other than the state of which the person is a citizen to step in and 'take over' protection if the home country fails to provide it. This new protection is referred to by the concept of asylum.[13] The 1951 Convention includes specific rules on the content of protection, i.e. the rights and obligations of recognised refugees in their host states.[14]

History of the Institution of Asylum
The modern institution of asylum holds its origins in the responses of the League of Nations to people in need post World War I. At this time, persons in need of international support were given a document stating this need, the so called Nansen passport, which then granted the holder certain rights in western countries.[15] In order to ease identification of persons in need of international protection several international agreements were adopted concerning recognition of refugees in the 1920s and early 1930s.[16] The Convention

---

[12] Despite many attempts to create a definition, international law holds no common definition of persecution. However, it is commonly acknowledged that only systematic infringements of basic human rights of individually chosen subjects can constitute persecution. For comments on the definition of persecution see Atle Grahl-Madsen, *The Status of Refugees in International Law Vol II* (Leiden 1972) 188–216 and for comments on the content of persecution in contemporary practice see Marx (2005a) chapter 2, paras 3 to 9.

[13] Black's Law Dictionary: Asylum: "A sanctuary, or place of refuge and protection…"

[14] Also the Qualification Directive, which in the European Union codifies the scope of protection, includes norms on the content of protection. Council directive on minimum standards for the qualification and status of third country nationals or stateless persons as refugees or as persons who otherwise need international protection and the content of the protection granted, Council directive 2004/83, OJ 29.4.2004 (L 304) 12.

[15] For remarks on the ancient history of asylum see Grahl-Madsen (1972) 7–21. On the history of refugee status see Goodwin-Gill (*et al.*) (2007) 15–50, Grahl-Madsen (1966) 9–27, Terje Einarsen, *Retten til vern som flykting I* (Bergen 1998) 103–287 and James C. Hathaway, "The Evolution of Refugee Status in International Law: 1920–1950" (1984/2) *The International and Comparative Law Quarterly*, 348–380.

[16] Arrangement with regard to the Issue of Certificates of Identity to Russian Refugees 13 LNTS 237 (1921); Arrangement with regard to the Issue of Certificates of Identity to Russian and Armenian Refugees Supplementing and Amending the Previous Arrangements 89 LNTS 47 (1926); Arrangement concerning the Legal Status of Russian and Armenian Refugees, 89 LNTS 53 (1928); Convention relating to the International Status of Refugees 159 LNTS 199 (1933) and the Convention Concerning the Status of Refugees coming from Germany 192 LNTS 59 (1938). These agreements were, however, not binding. All these documents did, in contrast to the modern refugee definition, was to define refugees on the basis of their belonging to a certain group – often nationality.

relating to the International Status of Refugees signed in 1933 included a legal obligation for signatories not to refoule refugees from their territory. However, inclusion of this obligation led to this convention receiving few signatures.[17] In 1948 the Universal Declaration of Human Rights was adopted, including Article 14(1) that states "Everyone has the right to seek and to enjoy in other countries freedom from persecution".[18]

In 1950 a resolution establishing the UNHCR and giving this organ an official mandate over refugees and stateless persons was passed in the United Nations.[19] Further, the Convention Relating to the Status of Refugees was signed in 1951, including an internationally valid refugee definition, provisions on non-discrimination and welfare as well as an important article prohibiting refoulement.[20] The convention imposed legal obligations on signatory states as well as placing the UNHCR in a position to overlook and guide use of the Convention. Through combining the definition of refugee and the principle of non-refoulement, refugees were granted protection from expulsion from signatory countries. In 1967 a protocol was added to the convention making the refugee definition universal time-wise.[21]

The Link between Asylum and Non-Refoulement
The main content of asylum is the obligation of the host country to protect the refugee from persecution and to offer a new link between state and citizen in place of the broken bond between the refugee and his or her home country. However, international law additionally includes substantive provisions on the rights of recognised refugees and, accordingly, on the obligations of signatory states. Thus, asylum also entails a certain standard of rights in the host country,

---

[17] The 1933 Convention Relating to the International Status of Refugees was ratified only by eight states. For a history of the particular convention see Robert J. Beck, "Britain and the 1933 Refugee Convention: National or State Sovereignty" (1999/4) *International Journal of Refugee Law*, 597–624.

[18] The Universal Declaration of Human Rights adopted and proclaimed by General Assembly resolution 217 A (III) of 10 December 1948. On Art 14 of the Convention in relation to asylum and refugees Grahl-Madsen (1972) 24.

[19] General Assembly Resolution 319 A (IV) (1949) and General Assembly Resolution 428 (V) (1950).

[20] *Supra* at 1. The Convention entered into force in 1954 and is still the prime legal instrument relating to recognition of refugee status. Altogether, 140 countries are today signatories to the Convention, including all EU Member States.

[21] Before the Protocol, the definition of refugee had been restricted only to apply to persons recognised under earlier conventions on the matter or whose claims for refugee status were based on events that had taken place prior to 1951. These restrictions were abandoned through the protocol. Protocol to the Convention Relating to the Status of Refugees, approved by the Economic and Social Council in Resolution 1186 (XLI) 18.11.1966 and UN General Assembly Resolution 2198 (XXI) 16.12.1966.

all of them, however, tied together by the intention of asylum to offer a new state as the protector of the refugee against persecution.[22] The concept of asylum accordingly entails a rather strong position of the alien in the host country. This, we will see, also impacts on evidentiary solutions found, as the stakes in asylum procedure are high, both for applicant and host state.[23]

Inherent to the environment of asylum and refugees is the rule of non-refoulement.[24] Put briefly, this rule invokes an obligation for states not to return persons to areas where they risk their lives or freedom, torture or other cruel, inhuman or degrading treatment as recognised on the one hand in a number of international agreements including the 1951 Convention.[25]

The Right to Asylum
None of the instruments adopted on the basis of international or regional law in the field of asylum and immigration provides for any right to be granted asylum. Nor is such a right established in customary law as international law recognises that state sovereignty prevails over the right to be granted asylum in all instances.[26] Most countries have also so far chosen not to incorporate asylum as a claim-right in their national legislation, but as a service-right, stipulating that "asylum can be granted" or that "asylum is granted" to refugees but still acknowledging the state's right to control immigration and the passing of individuals across its borders as stronger than the right to asylum.

1.3. *Subsidiary Protection*

Asylum through refugee status determination has established itself as the primary form of protection afforded to persons in need of protection. However, both because of the relatively narrow definition of refugees, the rigid

---

[22] James C. Hathway, *The Rights of Refugees under International Law* (Cambridge 2005) 75–153 and on the right to a permanent solution 913 ff.

[23] On the stakes in the asylum procedure see Ida Staffans: The Appellate Organ in the Asylum Procedure in (2006a/4) *Nordic Journal of International Law*, 89–119.

[24] See Goodwin-Gill *(et al.)* (2007) 232–284 and Hathaway (2005) 279 ff.

[25] Art 33 of the 1951 Convention, *supra* at 1; Art 3 of the Convention against Torture and Other Cruel, Inhuman or Degrading Treatment or Punishment, 10.12.1984, UNTS 24841; Art 3 of the European Convention on Human Rights, 4.11.1950, ETS 5. Also Clare Ovey & Robin C.A White, *European Convention on Human Rights* (Oxford 2006) 74–109.

[26] The same principles are found in the expression of the right to asylum in the Charter of Fundamental Rights of the European Union, OJ 7.12.2000 (C364) Art 18. In Hakan G. Sicakkan, "Political Asylum and Sovereignty-Sharing in Europe" (2008/2) *Government and Opposition*, 206–229, the author pragmatically reviews how interests of sovereignty affect access to and grant of asylum in Europe.

interpretation of this definition used by many states and the provisions in the 1951 Convention demanding certain rights to be granted to recognised refugees, many states and also the EU have in addition to asylum introduced so called subsidiary protection schemes.[27] This form of protection is not controlled by international law treaties or customary law, except for the basic prohibition of refoulement.[28] However, governing EU directives provide persons protected through subsidiary protection the same rights as persons granted asylum.[29]

Subsidiary protection is in practice granted to persons that fall outside the refugee definition but that still need protection from refoulement on the grounds of international law or, in the case of humanitarian protection, whose return would not be humane.[30] In most countries decisions on granting asylum and subsidiary protection are reached in the same administrative procedure, on the basis of the same material as is presented in support of the application for asylum. In terms of numbers, subsidiary protection is also often the primary national form of international protection.

2. *Refugee Status Determination in National Procedures*

Refugee status determination is carried out at national level in national asylum procedure.[31] National asylum procedure is thus a procedure designed to decide eligibility for international protection. Asylum procedure facilitates

---

[27] For a background to the European scheme for subsidiary protection see McAdam (2005) 461–516.

[28] The prohibition of refoulement is expressed, for instance, in the interpretation of the Torture Convention, *supra* at 25, Art 3 and the European Convention for the Protection of Human Rights, *supra* at 73, Art 3.

[29] The Qualification Directive is applicable not only to refugees but also to "persons who otherwise need international protection" and renders the same protection to both these categories of persons. The Qualification Directive, *supra* at 14, Art 2 (e) defines a person eligible for subsidiary protection as "a third country national or a stateless person who does not qualify as a refugee but in respect of whom substantial grounds have been shown for believing that the person concerned, if returned to his or her country of origin, or in the case of a stateless person, to his or her country of former habitual residence, would face a real risk of suffering serious harm as defined in Art 15, and to whom Art 17(1) and (2) do not apply, and is unable, or, owing to such risk, unwilling to avail himself or herself of the protection of that country."

[30] Humanitarian protection is used as a separate form of protection by some states. See for instance Finnish legislation on international protection, stating in section 88 (a) of the Aliens Act (301/2004) that humanitarian protection is granted, for instance, in situations of armed conflict or environmental catastrophes in the country of origin of the applicant.

[31] All European countries have national asylum procedures, whereas for instance Turkey, a non-signatory to the 1951 Convention, relies on the UNHCR for determination of refugee

necessary enquiries both of a general and individual character in order for the subject state to reach certainty on refugee or other protection status of the applicant.[32]

Asylum procedure is a procedure of an administrative legal character, as understood in the civil law system.[33] Aside from the fact of state practice, this also follows from relevant EU legislation, which as a starting point regards asylum procedure as an administrative procedure and a procedure of administrative judicial review in Member States.[34] Institutionally, this entails an authority as the first stage decision-maker. On appeal, the decision-making organ is an organ with competence in administrative justice, for instance a tribunal, court or board.[35]

The procedural regulation governing administrative procedure and administrative review procedures is often, especially in comparison to procedural laws on the civil or criminal front, not concerned with detailed procedural regulation and keeps its references to procedural issues on a fairly general level. An consequence of loose procedural regulation on the administrative level is that many countries have chosen to include procedural regulations in specific legislation relating to asylum and foreigners, typically the Aliens Act.[36]

---

status and practical measures in relation to asylum seekers in the country. See Council of Europe, *Asylum Seekers and Irregular Migrants in Turkey*, Report by the Committee on Refugees, Migration and Population, Doc. 10445 (Geneva 2005).

[32] The trend for asylum procedures in Europe is to move towards what are called "one stop shop" procedures, in which all grounds for residence permits to be granted are heard under the same procedure. Even if initiated as a claim for asylum, the procedure can thus end in residence permits to be granted for instance on the basis of employment, studies or family ties.

[33] Asylum is not considered to be one of the civil rights to which Art 6 of the European Convention on Human Rights, *supra* at 25, would apply. For the procedural implications of Art 6 on appeal rights and determination of a civil right in this respect, see Olle Mårsäter, *Folkrättsligt skydd av räten till domstolsprövning* (Uppsala 2005) 212–227. Rather, asylum is understood as belonging to the purely administrative framework.

[34] Council directive 2005/85, OJ 1.12.2005, (L 326) 13 on Minimum Standards on Procedures in Member States for Granting and Withdrawing Refugee Status. This directive is open for re-negotiations, see Proposal for a Directive of the European Parliament and of the Council on minimum standards of procedures in Member States for the granting and withdrawing of international protection COM (2009) 554/4 and Amended proposal for a Directive of the European Parliament and of the Council on common procedures for granting and withdrawing international protection status (Recast), COM(2011) 319 final.

[35] On obligations for facilitating asylum appeals in international instruments see Staffans (2006a).

[36] As we will see in Chapters IV – VI, the English, German and Finnish relevant substantive acts do include specific provisions on procedural and evidentiary issues.

In most cases, these special rules are complementary to general procedural norms, but in some instances specific rules can also contest general norms of administration. At the European level, both the Asylum Procedures Directive (APD) and the Qualification Directive (QD) also contain some relevant provisions in terms of procedural matters.[37]

Unsurprisingly, a debated and contested issue in relation to asylum procedures is the rights of the applicant – both procedure-wise and regarding, for instance, the right to housing and other benefits. Whereas international (and in many cases also national) law gives good references as to the rights of the refugee, the rights of a person only claiming this status are not quite as clear. On the one hand, it is clear that the asylum applicant is protected by the same rules as everyone else – against refoulement for example. Crucially, during examination of his or her application the applicant should be treated as a possible refugee with a claim to non-refoulement. Additionally, as James C. Hathaway recognises in his study of the rights of refugees, asylum applicants are also entitled to what is necessary in terms of basic living conditions.[38] On the other hand, there are some specific rights that international law, in particular the 1951 Convention, affords asylum seekers. Outstanding among these is the right of asylum seekers not to be punished for illegal entry to the state where asylum is applied for.[39] Thirdly, procedural rights included in relevant legislation, be it at national, international or EU level, are afforded the applicant.[40]

3. The Common European Asylum System

3.1. Background to the Common European Asylum System

Developments in the EC/EU in relation to asylum and refugees have been divided into three stages[41]. The first stage emerged in the 1980s and included creation of national but nevertheless intertwined responses to reception of

---

[37] *Supras* at 14 and 34.

[38] Hathaway (2005).

[39] The 1951 Convention, *supra* at 1, Art 31.

[40] However, Art 6 of the European Convention of Human Rights, *supra* at 25, does not apply to determination of refugee status procedure as the question is not of grant of a right to the asylum seeker in the spirit of the convention. Nuala Mole, *Asylum and the European Convention on Human Rights* (Council of Europe 2008) 56–57.

[41] This presentation of the phases of regionalisation of asylum responses is inspired by Rosemary Byrne; Gregor Noll & Jens Vedsted-Hansen, "Understanding Refugee Law in an Enlarged European Union" (2004/2) *European Journal of International Law*, 355–379.

foreigners in Europe. At this stage, the formations and principles of a common European response to asylum seekers were formed.[42] The second phase of regionalisation of asylum responses introduced measures to amend national approaches to regional approaches – though still mostly in the form of soft law recommendations and guidelines. The goal of this transformation was "to bring about a convergence of national asylum practices".[43] The third phase, which we are now seeing, aims at constructing common European regulations on asylum and refugees. From harmonisation of Member State policies and legislation the focus has now shifted to creating not only common principles and policies but also common procedures in the field.[44]

Whereas the early stages of European response in the area were characterised by isolated national policies and strategies, recent decades have clearly shown that states have found ways to respond collectively to the pressures of immigration. One of the core community concepts introduced early in the common debates on asylum, which also illustrates the mechanisms behind the evolution of European concepts in this field, was that of burden sharing and responses to mass influx.[45]

3.2. Relevant Legislation

The relevant EU instruments in relation to recognition of refugees on EU territory can be divided into two categories for the sake of clarity of presentation: First, let us look at the guiding primary legislation, general decisions and choices of development in the field of asylum and immigration. Secondly, we will review secondary legislation relevant for asylum procedure.

---

[42] Vigdis Vevstad, *Utvikling av et felles europeisk asylsystem* (Oslo 2006) 100–104.

[43] Byrne (*et al.*) (2004) 363 and Vevstad (2006) 104–108.

[44] A vast literature is available on the roots of harmonisation and integration of the laws and practices of EU Member States. This study does not encompass general considerations regarding harmonisation and European integration, but takes its starting point in developments in the specific field of asylum and immigration. For comments on general development of harmonisation see Legrand (1996) and Pierre Legrand, "The impossibility of legal transplants" (1997/4) *Maastricht Journal of European and Comparative Law*, 111 ff. Also, for a background to developments in private law, which heavily influence areas outside the common market, see Reinhard Zimmermann, "Roman law and the harmonisation of private law in Europe", in *Towards a European Civil Code*, eds. Arthur S. Hartkamp & Martin Hesselink (Nijmegen 2004) 21–42 and Mel Kenny, "Standing Surety in Europe: Common Core or Tower of Babel?" (2007/2) *Modern Law Review*, 175–196.

[45] On burden-sharing in the European asylum context see Eiko R. Thielemann, "Between Interests and Norms: Explaining Burden-Sharing in the European Union" (2003/3) *Journal of Refugee Studies*, 253–273 and Gregor Noll, "Risky games? A Theoretical Approach to Burden-Sharing in the Asylum Field" (2003/3) *Journal of Refugee Studies*, 236–252.

3.2.1. *General Framework*

The 1985 Schengen agreement, which entered into force through the Schengen Convention of 1990, introduced the concept of free movement of persons to Europe, presented principles and rules for the abolition of internal borders and provided for possibilities of free movement between signatory states.[46] During the 1980s and early 1990s, at the same time as Schengen was making its way into every day practice in Europe, a basis for contemporary EU legislation on asylum, refugees and immigration was developed through inter-governmental agreements between European states. The nature of these agreements was often linked to early attempts at burden sharing and to issues deepening implementation of the Schengen agreement between the states in question. One of the most significant agreements signed on an intergovernmental level during this time was the so called Dublin Convention agreed upon in 1990, which entered into force in 1997.[47] The Dublin agreement laid down rules on distribution of responsibility for assessing asylum applications in Europe, the main idea being that the first European country where the applicant arrived would be the sole country in which an application for asylum would be processed.[48]

The 1992 Treaty of Maastricht brought about a radical change in decision-making in the field of immigration and asylum in Europe.[49] Through this treaty, an "area of freedom, justice and security" was introduced in Europe so that the parameters were set for even closer integration of law and practice on the European level. The treaty of Maastricht not only introduced issues of immigration as a relevant and important question for cooperation between

---

[46] The first instrument abolishing internal border controls, the Schengen Agreement of 14 June 1985, was signed by the Benelux countries, Germany and France. Gradually, more states signed similar agreements and eventually the Schengen acquis was fully incorporated in Community law. For a list of instruments adopted since 1985 together forming the Schengen acquis see OJ 22.9.2000 (L 239), 0019–0062.

[47] Convention Determining the State Responsible for Examining Applications for Asylum Lodged in one of the Member States of the European Communities, OJ 15.6.1990 (C 254) 1.

[48] On the Dublin agreement and the associated rules for burden sharing, Gregor Noll, "Formalism vs. Empiricism: Some Reflections on the Dublin Convention on the Occasion of Recent European Case Law" (2001/1–2) *Nordic Journal of International Law*, 161–182 and Adam Hurwitz, "The 1990 Dublin Convention: A Comprehensive Assessment" (1999/4) *International Journal of Refugee Law*, 646–677. On the Dublin regulation within EU legislation see Christian Filzwieser & Barbara Liebminger, *Dublin II Verordnung das Europäische Asylzuständigkeitssystem* (Vienna 2006) and Jerry Bunker, "Burden Sharing or Burden Shifting? Asylum and Expansion in the European Union" (2006/2) *Georgetown Immigration Law Journal*, 293–322.

[49] Treaty on the European Union, signed 7.2.1992 and in force since 1.11.1993, 1992 OJ (C 191).

European states, but also brought about radically new implementation possibilities by introducing the Union frame of institutions. The Treaty of Maastricht, however, placed issues of refugees and asylum under the third pillar, lifting these areas on to the common policy agenda while still preserving the model of intra-governmental decision-making in the field.

In 1997 the expansion of European policy on immigration, refugees and asylum necessitated radical changes to the decision-making environment, calling for new instruments and tools for further work on migration management. The Treaty of Amsterdam, adopted in 1997 and in force since 1999, brought about these changes.[50] This treaty did for the Union in the field of migration what Maastricht had done for Europe, moving the asylum and refugee agenda from the third pillar, and state-to-state decision-making, to the first pillar, introducing community legislative competence in the field.[51] With the ground set for community decision-making, the European council meeting in Tampere 1999 set out to find a common agenda and a timeline for development of a Union asylum policy. With this goal in mind, it is hardly surprising that the outcome of the negotiations in Tampere has been decisive for introducing and creating a subject agenda for a common European asylum system within the EU.[52]

The conclusions established a time frame of five years (until 1.5.2004) by which time certain harmonising measures were to be introduced and adopted.[53] After that, a time of practical cooperation and harmonisation would take over, in order to establish a Common European Asylum System by 2010. The deadline was later amended to 2012.[54]

---

[50] Treaty of Amsterdam, signed 2.10.1997 and in force since 1.5.1999, 1997 OJ (C 340).

[51] Norms on Union competence in matters of asylum and immigration are today included in title IV of the Treaty, *ibid.*

[52] See the Presidency Conclusions from the Council Meeting in Tampere 15–16.10.1999.

[53] See Steve Peers, "EU Immigration and Asylum Law: Internal Market Model or Human Rights Model?", in *European Union Law for the 21st Century: Rethinking the New Legal Order*, ed. Takis Tridimas (Oxford 2004) 345 ff, where the author examines progress in the field of asylum and immigration through the view of competing legislative models.

[54] For general remarks on development including Schengen cooperation, the Treaty of Maastricht, the Treaty of Amsterdam and the Tampere conclusions and the implications of this legal framework on work towards a common asylum system, see Gisbert Brinkmann, "The Immigration and Asylum Agenda" (2004/2) *European Law Journal*, 182–199; Mohamed Elewa Badar, "Asylum Seekers and the European Union: Past, Present and Future" (2004/2) *International Journal of Human Rights*, 159–174 and Adrian Favell & Randall Hansen, "Markets Against Politics: Migration, EU Enlargement and the Idea of Europe" (2002/4) *Journal of Ethnic and Migration Studies*, 581–601 and Jens Vedsted-Hansen, "Common EU Standards on Asylum – Optional Harmonisation and Exclusive Procedures?" (2005/4) *European Journal of Migration and Law*, 369–376. Also Emek M. Ucarer, "Managing Asylum and European Integration: Expanding Spheres of Exclusion" (2001/2) *International Studies Perspectives*, 288–304.

During the first five years, targeted legislation was indeed adopted. A clear disadvantage for the negotiations was the exception made while introducing Union competence in the field in 1997 upholding requirements for unanimous voting in the Council on issues linked to immigration and asylum.[55] With reference to the often lengthy debates and rather hasty last minute adoptions of instruments, it is safe to say that while the legislation adopted entails elements for the construction of common standards and procedures and necessary tools for progress towards more unified approaches to asylum in Europe, they also constitute something of a patchwork of different national wills and strategies.[56] It is also clear that Union legislation due to the troublesome negotiation procedures includes broad margins of appreciation even regarding core aspects of common procedure. Thus, and as we will see, the harmonising effect of this legislation can be questioned.[57]

The first five year transition period ended in May 2004, entailing the beginning of the second circle encompassing practical integration and deepened cooperation between Member States, resulting in a common system and procedure.[58] In the shift between the first and second phase of developments the Hague programme was also agreed upon, entailing a continuum to the Tampere conclusions.[59] The action plan following the Hague programme entailed a road map for the sector of justice and home affairs in the EU.[60] The action plan and subsequent measures introducing steps to strengthen cooperation and harmonisation during the second phase of the Common European Asylum

---

[55] On the unanimous voting rules in asylum matters see Peter J. van Krieken (ed.), *The Asylum Acquis Handbook The Foundations for a Common European Asylum Policy* (Leiden 2000) 52–53. In Peers (2006) 47–59, the author analyses developments from the outset of unanimous voting to its abolition in favour of qualified majority voting.

[56] Elspeth Guild, "International Terrorism and EU Immigration, Asylum and Borders Policy: The Unexpected Victims of 11 September 2001" (2003/3) *European Foreign Affairs Review*, 331–346 studies the impact of the dichotomy between human rights protection and security interests on union legislation and practice, as one example of the strategies involved.

[57] Ida Staffans, "Convergence and Mutual Recognition in European Asylum Law" in *The Internationalisation of Law and Legal Education*, Jan Klabbers & Mortimer Sellers (eds.) (The Hague 2008) 149–168.

[58] See also the Green Paper on the Future of the Common European Asylum System presented by the Commission 6.6.2007, COM(2007) 301 Final, where the aims and stages of work towards a common system are spelt out taking into account the result of the first legislative phase. Elspeth Guild presents critical observations on developments and the structural approach to the CEAS in Elspeth Guild, *The Biopolitics of Refugee Law*, Paper presented at the Nordic Refugee Seminar, 5–6.2.2009.

[59] The Hague-Programme, Strengthening freedom, security and justice 13.12.2004, 16054/04.

[60] Council and Commission Action Plan implementing the Hague Programme on strengthening freedom, security and justice in the European Union, 12.8.2005, 2005/C 198/01.

System (CEAS) present, for instance, strengthened cooperation between Member States on exchange of knowledge and surveillance measures, reception and expulsion of asylum seekers to and from the Union, creation of European bodies such as the European Asylum Support Office, and measures in terms of internal resettlement and integration of refugees in Europe.[61]

Second stage developments also include introduction of ECJ competence in the field of asylum and immigration as a result of the adoption of the Treaty of Lisbon in 2009.[62] Partly in response to this added competence the ECJ in 2008 established an urgent claims procedure in order to be more effective in decision-making in certain fields.[63] Further, a move away from demands for unanimous voting was made in 2005 as the first stage of harmonisation came to an end and gave way to rules on qualified majority voting. Thus, second stage adaptations and additions to the legal framework are not hindered by the same requirements for unanimous voting as in the first round of negotiations.

In 2009 the third programme for the Justice and Home Affairs (JHA)-sector, the so called Stockholm programme, was agreed upon.[64] This programme features even more concrete measures in the field, such as external resettlement schemes for quota refugees, creation of common databanks and the like to support harmonisation and measures in the field of integration. Also, with

---

[61] Proposal for a Regulation of the European Parliament and of the Council establishing a European Asylum Support Office, COM(2009) 66 final. Views have indeed been expressed on the need to establish common decision-making organs. See for instance Ariel Meyerstein, "Returning the Harmonisation of EU Asylum Law: Exploring the Need for an EU Asylum Appellate Court" (2005/5) *California Law Review*, 1509–1555, which advocates the establishment of such a court. Similar opinions have also been raised by NGO:s in the field, such as the National Red Cross Societies of the Member States of the European Union. See *Opinion of the National Red Cross Societies of the Member States of the European Union and the International Federation of Red Cross and Red Crescent Societies* 12.11.2008.

[62] On the ECJ and asylum see Meyerstein (2005) and ECRE, *Analysis of the Treaty of Amsterdam in so far as it relates to asylum policy* (London 1997) 5–6.

[63] Regarding developments of ECJ competence and creation of the so called urgent procedure see Court of Justice of the European Union: Information for the Press, *A New Procedure in the Area of Freedom, Security and Justice: the Urgent Preliminary Ruling Procedure* 3.3.2008 and Allan Rosas, *Justice in Haste, Justice Denied? The European Court of Justice and the Area of Freedom, Security and Justice*, The Mackenzie-Stuart Lecture, University of Cambridge, 6.11.2008.

[64] Communication from the Commission to the European Parliament and Council: An Area of Freedom, Security and Justice Serving the Citizen, COM(2009)262/4. However, the Action Plan Implementing the Stockholm Programme reveals that many of the developments in the field of immigration and asylum are allocated to a rather distant future. Communication from the Commission to the European Parliament, the Council, the European Economic and Social Committee and the Committee of the Regions: Delivering an area of freedom, security and justice for Europe's citizens COM (2010) 171 final.

entry into force of the Treaty of Lisbon the Charter of Fundamental Rights, including in Article 18 a right of asylum and in Article 19 a prohibition against refoulement as well as the inclusion of asylum matters under the protection of a fair trial and effective remedy in Article 47, gained legal force and became relevant for everyday assessment of asylum applications in Europe.[65]

3.2.2. Secondary Legislation

As mentioned, 1999 saw the beginning of efforts to harmonise European asylum procedure through community legislation. Targeted legislation, mainly in the form of directives, has been adopted on various issues in connection to the asylum and immigration field.[66] Most legislation has been so called minimum standard legislation, setting out minimum standards of rights or benefits awarded to third country nationals in different positions, allowing Member States to adopt higher standards if they wish.

Adopted targeted legislation with relevance for appellate asylum procedures includes:

- Council Regulation Establishing the Criteria and Mechanisms for Determining the Member State Responsible for Examining an Asylum Application Lodged in One of the Member States by a Third-Country National (the so called Dublin II);[67]
- Council Regulation Concerning the Establishment of EURODAC for the Comparison of Fingerprints for the Effective Application of the Dublin Convention on the State Responsible for Examining Applications for Asylum Lodged in one of the European Union Member States;[68]
- Council Directive on Minimum Standards on Procedures in Member States for Granting and Withdrawing Refugee Status;[69]

---

[65] Charter of Fundamental Rights of the European Union, *supra* at 26.
[66] On the impact of directives on national legal orders see Outi Suviranta, *Virkamiesten ratkaisutoiminta ja Euroopan yhteisön oikeus* (Helsinki 1996) 87–96.
[67] Council regulation 343/2003 of 18 February 2003, 2003 OJ (L 50) 1.This so called Dublin II regulation is currently the object of renegotiation, see Proposal for a Regulation of the European Parliament and of the Council establishing the criteria and mechanisms for determining the Member State responsible for examining an application for international protection lodged in one of the Member States by a third-country national or a stateless person, COM(2008) 820 final.
[68] Council regulation 2757/2000, OJ 11.12.2000 (L 316) 1. This regulation is currently the object of renegotiation, see Proposal for a Council Decision on requesting comparisons with EURODAC data by Member States' law enforcement authorities and Europol for law enforcement purposes, COM(2009) 342 final.
[69] *Supra* at 34.

- Council Directive on Minimum Standards for the Qualification and Status of Third-Country Nationals and Stateless Persons as Refugees or as Persons Who Otherwise Need International Protection and the Content of the Protection Granted.[70]

Additionally, directives have been adopted on reception standards[71], temporary protection[72] and the European Refugee Fund[73]. Further, a draft directive on common procedures for returning illegally staying third-country nationals was presented in 2005.[74]

4. *Asylum in Context*

The institution of asylum is a part of international and regional European law. Asylum is an instrument of protection that is deeply rooted in international law and history. The ties between asylum and other elements of society are also easily noted at the European level, where asylum procedures are supported by a vast framework of rules. Asylum understood as an instrument for protection and as an institution of international and regional law offers the first material framework for study. As we will see, the institution of asylum itself, as well as the perception of refugee protection in the countries included in the comparative study, indeed offers implications of relevance for limitations in a study of evidentiary assessment. In order to understand the functions of asylum in an evidentiary context, it is nevertheless important also to understand the deeper functions of this institution – the purpose, the history and the environment of asylum.

---

[70] *Supra* at 14 and Proposal for a Directive of the European Parliament and of the Council on minimum standards for the qualification and status of third country nationals or stateless persons as beneficiaries of international protection and the content of the protection granted COM (2009) 551.

[71] Council directive 2003/9, OJ 27.1.2003, (L 31) 18.

[72] Council directive 2001/55, OJ 20.7.2001 (L 212) 12.

[73] Council decision 2000/596, OJ 28.9.2000, (L 252) 12 and Council decision 2004/904, OJ 2.12.2004, (L 381) 52.

[74] Proposal for a Directive of the European Parliament and of the Council on common standards and procedures in Member States for returning illegally staying third country nationals, 1.9.2005, COM(2005) 391 final.

Chapter III

Asylum and Evidence

1. *Evidentiary Framework for the Study*

1.1. *What Is Assessment of Evidence?*

In the analysis carried out in this book the substantive framework, asylum procedures, is studied with aid of the theoretical framework made up of standards and assessment of evidence. Assessment of evidence is, as we have seen, an integrated part of all judicial decision-making: In all circumstances when law is to be applied, a decision has to be made on what the law is to be applied to – we need to know the reality against which the law is projected. Regardless of whether decision-making is of an administrative, criminal or civil character, the law needs a reality to work with.

And realities are difficult to grasp. Different perceptions of reality exist, as do different ways to value and weigh circumstances. This makes objective and common agreements on reality difficult to achieve. The remedy for this in legal decision-making has been legal prerequisites for analysis of reality: The law dictates the elements that must be present in order for the law to apply to the individual context. The law thus guides the assessor towards what is significant.[1] And in order for the law to be effective judicial decision-making as a regulatory means requires that the reality to which legal prerequisites are applied is the same reality that is shared by and commonly perceived in society, and with reference to which the law has been made. Hence, only after creating an

---

[1] This does not, of course, mean that we always reach common agreement on when these legal prerequisites are at hand. And in addition to differences in perceptions of reality, differences also occur in perceptions of the elements of law and legal prerequisites. See also Bengt Lindell, *Civilprocessen* (Uppsala 1998) 484–487, for questions relating to perceptions of legal prerequisites. However, in Karl H. Kunert, "Some Observations on the Origin and Structure of Evidence Rules Under the Common Law System and the Civil Law System of 'Free Proof' in the German Code of Criminal Procedure" (1966/1) *Buffalo Law Review*, 122–164 at 123, proof is given that an inverted approach is also possible when the author presents that the second step in any evidentiary assessment concerns assessing whether the information that the evidence gives can be accepted as reality.

understanding of reality in accordance with this common perception can the decision-maker decide whether certain legal prerequisites are met and if certain legal provisions are thus applicable to this reality.[2] And in order to form a solid knowledge of what is real, the decision-maker gathers knowledge.[3] As a result of different perceptions and interests vested in decision-making, the knowledge presented to the decision-maker may not always be clear and unchallengeable. Nevertheless, it is a task for the decision-maker to form a picture of relevant events and elements. Consequently, it is also a task for the decision-maker to identify the methods for coming to the right conclusions about the state of reality on the basis of sometimes contradictory information and knowledge.

Hence, evidentiary assessment is the part of decision-making that strives to understand the reality against which legal rules and principles are to be projected.[4] Whereas evidentiary assessment in itself is an utterly theoretical part of decision-making, the object and the instruments for this work are highly concrete and the main substance with which the decision-maker works consists of bits and pieces of reality.

1.2. *Questions of Interest and Debatable Solutions*

Diverging interests in the procedure often lead to diverging perceptions of reality. Also, divergent interests or points of references may lead to debates about the most efficient and correct method for going about evidentiary assessment – which, if dressed down, is a debate about the correct way to perceive and de-construct reality.

Whereas legal developments over time have brought about agreements on and conclusions regarding certain elements of evidentiary assessment, such as the burden and standard of proof in various contexts[5], no institutionalisation

---

[2] Saranpää (2010) 17 ff argues for the necessity of evidentiary standards as guarantees of legal security.

[3] As we will see in later chapters, collecting information is undertaken in different ways in different forms of procedure and is partly governed by legal limitations and rules. For an explanation of the responsibility of the judge towards evidence in criminal procedure, see Pölönen (2003) 397.

[4] On the tasks of evidentiary assessment, see Jonkka (1993) 24–32, where tasks are described generally from a criminal procedural point of view. See also Bengt Lindell, *Sakfrågor och rättsfrågor* (Uppsala 1987) 35–41, where evidence and evidentiary assessment is examined as a distinct element in judicial procedure.

[5] Evidentiary assessment has been more or less institutionalised over time. The line has generally gone from heavily restricted and limited assessment towards more open and free procedural rules. Pölönen (2003) 181–238 gives an elaborate account of institutionalisation as to forms of evidence allowed in criminal procedure.

has been able to grasp the very core of assessment – weighing and balancing information and knowledge. The debate on this matter has often concerned issues linked to the difficulty in combining the abstract and utterly human task of weighing information provided in a judicial procedure with rigid rules on right and wrong.[6]

This study does not involve itself in general discussions on the perception of reality. It does not argue that the solutions here presented are the only plausible or the sole correct paths to perception. Nevertheless, it will in order to define the keys of comparison in their subject environment provide an example of how evidence can be assessed and how evidentiary standards can be used in the appellate asylum procedures. The methodological basis for evidence theory as used in this study is accounted for in the introduction to the material analysis of evidence in asylum procedures, in chapter IV.7 below. Suffice to state at this stage that the method chosen emphasises a functional approach to assessment of evidence, taking into account the effect of institutional and other pragmatic elements and recognizing the need for a clear strategy for evidentiary assessment.

1.3. *Evidence in Administrative Context*

As stated, the keys for comparison in this study are made up of evidentiary tools and standards that exist, even though not alike, in all European asylum procedures.[7] And in order to use these keys and points of reference a certain and specified framework is required – for the purposes of this study, the European appellate asylum procedure.[8] These procedures, forming the objects for this

---

[6] See for instance Lindell (1998), who dismisses certain methods of assessment as too mathematical in relation to the issues that are to be investigated. See also Dan Frände, *Finsk straffprocessrätt* (Helsinki 2009) 363–370 where evidentiary assessment is grasped in an utterly pragmatic way, despite incorporation of elements from statistical models of assessment.

[7] The choice of comparative keys has been made with full knowledge that the structures of procedures are different, but with a firm belief that these keys are evidence and necessary in all forms of asylum procedure. See Kay Hailbronner, "One Single Procedure", in *The Emergence of a European Asylum Policy*, eds. Philippe de Bruycker & Constanca Dias Urbano De Sousa (Brussels 2004), in which the author structures the field of asylum procedures according to the reach and inclusiveness of the procedure and Gregor Noll, *Negotiating Asylum: The EU Acquis, Extraterritorial Protection and the Common Market of Deflection* (Dordrecht 2004) 213–215, where division follows the institutional framework of procedures.

[8] Da Lomba (2004) contains an account of the institutional and procedural frameworks of asylum procedures in the EU Member States as of 2004. See Rosemary Byrne, Gregor Noll & Jens Vedsted-Hansen (eds.), *New Asylum Countries? Migration Control and Refugee Protection in an Enlarged European Union* (The Netherlands 2002), for references to the outsets for asylum procedures in some of the new Member States, 64–66 (Poland), 85–92 (The Czech Republic), 146–157 (Hungary), 246–249 (Lithuania), 276–277 (Latvia), 292–294 (Estonia).

study, are procedures of what continental systems would call administrative justice. Thus, a context for comparison of points of reference can be found in procedural solutions found in the administrative environment for evidentiary features of decision-making. The characteristic legal climate of the administrative framework determines the outsets for the evidentiary features that are to be examined, regardless of the domestic classification of the procedure.

Institutional Framework

The concept 'administrative appellate body in European asylum procedures' includes a varied field of organs and bodies, for example courts, boards and organs within the first instance authority.[9] Administrative courts are increasingly used as appellate organs in asylum procedure, provided that the country of use has a system in place for such courts.[10] Within this group, a distinction can be drawn between countries employing special administrative courts for asylum matters, whose sole task is to review asylum decisions, and countries employing general administrative courts in asylum procedure, in which case asylum decisions are only one of many administrative case types for review by the court. A third possibility also exists: Countries may employ some or one of the general administrative courts in order to create a general administrative court with special competence over asylum decisions. In such cases asylum procedure is concentrated in one or many general court(s) that receive additional funding and means in order to cope with these decisions.[11]

---

[9] All procedures included in present comparative study use courts in their appellate asylum procedures. On institutional choices in appellate asylum procedure, see Staffans (2006a).

[10] Clearly, the choice of institutional model for the appellate organ depends on the general administrative traditions in the country in question, and institutional models are many: both Finland and Germany make use of general administrative courts as appeal instances in asylum claims. In Denmark the task of review is entrusted to the Refugee Board, an independent board (in its own words, "court-like") which automatically reviews all negative decisions from first instance and whose decisions cannot be subject to further review. After first instance decisions by the Ministry of the Interior in the Czech Republic, appeals can be lodged with an administrative committee consisting of state and NGO representatives. This committee thus functions as the second instance and makes recommendations to the ministry on the possible need to alter earlier decisions. The UK, in turn, abandoned their earlier appeals system, featuring both adjudicators and administrative bodies in 2004, in favour of a single-track procedure. Today appeals in asylum cases can be lodged with the First-Tier and Upper Tribunal, a semi-specialised administrative court. Also, there are appellate organs that are internal to the first decision-making authority. However, Community legislation opposes this form of appellate body in asylum procedures. Battjes (2006) 328–329. For information on appeals organs in European asylum procedures see Da Lomba (2004) 187–189, 213–217.

[11] On the procedural implications of court structure in asylum matters, see Staffans (2006a) 105–118.

Regardless of the nature of the court, one characteristic of this solution is that the court follows procedural rules laid down in general laws on administrative appellate procedures, and that the procedural norms governing appellate asylum procedure are thus not specific to the asylum context.[12] In addition to general procedural acts, special laws on asylum matters may include relevant procedural norms.

Aside of the nature of the court, also the mandate of the court can vary between different countries. While the task is shared, to review and provide legal certainty in asylum cases, the mandate between appellate procedures may differ in accordance with the division between questions of law and questions of fact.[13] Some appellate instances in asylum procedures are only confined to reviewing questions of law. Others again review decisions in relation to questions of both law and fact. Nevertheless, as the European Court of Human Rights has held that the requirement for effective remedy indeed includes a requirement for at least one possibility to review on grounds of both fact and law, first instance appellate procedures normally give access to review of as well facts and law. In upper instances, limitations and variations occur.[14]

Procedural Framework
A clear but still important feature of asylum decision-making in administrative appellate organs is that this decision-making is of a legal nature, regardless of institutional framework.[15] The methods applicable to both reasoning

---

[12] On common procedural features of European asylum procedures see Battjes (2006) 289–365 and Johannes van der Klaauw, "Towards a Common Asylum Procedure", in *Implementing Amsterdam: Immigration and Asylum Rights in EC Law*, eds. Elspeth Guild & Carol Harlow (Oxford 2001) 165–193.

[13] When looking at evidentiary standards in procedures, it is not always self-evident if these are questions of fact or law. Surely, collection of evidence has much to do with establishing facts. Evidentiary assessment and review is, on the other hand, often to be seen as involving questions of law. However, as most asylum procedures at first instance are also concerned with questions of law as questions of fact, the implications of the dichotomy are central only in the upper appellate procedure. On the division between questions of fact and questions of law see Lindell (1987) 364–384.

[14] See *Potocka and Others v. Poland*, Appl. No. 33776/96, Council of Europe: European Court of Human Rights 4 October 2001, para 57. A further question relating to the limits of the power of the appellate organ which is of special importance in asylum procedure relates to the issue of suspensive effect at appeal instance. On the issue of suspensive effect in European asylum procedures see Noll (2004) at 220–222. See also ECRE, *Memorandum to SCIFA – Improving the Functioning of the Dublin System* ECRE document AD7/8/2006/EXT/CW/RN (2006), 2–3.

[15] Administrative decision-making is not to be confused with pure political or policy-orientated decision-making. It is important to note that the aims and goals of decisions in these fields, as well as the means for and outsets of decision-making are different and that whereas

and decision-making are legal, and the decision-maker needs to be able to give an account of the reasons for the decision in legal terms. It is clear that basic requirements for legal decision-making, such as legal certainty and the need for reasoning in decisions also have an impact on evidentiary norms and on evidentiary practice. Most clearly, perhaps, the requirements for account-ability, reasoning and other elements of legal certainty place a requirement with the decision-maker to be able also to give an account of evidentiary assessment. Here, models and methods of evidentiary assessment appear in the picture.

A distinct feature of the framework of administrative procedures is that one cannot speak of a clear cut two-party procedure, at least not in the same sense as in criminal or civil procedure.[16] Partly, this depends on emphasis on the role of the appellate organ as the assessor of legality in addition to the role of solver of inter-party disputes. Additionally, the position of strength between the parties is often in administrative justice unequal, a fact that in turn has effects, for instance, on distribution of responsibilities for presenting evidence in the procedure.[17] It should be noted that the impact is two-sided: There is both an impact on the evidentiary tools and means by the special relationship between the parties to the procedure, and an impact by the evidentiary requirements of the procedure on the positions and relationships of the parties.[18]

---

administrative decision-making, especially in authorities, clearly includes elements of these other forms of decision-making, administrative judicial procedure is far from political or policy-orientated. On the distinctions in methods, aims and goals between administrative conduct and administrative procedure see Mäenpää (2007a) 9–13. See also Carol Harlow, "Proceduralism in English Administrative Law", in *The Europeanisation of Administrative Law – Transforming national decision-making procedures*, ed. Karl-Heinz Ladeur (Darmouth 2002) 46–67, for an account of procedural distinctions in common law administrative proce-dures, distinguishing these from political or policy-orientated decision-making.

[16] For comparison see Mäenpää (2007a) 193–195 on the distinction between administrative procedure and criminal procedure and same, 178–189 for civil procedure, where the author also refers to the possibilities of state entities as parties to civil proceedings.

[17] Cpr Christian Diesen & Annika Lagerqvist Veloza Roca, *Bevisprövning i förvaltningsmål* (Stockholm 2003) 80–84, which considers the burden of investigation in administrative pro-cedures in the light of examples from civil and criminal procedures and which advocates also allocating to the state party objective responsibility for the robustness of investigations.

[18] The burden of investigation, for instance, works both ways. On the one hand, it is because of the distinctive character of the inter-party relationship that this burden also has an impact on the actions of the parties, regardless of the placement of burden of proof. On the other hand, responsibility for robustness affects the relationship of the parties by tying them closer together than they would be for instance in civil procedure. *Ibid.*

Moreover, the regulatory framework for administrative justice procedures is commonly of a different calibre to procedural norms for other forms of judicial procedure. The reasons for this may be many; the role of administration is more focused on general aims and conditions of good governance than other judicial procedures, the consequences of 'wrong decisions' in administration and thus the need for legal certainty in the procedure have not been discussed as much as in other forms of procedure and the much more developed doctrine on criminal and civil procedure. The administrative legislator uses different methods than the legislator of civil and criminal procedures.[19] Thus when examining and analysing administrative procedural norms it must be remembered that the general rules of administrative judicial procedure are all but exhaustive. It must also be noted that the aim of more specific legislation on different types of administrative matters may focus on issues different to the focal points of general legislation and of procedure in general, and that these particular legal frameworks often also include procedural norms and rules.[20] Hence, the general picture and the correct understanding of norms are only gained by an inclusive and type-sensitive approach.

Finally, the last point to be made in relation to the general framework for evidence in administrative judicial procedure is not perhaps as much of procedural importance as of interest to the researcher and analyst of evidentiary features in administration. This refers to the common semantic use of knowledge and information as synonyms for evidence when speaking about administration.[21] Nevertheless, in the same manner as in criminal or civil procedures, information and knowledge in administrative justice procedures evolve into evidence when presented for and accepted by the appellate organ. The clearest time for this is when knowledge and information becomes relevant for the procedure, and the very last timeline for this transformation is in connection with use of this knowledge and information in the motivations to the decision.

---

[19] Mäenpää (2007a) 23–43.

[20] See for instance asylum procedure in Finland and Sweden where general administrative acts (Finland: Act on Administrative Procedure 586/1996, Sweden: Act on Administrative Procedure 1971/291) and specific legislation on asylum (Finland: Aliens Act 301/2004, Sweden: Aliens Act 2005/716) govern asylum procedure. Both general and specific laws include provisions affecting procedural standards and evidentiary assessment.

[21] See for instance Mäenpää (2007a) where features that in other forms of judicial procedure would be referred to as evidence are referred to as knowledge, investigations, and information. However, see also Diesen (*et al.*) (2003), where evidentiary semantics throughout the study are used with reference to administrative procedures. In this study, I have chosen to use evidence as a concept separate from that of information and knowledge, implying that information has been given a special procedural position in asylum procedure. However, it is clear that evidence, by its nature, consists of information and knowledge.

2. Evidence in Asylum Procedure

2.1. The Role of Evidence in Asylum Procedure

The role of evidence in asylum procedure is accentuated in comparison to many other administrative justice procedures. On the one hand, the object for the procedure is, as we will see, highly specific and tied to individual features of the applicant, which emphasises the role of evidence presented and decreases the importance of tacit knowledge by the decision-maker.[22] On the other hand, many difficulties are involved in both presentation and evaluation of evidence in asylum procedure, for instance due to cultural differences and the fact that the evidence is aimed at predicting the future.[23] Thirdly, special attention also needs to be paid to use of information in asylum procedure due to the relatively complicated nature of the evidence presented itself. Clearly, some of the evidence presented is rather 'traditional' in the sense that it consists of documents or other material sources. But even if this is the case special factors regarding for instance state security makes handling the knowledge challenging at times.[24] However, the most important evidence in asylum procedure is generally the oral evidence delivered by the applicant in so called asylum interviews – transferred to higher instances in the procedure via the interview record. As we will see, interpreting and evaluating oral evidence, not easy even under optimal circumstances, is very challenging in asylum procedure due to differing factors between the asylum applicant and the assessor. Hence, reliance on assessment of credibility in asylum procedure is both important and contested.[25] Furthermore, the nature of evidence in asylum procedure in general is different from the nature of information in other procedures, both due to the stakes vested in the procedure and the different types of sources of information. Besides, the relationship between the parties is

---

[22] As to focus on the individual in asylum procedures see Einarsen (1998) 433–440; Goodwin-Gill (*et al.*) (2007) 35–41 and Kourula (1997) 87–90. See also Sabine Weidlich, "First Instance Asylum Procedures in Europe: Do Bona Fide Refugees Find Protection" (2000/3) *Georgetown Immigration Law Journal*, 643–672 at 645 ff.

[23] See Weidlich (2000) 644–645.

[24] See Virgil O. Wiebe, *Maybe You Should, Yes You Must, No You can't. Shifting Standards and Practices for Assuring Document Reliability in Asylum Cases* University of St. Thomas School of Law Legal Studies Research Paper No. 06–18 (2006).

[25] On assessment of the asylum interview see Sofia Mineur, "Förhör i flyktingärenden", in *Prövning av flyktingärenden*, eds. Christian Diesen & Johanna Börkman (Stockholm 1998) 267–296 and Cécile Rousseau, Francois Crépeau, Patricia Foxen & France Houle, "The Complexity of Determining Refugeehood: A Multidisclipinary Analysis of the Decision-making Process of the Canadian Immigration and Refugee Board" (2002/1) 15 *Journal of Refugee Studies*, 43–70.

special due to the difference in procedural strength and the possible drastic consequences of decisions. To conclude, it must be noted that while evidence plays a vital role in the procedure in asylum cases, establishing reality for the purposes of the particular matter is very challenging.

2.2. Particular Evidentiary Features

2.2.1. High Stakes and Vested Interests

Firstly, it is important to note that the interests vested in asylum procedure by both state and applicant may be not only of a different nature but also of a higher ranking than in many other administrative procedures.[26] Additionally, asylum procedure in particular involves relative difficulty with which these interests are identified. The interests (in other words, the risks of the decision[27]) affect both presentation and production of evidence and its assessment.

From the standpoint of the applicant, the reason for applying for asylum and, further, the reason for challenging a negative decision can be as low as social welfare for the duration of the asylum procedure or the possibility to spend some time in a foreign country. On the other side of the scale, the interest of the applicant can be as high as future persecution or the right to life and freedom. Most applicants' interests fall somewhere in between these poles and are not as clearly defined. Furthermore, many applicants may have combined reasons or may not entirely understand or be able to acknowledge their stakes themselves.

From the standpoint of the other party, the receiving state, interest in the procedure is also high. In most European countries recognised refugees are afforded far-reaching rights and long term or permanent residence permits.[28]

---

[26] For general comments on the interests vested in asylum procedure by the parties, see Staffans (2006a) 90. Also Noll (2000) 82–84.

[27] The expression "risks of the decision" is here used in another meaning than the one used by evidentiary law when defining the meaning of burden of proof – allocation of risk of a negative decision in the event of the evidence not reaching the standard of proof. "Risk" here refers to subjective risk connected to claims in the procedure.

[28] Practice among European countries varies in relation to the extent of the residence permit afforded recognised refugees: Germany, for instance, issues refugees a three year residence permit, after which time the grounds for residence permit are investigated anew, whereas Sweden generally issues recognised refugees with permanent residence permits immediately after recognition. As we have seen, the very idea with asylum is to resettle refugees, thus providing a durable solution for them. Also, the rules binding European states at the level of international law clearly state that refugeehood is continuous unless the applicable rules on cessation apply. Battjes (2006) 267–269. On the relationship between temporary protection in Europe and durable solutions, see Goodwin-Gill (*et al.*) (2007) 340–345, showing that temporary protection is an exception in cases of max influx, which also is the view of the Directive, and that this is a bridge between pragmatic issues and durable solutions. See also Kourula (1997) 307–319.

Through deciding on applications, the receiving state thus also decides on welcoming a new member to its society, with all that this entails in terms of integration and economic investment. Today, issues relating to safety and state security, as well as considerations regarding the costs of assessing claims also form natural parts of the interests of the state in asylum procedure.[29]

The interests of the applicant are usually not easily identified. On the one hand, the applicant may not be able to articulate these. On the other hand, the applicant may not want to articulate these.[30] And, thirdly, even for applicants who are willing and able to articulate their interests, their understanding of these is not an easy task due to the same difficulties as in general assessment of information.

Clearly, difficulty in identifying the interests vested in the procedure has an impact on asylum procedure and related assessment of evidence. It invites misuse and abuse of the procedure by both parties, which in turn reflects on evidentiary assessment as a requirement for extra care. And as we will see later, the elements of this identification work (in other words, evidentiary assessment) are filled with complex issues not relating directly to any forms of abuse or misuse, but to the extraordinary nature of the evidence presented.

2.2.2. *Position of Parties in Appellate Asylum Procedure*

The outset in administrative appellate procedures is an asymmetry between the parties due to the procedural setting of an individual versus a state party. However, this asymmetry is further accentuated in asylum procedure.

Firstly, it should be recognised that the applicant suffers from a handicap through the fact of being a stranger to the country and culture in which the application is processed and where the appeal is examined.[31] For the applicant, the setting as such with judicial organs and 'implicit knowledge' about, for instance, the expectations of courts or tribunals, may be completely new. The state party, on the other hand, knows the system very well. The applicant is

---

[29] See the Swedish report Statskontoret, *En tydligare styrning av Migrationsverket* 2004:20, 33–34 in which costs for asylum seekers during the procedure have been calculated: For an asylum seeker in a reception centre the cost was 237 SEK / day, for an asylum seeker in group care 1009 SEK / day and for an asylum seeker in detention 2419 SEK / day in 2004. See also Noll (2000) 101–107.

[30] Clearly, a common reason for not wanting to articulate interests is that the interests do not amount to grounds for asylum or, perhaps, any other form of residence permit.

[31] On the implications for evidentiary assessment arising from cultural differences between the applicant and the assessor / decision-maker, see Michel-Acatl Monnier, "The Hidden Part of Asylum Seekers' Interviews in Geneva, Switzerland: Some observations about the socio-political construction of interviews between gatekeepers and the powerless" (1995/3) *Journal of Refugee Studies*, 305–325; Mineur (1998) 271–286 and Rousseau (*et al.*) (2002).

segregated both by factors of culture and language but also in some cases as a result of prior encounters with the authorities.[32] In relation to the evidence, it is thus clear that these differences have to be recognised and that the decision-maker must be able to see beyond these in order for evaluation to be valid and suited to the environment.

However, the applicant is at times legally represented.[33] Even if the lawyer is accustomed to the 'culture of the procedure' and the applicant is thus provided with a bridge between the two camps, difficulties arise as, in turn, interaction with the lawyer can be troublesome. Thus, even when represented legally the applicant is always set apart from the procedure due to differences in language and culture and is hence placed in a further weakened position towards the state party.

Inevitably, this involves use of interpreters in asylum procedure.[34] Both in oral hearings before the appellate court and possibly in interaction with a lawyer the applicant communicates through an interpreter. Regardless of the skill of the interpreter, it is clear that indirect communication is always inferior to direct communication and that use of interpreters adds to the risk of possible misunderstandings in the procedure.[35] This is especially important to bear in mind considering the vast importance of oral evidence in asylum procedure.

2.2.3. *Prognostic Decision*

Another distinct feature of asylum procedure that affects evidentiary assessment is the link to predictions of the future in determining refugee status. As mentioned, refugee status is awarded to persons with a well-founded fear for

---

[32] Difficulties in this respect arise from the fact that perpetrators of persecution are often authorities and representatives of states. On psychological implications of asylum procedure as a setting see Jane Herlihy, "Evidentiary Assessment and Psychological Difficulties", in Noll (2005a) 123–137.

[33] On the experiences of legal professionals working with asylum cases see Maria Appelqvist, "Refugee Law and Case Lawyering: A Swedish Study of the Legal Profession" (2000/1) *International Journal of Refugee Law*, 71–89.

[34] The right to use of interpreters and translation in asylum procedure is also guaranteed by EU law. See the Council directive 2005/85, OJ 1.12.2005, (L 326) 13 on Minimum Standards on Procedures in Member States for Granting and Withdrawing Refugee Status, Art 10 (b). This directive is open for re-negotiations, see Proposal for a Directive of the European Parliament and of the Council on minimum standards of procedures in Member States for the granting and withdrawing of international protection COM (2009) 554/4 and Amended proposal for a Directive of the European Parliament and of the Council on common procedures for granting and withdrawing international protection status (Recast), COM(2011) 319 final.

[35] See Eva Smith, "Bevisoptagekse og bevisvurdering", in *Asyl i Norden*, Dansk Flyktinghjälp (Copenhagen 1990) 89–101, which provides an exhaustive scheme of possible traps involved in use of interpreters in judicial procedures.

being persecuted if returned to their home country. This means that evidence is collected to assess the possibility of something happening in the future. Thus, evidentiary assessment does not refer in the same manner as, for instance, in criminal procedure, to an event that has already produced evidence. Clearly, a possibility of persecution has to have arisen before a decision on the application is taken, and evidence of this must thus be brought before the court. However, persecution itself may be something only expected and not already experienced.[36]

The impact of this feature on the material evidence is clearly that the existing evidence does not point at persecution in itself but at the likelihood of it occurring in the future. And as likelihood is an abstract entity of which the nature and elements may vary, the nature of the evidence may differ from case to case. Moreover, as the object of the proceedings is to assess the possibility or likelihood of something that may occur, the possibility used as a measurement in assessing the evidence is not a possibility of future persecution, but a possibility of the likelihood of future persecution.

Clearly, the abstract notion of likelihood and the prognostic elements of the theme of proof do have implications for evidentiary assessment. The futuristic element as the object of the evidence clearly implies a vagueness in the evidence as well. As the object is not clear and structured and may be composed of very different elements, the evidence for this may vary considerably. It is, so to speak, not easy to know what you are looking for. The object of the evidence must thus be determined during evidentiary assessment, not before.

2.2.4. *Forms of Evidence*

Lastly, let us review the forms of evidence mostly used in asylum procedure and the evidentiary implications of these forms. This survey is not exhaustive and as in all other procedures the forms of evidence presented may vary greatly and are closely tied to the individual case. As we will see, there are complexities tied to assessment of evidence in asylum procedure also as a result of the very nature of the evidence often used.

First of all there is the asylum interview held by the first instance authority and possible oral testimony at appellate instance. In some countries the interview is conducted according to a pre-established set of questions, while in

---

[36] On the predictive character of assessment, see Weidlich (2000) 644–645. See also Jean-Yves Carlier, Dirk Vanheule, Klaus Hullman & Carlos Peña Galiano (eds.), *Who is a Refugee? A Comparative Case Law Study* (The Netherlands 1997), chapter 1.2.3 which refers to the degree of risk required in different asylum procedures.

others the interview is more spontaneous.[37] The aim of the interview is to produce information on grounds for protection of the applicant and by expressing these to provide the decision-maker with information on the circumstances of the individual case. Thus, at the same time as oral testimony delivered in the interview forms part of the evidence in the procedure, it also has a further function essentially as a deliverer of initial information about the case.[38] As claims for asylum are to be decided upon individually and as grounds for refugee status are closely linked to the individual, the asylum interview is also a source of information for the decision-maker and the assessor of claims as to what circumstances might be of importance in the individual case. Thus, at the same time as oral testimony from the interview has the position of evidence in relation to the final decision, one of its main functions is to initiate investigations and to point investigators in the right direction.

In both doctrine and practice it has long been recognised that assessing the interview has to involve special consideration due to the particular situation of the applicant, the unequal position of the parties and the possible practical or psychological hindrances for the applicant in delivering good testimony from the standpoint of the theme of proof.[39] Furthermore, it has also been recognised that help in carrying out interviews in a valid manner and in assessing the information gained from these may be obtained for instance from general (and special) doctrine on witness psychology and interrogation tactics presented within the framework of criminal law or with the aid of medical assessments of the applicant's condition.[40] It should further be noted that the record of the interview is most often used as evidence in appellate procedure.

---

[37] The APD includes requirements for a personal interview as well as for a record of the interview. APD, *supra* at 34, Arts 12–14. However, Member States implement these requirements very differently. In UNHCR, *Improving Asylum Procedures Comparative Analysis and Recommendations for Law and Practice* (Geneva 2010), divergences between implemented norms are analysed comparatively.

[38] All evidence adds to the information in the case and the informative function is inherent to the nature of evidence. In asylum procedure the interview nevertheless plays an accentuated role as the catalyst of investigations due to the personal nature of the theme of proof and the difficulty in obtaining documentary evidence.

[39] Nienke Doornbos, "On Being Heard in Asylum Cases – Evidentiary Assessment through Asylum Interviews", in Noll (2005 a) 103–122. See also Mineur (1998) 267–296; Ruosseau (*et al.*) (2002) and Smith (1990).

[40] For a general assessment of asylum procedure in the eyes of criminal procedure see Popovic (2005) 27–53. See also Jane Herlihy, Peter Scragg & Stuart Turner, "Discrepancies in autobiographical memories – implications for the assessment of asylum seekers: Repeated interview study" (2002) *British Medical Journal*, 324–327.

Aside from the asylum interview, we will see that at times the appellant is also given the possibility in appellate procedure to deliver oral testimony before the appellate decision-making body. Oral testimony is then, aside from the record of the first instance authority, directly used as evidence in appellate procedure. The conduct of the oral hearing is, as we will see, utterly dependent on the legal environment in which claims are assessed.

On the part of the applicant, almost any form of evidence can be and is presented in addition to oral testimony. Commonly, this includes different types of document relating to the political or social activities of the applicant or to their family relations and personal background.[41] Additional material evidence of other types than documents is frequently presented and may be linked to e.g. prior mistreatment or the social context of the applicant. Further, information from the local media or from special rapporteurs may be presented to highlight local events or incidents. Besides, other types of material evidence and testimony from persons close to the applicant may be used in procedures.

Sources of information often used by state parties to asylum procedure are so called country reports.[42] These are general reports on the economic, political and social situation in a country or a region, either by international organisations or by governments. Clearly, these reports often give valuable information on the state of matters in the applicant's region of origin. Nevertheless, it is also clear that these reports are made without reference to individuals and thus must be seen as providing general information that needs to be completed with case-specific information. Furthermore, use of state reports as sources of information always requires an understanding of the background to the report and the possible interests of the author.[43]

In addition to general state reports, more specific data on issues in the home regions of applicants may also be presented by states. Such information may stem from fact finding missions conducted by the receiving state, from investigations by local representatives of the state or from other less official channels. Common databases and other sources are frequent, especially

---

[41] See also the list of compulsory elements of proof that must be included in any asylum assessment according to the European legislator, as included in the QD, Art 4 (3). Council directive on minimum standards for the qualification and status of third country nationals or stateless persons as refugees or as persons who otherwise need international protection and the content of the protection granted. Council directive 2004/83, OJ 29.4.2004 (L 304) 12.

[42] See Ann Sofie Rudolph, "Sakkunniga som bevismedel i flyktingärenden", in *Prövning av flyktingärenden*, ed. Diesen (Stockholm 1998) 299–245. Some of the most frequently used country reports in asylum procedures in Europe include reports from the U.S. Department of State and reports by the British Foreign and Commonwealth Office.

[43] See Rudolph (1998).

within the EU.[44] Again, when assessing such evidence, and also when deciding on which paths of investigation to pursue on the basis of information acquired, the background interests and reasons for specific reports must be taken into account.

Additionally, just as in the case of the applicant, there are very few limits to the nature of evidence that may be presented by the state both in relation to the general circumstances in the applicant's region of origin and in relation to more case specific circumstances.

2.2.5. *Confidential Evidence*

The last issue to be mentioned, and one that makes the evidentiary situation in asylum procedures somewhat peculiar, is the amount and types of classified information used as evidence. If considering the possible interests of state security in relation to individual asylum applicants and the possible state interest in relation to sources of information, quite apart from some of the information itself, it becomes quite clear that some information used as evidence may be of a classified nature. This is not special to asylum procedure, since many other judicial procedures also operate with classified information as evidence and since it is commonly acknowledged that classification of evidence can for different reasons at times be permissible as exceptions to the general rule on openness in decision-making. On the other hand, classification of information in asylum procedures is distinct in the sense that it often relates to interests of state security. The importance of this distinction is related to the fact that information classified on grounds of state security is often also classified in relation to the parties, whereas regular classification is often the result of party interests, in which case the information is thus open to the parties.[45]

---

[44] At the moment much of the energy of the EU in issues of asylum and immigration is focused on the creation of common sources of information and training. See Multiannual Programme for an area of Freedom, Security and Justice serving the citizen (Stockholm Programme), Communication from the Commission to the European Parliament and Council: An Area of Freedom, Security and Justice Serving the Citizen, COM(2009)262/4, and also Communication from the Commission to the Council and the European Parliament on Strengthened Practical Cooperation: New Structures, New Approaches: Improving the Quality of Decision Making in the Common European Asylum System, 17.2.2006, COM(2006) 67, and the Council and Commission Action Plan implementing the Hague Programme on strengthening freedom, security and justice in the European Union, 10.6.2005, COM(2005) 491.

[45] An example can be taken from Finnish legislation: The Finnish Act on the Openness of Government Activities (Laki viranomaistoiminnan julkisuudesta 621/1999) states in Article 24 (24) that as a starting point all documents relating to refugees and asylum seekers are classified by nature. The Act further stipulates that documents concerning foreign relations are classified (Article 24 (1)). With reference to general interest and public safety, such documents

Hence, classification of information as secret for reasons of state security can withdraw information from the evidence communicated between the parties in the procedure. In some cases this may imply that the information is referred to transparently but without disclosing the classified parts in any detailed way either in the procedure or in the decision, thus preventing the applicant from reacting to the information. On the other side of the scale there are cases where the existence of information is disclosed to the applicant neither in the procedure nor in the decision, so that the reasons for the decision may be unreachable and impossible for the applicant to understand.

3. Evidence in EU Asylum Law

Aside of pragmatic concerns regarding the particular nature of evidence in assessment of refugee status, evidentiary practice in European national appellate asylum procedures is also influenced by requirements posed by the European Union. Secondary Union legislation in the field of asylum does indeed concern itself with some issues of a procedural character. Further, general principles of EU law to also impact on the normative framework for evidence in appellate asylum procedures in Europe.[46]

3.1. General Principles of EU Law

It has been stated that evidence in asylum procedures is loosely regulated as well in national as regional context. Also EU law has been reluctant to offer detailed rules on evidence. On the one hand, this follows from the same reasons linked to the nature of administrative law as in national procedures. On the other hand, EU is hesitant to interfere with national procedural rules as a matter of principle. As procedural guidance from EU level often is scarce, the importance attached to general principles of EU law, which are applicable to national norms also outside the scope of direct EU normative guidance and which, thus, set the limits for national margins of appreciation grows.

---

can also be excluded from the documents communicated to the applicant under Article 11 (2) of the Act. Thus, the applicant has no right to knowledge of the contents of, for instance, particularly sensitive intelligence information relating to his or her application. See also KHO 2007:47, where the Finnish Supreme Administrative Court decided to withhold information from the asylum applicant / appellant on this ground.

[46] For an outline of the "specificities" of the asylum procedure that EU legislation must also acknowledge see Michael Kagan, "Is Truth in the Eye of the Beholder?" (2003/3) *Georgetown Immigration Law Journal*, 367–415 and Rousseau *(et al)* (2002) 43–70. On the secondary legislation of the Union see Olga Ferguson Sidorenko, *The Common European Asylum System* (The Hague 2007) 41–124.

The EU principle of procedural autonomy of national legal systems has its beginning in the case law of the European Court of Justice (ECJ). ECJ stated in 1989 in *Rewe-Zentralfinanz eG and Rewe-Zentral AG v. Landwirtschaftskammer für das Saarland* that responsibility for procedural matters also in cases purporting rights and obligations stemming from EC law is primarily placed with national entities and that EU competence and responsibility in these matters is only of secondary nature.[47] The ruling stated that the court cannot, in the absence of detailed EU procedural norms, require that national procedural rules are amended. However, in jurisprudence the court has later made clear that the national procedural autonomy, nevertheless, is dependent on the principles of equivalence and effective remedy and that also national remedies must acknowledge and function in accordance with these principles.[48] In *R. V. Secretatry of State for Transport, ex parte Factortame Ltd. and Others* ECJ ruled on the primacy of the principles of effective remedy and equivalence over the national procedural autonomy.[49] It stated that to the extent that national remedies infringe on these principles, national procedural autonomy falls, also when the remedies are of administrative character.[50]

Hence, in practice, these requirements imply that all national procedural rules, regardless of whether they stem from EU or national legal sources and regardless of whether they concern asylum or any other form of judicial procedure, must conform with the goals of effectiveness and equivalence as presented by principles of EU law. Thus, in relation to the asylum procedure the immediate effect of the principles is that all norms regulating the procedural aspects of the procedure, including evidentiary matters, must be in conformity with the principles.

---

[47] C-33/76 *Rewe-Zantralfinanz eG and Rewe-Zentral AG v. Landwirtschaftskammer für das Saarland* European Communities: European Court of Justice, 16 December 1976.

[48] On the principle of procedural autonomy generally see Paul Craig & Gráinne de Búrca, *EU Law Text, Cases and Materials* (Oxford 2008) 306 ff. See also the Opinion of Advocate General Stix-Hack in C-244/00 *van Doren + Q. GmbH v. lifestyle and sportswear Handelsgesellschaft mbH*, paras 34 and 48 ff, where the Advocate General in relation especially to the burden of proof considers the relationship between national procedural autonomy and principles of effectiveness and equivalence.

[49] C-213/89 *R. v. Secretary of State for Transport, ex parte Factortame Ltd. and Others*, European Communities: European Court of Justice, 19 June 1990.

[50] Thomas von Danwitz, *Europäisches Verwaltungsrecht* (Heidelberg 2008) 530–531. See also Helen Oosterom-Staples, "Effective Rights for Third-Country Nationals?" in *A Right to Inclusion and Exclusion? Normative fault lines of the EU's area of freedom, security and justice*, ed. Hands Lindahl (Oxford 2009) at 75 ff, where it is argued that EU so far has refrained from interactivity with national procedures of justice in the form of procedural harmonisation in the name of procedural autonomy, and that the only requirements for procedures from EU are imposed in the form of general requirements for equivalence and effectiveness.

The principle of equivalence is defined as requiring that "the remedies and forms of action available to ensure the observance of national law must be made available in the same way to ensure the observance of Community law".[51] Thus, national remedies used in relation to rights and obligations as arising from national law, must be available also for the person who wish to enforce rights arising from EU law. In practice this principle requires courts and other instances of judicial remedies to extend their competence also to the EU sphere. Further, the remedies in place for redress for infringements of rights arising from EU law must not be discriminated against in the national judicial order.[52] Remedies must be equal both formally and practically.

The principle of effective remedy and effective judicial protection, again, refers to requirements for practical possibilities to access to justice.[53] Member States cannot, according to this principle, make access to national judicial remedies for persons whose rights under EU law have been infringed impossible or too difficult in practice.[54] The principle deals with as well formal as practical obstacles for access to justice, and has effect on deadlines, requirements for procedure etc.[55]

The principle of effectiveness has also been assessed by the ECJ with reference to standards of evidence.[56] In *Laboratoires Boiron SA v. URSSAD de Lyon* the ECJ considered the scope and placement of the burden of proof. The court stated that the placement of the burden of proof, including a formal requirement for presentation of particular evidence in order

---

[51] Craig *(et al)* (2008) 307.

[52] C-228/98 *Dounias v. Ypourgio Oikonomikon*, European Union: European Court of Justice, 3 February 2000.

[53] On the definition of the principle and also its development see Craig *(et al)* (2008) 313–325.

[54] See also Eveline Brouwer "Effective Remedies in EU Migration Law" in *Whose Freedom, Security and Justice? EU Immigration and Asylum Law and Policy* (eds.) Anneliese Baldaccini, Elspeth Guild & Helen Toner (Cornwall 2007) 57–84 at 74 ff for an account of the principle of effective remedy and equivalence in immigration matters.

[55] In C-14/83 *Von Colson and Kamann v. Land Nordrhein-Westfalen* (1984) ECR 1981 the ECJ established that the principle requires that national remedies, in addition to being practically accessible, also have to be adequate and effective. In C-120/97 *Upjohn v. The Licensing Authority*, European Union: European Court of Justice, 21 January 1999 and C-430–431/93 *Van Schihndel & Van Veen V. Stichting Pensioenfonds voor Fysiotherapeuten*; European Communities: European Court of Justice, 14 December 1995 it was stated that national courts must have the procedural possibility to apply principles of EU law in their work and national norms implementing EU law must in each particular case brought before a court be assessed to see whether the exercise of a EU legal right is made too difficult in the individual case.

[56] von Danwitz (2008) 540, states that no direct rules for standards of evidence has been given in the light of mentioned principles, and that in this field, the principle of procedural autonomy has primacy.

to dispatch of the burden of proof, on a particular party to the procedure is not in compliance with the principle of effectiveness, if the placement renders it excessively difficult for this party to produce the formally required proof and hence dispatch of the burden of proof.[57] Rather, if it is excessively difficult for the party to dispatch of the burden of proof, the court should consider procedural activity to produce the required document either itself or by asking other parties to produce the proof. Thus, the principle of effectiveness implies that also requirements and standards of evidence must be placed so that it is not excessively difficult for the parties to dispatch of their formal evidentiary obligations. Further, the principle of effectiveness implies a requirement for statement of reasons for any decision in national judicial procedures.[58] This can be interpreted as a requirement also for some form of strategy in the assessment of evidence.

Taking into consideration the principle of national procedural autonomy, it is noteworthy that EU has commenced on regulating the Common European Asylum Procedure also procedurally. In this endeavour, EU has put in place direct procedural rules for as well first-instance as appellate organs of an administrative procedure in the Member States, instead of relying to a higher degree on the effect of general principles of EU law.

Charter of Fundamental Rights

The Charter of Fundamental Rights is as of the Lisbon treaty binding as primary legislation in the EU.[59] The Charter does not include principles *per se* but expresses binding rules for Member States. The Charter contains two important rules that are of direct importance to Member States' national appellate asylum procedures and, thus, for this study.

The Charter in Article 18 codifies the right to asylum. The Article reads:

Article 18

The right to asylum shall be guaranteed with due respect for the rules of the Geneva Convention [...] relating to the status of refugees and in accordance with the Treaty establishing the European Community.

---

[57] C-526/04 *Laboratoires Boiron SA v. URSSAF de Lyon*, European Union: European Court of Justice, 7 September 2006. See also von Danwitz (2008) 533–534, where a "Untersuchungsgrundsatz" is examined in the EU legal order. See also, on the subject of the burden of proof and national procedural autonomy *van Doren + Q. GmbH v. lifestyle + sportswear Handelsgesellschaft mbH*, supra at 48.

[58] C-70/95 *Sodemare SA, Anni Azzurri Holding SpA and Anni Azzurri Rezzato Srl v Regione Lombardia*. European Communities: European Court of Justice, 17 June 1997.

[59] For remarks on the relationship between the Charter of Fundamental Rights, *supra* at 74, and EU secondary legislation see Craig *(et al)* (2008) 412 ff.

Article 18 establishes the right to asylum in the Union and, further, gives the 1951 Convention a strong position in EU law. For appellate asylum procedures, the Article reaffirms the importance of international law's influence on the interpretation also of EU legal standards through the validity of the 1951 Convention.

Further, and of procedural importance, the Charter in Article 47 provides for the right to an effective remedy and a fair trial. The Article reads:

> Article 47
>
> Everyone whose rights and freedoms guaranteed by the law of the Union are violated has the right to an effective remedy before a tribunal in compliance with the conditions laid down in this Article.
>
> Everyone is entitled to a fair and public hearing within a reasonable time by an independent and impartial tribunal previously established by law. Everyone shall have the possibility of being advised, defended and represented.
>
> Legal aid shall be made available to those who lack sufficient resources in so far as such aid is necessary to ensure effective access to justice.

Article 47 of the Charter of Fundamental Rights codifies Union requirements on effectiveness in judicial remedies and provides for rights relying on as well Article 6 as Article 13 of the European Convention on Human Rights (ECHR). As said, Article 6 of the ECHR is not applicable to asylum procedures, whereas Article 13 indeed is. In the Charter of Fundamental Rights no such differentiation is made, and the rights awarded by Article 47, including as well due process as effective remedy, are applicable also to asylum seekers.[60] The enforcement of this Article has led to amendments to existing legal provisions in secondary legislation, for instance on the right to legal aid for asylum seekers – a requirement for effective access to justice.[61]

3.2. *The Qualification Directive and Evidence*

The QD indeed provides some limitations and frames for evidentiary assessment in Member State asylum procedures.[62] One of the first things to be noted

---

[60] See also Xavier Groussot, *General Principles of Community Law* (Groningen 2006) 63–66, where the author considers the relationship between Community law and the ECHR.

[61] In the amendments proposed to the APD, Arts 15 and 39 in legal aid and effective remedies are amended with direct reference to increased procedural requirements as a result of the Charter of Fundamental Rights. *Supra* at 34.

[62] Gregor Noll has written an elaborate paper for the UNHCR where the directive's implications for evidentiary assessment are examined in detail. Gregor Noll, *Evidentiary assessment and the EU qualification directive* New Issues in Refugee Research UNHCR Working Paper No. 117 (Geneva 2005c).

about dealings with evidence and knowledge in this directive is that it places great emphasis on the individual nature of evidentiary assessment.[63]

The QD effectively determines the theme of proof for asylum procedures in the Member States as it defines the concept of refugee. The definition of refugeehood as included in the directive draws on the 1951 Convention.[64] The QD in Article 2 (c) defines a refugee as a

> third country national who, owing to a well-founded fear of being persecuted for reasons of race, religion, nationality, political opinion or membership of a particular social group, is outside the country of nationality and is unable or, owing to such fear, is unwilling to avail himself or herself of the protection of that country, or a stateless person, who, being outside of the country of former habitual residence for the same reasons as mentioned above, is unable or, owing to such fear, unwilling to return to it...

The definition of the QD is similar to that of international law. Nevertheless, the QD includes articles which guide interpretation of the definition divergently to interpretation of the 1951 Convention definition.[65] This concerns for instance actors recognised as providers of protection.[66] Further, a decisive difference lies in the fact that the QD in Article 2 (c) only recognises third country nationals as aliens eligible for refugee status.[67] Further, the QD spells out the 'EU-interpretation' of the elements of this definition, thus framing the theme of proof for asylum procedures more closely than the 1951 Convention.[68]

---

[63] See for instance preamble part 26 and Arts 2 c and 4 (2) of the Directive, *supra* at 41.

[64] For general comments on the Qualification Directive see Steve Peers & Nicola Rogers (eds.), *EU Immigration and Asylum Law* (Leiden – Boston 2006) 323–366 and Jane McAdam, "The European Union Qualification Directive and the Creation of a Subsidiary Protection Regime" (2005/3) *International Journal of Refugee Law*, 461–516. For a contrast to the ideas put forward in the Directive, see the Proposal for a new European convention on refugee protection as presented in Vigdis Vevstad, *Refugee Protection A European Challenge* (Oslo 1998) 285–291.

[65] On interpretation of the Directive see for instance Battjes (2006) 219–275 and Reinhard Marx, *Handbuch zur Flüchtlingsanerkennung – Erläuterlungen zur Richtlinie 2004/83/EG* (Frankfurt a M 2005b).

[66] Qualification Directive, *supra* at 41 Art 7(1)9) includes other entities than the state as possible providers of protection.

[67] This restriction could be criticised for in fact being a regional derogation from the 1951 Convention and for thus contesting the universal nature of refugee status as created in the 1951 Convention and promoted by the UNHCR. Further, see also Elspeth Guild, "Seeking Asylum – Storm Clouds Between International Commitments and EU Legislative Measures" (2004/2) *European Law Review*, 198–218, for comments on the challenges involved in creating a subsidiary protection scheme alongside asylum in Europe.

[68] The articles deal with definitions of agents of persecution and protection, and of acts of and reasons for persecution. Some definitions do not match the exact scope of Member State obligations arising from international law. See Battjes (2006) 274–288 and ECRE, *ECRE Information Note on the Council Directive 2004/83/EC of 29 April 2004* (London 2004).

The QD also takes stands on the burden of proof, evidentiary robustness, evidentiary assessment and the standard of proof. The most interesting part of the directive in terms of evidence, and also the part mostly affecting the abstract element of decision-making, is included under Article 4 of the QD, which reads as following:[69]

Assessment of facts and circumstances

1. Member States may consider it the duty of the applicant to submit as soon as possible all elements needed to substantiate the application for international protection. In cooperation with the applicant it is the duty of the Member State to assess the relevant elements of the application.

2. The elements referred to in of paragraph 1 consist of the applicant's statements and all documentation at the applicants disposal regarding the applicant's age, background, including that of relevant relatives, identity, nationality(ies), country(ies) and place(s) of previous residence, previous asylum applications, travel routes, identity and travel documents and the reasons for applying for international protection.

3. The assessment of an application for international protection is to be carried out on an individual basis and includes taking into account:

(a) all relevant facts as they relate to the country of origin at the time of taking a decision on the application; including laws and regulations of the country of origin and the manner in which they are applied;

(b) the relevant statements and documentation presented by the applicant including information on whether the applicant has been or may be subject to persecution or serious harm;

(c) the individual position and personal circumstances of the applicant, including factors such as background, gender and age, so as to assess whether, on the basis of the applicant's personal circumstances, the acts to which the applicant has been or could be exposed would amount to persecution or serious harm;

(d) whether the applicant's activities since leaving the country of origin were engaged in for the sole or main purpose of creating the necessary conditions for applying for international protection, so as to assess whether these activities will expose the applicant to persecution or serious harm if returned to that country;

(e) whether the applicant could reasonably be expected to avail himself of the protection of another country where he could assert citizenship.

4. The fact that an applicant has already been subject to persecution or serious harm or to direct threats of such persecution or such harm, is a serious indication of the applicant's well-founded fear of persecution or real risk of suffering serious harm, unless there are good reasons to consider that such persecution or serious harm will not be repeated.

---

[69] This presentation leans on the analysis in Noll (2005c).

5. Where Member States apply the principle according to which it is the duty of the applicant to substantiate the application for international protection and where aspects of the applicant's statements are not supported by documentary or other evidence, those aspects shall not need confirmation, when the following conditions are met:

(a) the applicant has made a genuine effort to substantiate his application;

(b) all relevant elements, at the applicant's disposal, have been submitted, and a satisfactory explanation regarding any lack of other relevant elements has been given;

(c) the applicant's statements are found to be coherent and plausible and do not run counter to available specific and general information relevant to the applicant's case;

(d) the applicant has applied for international protection at the earliest possible time, unless the applicant can demonstrate good reason for not having done so; and

(e) the general credibility of the applicant has been established.

The Qualification Directive is at time of writing opened for negotiation and a recast Directive was issued in October 2009.[70] In the recast, Article 4 is not amended.

Section 1 of this Article introduces facultative obligations for the applicant to provide information for the decision-maker by stating that Member States may considered it the duty of the applicant "to submit as soon as possible all elements needed to substantiate the application for international protection". The section does not refer to these facultative obligations of the applicant in the words of submitting "evidence" or "information", but only in relation to the "elements needed to substantiate the application". In Article 4 (2), the scope of these elements is defined as including statements by the applicant and possible detailed documentation regarding the grounds for asylum and issues in relation to the claim for asylum, such as for instance information about the applicant's relatives, identity, nationality, country and place of previous residence. The QD also lists themes such as travel routes and travel documents as elements of importance. Thus, the assessment purported in the Article and to which the facultative obligation of the applicant refers is not merely assessment of claims for international protection by applicants, but also grounds for responsibility over assessment of these claims and burden sharing between Member States.

---

[70] Proposal for a Directive of the European Parliament and of the Council on minimum standards for the qualification and status of third country nationals or stateless persons as beneficiaries of international protection and the content of the protection granted COM (2009) 551.

The facultative obligation to present the "elements of the claim" as stated in Article 4 (1) of the QD must in practice be interpreted as an obligation which the Member States can impose on the applicant to shed light on the grounds for international protection. This can be done for instance through oral testimony at interview. Further, the obligation includes efforts to substantiate the grounds for protection by presenting material evidence if possible.

The second sentence in Article 4 (1) states that the assessment of relevant factors shall be carried out in cooperation between the applicant and the authority. This rule relates to the method for evidentiary assessment and the manner in which the decision-maker indeed weighs and balances the information and knowledge provided.

The relevant question in the interpretation of the second sentence of Article 4 (1) concerns what is understood by "cooperation". It has been stated that this is to be interpreted as a facultative rule obliging the state to communicate all materials to the applicant, as communication is a primary form of cooperation in the procedure.[71] It can also be understood less rigidly as a reminder that fact-finding and decision-making in asylum claims is an endeavour where neither party can succeed alone. It is an imperative both for the authorities and for the applicant to cooperate as far as possible in investigation and decision-making.

Article 4(3) stipulates firstly an obligation to assess all asylum claims on an individual basis. As we have seen above, individual assessment is one of the cornerstones of the course of evidentiary assessment as described and decided on in the directives. However, this section also includes a list of components that the QD considers relevant to assessment of applications for asylum. Thus, Article 4(3) provides norms for the amount and quality of information that must be considered when deciding on applications for asylum.

The list provided in Article 4(3) is not exhaustive but lists the very minimum of circumstances to be taken into account when assessing claims for international protection and includes elements such as facts about the country of origin, including information about laws and regulations and their application, relevant statements and evidence presented by the applicant, the individual and personal circumstances of the applicant, information about activities undertaken outside the country of origin and about the background of the applicant and their possible connections to other countries. Member States and individual decision-makers are naturally free to consider also material outside this scope.

It is striking that the information provided by the applicant is listed as one of the elements that need to be taken into account when making decisions on

---

[71] And if this is impossible, to leave out incommunicable evidence from examination. Noll (2005c) at 4.

asylum, since clearly all information gathered must be assessed, regardless of the source.[72] And since the QD itself stipulates an obligation for the applicant to cooperate in production of evidence, it would seem self evident that the evidence thus presented in accordance with this obligation is also to be assessed. Nevertheless, one must be aware not to place the evidence provided by the applicant in a special 'compartment' because of the special listing of this information. Clearly, the source of information is one of the things to be considered when assessing evidence; however, this is the case regarding all evidence, not only information provided by the applicant.[73]

Lastly, Article 4(4) deals with as well the importance and comparable weight of a sub-theme of proof in the evidentiary assessment, and standard of proof. The Article states that prior persecution is a "strong indicator" of a well-founded fear of persecution unless there are "good reasons" to consider that the persecution will not be repeated. In terms of evidentiary weight, the Article states that prior persecution must be given particular weight in determining the protection needs of an applicant. As a strong indication implies a high probability, the norms must be seen as shifting the burden of proof when prior persecution can be shown. If prior persecution can be proven, the applicant must be granted protection if the state cannot provide good reasons for that this prior persecution will not be repeated.

This section is a direct reference to the situation of a shifted burden of proof in the form as traditionally embraced in German law.[74] Use of prior persecution

---

[72] QD, *supra* at 41. Art 4 (3) (b): "The assessment of an application for international protection is to be carried out [....] taking into account the relevant statements and documentation presented by the applicant including information on whether the applicant has been or may be subject to persecution or serious harm".

[73] In order for the theoretical tools for assessing evidence to function properly in practice, there can be no "prejudices" about the evidence, for example on the grounds of its sources, before assessment begins according to the scheme for use of tools. See Jonkka (1993) 125–132, where the author elaborates on the impact of prejudices on evidentiary assessment and Lars Heuman, *Bevisbörda och beviskrav i tvistemål* (Stockholm 2005) 416–430, where the author analyses the implications of initial comprehensions of probability in assessments involving considerations of probability.

[74] Juliane Kokott, *Beweislastverteilung und Prognoseentscheidungen bei der Inanspruchnahme von Grundrechten und internationalen Menschenrechten*, Beiträge zum ausländischen öffentlichen Recht und Völkerrecht (Berlin – Heidelberg – New York 1993) 362–363, BVerfG (2.7.1980) 54, 341 (361) 1980 and Reinhard Marx, *Aufenthalts-, Asyl- und Flüchtlingsrecht in der anwaltlichen Praxis* (Frankfurt a M 2007) 1120–1122, examining the implications of German practice for EU legislation in this respect. BVerwGE (27.4.2010) 10 C 5.09 reaffirms the position of the principle in German practice and, as a result of the inclusion of the principle in EU law, broadens its scope of application in German asylum practice. For comments on the value attached to prior persecution in the Directive see Battjes (2006) 227 and Noll (2005c) 11–12.

as a special element in RSD is nevertheless not a national invention, since international law and for instance the UNHCR Handbook guiding interpretation of the 1951 Convention directly refer to prior persecution as also a "strong indicator" of future persecution.[75] However, the direct reference to particular standards of proof for the mechanism is a feature developed in German practice.

Article 5 relates to the so called benefit of the doubt and states that statements by the applicant (oral testimony) are to be seen as sufficient proof of a well-founded fear of being persecuted in some circumstances.[76] A condition for this is that the statements of testimony, if taken as a basis for decision, fulfil the requirements of the theme of proof and are linked to the refugee status of the applicant. Further prerequisites for relying solely on statements by the applicant are that that no other evidence is available (a), that the applicant has submitted all relevant elements (b), that the statements are coherent and plausible (c), that the applicant has applied for asylum at the earliest possible time (d) and that the general credibility of the applicant has been established (e). Of these prerequisites, all but (d) are rather self-evident in elaborations on the place of evidence in assessment. It is natural that issues such as reliability of the source and the evidence itself and possible intentions to not 'tell all' have an impact on assessment of evidence. However, that the applicant has applied at a special time seems to have little to do with assessment as such.[77]

Conclusively, the QD includes provisions that affect both the more material outsets for assessment of evidence (through for instance deciding on what circumstances must be investigated) and the abstract side of assessment (through for instance stipulating the evidentiary weight of certain elements). Thus, in Europe the QD forms an important part of the legal context and framework for evidentiary standards in asylum procedures.

3.3. *The Asylum Procedures Directive and Evidence*

The second relevant EU directive, the Asylum Procedures Directive, does not in the same manner as the QD include direct rules on assessment of evidence but nevertheless includes provisions that indirectly affect evidentiary

---

[75] UNHCR (1992) para 45.
[76] QD, *supra* at 41, Art 4 (5): "… Where aspects of the applicant's statements are not supported by documentary or other evidence, those aspects shall not need confirmation, when the following conditions are met…".
[77] See Noll (2005c) 12–13.

assessment.[78] Also the APD is at the time of writing open for negotiations and a first recast Directive was issued in October 2009.[79] This recast Directive was not successful in negotiations and the Commission has in June 2011 subsequently issued a recast proposal for an updated version of the Directive.[80]

Article 8 of the APD concerns as well the requirement for individual examination of applications as quality of evidence. The Article reads:

Article 8

Requirements for the examination of applications

1. Without prejudice to Article 23(4)(i), Member States shall ensure that applications for asylum are neither rejected nor excluded from examination on the sole ground that they have not been made as soon as possible

2. Member States shall ensure that decisions by the determining authority on applications for asylum are taken after an appropriate examination. To that end, Member States shall ensure that:

(a) applications are examined and decisions are taken individually, objectively and impartially;

(b) precise and up-to-date information is obtained from various sources, such as the United Nations High Commissioner for Refugees (UNHCR), as to the general situation prevailing in the countries of origin of applicants for asylum and, where necessary, in countries through which they have transited, and that such information is made available to the personnel responsible for examining applications and taking decisions;

(c) the personnel examining applications and taking decisions have the knowledge with respect to relevant standards applicable in the field of asylum and refugee law.

---

[78] The mere fact that the QD includes both numerously and substantially more provisions with an impact on evidentiary assessment than the procedural directive, the APD, is interesting. This can be seen as implying a transfer of evidentiary responsibility from the area of states and state parties to asylum procedures to the area of the applicant. See also Noll (2005 b) 197–214.

[79] *Supra* at 34. Similar to in the negotiations regarding the first APD Germany has been highly reluctant to accept changes to the directive. The difficulties in negotiations has led to tensions also between the EU institutions, and at the time of writing is still unclear whether the Commission will issue a new proposal in 2011 or if the 2009 proposal will be elaborated on. Kees Groenendijk, "The Long-Term Residents Directive, Denizenship and Integration" in Baldaccini (*et al*) (2007) 429–450 at 433, describes some of the difficulties for Germany in negotiations on EU legal norms.

[80] *Supra* at 34.

3. The authorities referred to in Chapter V shall, through the determining authority or the applicant or otherwise, have access to the general information referred to in paragraph 2(b), necessary for the fulfilment of their task.

4. Member States may provide for rules concerning the translation of documents relevant for the examination of applications.

The Article emphasizes the individuality of asylum claims and the importance of individual assessments of claims. The Article further states that decision-making is to be undertaken objectively and impartially, which gives important outsets for the evidentiary assessment. A minimum requirement for the method chosen for the evidentiary assessment is according to the Article that is supports the objectivity of the assessment.

Further, the Article provides rules for the quality of evidence in the asylum procedures. Information must, according to the article, be obtained from the UNHCR and other sources about the general situation in countries of origin. It also requires the information to be precise and up-to-date.[81] This rule hence makes a direct reference to the quality of evidence to be used in Member States.

In the recast proposal for amendments to the APD, the Article also provides rules for communication of evidence and the use of expert evidence. These rules place further demands on quality of evidence. Recast Article 23 states that the up-to-date and precise information acquired in accordance with the Article must be made available to the applicant and the legal adviser if the information is used in the decision. Recast Article 10 states that decision-makers must have the possibility to make use of expert evidence when making a decision.[82]

Furthermore, Article 12 of the APD provides for a right to an interview for applicants, whose applications are considered in regular procedures.[83] The Article emphasises the interview as a source of information and as evidence in the asylum procedure. Nevertheless, the same Article also states that in assessing claims for asylum the fact that an asylum-seeker has failed to appear at interview may be taken into account.[84] Even if rather vague language, "may", is used in this provision, clearly the intention is to attach evidentiary value to the circumstance of not appearing at interview and following from this the

---

[81] See Battjes (2006) 307–315.

[82] As the recast proposal is still under negotiations, these may not be the final provisions of the directive.

[83] The Article nevertheless also allows for vast derogations from the principle of the right to an interview in accelerated procedures and in cases where positive decisions can be made without an interview. For an analysis of implementation see UNHCR 2010.

[84] APD, *supra* at 34, Art 8 (3) (6).

stipulation also makes clear that the doings and behaviour of the applicant during the asylum procedure are themselves to be seen as valid evidence in the procedure.

Article 15 of the APD concerns applicant's rights to legal assistance in the procedure, which we will see can be of crucial importance for the quality of evidence presented. The Article states that legal assistance at the cost of the applicant must be allowed to all applicants. It, further, requires the Member States the opportunity to provide for free legal assistance for appellate procedures following negative decisions. However, Article 15 (3) states that such free legal assistance can be limited to the following situations:

(a) only for procedures before a court or tribunal in accordance with Chapter V and not for any onward appeals or reviews provided for under national law, including a rehearing of an appeal following an onward appeal or review; and/or

(b) only to those who lack sufficient resources; and/or

(c) only to legal advisers or other counsellors specifically designated by national law to assist and/or represent applicants for asylum; and/or

(d) only if the appeal or review is likely to succeed.

Success of the appeal as a prerequisite for free legal assistance requires legal representatives and authorities to before the appellate procedure make an assessment as to the possibilities for the appeal to succeed. It goes without saying that this introduces a vast amount of uncertainty to the procedure. In the first recast of the APD, the possibilities to limit free legal assistance only to cases that are likely to succeed were abandoned, but were reintroduced in the second June 2011 recast proposal.

Lastly, APD Article 39 refers to the right to an effective remedy also in asylum matters.[85] It requires Member States to "ensure that applicant for asylum have the right to an effective remedy before a court or tribunal" for decisions on their applications for asylum. The Article thus places restrictions on the institutional framework for asylum procedure in Member States and introduces the general principle of effective remedy to the asylum field. In the negotiations on the recast proposals put forward by the Commission, the articles concerning effective remedy have been object for lengthy debates in Council.

---

[85] See Brouwer (2007) 65, where the author describes the legislative process of this article.

Chapter IV

Evidence in the European Appellate Asylum Procedure

1. *Aim and Method*

The following chapter outlines how evidentiary standards can be used in a European appellate asylum procedure. The purpose of this exercise is not to create a model procedure optimal in all evidentiary standards but to provide points of reference for comparative analysis. The aim with the chapter is, thus, to define keys of comparison for the reader and to give an example of their use in the asylum environment. Relevant international and regional frameworks are taken into account.

In choice of method for the analysis of how the evidentiary standards function in the asylum environment the options are many. One could rely on purely dogmatic structures, taking into account solely direct normative references in international and regional frameworks. Another option would be to take an outset in procedural aims, such as procedural economy or risk management to establish optimal standards in order to find working solutions for how evidence functions in the asylum environment. However, the method chosen accentuates the importance of pragmatic impact and aims at solutions that emphasise reliability of decisions and robustness of evidence.[1] The approach is dogmatic-functionalist in that the choice of methodology for evidentiary assessment places an emphasis on the possibilities for optimal material knowledge and information.

The choice of method for the definition of keys of comparison is influenced by two discussions on evidentiary theory, which stand fairly close to each other. On the one hand, Hannu Tapani Klami and his fellow researchers have in the Finnish context presented a highly analytical theory of evidence.[2] Klami places emphasis with concepts like certainty, also statistical certainty, as

---

[1] See also Mårten Knuts, "Lectio" (2010/3) *Tidskrift utgiven av Juridiska Föreningen i Finland*, 285–292, where the author elaborates on a functionalist approach to legal research.
[2] The evidentiary theory advocated by Klami and his research group is given a thorough presentation in Hannu Tapani Klami, Minna Gräns & Johanna Sorvettula, *Law and Truth A Theory of Evidence* (Helsinki 2000).

opposed of truth and with empirical argumentation in the analysis of questions of proof. He also places weight with pragmatic impact on evidentiary solutions for instance institutional frameworks.[3] Klami often uses elaborate mathematical schemes in strivings to ensure reliability in the evidentiary assessment. On the other hand, there is the traditional and highly influential Swedish debate on evidentiary theory, the use of evidence and possibilities for legally defining evidentiary issues.[4] In this debate, Per Olof Ekelöf has presented theories based on the value of evidence, on which Klami, again, built some of his reasoning.[5] Christian Diesen has in the Swedish debate presented views on evidentiary assessment that accentuate the connection between quantity and quality of evidence.[6] The impact of these theories will be further discussed in relation to evidentiary assessment below.

These theories form the basis for the understanding of the evidentiary assessment for the purposes of this study for two reasons. These theories have been discussed vividly in the Nordic countries, where also most of the research for this book has been conducted.[7] Further, these theories combine theory with practice. In discussions on Nordic evidentiary theories, pragmatic concerns are linked with theoretical schemes creating an understanding of evidentiary theory as a supplement and aid in practical evidentiary assessment. Particularly in challenging evidentiary environments, the 'teamwork' between pragmatic concerns and theoretical support is crucial.

It must, nevertheless, be noted that above mentioned theories and analysis have not been implemented in this study in their extremes, but, as said, form a basis for the understanding of how evidence is and can be used.[8] For example, the use of purely statistical models and mathematical calculations as Klami

---

[3] Klami (1986) 6–11.

[4] The discussion includes, amongst others, Per Olof Ekelöf, Henrik Edelstam & Lars Heuman, *Rättegång – fjärde häftet* (Stockholm 2009), Lars Heuman, *Bevisbörda och beviskrav i tvistemål* (Stockholm 2005), Per Olof Bolding, *Går det att bevisa?* (Stockholm 1989), Lindell (1998) and Lindell (1987) to mention some. Pölönen offers an analysis of the Swedish debate including the links of this discussion to the Finnish debate. Pölönen (2003) 150–162.

[5] Per Olof Ekelöf (*et al*) (2009). Nevertheless, Klami also critically studied the theory as presented by Ekelöf. See for instance Hannu Tapani Klami, "Kommentarer till diskussionen om bevisvärde och bevisbörda" in *Rätt och sanning* ed. Hannu Tapani Klami (Uppsala 1990) 67–70.

[6] Christian Diesen, *Utevarohandläggning och bevisprövning i brottmål* (Stockholm 1993) and Christian Diesen, "Grunderna för bevisvärdering" in *Bevis. Värdering av erkännande, konfrontationer, DNA och andra enstaka bevis* Christian Diesen, Johanna Björkman, Fredrik Forsman & Peter Jonsson (Stockholm 1997) 13–81. In Finland Dan Frände, *Finsk straffprocessrätt I* (Helsingfors 1999) has made use of the approach.

[7] Klami (1986) 12–13 notes that the discussion, nevertheless, has been clearly more vivid in Sweden than in Finland.

[8] Also Ryynänen states that combinations of theories can be used in the study of administrative procedures. Ryynänen (2000) 97.

often advocated has not been seen as fruitful.[9] Nevertheless, Klami's call for an evidentiary backbone and structure in the evidentiary assessment is important.[10] Also, strivings towards optimal understanding of the material reality as a guiding star for solutions made in evidentiary assessment is embraced.[11]

2. *Theme of Proof*

An examination of evidentiary structures must necessarily include a definition of the theme of proof. The theme of proof is decisive for correct application to the individual case of burden of proof, standard of proof and all other evidentiary concepts.

The theme of proof will be referred to in the study but will not be used as a key of comparison. Hence, the concept will not be analysed outside the pure definition that is required in order to understand the evidentiary assessment. Also in relation to the definition, many discussions on interpretation and scope are omitted. The reason for not engaging in comparative study using the theme of proof is linked to the nature of the study as primarily procedural-evidentiary. An opening up of the theme of proof and a closer analysis of this concept and its position in the evidentiary framework would have required a more elaborated refugee law –based approach.

The theme of proof is for the purposes of this study understood and interpreted as implying the aim or goal of collecting information and knowledge.[12] The theme of proof defines the objective for the judicial procedure. The theme of proof defines the substantive aim of evidentiary work and gives the procedure a frame of reference. The theme of proof also presents matters of fact relevant for the procedure.[13]

---

[9] Klami, for instance, supports the use of "computer-aided decision-making models". Klami (*et al*) (2000) 39.

[10] Dag Prawits has stated that the task of theories of evidence is to answer questions relating to rational argumentation in the legal context. Dag Prawitz: Några filosofiska synpunkter på rationell argumentation i juridiken in Aleksander Peczenik, Dag Praqitz, Torstein Eckhoff, Lars Lindahl & Jan Hellner: *Rationalitet och empiri i rättsvetenskapen* Juridiska Fakulteten i Stockholm skriftserien nr 6 (Stockholm1985) 24.

[11] *Ibid* at 81 ff.

[12] For definitions of the theme of proof as a concept see Juha Lappalainen, Dan Frände, Erkki Havansi, Risto Koulu, Johanna Niemi-Kiesiläinen, Anna Nylund, Jaakko Rautio, Juha Sihto & Jyrki Virolainen, *Prosessioikeus* (Helsinki 2007) 484–490, in particular 484–485. Also Ian H. Dennis, *The Law of Evidence* (London 2007) 116–119.

[13] For general comments on the tasks of the theme of proof in criminal and civil procedure see Juha Lappalainen, *Siviilioikeus II* (Helsinki 2001) 130; Klami (2000) 17–19; Pölönen (2003) 103–105 and Jonkka (1993) 31–33. Especially on the theme of proof in administrative conduct see Diesen (*et al.*) (2003) 49–61, emphasising the impact of future predictions on the theme of proof in many fields of administrative conduct.

In order to pinpoint the theme of proof in appellate European asylum procedure, the backbone must be taken in the refugee definition as applied in the Qualification Directive.[14] The theme of proof for RSD in European asylum procedures is found in Article 2 (c) of the directive, which defines a refugee as a

> third country national who, owing to a well-founded fear of being persecuted for reasons of race, religion, nationality, political opinion or membership of a particular social group, is outside the country of nationality and is unable or, owing to such fear, is unwilling to avail himself or herself of the protection of that country, or a stateless person, who, being outside of the country of former habitual residence for the same reasons as mentioned above, is unable or, owing to such fear, unwilling to return to it...

As we have seen, this definition draws on the 1951 definition and requires:

- that the applicant is a third country national;[15]
- that the applicant belongs to a certain group in his home country and that this is due to the applicant's religion, race, nationality, social group or political opinion;[16]
- that there is a well-founded fear that the applicant will be persecuted in his or her home country;[17]
- that this fear is linked to the group belonging; and

---

[14] Council directive on minimum standards for the qualification and status of third country nationals or stateless persons as refugees or as persons who otherwise need international protection and the content of the protection granted. Council directive 2004/83, OJ 29.4.2004 (L 304) 12. See also Proposal for a Directive of the European Parliament and of the Council on minimum standards for the qualification and status of third country nationals or stateless persons as beneficiaries of international protection and the content of the protection granted COM (2009) 551.

[15] The geographical limitation to the definition in EU law can be seen as constituting a geographical derogation to the refugee definition from the 1951 Convention, also binding on all Member States.

[16] The interpretation and scope of the nexus-criteria is ever evolving. See Hathaway (1991) 135–188 and Goodwin- Gill (*et al*) (2007) 70–90 for comments on the scope of the criteria.

[17] As well the meaning of well-founded fear and persecution as concepts have been debated. The requirement for well-founded fear has been seen as implying as well a subjective as objective element, implying a generalized and inclusive approach to the assessment of well-foundedness. In Gregor Noll, "Evidentiary assessment under the refugee convention: Risk, pain and the intersubjectivity of fear" in Noll (2005a) 141–159, the impact of the concept of well-founded fear on amongst others evidentiary assessment is explored and the inclusiveness of the assessment is emphasized. The applicant's own assessment is an important, integrated part of the concept. See also Hathaway (*et al*) (2005) and and The Michigan Guidelines on Well-Founded Fear as presented at the Third Colloquium on Challenges in International Refugee Law, University of Michigan Law School, 26-28.3.2004.

- that the applicant due to the well-founded fear for persecution as a consequence of group-belonging does not wish to or cannot avail himself or herself of the protection of the home country.[18]

These are thus the elements that need to be subjected to scrutiny by the appellate organ and that constitute the general theme of proof for the asylum procedure. The reviewing organ must review both the interpretation of these elements presented by the first instance decision-maker and the conclusions regarding them made on the basis of the facts gathered in the case.[19] Only then can a conclusion regarding the legality of the decision under review be made.[20]

3. Burden of Proof

Burden of proof will be used as a key of comparison for the purposes of analysing evidentiary elements of national appellate asylum procedures. In the same manner as all theoretical tools to be used in this study, burden of proof is closely linked to the other instruments. Thus, while here presenting burden of proof as distinct from issues relating to robustness, models for evidentiary assessment and standards of proof, these elements are in practice intertwined.

3.1. Definition

The burden of proof has been defined as the "necessity or duty of affirmatively proving a fact or facts in dispute on an issue raised between the parties in a cause" or as the "obligation of a party to establish by evidence a requisite

---

[18] On the responsibility to protect in refugee law Hathaway (1991) 101–105 and also Goodwin-Gill (*et al*) (2007) 123–129.

[19] Which, in turn, implies that both assessment and interpretation of the information and knowledge gathered in relation to the definition *and* questions of legally correct interpretation of the definition and the rules and standards relating to evidence can be subject to review.

[20] Aside of the subject theme of proof, the reviewing instance also considers formal requirements on administrative conduct, e.g. whether the decision-making in first instance has been formally correct and in accordance with applicable rules. This consideration may include considerations as to formal requirements on fact-finding, communication and the applicability of general principles of administrative conduct. In Olli Mäenpää, *Hallinto-oikeus* (Helsinki 2003) 199–214 and 255–330, formal requirements on decision-making in administrative conduct are considered. Aarre Tähti, *Periaatteet Suomen hallinto-oikeudessa* (Helsinki 1995) 331–381, considers the applicability and formal requirements posed by general administrative principles. Diesen (*et al.*) (2003) 62–114 examines formal requirements on fact-finding. For a detailed account of communcation in administration on a general level, see Niels Eilschou Holm, *Det kontradiktoriske Princip i Forvaltningsprocessen* (Copenhagen 1968).

degree of belief concerning a fact".[21] In more elaborate terms, the burden is defined as the obligation to prove the claims in the procedure or as the risk of suffering negative consequences as a result of insufficient proof of these claims.[22] In other words, the burden of proof tells us where the starting point and the 'status quo' of the procedure are placed.[23]

In refugee status determination the burden of proof concerns the question for which party it is to prove something in the procedure. Is it for the asylum-seeker to prove that he is a refugee, or is it for the state to prove that he is not?

From these definitions it becomes evident that the concept of burden of proof can be understood in at least two ways: Firstly, the more general understanding of burden of proof implies understanding the burden as also encompassing considerations relating to production and presentation of evidence.[24] This understanding places emphasis on the connection between the abstract risk of suffering negative consequences due to insufficient proof and the practical obligation of producing and presenting sufficient proof. This broader understanding of the burden of proof also holds within considerations relating to the standard of proof: Only the standard of proof can determine when the burden of proof shifts and which of the parties in the end has to suffer the negative consequences of underweight evidence. Secondly, a narrow understanding of the burden of proof incorporates only the distribution of risk of negative consequences under the burden and is not interested in connections to obligations of presentation and production of evidence or in connections to the standard of proof.

Thus, aside of the question regarding which of the parties carries the burden of proving a need for protection, the burden of proof can also be understood as including questions regarding what is practically necessary in order to meet the requirements of this burden.

---

[21] Definitions in Black's Law Dictionary, West Publishing, Centennial edition 1991.

[22] For definitions of the burden of proof as the burden of suffering negative consequences in as well civil as criminal procedure see Lappalainen (*et al.*) (2007) 575–576; Pölönen (2003) 132–133 and Klami (*et al.*) (1987) 71–72. See also Adrian Keane, *The Modern Law of Evidence* (Oxford 2006) 82–108 placing definition of the burden of proof in a common law context indicating the "umbrella effect" of the civil law definition in relation to the common law understanding of the concept.

[23] On burden of proof particularly in criminal proceedings see Lappalainen (*et al.*) (2007) 590–595 and Paul Roberts & Adrian Zuckerman, *Criminal Evidence* (Oxford 2010) 224 ff., where the authors studies possible variations of the concept of burden of proof.

[24] See for instance Lappalainen (*et al.*) (2007) 575–580 and Ekelöf (*et al.*) (2009) 72–81, where the broader understanding of the concept becomes apparent. See also Ekelöf (*et al.*) (2009) 93–94, where the connection between burden of proof and burden of allegation is presented.

A reference to the shifted burden of proof is here called for, as European asylum procedure indeed also makes use of such burdens. The burden of proof is shifted when the original holder of the duty has managed to satisfy the obligations connected with the burden and has thus succeeded in shifting the burden and the status-quo of the procedure to the detriment of the other party.[25] The burden of proof can shift between the parties several times during judicial procedure, all depending on the relationship between evidence presented and the required standard of proof.[26]

For the purpose of the comparative study undertaken in this book, the use of the burden of proof will be identified and explored in the appellate asylum procedure of three European countries. Questions will be raised regarding how national procedures place the burden of proof (Which party to the procedure suffers negative consequences as a result of insufficient proof of the claims in the procedure, where is the starting-point of the procedure?) and what national procedures understand with the burden of proof (What must the party with the burden of proof do to dispatch of this burden?).

3.2. Normative Frames for the Burden of Proof in European Asylum Procedures

International refugee law does not present direct rules regarding the placement or the content of the burden of proof in asylum procedures. UNHCR, however, often considers that the burden of proof in asylum procedures is placed with the asylum-seeker.[27] In establishing the content of the burden of proof UNHCR takes into account the difficulties for asylum-seekers in presenting evidence. It is argued that the refugee must make "reasonable effort to establish the […] accuracy of the facts on which the claim is based." However, the "decision-maker must share the duty to ascertain and evaluate all the relevant facts" including assessment of COI.[28]

EU law includes a facultative rule stating in QD Article 4(1) that "Member States may consider it the duty of the applicant to submit as soon as possible all elements needed to substantiate the application for international protection." Article 4(2) lists the elements referred to as "the applicant's statements and all documentation at the applicants disposal regarding the applicant's age,

---

[25] On false burden of proof see Ekelöf (*et al.*) (2009) 87–88.

[26] Saranpää (2010) 92–99, examines the relationship between a shifted burden of proof and burden of allegation.

[27] UNHCR (2002) 4: "It is normally considered that the burden of proof, or the obligation to prove a claim or allegation, lies with the applicant." Also Goodwin-Gill (*et al*) (2007) 54 and UNHCR (1992) para 196.

[28] UNHCR (2002) 4–5.

background, including that of relevant relatives, identity, nationality(ies), country(ies) and place(s) of previous residence, previous asylum applications, travel routes, identity and travel documents and the reasons for applying for international protection."[29]

The facultative rule in QD 4(1) does not concern a burden of proof *per se*. The rule does not state that it is the applicant who suffers negative consequences if the theme of proof cannot be established. Thus, the Article is rather to be interpreted as a rule of assertion, making it the obligation for the applicant to declare reasons for asylum, than as a rule on the burden of proof.[30] Nevertheless, the Article does, indeed, provide for the possibility to place a responsibility for production of evidence with the applicant. Such responsibility can be considered part of the burden of proof.

EU law, further, includes a norm on shifted burdens of proof. Article 4(4) of the QD states that "The fact that an applicant has already been subject to persecution or serious harm or to direct threats of such persecution or such harm, is a serious indication of the applicant's well-founded fear of persecution or real risk of suffering serious harm, unless there are good reasons to consider that such persecution or serious harm will not be repeated." As "serious indication" must be interpreted as a high probability, the Article effectively implies that EU law has identified one important situation where it is mandatory for national asylum procedures to consider the burden of proof shifted.

Even though normative international law is silent on the matter and EU presents only a facultative rule for a burden of assertion, some commentators at the international level as well as at the EU-level place the initial burden of proof with the applicant.[31] This position is not self-evident, but must be positioned against a general understanding of the purpose of the asylum-procedure.

On the one hand, the asylum procedure can be understood as a means for the state to ensure that the principle of *non-refoulement* is upheld. According to this understanding the state, in the national asylum procedure and through assessing the need for protection in the individual case, makes sure that no-one is removed from its territory in violation of binding international norms on *non-refoulement*. The asylum procedure thus functions as a procedure where restrictions, in the form of removal, can be imposed on an individual after careful consideration of the consequences. If such approach is taken to the asylum procedure, it could be argued that it is for the state to prove that

---

[29] Qualification Directive, *supra* at 14.
[30] Also Noll (2005c) 5.
[31] UNHCR (2002) 4–5 and Goodwin-Gill (*et al*) (2007) 54.

the applicant is not a refugee, insofar the negative decision includes a order for removal.[32] According to this understanding the burden of proof could be placed with the state, as the primary purpose of the procedure is for the state to ensure safe returns and not for the individual to be granted benefits. The placement of the burden of proof would follow a general administrative principle stating that the burden for benefits is placed with the applicant while the burden for restrictions is placed with the state.[33]

On the other hand, the asylum procedure can be understood as a procedure where the individual applies for and is possibly granted the benefit of asylum. The task for the procedure according to this understanding is not primarily linked to *non-refoulement*, which nevertheless is a component of the procedure, but to the benefits of asylum as a legal instrument. Seen in this way, it is natural that the burden of proof is placed with the applicant, since the purpose of the procedure is linked to the granting of a benefit rather than to imposing a restriction. As a result of the fact that benefits are only awarded to persons meeting the prerequisites provided for by law, the starting point in the procedure is taken in the position that the existence of the prerequisites must be proven and hence the burden of proof is placed with the individual and applicant for the benefit.[34]

3.3. *Burden of Proof in an Appellate European Asylum Procedure*

The burden of proof in a European asylum procedure can normatively be placed as well with the applicant as the state, depending on how the procedure is perceived. However, if asylum procedure primarily is understood as

---

[32] Noll (2005d) 141 uses this notion of asylum procedure when writing in relation to procedural requirements posed by the 1951 Convention: "If a state wishes to remove a person who claims to be a refugee, it has to assess whether of not the conditions of Article 33 (1) CRS are satisfied [...]."

[33] Diesen (*et al.*) (2003) 63 describes this principles. Also Albert Kiralfy, *The Burden of Proof* (Abingdon 1987)191 ff. See however also Aoife Duffy, "Expulsion to Face Torture? *Non-refoulement* in International law" (2008/3) *International Journal of Refugee Law*, 373–390, at 380, where the author considers burden of proof from the point of view of practice from the Committee Against Torture. Her conclusion is that also in the practice of this Committee, the burden of proof is placed with the applicant.

[34] In contrast, the state carries the responsibility of proving that conditions exist for measures implying infringements on the personal freedom of a person. In terms of starting points the same can be said in different words: One starting point is that the right to a particular benefit does not exist (so that the individual claiming the benefit must prove that the right exists) and another is that the conditions for measures of infringement towards a person do not exist (so that the state must show that they indeed do exist). *Ibid.*

a procedure where the benefit of asylum is granted to an applicant – which is the view embraced by this study, the starting-point can be taken in that the person claiming the right to the benefit, the asylum seeker, carries the burden of proof. Accordingly, the initial position in an asylum procedure concerned with granting a benefit is that the conditions for the granting of asylum do not exist and the applicant faces the challenge of shifting this starting point. This allocation is in conformity with as well international law as EU law. As we have seen, the burden of proof can shift during assessment so that if the applicant achieves the standard of proof required for the burden to shift, the state then has to prove that the prerequisites for asylum do not exist.

Allocation of the initial burden of proof with the asylum-applicant can, thus, also be the starting point for appellate asylum procedures. According to this view, it is a task for the appealing applicant to prove the wrongfulness of the first instance decision by proving that the preconditions for asylum do exist, contrary to what the appealed decision says.

The placement of the burden of proof with the applicant can naturally be contested. We have seen that the notion of asylum procedure as a procedure concerned with granting a benefit is not self-evident. The placement of the burden with the applicant does not take into consideration the notion of asylum procedures as procedures imposing restrictions. It could, further, be claimed that the difficult evidentiary environment combined with weighty interests of the individual calls for a relief of the burden on the applicant, also when the procedure concerns a benefit:

As we have seen before, asylum procedure is characterised by a difficult evidentiary situation, inequality between the parties to the procedure and a strong political tie. Additionally, the procedure strives towards determining a likelihood of future persecution, making both the theme of proof and evidentiary assessment in general vague and abstract.[35] However, the predictive character of evidentiary assessment in asylum procedure and the impact of policy-oriented interest on the procedure are not directly linked to either one or other of the parties. These are elements that influence the procedure more generally and that must be taken into consideration throughout assessment – not because they speak directly to the benefit of either of the parties but because they complicate evidentiary assessment.

In the same way, difficulties in producing and presenting evidence are not directly linked to either party and are, moreover, even further divided through

---

[35] Also, there is the inclusion of as well a subjective as objective element in the assessment of fear, implying a further element to be aware of. *Supra* at 17.

the responsibility of the state agent to investigate the matter objectively.[36] It could nevertheless be argued that difficulties in producing evidence have negative implications for the party left with the burden of proof – especially if this is linked to the burden of presenting evidence. However, first and foremost these disadvantages are disadvantages of the court, making it more difficult to come to a correct decision in the matter on a general level.

As the difficulties do not affect only one of the parties, but are inherent to the procedure generally, they cannot be seen as reasons for shifting the initial burden of proof away from the applicant or appellant. Many of these features affect the parties equally and only place an obligation with the assessor of evidence for particular awareness in general assessment. Further, the most discriminatory inequality relates to issues of procedural strength and differences in cultural understanding. These are issues that are effectively also dealt with outside the burden of proof, for instance through introduction of strong procedural safeguards for the weaker party.[37] Thus, while it is clear that features of the procedure indeed place the appellant in an inferior position, the implications of these features are not grave enough to call for a complete shift of allocation of the burden of proof. Rather, they require procedural safeguards and an awareness of the unequal position to be introduced to asylum procedure. Thus, also after considering the particular features of the asylum procedure the burden of proof can still be placed with the appellant. Taking into account the difficult evidentiary situation for the appellant, this requirement cannot, however, be too rigid. Also the state party and the decision-maker have responsibilities towards the production of evidence.

---

[36] The responsibility of the state party to investigate and present evidence objectively is derived from the duty to investigate, which could be considered to follow the state party from the decision-making role of the first instance to the role as a party at the second, appellate instance. See Mäenpää (2007a) 367–379. Nevertheless, stakeholders especially in English asylum procedure point out that the obligation of objectivity does not imply that the first instance authority would file self-incriminatory evidence at the appellate stage.

[37] European norms have, for instance, enforced the right to interpreting and legal representation in asylum procedure. In the proposals for amended Directives presented 21.10.2009, these rights are also enhanced at the level of appellate procedures. Council directive 2005/85, OJ 1.12.2005, (L 326) 13 on Minimum Standards on Procedures in Member States for Granting and Withdrawing Refugee Status, Art 10 (b), Arts 10, 13 and 15. See also Proposal for a Directive of the European Parliament and of the Council on minimum standards of procedures in Member States for the granting and withdrawing of international protection COM (2009) 554/4 and Amended proposal for a Directive of the European Parliament and of the Council on common procedures for granting and withdrawing international protection status (Recast), COM(2011) 319 final, Art 18.

4. *Evidentiary Robustness*

The burden of proof necessitates that evidence is produced in the procedure. The duty to produce evidence reflects the responsibility for producing and presenting material evidence in support of certain claims. How much evidence has to be presented in all in the procedure is determined by the required robustness of the evidence, which in turn is determined by the nature of the judicial procedure.[38] What evidence is to be presented also depends on the procedure. Finally, the beneficiary of the evidence presented is determined by the burden of proof.

4.1. *Definition of Concepts*

Evidentiary robustness and the duty to present evidence are concepts used in order to examine fact-finding processes in judicial procedures. However, these particular concepts are not nearly as clearly defined as the burden of proof. Nor can these concepts be measured or identified with the same clarity as the burden of proof. Nevertheless, through defining the meaning of these concepts and through understanding their role in evidentiary assessment, their significant importance and their role as the basis of evidentiary assessment becomes evident.[39]

Responsibility for Evidentiary Robustness
The concept of responsibility for establishing facts is commonly used within civil law administrative doctrine.[40] The concept refers to an obligation to investigate the matter at hand to a certain point and to strive to establish the facts.[41] However, in order for analysis of the burden to be meaningful the concept has to be split up into smaller parts: one part encompassing the material and practical establishment of facts (production and presentation of

---

[38] The term used here "robustness" refers to the concept of "robusthet" as presented by, amongst others, Ekelöf, Diesen and Schelin. Ekelöf (*et al.*) (2009) 187–189, Lena Schelin, *Bevisvärdering av utsagor i brottmål* (Stockholm 2006) 50–53 and Diesen (1993) 548–552.

[39] Mäenpää (2007a) 367–388; Diesen (*et al.*) (2003) 80–89 and Ryynänen (2000) 58–62 all relate to the importance of the acquirement of information in judiciary procedures. Also the evidentiary theory presented in Heuman (2005) relies mainly on acquisition of sufficient evidence as the basis for all evidentiary work.

[40] Diesen (*et al.*) (2003) 80–83.

[41] It is, however, partly misleading to speak of a "burden" in this respect, as failure to meet the requirements imposed by the burden does not, in the administrative environment and in contrast to criminal procedure, entail negative consequences for the party on whom the burden is placed.

evidence) before the decision-maker and a second part encompassing the obligation to ensure sufficient investigation of the matter at hand (evidentiary robustness).

The first part of the concept refers to rules and principles providing a duty for a party to the judicial procedure to present evidence before the decision-maker. For instance, a principle common to many forms of procedure is that the party making a claim has to present evidence in support of this. The duty may be placed with several parties to the procedure at the same time.

The second part of the responsibility, the obligation to ensure establishment of facts through sufficient investigation, refers to a general responsibility for robustness in investigations. Even if duties to present evidence are allocated to different party, there may, in addition, be a general responsibility for that enough information is entered into the procedure. In certain procedures it is for the parties to the procedure to decide on the required robustness[42], and at times it is for the court or decision-maker[43].

In relation to the asylum procedure, the first part of the responsibility to establish facts concerns for whom in the procedure it is to practically present evidence and knowledge about facts of importance in order to establish whether the applicant is a refugee. Who has to present evidence about past events, information about the situation in the home country and the individual circumstances of the applicant, and other relevant information? The second part of responsibility concerns for whom it is to ensure that the decision-maker has information about all material issues before making a decision, and when one can say that the decision-maker has enough information to be able to make a sufficiently good decision.

Robustness

The requirement for evidentiary robustness must also be defined. How much and what information, knowledge and evidence must be gathered and examined in order for the responsibility to establish facts to be fulfilled. Is it possible to determine when knowledge is adequate both in amount and quality? And can separate requirements on amount and quality be imposed?

Thus, using evidentiary robustness as a key of comparison, this study will ask for whom it is to present evidence in the appellate asylum procedure, who has the responsibility for that enough information is provided the decision-maker and what is enough information in the particular procedure.

---

[42] This is particularly the case if the focus is on the procedural truth. For comments from civil procedure see Lappalainen (*et al.*) (2007) 499–502, Jonkka (1993) 67–69 and 74–76 and Diesen (*et al*) (2003) 80–81.

[43] See Schelin (2006) 50–51, for robustness in criminal procedure.

4.2. Development of Concepts in Appellate Administrative Procedures

As the administrative environment is distinct from criminal and civil procedures, it is well worth to explore the concepts mentioned above in the particular administrative framework. Firstly, how is the general responsibility for robustness met in the appellate administrative procedure?

Responsibility for Evidentiary Robustness
In appellate administrative procedures, allocation of a general responsibility for establishing facts can be solved in at least three ways: Allocation with the court or tribunal, with the appellant or with the first instance authority. Additionally, allocation can of course be joint so that responsibility is thus joint.

If starting with the position of the appellant, it can be acknowledged that it may not be in the interest of the appellant to conduct thorough investigations and that the appellant's means for ensuring in practice that requirements as to establishing facts are met are small. Further, the appellant is not in all circumstances aware of the evidence collected and does not have the practical possibility to evaluate the general sufficiency of the knowledge of the court. These circumstances make it difficult to place responsibility on the shoulders of the appellant.

Turning then to the administrative authority possibly present in appellate proceedings, it must be recognised that this party indeed has a certain interest in defending prior decisions in the matter at hand.[44] It is clear that, assuming no major changes to the facts have occurred, the position of the administrative authority must be that the facts have been sufficiently established, that robustness is sufficient and that investigations have led to a correct decision. Thus, clear contradictions exist between the interest of the first instance authority as a party to the procedure and the interest of the procedure itself. However, it is also true that the first instance authority may in many instances be better equipped effectively to ensure a certain standard of investigation than for instance the appellate instance court. The authority is often specialised in its field and has better resources, means and contacts than the court for establishing facts.[45]

---

[44] On the relationship between public power and responsibilities for investigation see Kauko Heuru, *Hyvä hallinto* (Helsinki 2003) 113–115; Aer (2000) 78–86 and Diesen (*et al.*) (2003) 13–15.

[45] Practical possibilities for ensuring robustness also vary due to the nature of the decision-maker at second instance. In particular, general courts may have little possibility for special fact-finding whereas for instance specially established tribunals or boards are often equipped with entire departments for fact-finding. See Staffans (2006a).

The final possible allocation is with the court. The court clearly has an inter-est in ensuring that facts are adequately established as a result of its role as the executive of power in the procedure. This interest is *per se* free from ties to background interests in individual matters, as the court has not been involved in earlier stages of the procedure and thus has nothing to gain or lose with respect to prior decisions.[46] The court also has effective means to ensure prac-tical robustness as it can delegate practical work to the parties.

Thus, whereas allocation of responsibility with the parties to the procedure would be challenging in terms of interest and efficiency, these challenges do not arise in respect of the court. On the contrary, the theoretical possibilities for the court to serve the procedure in this respect are in fact increased by the duty of the court to actually come to a conclusion in the matter and are not hindered by issues linked to interests or restraints on efficiency.

However, it is not enough that responsibility for ensuring that facts are ade-quately established is allocated. There must, secondly, be a practical duty to present and produce evidence.[47] This is the 'practical mode' of responsibility for sufficiency in investigating the relevant circumstances and holds within the obligation to present material evidence in the procedure.

An important legal principle must be kept in mind when assessing alloca-tion of the duty to present and produce evidence. This is the procedural prin-ciple that claims should be supported and that it is for the party making those claims to substantiate them.[48] This principle is valid in criminal procedures as a general rule, implying that it is for the prosecutor to substantiate its demand for punishment (even if criminal procedure additionally includes an obliga-tion for the prosecutor to present evidence objectively), and for the defendant to substantiate claims that he or she presents.[49] Furthermore, the role of the

---

[46] Another issue is the political implications of decisions by the decision-maker for the appellate body itself and the effects of such considerations on the procedure. Further, even local effects such as effects on the decision-maker's career may at times impact. *Ibid.*

[47] Production of evidence refers to instances where a party finds, identifies and presents evi-dence to the decision-maker. For general considerations on the role of this concept in the evidentiary environment see Ekelöf (*et al.*) 34–38. See also Heuman (2005) 182–223, where presentation of evidence is taken as the starting point for creating a general theory of evidence.

[48] Lappalainen (*et al.*) (2007) 580 and Klami (*et al.*) (1987) 82, where the first step in evidentiary assessment is to consider if the party making a claim has been able to support this to the level of standard of proof. See also Lindell (1998) 505.

[49] The field is somewhat more complicated than this clear cut statement on obligations to pre-sent and produce evidence in criminal procedure – but as a ground rule this is efficient. For more elaborate discussion on the duty to present and produce evidence in criminal procedure see Pölönen (2003) 82–85 and 123–125 and Schelin (2006) 43–47.

principle is also evident in civil proceedings regardless of whether the proceedings rely on discretionary or mandatory norms.[50] However, the discretionary nature of the proceedings tends to emphasise this principle, as there is no counter-weight to the principle in the form of responsibility towards material probability.

There is no reason for this principle not also to apply to administrative justice proceedings, at least when understood as a principle, not as a strict rule. Thus, the starting point in relation to robustness in administrative justice procedures must also be taken in the responsibility of the court to ensure establishment of facts and in the principle that it is for the party making a claim to substantiate this by means of evidence. It is clear that one of the means that the court can use to exercise its responsibility towards robustness is to call for the parties to the procedure to present evidence in support of their claims, in which scenario these two outsets meet in practice.

Robustness
Christian Diesen has described requirements for robustness as referring both to the amount, the objectivity, the trustworthiness and the usefulness of knowledge and information gathered.[51] Robustness understood in this sense refers to the totality of the quantitative and qualitative requirements placed with the investigatory function of knowledge and information made available to the court through the evidence in any individual procedure.

Let us take the starting point for examining the precise content of the requirement for evidentiary robustness in the criminal procedure.[52] Criminal procedure is characterised by weighty interests, a well-guarded presumption of innocence and a strong requirement for certainty and rightfulness in decision-making. No direct threshold or standard has been presented as the precise requirement for robustness in criminal procedure. Nevertheless, it has been stated that investigations are sufficiently solid when they encompass all known issues involved in the case and when no relevant knowledge is left unexplored.[53] Robustness implies that all issues of interest to the procedure

---

[50] See also Ekelöf (*et al.*) (2009) 93–94 regarding the relationship between burden of proof and burden of allegation.

[51] Diesen (*et al.*) (2003) 81–83 and Diesen (1998) 160–162.

[52] The reason for choosing criminal procedure as an example is that the procedure represents an extreme in relation to requirements for legal certainty and correct decision-making, so that the requirements of robustness in this particular procedure are weighty, thus clearly highlighting the position of robustness.

[53] Ekelöf (*et al.*) (2009) 187–189, Lindell (1998) 432–433 and Pölönen (2003) 126. See also Diesen (1993) 265–284.

have been investigated and that information has been gathered about all circumstances that might have an impact on the 'piece of reality' to be perceived by the court.

If robustness is perceived in this manner, the following question arises: How do we know what is of importance to the matter, and how do we know when all issues and circumstances of importance to the matter have been explored? Pölönen offers a model for this analysis, again within the context of criminal procedure: Firstly, there are claims by the prosecutor. All circumstances presented as relevant to those claims have to be explored and investigated. Secondly, there are claims by the defendant. All circumstances and issues related and relevant to the claims of the defendant also need to be explored and supported by evidence. And finally, there is the entirety of the case and all issues that may be of importance to the matter aside from the circumstances presented in the claims of the parties to the procedure. Thus, it has also to be considered whether other circumstances may be of importance for a proper holistic and broader picture of the matter.[54]

Moreover, Pölönen does not see the requirement for robustness as a rigid requirement: The practical implications of the requirement may vary, depending on the type of case and on the defendant's need for procedural certainty.[55] The higher the stakes in the procedure and the weightier the interests vested in the procedure, the tighter the practical implications of the requirement for robustness.

When considering the practical scope of the requirement for evidentiary robustness in the administrative judicial environment, the aim of appellate administrative procedure must be kept in mind. The aim of evidentiary work is also to assess the parties' claims, including assessment of the theme of proof, so that the practical implications of the requirement for robustness must thus be examined against this background. Referring to the model presented by Pölönen but transferring it to the context of administrative justice, evidentiary robustness can be measured by assessing coverage of the following elements: Firstly, all the relevant circumstances that the appealing party draws on in his or her claims must have been examined in a qualitatively acceptable manner. Secondly, there must be qualitatively acceptable knowledge of the circumstances and issues that have been relevant for the first instance decision and which thus constitute the response to the claims presented by the appealing party. Additionally, qualitatively acceptable evidence must be presented in respect of all circumstances and issues relevant to possible additional claims

---

[54] Pölönen (2003) 126.
[55] *Ibid* at 127.

by the 'defendant', i.e. the first instance authority, in the procedure. Lastly, the court has to conduct a general survey of the case, evaluate the theme of proof, and in a qualitatively acceptable manner explore possible other issues and circumstances that are not directly linked to the claims and responses of the parties, but which are still of relevance to the theme of proof in the matter at hand.[56]

4.3. *Normative Frames for Evidentiary Robustness in European Asylum Procedures*

International law does not pose direct rules regarding general responsibility for robustness, the duty to present evidence nor the required robustness of investigations. The 1951 Geneva Convention does not include norms on procedural aspects of the asylum procedure.

Nevertheless, guidelines can be found in the UNHCR Handbook and also in international practice. The UNHCR Handbook recognizes that no direct rules in international law are provided for the procedural aspects of RSD, but states regarding the establishment of facts that it is for the applicant to as well put forward relevant facts and "make an effort to support his statements by any available evidence" and to "supply all pertinent information concerning himself and his past experience in as much detail as is necessary".[57] The Handbook, however, also recognizes that material proof is not often available in RSD.[58] Further, the Handbook concludes that due to the difficult evidentiary environment, it may also be for the "examiner to use all the means at his disposal to produce the necessary evidence in support of the application".

Hence, the UNHCR Handbook places some form of general responsibility for robustness with the examiner. Also, a duty to present evidence, limited by the difficult environment of the asylum procedure, is placed with the applicant.

Concerning the requirement for robustness the UNHCR Handbook states that "Very frequently the fact-finding process will not be complete until a wide range of circumstance has been ascertained".[59] Hence, the Handbook is inclusive in its approach to the requirement for robustness.

In relation to subsidiary protection, the European Court of Human Rights has in some cases taken stands also in relation to robustness. In *Salah Sheehk* the European Court of Human Rights emphasised the role of qualitative evidentiary robustness in matters concerning international protection.

---

[56]   See Diesen (*et al.*) (2003) 81–83.
[57]   UNHCR (1992) paras 195 and 205.
[58]   *Ibid* at para 196.
[59]   *Ibid* at para 201.

The Court stated that attention must, when examining the need for protection in the light of information provided, also be paid to the objectivity of both individual sources and the material in its entirety.[60] In *Vilvarajah* the Court has also determined that the Court itself has a general responsibility for robustness as the Court must take into account all material placed before it "or, if necessary, material obtained *proprio motu*" in determining breaches of Article 3.[61] The ECHR particularly in matters of international protection thus also places a general responsibility for robustness with the examiner.

In opposite of international law, EU law, again, indeed includes direct norms also on matters of robustness and investigations in secondary legislation. These norms reflect also the influence of general principles of EU law on secondary legislation.

The QD in article 4 (1) states that Member States may consider it the duty of the applicant to submit evidence in support of his claims.[62] This facultative rule gives Member States formal possibility to regulate on the duty to present evidence. The rule is not mandatory, and thus gives the Member States the possibility to provide for other solutions to the production of evidence. As Noll has noted, the obvious alternative is for the examiner to provide evidence.[63]

Further, the QD in Article 4 (2) provides a list of elements, regarding which the applicant may be considered to have a duty to provide evidence. The list includes "statements and all documentation at the applicants disposal regarding the applicant's age, background, including that of relevant relatives, identity, nationality(ies), country(ies) and place(s) of previous residence, previous asylum applications, travel routes, identity and travel documents and the reasons for applying for international protection." Even if it clear that the list itself does not constitute either a maximum level or minimum level of robustness, the list, nevertheless, provides information on which matters are considered to be of importance in the asylum procedure and thus affect the assessment of whether required robustness in the individual case has been achieved. Further, also Article 4 (3) lists components that must be part of the assessment of applications for asylum. Country of origin –information, statements and evidence provided by the applicant, individual and personal circumstances of the applicant and activities outside of the country of origin are mentioned. At least partly, also this section thus adds to the requirements on robustness.

---

[60] *Salah Sheekh v. The Netherlands*, Appl. No. 1948/04, Council of Europe: European Court of Human Rights, 11 January 2007, para 136.

[61] *Vilvarajah and Others v. The United Kingdom*, 45/1990/236/302–306, Council of Europe: European Court of Human Rights, 26 September 1991, para 107.

[62] QD, *supra* at 14.

[63] Noll (2005c) 4–6.

The Asylum Procedures Directive, again, does not provide norms regarding the distribution of tasks, duties or responsibilities towards robustness. However, the directive includes norms regarding required quantitative and qualitative robustness. In Article 8 (2) (b) the directive requires that "precise and up-to-date information is obtained from various sources, such as the United Nations High Commissioner for Refugees (UNHCR), as to the general situation prevailing in the countries of origin of applicants for asylum and, where necessary, in countries through which they have transited".[64] This Article concerns, on the one hand, qualitative robustness through emphasizing the need for precise and up-to-date evidence. On the other hand, the Article also concerns quantitative robustness as it requires information from various sources.

Further, the APD provides for a right to an interview, which also affects as well qualitative as quantitative standards of investigation, and in Article 15 the right to legal aid is provided for, a right that may be of crucial importance for the applicant's factual possibilities to produce evidence.

4.4. *Evidentiary Robustness in an Appellate European Asylum Procedure*

The procedural setting of appellate asylum procedure is, as we repeatedly have seen and as recognized by relevant international and regional norms, affected by the distinct features of the asylum environment primarily with an emphasis on the subjectivity of the parties to the procedure. Further, the rather distinct practical environment for presenting and producing evidence clearly has an impact on the nature of the requirement for robustness. The subjectivity emphasised together with difficulties in retrieving information and knowledge lead to calls for special attention on the one hand to the legal certainty of the parties and on the other hand to evidentiary robustness. Additionally, the special features that have been presented can also be interpreted as calling for extra care in decision-making and evidentiary assessment in order to ensure that the examination made is qualitatively acceptable.[65]

---

[64] APD, *supra* at 37.

[65] The special circumstances of the procedure and their effect on responsibility for investigative robustness is in practice evident in many of the procedural rules prevailing in administrative procedures in asylum matters. For instance, the procedural rules for the English Asylum Chamber of the First- Tier Tribunal allow for all evidence to be given "of any fact which appears to be relevant to an appeal or an application for bail, even if that evidence would be inadmissible in a court of law". See The Asylum and Immigration Tribunal (Procedure) Rules 2005, Statutory Instrument 2005 No. 230 (L.1), section 51, in force also in relation to the First-Tier Tribunal by virtue of Statutory Instrument 2010 No.21 Tribunals and Inquiries: The Transfer of Functions of the Asylum and Immigration Tribunal Order 2010, in force 15.2.2010.

Thus, the position of the court as the neutral deciding member of the procedure is, in the appellate asylum procedure, emphasised due to the stressed subjectivity of the parties and the enhanced possibilities of this subjectivity also shining through in evidentiary assessment due to the rather difficult practical evidentiary situation. Any allocation of responsibility to ensure robustness other than with the court seems impossible as a result of these circumstances in asylum procedure. Moreover, entrusting to the court the responsibility to ensure robustness in investigations may in fact further encourage the court to proceed with care in evidentiary assessment and also to pay attention both to quantity and quality of material outside the gathering process.[66]

Further, the practical obligation to produce and present evidence has been considered. In relation to administrative conduct in asylum matters as well international as European law place a duty to produce and present evidence in support of the claims for asylum with the applicant, and an additional duty with the decision-maker to produce evidence if required by the demands on robustness. Hence, in practice all actors involved in the appellate procedure have a responsibility to present evidence: The appellant in support of the claims of the appeal, the other party to the procedure in support of the legality of the first decision and the decision-maker as a secondary obligation if no other means of producing sufficiently solid knowledge is apparent.

One of the distinctive features of appellate asylum procedure is, as we have seen, that the positions of power and the practical possibilities to produce evidence may vary greatly between the parties. Generally, the appellant has a rather weak position in comparison with the state representative. Thus, whereas the appellant has the advantage of being directly tied to the issues and circumstances of substantive relevance to the procedure, the state representative has an advantage in better practical possibilities for producing and presenting evidence. The traditional means of dealing with this inequality between the parties from the asylum perspective has been through the so called benefit of the doubt allowed the applicant at all stages of asylum procedure, implying that sufficient evidence robustness-wise and in terms of burden of proof has been produced by the applicant if he or she can deliver trustworthy oral testimony concerning the claim for asylum.[67] This practice has also been recognised in relevant European law.[68]

---

[66] See Diesen (*et al.*) (2003) 80–83 and 87–89.

[67] UNHCR (1992), paras 196 and 203–204. See also Noll (2005b) 197 ff, for a broader perspective on issues relating to inclusion and evidentiary assessment.

[68] QD, *supra* at 14, Article 4 (5).

The responsibility for establishing facts that is tied to the court in appellate asylum procedure in practice transforms partly into a practical obligation to ensure that the quality of information gathered is acceptable so that the unequal positions of the parties to the procedure have not been transferred to unequal standards in the evidence. As a result of this responsibility, the court is also in practice entrusted with the task of ensuring that sufficiently solid material is presented as needed. Thus, the responsibility of the court includes an obligation to see to it that information from both ends of the matter is gathered and that both the appealing party and the counter-party are represented in the evidence. Bearing in mind that the uneven position between the parties, especially in asylum matters, tends to also affect possibilities to produce evidence, it becomes clear that the responsibility of the court in this respect is enhanced. Drawing on the practice of the benefit of the doubt, the decision is at least guided by the fact that testimony must be taken seriously and can in itself be decisive in the matter.

Hence, the conclusion must be that only a vague primary responsibility can be established for the appealing party to produce and present evidence in support of their claims and a corresponding responsibility for the counter-party to produce evidence. In the end, it is a task for the court to ensure, in the name of sufficient robustness, that the parties produce the information needed for the procedure. Ultimately, the court thus has power over distribution of this responsibility.[69]

The final concept examined was the requirement for robustness. A formula for understanding robustness in context was introduced: The basis is solid and robust if it sheds qualitatively adequate light on issues and circumstances of importance to the claims of the appealing party, on issues and circumstances of importance to possible counter-claims and on other issues and circumstances that on a more general level are of importance to the holistic picture of the individual matter. Thus, the requirement for robustness encompasses both qualitative and quantitative points of reference.

In relation to qualitative requirements, it is worth emphasising that the peculiarities of asylum procedure require that the court pays special attention to the objectivity and reliability of the evidence. The issue has also been raised by the European Court of Human Rights.[70] Both the strong interests present in the procedure, the unequal positions and the political ties inherently pose risks for quality of evidence. Moreover, the nature of the evidence itself and the form it is presented in often also place high demands on the decision-maker for correct evaluation of background features and elements. On the quantitative side, it must also be recognised that the difficult practical evidentiary climate of appellate asylum procedure may at times pose a

---

[69] Mäenpää (2007a) 384–388 discusses court activity in administrative setting.
[70] See also *Salah Sheekh, supra* at 60 and *Vilvarajah, supra* at 61.

hindrance for all-inclusive investigations and that the decision-maker has on the one hand to be aware of this in the practical task of ensuring robustness and on the other hand to be aware that the threshold for acceptability must not be set at an unrealistic level.

Quantitative robustness can be achieved through inclusive investigations and through inclusion of evidence in relation to the claims of both the appellant and the other party to the proceedings. Additionally, the court needs to take a holistic view of the matter and to include evidence on other possible important circumstances. The qualitative standard can on the other hand be achieved through thorough consideration of the evidence gathered, the means of gathering relevant information, and careful assessment of the evidence. The contradiction between a difficult evidentiary situation, including when it comes to presentation of evidence, and the high requirements of procedural certainty must be met with respect by the decision-maker.

5. *Methods of Evidentiary Assessment*

5.1. *Definition of Concept*

Evidentiary assessment as a general concept is used to describe the intellectual process of assessing and reaching conclusions on the basis of knowledge gathered. It includes considerations regarding the applicable burden and standard of proof, the robustness of evidence presented as well as regarding other elements of production and assessment of information. In this general respect, evidentiary assessment is thus to be understood as describing the whole evidentiary process included in judicial procedures from determining the theme of proof to assessing the robustness and implications of the evidence.

However, in a more specific meaning, evidentiary assessment can also be understood exclusively as the weighing and balancing of evidence acquired in order to come to a conclusion regarding the theme of proof. In this particular meaning, evidentiary assessment excludes general considerations regarding burden of proof, robustness or standard of proof and is only interested in what the evidence produces in terms of information. This specific form of assessing the evidence takes place prior to assessing whether the required standard of proof is reached, and in close connection to considerations regarding burden of proof.[71]

---

[71] For general comments on evidentiary assessment see Lappalainen (*et al.*) (2007) 573–574 and for elaboration on the different elements of evidence and their interrelation, same, 458–465. Also Diesen (1993) 381–483 and Schelin (2006) 99 ff. Jonkka (1993) 99–122 analyse assessment of parts of proof within the greater framework of evidentiary assessment.

When examining evidentiary assessment in the latter meaning, it is not possible to sidestep the issue of choice of method. A strategy is needed for analysing the evidence and determining if and how the evidence in the individual case meets the required standard of proof. Methods of evidentiary assessment as a concept refers to this particular structure of practical and intellectual work that the decision-maker carries out when trying to grasp the entirety of knowledge gathered in an individual case in order to determine the correct application of law.[72] Methods could be described as road-maps guiding the decision-maker through evidentiary assessment.[73] This journey comprises at least the following steps: an assessment of the importance and relevancy of each piece of evidence, estimates as to the effects of inter-relevance of different parts of the evidence, assessments of the significance of what cannot be supported by evidence and finally establishing a general view on what the evidence says about the theme of proof.[74]

In the comparative study the method for evidentiary assessment in its specific meaning will be used as a key of comparison through analysis of how decision-makers come to conclusions based on the evidence before them, how the evidence is weighed and if there are common strategies in legal systems for how the evidentiary assessment is undertaken.

5.2. *Choice of Method*

So, what are the choices? Clearly it is impossible here to give an account of all possible methods and models for evidentiary assessment. Furthermore, the object of this study is not to explore the possible application of different methods to asylum procedure, but to study the actual application and its implications. However, in the following some outlines regarding possible frameworks and their developments will be presented, leaving detailed analysis of these models for other researchers.[75]

---

[72] For an outline of the theoretical elements of evidentiary assessment see Schelin (2006) 27–42 and Diesen (*et al.*) (2003)115–118. See also Lindell (1998) 484–486, where the author examines the objective for assessment – evidence – as a self evident part of the constellation.

[73] The operative sphere for these methods is not all inclusive. At times there is no need for elaborate methods in order to reach a conclusion regarding the state of matters. However, when recognizing that uncertainty in decision-making is both inevitable and permitted, methods of evidentiary assessment find their natural role in the actions of the decision-maker.

[74] See Jonkka (1993) 20–24, where the author provides a practical outline of the steps included in evidentiary assessment.

[75] Besides methods of evidentiary assessment, abstract models of the same character have been presented regarding placing the burden of proof. See Heuman (2005) 41–60. While it is clear that the challenges that influence placing the burden of proof may also be taken into account in evidentiary assessment, these types of models and theories are nevertheless clearly distinct.

Firstly, some methods rely on calculations of probability. These are methods based on more or less scientific reasoning regarding determining the impact of the evidence. Probability-based models and methods are strongly connected to calculations of statistical probability relevant for scientific research and rely at least partly on mathematical approaches to evaluating evidentiary value. The strategies at times use rather elaborate schemes for coming to objectively verifiable conclusions about the probability of the theme of proof in the light of the evidence available in the case (or *vice versa* if one so wishes).[76]

Methods of statistical probability have been extremely influential over recent decades and were for a long time the leading approach towards evidentiary assessment, at least in the Nordic countries. Two main disciplines within the field may be identified: The value method and the theme method. The value method springs from the teachings of Ekelöf and takes its starting point in questions such as: What is the relationship between the evidence and the theme of proof? What are the probabilities for the evidence, given the theme?[77] The theory aims, in abstract words, at deriving the evidence from the theme of proof. Thus, the method to a large extent emphasises causality between the theme of proof and the evidence, as no value can be given to the evidence if it is not established that some level of causality exists: The evidence must be a result of the theme of proof in order for it to be meaningful. Central focus points are the correct definition of the theme of proof and careful consideration of the reliability of individual evidence. The value method incorporates the possibility of uncertainty in all calculations.

The theme method has its basis mainly in the writings of Bolding and Lindell and relies to an equally large extent on statistical models for estimating probabilities.[78] The difference compared to the value method is that the theme method is interested in the probability of the theme, given the evidence. *In concreto*, the theme method asks for the statistical probability that the theme of proof follows from the existence of the evidence established. Again, careful consideration of the reliability of the pieces of evidence is central to the functioning of the method. Another characteristic of the method is that it works with a two-sided probability, saying that the evidence either speaks for

---

[76] For general presentations of statistical methods see Pölönen (2003) 150–758, Klami (2000) 27–49 and Lindell (1987) 144–150. Also in Saranpää (2010) 203–225, are statistical models in the Scandinavian discourse presented and compared.

[77] Evidentiary assessment according to the value method is presented in Ekelöf (*et al.*) (2009) 180–218.

[78] See for instance Per Olof Bolding, *Bevisbörda och beviskrav* (Lund 1983) 8–13 and Lindell (1987) 171.

or against the theme of proof. No room is allowed for uncertainty or possible evidence not included in the material of the individual procedure.

The critique aimed at all theories relying on statistical approximations of probabilities contained in evidence has mainly been related to the impossibility of combining law, judicial procedures and human behaviour (the decision-maker's as well as that of the parties) with scientific models for mathematical calculations of probability.[79] Nevertheless, these theories continue to influence discussions on evidentiary assessment.

Secondly, Diesen (and later Pölönen) has developed methods for evidentiary assessment relying on *falsification of hypotheses.*[80] The basis for this method lies in a system of pin-pointing the facts presented by the evidence and then through falsification of different hypotheses to come to a conclusion regarding the theme of proof. In practice, the assessor thus tries to identify different hypothetical scenarios in the matter at hand and to use the evidence either to verify or falsify as many of these as possible. This method presents a practical tool for establishing evidentiary value for existing information in individual cases. However, a prerequisite for the method's usefulness is that the material basis is solid and that the knowledge incorporated in the material is broad enough to enable the approach to lead to accurate conclusions.

The practical implication of the model is a scheme for determining the collective value of the evidence by establishing and falsifying different hypotheses. Establishment is in itself an important part of evidentiary assessment, as eligibility for the hypotheses requires all the evidence gathered to fit into the proposed scenario. Thus, by establishing and falsifying/verifying different hypotheses against the background of knowledge in the evidence, a certain standard can be attached to the remaining possibilities.

In the choice and application of a method in a certain procedure, a range of elements that impact on the evidentiary field must be taken into account. These elements concern, for instance, the availability of evidence; the risks and interests vested in the procedure; and the quality of the evidence.

---

[79] See for instance Lindell (1998) 466–482 highlighting comparison between evidentiary assessment of judicial procedures and mathematical approximations. See also Anders Stening, "Konflikt mellan två bevismodeller" (1979/4) *Svensk Juristtidning*, 283–296, for discussion of the differences between the theme method and the value method, with the author finally supporting the latter.

[80] See Diesen (1993) 598–634 and Pölönen (2003) 158–179. For a critical approach to the method presented by Diesen particularly from the point of view of criminal procedure, see Helena Vihriälä, "Diesenin metodin soveltamisesta tuomioistuimen ratkaisutoiminnassa talousrikoksissa", in *Rikostuomion perusteleminen*, eds. Mika Huovila, Raimo Lahti & Timo Ojala (Helsinki 2005) 281–300.

5.3. Normative Frames for the Choice of Method for Evidentiary Assessment

Whereas international norms are silent also regarding choice of method for evidentiary assessment, guidance as to international practice can, again, be retrieved from UNHCR standpoints and case-law:

The UNHCR Handbook does not make direct reference to requirements on the method for evidentiary assessment. However, it does guide the assessor by stating that "Untrue statements by themselves are not a reason for refusal of refugee status and it is the examiner's responsibility to evaluate such statements in the light of all the circumstances of the case".[81] UNHCR has also in their own research emphasised that the decision-maker in the asylum procedure must consider all evidence provided, that the evidence must be considered as a whole and not just as parts in isolation. Further, the Handbook also states that it is for the decision-maker to "establish the objective and the subjective elements of the case".[82] Also this requirement relates to the method for evidentiary assessment as it seems to require some form of distinctiveness in the assessment, despite prior requirements for a generalized evidentiary assessment. UNHCR thus advocates an inclusive method for assessment, where causality and links between evidence is taken into due account.

Further, the UNHCR Handbook expresses its view on evidentiary assessment by stating that determination of refugee status is to take place in two stages: "Firstly, it is necessary to ascertain the relevant facts of the case. Secondly, the definitions in the 1951 Convention and the 1967 Protocol have to be applied to the facts thus ascertained".[83] The expression used by UNHCR does not endorse the clear separation between historical facts and prognosis. Rather, the two phases referred to by the UNHCR must be seen as one phase including the facts of the matter at hand and conclusions drawn from this and a second phase including considerations as to whether the conclusions drawn from the facts are subsumable to the refugee definition in the 1951 Convention.

In *Chahal*, a case concerning international protection and *non-refoulement*, the European Court of Human Rights implied that non-existence of evidence is also to be considered as proof of something and that non-existence of evidence must be taken into account as a factor in the evidentiary assessment.[84] The court, hence, makes clear that insecurities and the unknown have their

---

[81] UNHCR (1992) para 199.
[82] UNHCR (1992) para 205
[83] UNHCR (1992) para 29.
[84] *Chahal v. The United Kingdom*, 70/1995/576/662, Council of Europe: European Court of Human Rights, 15 November 1996, para 103.

given place in the assessment of evidence in cases of international protection. The introduction of the unknown to the evidentiary assessment directly affects the method of assessment.

The EU legal order does not *per se* place requirements on the choice of method for evidentiary assessment. However, the APD in Article 8 (2) (a) requires that the assessment of any application for asylum shall be objective and individual and impartial.[85] Rather than a requirement for a particular method, this Article can be seen as a requirement for the use of a method. The examiner and decision-maker must have objective and impartial standards for the evidentiary assessment in the individual case. Further, APD Article 9 (2) states that Member States shall ensure that rejected applications are reasoned on points of fact and law. As we have seen, the requirement for reasoning of decisions requires that the evidentiary assessment is conducted in a manner that the decision-maker is able to explain through the reasoning.

5.4. *Method of Evidentiary Assessment in an Appellate European Asylum Procedure*

Looking specifically at asylum procedure one must once again identify distinct features of the procedure that influence the choice of method of assessment. Such features are found amongst others in the prognostic element involved in evidentiary assessment, the accentuated difference in procedural strength between the parties and practical problems related to acquiring and presenting evidence in the procedure.

The prognostic element of assessment has to do with the fact that the material question in refugee determination concerns the likelihood of future persecution. The implication of the risk element on choice of assessment method thus introduces uncertainty to assessment. This uncertainty is emphasised by difficulties in acquiring evidence that often result in a very scarce evidentiary base for assessment. The prognostic character, persecution as a concept, cultural differences and long geographical distances, to name a few elements, all add to the difficulties for the decision-maker in coming to a conclusion based on evidence. The direct implication of these challenges is the creation of an environment for assessment that includes not only a scarce evidentiary base but also vast uncertainty.

As we have seen, also the ECtHR has recognised the momentum of uncertainty by stating that the non-existance of evidence is a factor of importance in

---

[85] APD, *supra* at 37.

the evidentiary assessment in matters of international protection.[86] Hence, also the unknown must be taken into account in the inclusive assessment as advocated by international commentators. The inclusion of a known momentum of uncertainty in evidentiary assessment clearly hinders evidentiary methods of assessment not familiar with the concept of uncertainty from being used as support in evidentiary assessment. Thus, the theme method as a method for assessment is excluded.[87]

Difficulties in acquiring material evidence are integrated in the identified uncertainty that forms part of any asylum procedure. However, this difficulty also has other impacts on choice of assessment method. The asylum environment poses a challenge to methods relying on statistical approaches to evidentiary assessment due to the weakness of the 'population' of statistical data in assessment which results from the scarce evidentiary material. The results of assessment may simply not be reliable, even if accepting uncertainty in relying on human patterns of behaviour as part of the method. However, the hypothetical approach defended by Diesen and others can also be criticised on the very same grounds. Scarcity of material evidence makes it close to impossible to rule out enough possibilities in order to achieve a high standard of proof in the individual case, especially keeping in mind that reliability of available evidence is not always clear. Even if this perhaps is ultimately a question about the appropriate level of the standard of proof, it must be recognised that all methods available face a challenge in asylum procedure.[88]

All things considered, and especially taking into account the impact of the unknown which also the ECtHR has pointed out, it is clear that the theme method is not a valid choice for appellate asylum procedure, while the method requires a solid base and good evidentiary conditions to work properly. In contrast, the value method has a defined format for dealing with evidentiary uncertainties and the unknown and thus seems to represent the most feasible alternative for asylum procedure. Nevertheless, it is clear that even in implementing this method of assessment in asylum matters, consideration must be taken of the features and the challenges of asylum procedure in its distinct form.

---

[86] *Supra* at 84.
[87] The theme method does not recognise uncertainty as an element in evidentiary assessment. For a particular analysis of the role of uncertainty, see Klami (2000) 35–40.
[88] Diesen explicitly recognises the need for robustness and a good material basis for decisions as a prerequisite for using falsification of hypotheses as a method of evidentiary assessment. Diesen (1993) 553.

5.5. *Credibility Assessment as an Integral Part of Assessing Evidence*

It is clear that the central position of credibility and the assessment of credibility in asylum procedure must be taken into account when reviewing evidentiary assessment at appellate level.[89] Due to the extraordinary significance of the asylum seeker's oral testimony in the asylum environment, credibility assessment and its effects are important in asylum procedure. However, from this it does not directly follow that particular devices or methods for assessing credibility must be construed.[90] The role of credibility may affect choice of method of evidentiary assessment and the assessment itself but established elements of evidentiary assessment and the methods already available are also quite capable of dealing with this particular feature. Assessing credibility can have different impacts on general evidentiary assessment, depending on which method is used for evidentiary assessment.[91] If the assessor has taken the standpoint that evidence is either for or against the theme of proof, the credibility assessment will often determine on which side of this dichotomy the evidence is placed. For other assessors, evidence can be more or less credible so that the impact of credibility assessment on the general standard of proof can be simultaneously positive and negative.[92]

---

[89] On the importance of credibility assessment in the asylum environment see Noll (2005b) 197–214 and Juliet Cohen, "Of Credibility: Omissions, Discrepancies and Errors of Recall in the Testimony of Asylum Seekers" (2001/3) *International Journal of Refugee Law*, 293–309.

[90] Cpr James A. Sweeney, "Credibility, Proof and Refugee Law" (2009/4) *International Journal of Refugee Law*, 700–926, where the author argues that questions of credibility should not be seen as questions of evidentiary value, but rather as questions of admissibility of information in the procedure. This study does not embrace the idea that methods of evidentiary assessment would not also be of importance in the stages of admitting information or evidence in the procedure. It is argued that the act of admitting information in the procedure (which, as spelled out in chapter IV in particular can constitute an important part of RSD) must also include assessment of information and thus can, depending on the procedure and its traditions, constitute a step in evidentiary assessment. It is argued that sidestepping credibility as a question of evidentiary value and isolating credibility as a separate matter is indeed possible, but not necessary.

[91] For accounts of credibility assessment as a part of evidentiary assessment see Klami (*et al.*) (1987) 63–70.

[92] Gregor Noll has in particular interpreted credibility assessment in asylum procedure as a part of a greater strategy to revive Christian traditions of confession in judicial decision-making. See Gregor Noll, "Salvation by the Grace of State? Explaining Credibility Assessment in the Asylum Procedure", in Noll (2005a) 197–214 and Gregor Noll, "Asylum Claims and the Translation of Culture into Politics" (2006/3) *Texas International Law Journal*, 491–501. This view is clearly detached from the strict view of credibility assessment of oral testimony and documentary evidence as an integrated part of objective evidentiary assessment.

In practice, one of the most central features of asylum procedure is credibility assessment of the oral testimony delivered by the asylum applicant and of the applicant him- or herself. As evidence collected in asylum procedure is often scarce and as the testimony of the applicant often has a key role to play since it is the only direct link to knowledge about events in the matter at hand, it is vital that its value for decision-making is determined carefully. Central to this determination is establishing whether the testimony is credible or not.[93]

If the testimony is credible and can be treated as evidence about circumstances of weight for the matter at hand, its information value is vast. Also, as we have seen in connection to the benefit of the doubt earlier, a credible statement by the applicant is in itself enough to discharge the burden of proof for the applicant. On the other hand, if the testimony is not credible the effects on evidentiary procedure are at least twofold: Firstly, this makes the evidentiary scene even scarcer and that it becomes very much more difficult to obtain information and knowledge about the possible refugee status of the applicant. Secondly, the credibility finding in itself may be seen as evidence in the procedure, mainly in the form of behaviouristic evidence as to the intentions of the applicant.

Nevertheless, it is important to separate credibility assessment from general evidentiary assessment in asylum procedure and to consider credibility as a factor impacting on the value and weight of the evidence, but not on the theme of proof itself. The effect of testimony that is not credible is that the value of that testimony for evidentiary assessment is low or none, not that the theme of proof cannot be established.[94] Hence, credibility assessment is not itself linked to assessment of the refugee status of the applicant – credibility is not a prerequisite for refugee status.[95]

Drawing on the connection between credibility and refugee status, it must also be recognised that applicable European Union legislation determining the theme of proof for asylum procedures in the region emphasises the role of credibility in the procedure: Article 4 part 5(e) of the QD refers to application of the benefit of the doubt in the procedure and states that aspects of the

---

[93] Clearly, this is not unique to asylum procedure. Questions of reliability and credibility are present in all evidentiary assessments. For comments in the asylum context see Wiebe (2006). With regard to other forms of judicial proceedings see Klami (2000) 64–72 and Jenna Haapasalo, Kari Kiesiläinen & Johanna Niemi-Kiesiläinen, *Todistajanpsykologia ja todistajankuulustelu* (Helsinki 2000) 136–145. For an interesting parallel with credibility assessments in international criminal law see Rosemary Byrne, "Credibility in Changing Contexts: International Justice and International Protection", in Noll (2005a) 179–194.

[94] UNHCR (1998) 3.

[95] Cpr Sweeney (2009) and the discussion on inadmissibility versus evidentiary value.

statement of the applicant that are not supported by other evidence do not need confirmation if the "general credibility of the applicant has been established". Here, the reference is not to the credibility of a statement by the applicant but to the general credibility of the applicant as a person. Thus, in addition to assessment of the applicant's statement, which in all events must be carried out as a natural part of evidentiary assessment, credibility assessment is also moved out from evidentiary assessment and given independent importance for the 'character' of the procedure in the individual case. However, not even in this context is the credibility finding decisive for establishing the theme of proof. Its effects are limited to use of the benefit of the doubt.[96]

In appellate asylum procedure, the role of credibility assessment adds to the uncertainties of the procedure. Credibility is difficult to define and establish, and indications regarding credibility are seldom definitive. Thus, the main impact of the role of credibility assessment in appellate asylum procedure on choice of method of evidentiary assessment further emphasises the elements of uncertainty already mentioned. Following the logic presented in relation to other elements of uncertainty, it is clear that methods drawing attention to efficiency, robustness and the inductive elements of assessment are better suited than methods ignoring the role of uncertainty or possibilities of change.

6. *Standard of Proof*

The last element of evidentiary assessment to be used as a key of comparison is the standard of proof.[97] Standard of proof is a measure of probability or intensity of knowledge in the procedure and is employed in order to analyse the sufficiency of this knowledge.[98]

6.1. *Definition*

The concept of standard of proof may be understood as referring to two different standards in evidentiary assessment, depending on whether the view is taken from the information in the individual case or from an angle referring to the result of the procedure: on the one hand, each judicial procedure has a

---

[96] Also Noll (2005c) 13, where the author points to the inherent risks with uncertain interpretation of the concept of "credibility".

[97] For general comments on the standard of proof see Lindell (1998) 508–517 and Diesen (1993) 501–506.

[98] For general remarks on the standard of proof see Schelin (2006) 47 ff, Lappalainen (*et al.*) (2007) 588–590, Pölönen (2003) 139–143 and Ekelöf (*et al.*) (2009) 81–83.

required standard of proof for certain legally determined consequences for the theme of proof to gain force. In other words, the standard of proof in this context is a measure of how sure the decision-maker has to be of the theme of proof in order for the circumstances of this theme to be legally valid and for the consequences of the theme of proof to enter into force.

On the other hand, standard of proof can also be understood as referring to certainty about the theme of proof that in fact is achieved in the individual case, regardless of whether this meets the required standard of proof for certain consequences of the theme of proof. Often the standard of proof is presented either semantically (e.g. probable, on a balance of probabilities) or with mathematical precision (e.g. probabilities of 10 % or 20 %).[99]

In asylum procedure, the standard of proof in the individual matter concerns the level of certainty that the decision-maker has reached about that refugee status of the applicant. As a general concept in the asylum context, the standard of proof relates to how certain the decision-maker must be, according to either outer or internal requirements, about the refugee status of the applicant in order to award the applicant this status.

Concrete and case-by-case standard of proof and certainty about the theme of proof differ from case to case. In some cases the decision-maker can, after careful assessment of the evidence, be completely sure about the correctness of the theme of proof and in some cases it is possible to be completely sure of the opposite. However, most judicial decisions are based on a standard of proof in the individual case that does not reach any of these poles but where the decision-maker is more or less certain about the theme of proof.

Besides, the required standard of proof varies between groups of decisions and between different forms of judicial procedure. The threshold included in the standard of proof is relatively clearly defined in criminal law. In most western legal systems the applicable threshold lies at the level of "beyond reasonable doubt".[100] This is a standard at a relatively high level, implying that the decision-maker needs to be convinced to a very high degree before passing a sentencing judgment. In civil procedure the required standard of proof for 'tipping over' the burden of proof and shifting the starting point of assessment to the facts of the theme of proof is less clear. Civil procedure simply encompasses very many different types of matter, so that no general threshold like

---

[99] See also Lindell (1998) 508–521 where semantic expressions of the standard of proof are put to the test. Clearly, the mathematical expression of the standard is linked to a view of evidentiary assessment as manageable through statistics and calculations of probability.

[100] For an outline of the criminal procedure threshold in the Nordic countries, see Pölönen (2003) 140–143. See also Roberts (*et al.*) (2010) 253 ff for an outline of the implications of the threshold in English law.

the one in criminal procedure can be set.[101] In administrative procedures, too, the required standard of proof varies between different forms of administrative procedure.

In the comparative study an analysis will be carried out as to the applicable threshold for RSD in national appellate asylum procedures and how this threshold is construed.

6.2. Establishing the Standard of Proof

A number of complicating features for the determination of the standard of proof often occur in judicial procedures and perhaps especially in difficult cases where the need for theoretical support in evidentiary assessment is the greatest.

It must be recognised that the tie between burden of proof and standard of proof is tight and that the interrelation and interdependency between these concepts is strong, as in practice the standard of proof determines when the burden of proof shifts. This also means that in the same way as the burden of proof can shift between the parties to the procedure, the standard of proof may become relevant to 'both sides of the theme of proof'.

The tendency of the standard of proof to change during the procedure entails demanding and complicated decision-making for the court. The complexity of assessment makes it evident that a clear and uncomplicated understanding of the applicable threshold at the theoretical level is a key to successfully managing the part of evidentiary assessment that relates to the standard of proof. Thus, the theoretical priority versus the practical finality of the standard of proof as a concept is motivated.[102]

Also, the standard of proof is the evidentiary tool that perhaps most closely ties together the theoretical and the practical outsets for evidentiary assessment. Whereas assessing the weight of the evidence and practical determination of the standard of proof in this context is utterly practical – even if conducted with the aid of theoretical tools available for evidentiary assessment – identifying the applicable threshold for the matter at hand is again exclusively theoretical. The threshold needs to be established without links to the evidentiary situation in the matter at hand, as the threshold is to serve as

---

[101] Lappalainen (*et al.*) (2007) 572–573 and 589, where the author concludes that many elements that also influence allocation of burden of proof in civil procedure affect the level of the threshold to be determined between different case types. Also Ekelöf (*et al.*) (2009) 154 ff.

[102] Heuman (2005) at 66–67, points out that the threshold in most instances is determined before practical evidentiary assessment in order to give the assessment structure; Lindell (1998) at 517–518 refers to the implications of standard of proof for legal certainty.

an indicator of legal certainty in the matter, restraining the decision-maker from making decisions on the reliability of the theme of proof without objective support.[103]

So, how is the required threshold established? Some features with an impact on the standard of proof can clearly be identified: Both the interests of the parties to the procedure and the possible consequences of the decision are bound to affect the level of the threshold. Generally, the level of the threshold implies a choice between the risk of wrong decisions holding the theme of proof for a fact and the risk of wrong decisions stating that the theme of proof is not established.[104] Considerations on risk, on the functions of the material law at hand and on the role of the parties, are made in relation to the case-type at hand and not in relation to the individual case.[105]

6.3. *Normative Frames for Standard of Proof in European Asylum Procedures*

In doctrine the need for separate standards of proof for refugee status determination and the use of *non-refoulement* has been examined.[106] The question of separation of standards relates to the possibility to view the asylum procedure either as a procedure granting a benefit or imposing a restriction, which has been presented earlier.[107] Nevertheless, the conclusion in doctrine has been that a general standard of proof can be applied, disregarding the benefit versus restriction dichotomy, particularly if focusing on *non-refoulement* in relation to refugee status. It is stated with a view to the travaux preporatories of the 1951 Convention, that the link between asylum and *non-refoulement* is strong and that no distinction is made between "refugee status and the entitlement to *non-refoulement*". Hence, a general standard of proof can be applied.

International conventions do not provide explicit rules on the standard of proof in asylum procedures. However, the 1951 Convention in its definition of

---

[103] However, concerns have been expressed about the possibility that too rigid and complicated recommendations relating to the standard of proof may in fact be hazardous to legal certainty. Pölönen (2003) 142. See also Lindell (1998) 518 for an outline of the importance of objective standards for legal certainty in individual cases. Heuman points out that the threshold in Swedish practice is established without any link to material cases. Heuman (2005) 64.

[104] On risk calculations in relation to standard of proof, see Lindell (1998) 508–510. Also Pölönen (2003) 141.

[105] See also Lindell (1998) 517–518 on the implications of standard of proof for legal certainty and the impossibility of case by case establishment of standard of proof.

[106] Goodwin-Gill (*et al*) (2007) 433–434.

[107] *Supra* chapter IV. 3.

refugee-status states, that the fear for being persecuted must be well-founded.[108] In doctrine, this requirement has been interpreted as requiring a potential risk for being persecuted.[109] The requirement of the definition for well-foundness thus in itself concerns the probability for future persecution, a part of the general theme of proof for refugee status, but not the standard of proof for the theme of proof in its entirety.

Nevertheless, also UNHCR links the requirement for a standard of proof in RSD to the requirement in the refugee definition for well-foundness of fear. UNHCR states that "the standard required is less than the balance of probabilities required for civil litigation matters. It is generally agreed that the risk for persecution must be proved to be "reasonably possible in order [for the fear] to be well-founded".[110] The statements reflect the view of the UNHCR regarding particularly the standard of proof for persecution as an element of the theme of proof.

Doctrine has, partly leaning on case-law regarding *non-refoulement* in the European Court of Human Rights and partly leaning on doctrine from common law countries, put forward standards or proof for the general theme of proof in the asylum procedure at the levels of a "serious possibility", "good reason" or "reasonable likelihood".[111] These have been explained to require a level of proof below the balance of probabilities, which, hence, would place the standard of proof for RSD at a level well below 50 % probability.[112]

As in international law also EU law refrains from explicitly posing a general standard of proof for the process of RSD, but includes the requirement for well-foundness in the definition of refugee status in Article 2 of the

---

[108] Convention relating to the Status of Refugees, Adopted on 28 July 1951 by the United Nations Conference of Plenipotentiaries on the Status of Refugees and Stateless Persons convened under General Assembly resolution 429 V of 14 December 1950, entry into force 22 April 1954, 189 UNTS 150. All EU Member States have signed the Convention.

[109] Hathaway (1991) 65–70.

[110] UNHCR (1998) 3.

[111] Gorlick (2003) 367–370; Hathaway (1991) 78 ff. Opinions on standard of proof in international refugee doctrine also rest partly on the case law of the European Court of Human Rights. See *Cruz Varas and Others v. Sweden*, 46/1990 /237/ 307, Council of Europe: European Court of Human Rights, 20 March 1991, paras 67 and 69, in which the Court refers to the standard in relation to breaches of Article 3 of the Convention at the level of "real risk". In *Chahal v. The United Kingdom, supra* at 84, paras 74 and 80 and *Saadi v. Italy*, Appl. No. 37201/06, Council of Europe: European Court of Human Rights, 28 February 2008, para 139, the Court held that the standard of proof at the level of real risk is not dependent on external factors such as national security concerns.

[112] For a thorough examination of the empirical impact of the level of balance of probabilities, see Saranpää (2010) 228 ff.

Qualification Directive. However, EU, nevertheless makes explicit reference to the standard of proof in relation certain instances of a shifted burden of proof. This reference includes a requirement for a particular standard of proof in certain circumstances:

Article 4 (4) of the Qualification Directive reads:

> The fact that an applicant has already been subject to persecution or serious harm or to direct threats of such persecution or such harm, is a serious indication of the applicant's well-founded fear of persecution or real risk of suffering serious harm, unless there are good reasons to consider that such persecution or serious harm will not be repeated.

Thus, according to EU law and as a result of the strong expression "serious indication", if prior persecution has been proved in the individual case, the burden of proof shifts to the state. It is after this shift the burden of the state to prove, to a standard of proof at the limit of "good reasons" that the prior persecution will not be repeated.[113]

The standard of proof advocated in QD Article 4 (4) concerns specific elements of RSD, more particularly the continuity of persecution. Thus, the standard does not relate to the general theme of proof for RSD. Further, it is clear that before the burden of proof has shifted, and the standard of proof addressed in the Article becomes relevant, the applicant must show that prior persecution has occurred. The directive does not give guidance as to the standard of proof applicable for the applicant to show prior persecution.

6.4. *Standard of Proof in an Appellate European Asylum Procedure*

Christian Diesen has argued that the standard of proof in administrative procedures cannot be compared to the standard of proof used in other types of judicial procedure.[114] According to Diesen, this is impossible since assessment assembling the knowledge and information in the matter at hand in administrative procedure includes assessing many other things than evidence such as considerations of suitability and appropriateness. Thus, in administrative procedure the standard of proof that results from evidentiary assessment is a measure of something different than the implications of evidence.

This may, perhaps, be a valid concern in relation to study of the standard of proof in administrative conduct. However, taking the step from administrative conduct to administrative review procedures, things change. The theme of

---

[113] Noll sees this rule as an alleviating evidentiary rule, not as a shifted burden of proof. He also elaborates on the meaning of "good reason". Noll (2005c) 11–12.

[114] Diesen (1998) 175 ff.

proof in administrative review procedures is included in the procedure along-side considerations arising from the claims of the parties as to the lawfulness of the first instance decision. Clearly, the framework for lawfulness includes both material and formal elements of the first instance decision and thus also encompasses possible considerations on appropriateness carried out at first instance. As assessment at appellate instance is bound by rigid concerns on legal certainty and accountability, which in themselves can take matters of appropriateness into consideration, the concern that the standard of proof would not be useful to administrative justice procedures can be dismissed.[115] However, it must be kept in mind that appellate assessment and the theme of proof itself may very well include review of the use of margins of appreciation at first instance and that the standards set for appellate procedure in them-selves can take into consideration matters of fairness and justice.

In doctrine a general threshold for appellate administrative procedure has been presented and contested. According to Diesen, a general threshold of 75 % certainty can be identified in administrative procedure.[116] This implies a level notably lower than in criminal procedure, but not as low as accepting 'overweight' or 'balance of probabilities' as a ground for decisions. Semantically, a level of 75 % would imply a level of certainty referred to as 'probable'.

For the standard of proof particularly in the asylum environment, relevant characteristics that may affect the threshold are primarily the uncertainty of evidentiary assessment already emphasised, the high stakes possibly vested in the procedure, and the positions of the parties. In sum, the effect of these ele-ments on the standard is, following the logic presented above, to lower it. An argument for raising the bar may be found in the interests of the state in the procedure.

When assessing the impact of these elements that increase the uncertainties of the evidentiary environment, risk calculations come into play. Combining the risk with the claims of the procedure, the setting for the calculation becomes the following: Would you rather have more decisions incorrectly stating that the first instance decision is legal (implying a high standard) or more decisions incorrectly stating that the first instance decision is not legal (implying a low standard)? Alternatively the impact of the level of the required standard of proof can be addressed through assessing the desired level of dif-ficulty for quashing the first instance decision.[117] This scheme follows from the

---

[115] Mäenpää (2007a) 44–45 and 71–74 on the target and aims for appellate administrative procedures.

[116] Diesen (*et al.*) (2003) 99–102.

[117] The higher the difficulty, the higher the requirement for the standard of proof and the greater the possibility for wrong decisions in the procedure.

setting of administrative procedure; either an individual appealing against a decision not granting them a benefit or an individual appealing against a decision obliging them to do something and also represents inclusion of concerns relating to fairness and justice in the procedure.

Taking into account that a key function of administrative review procedure is to provide legal certainty for the individual and that the positions in the procedure are those of an individual against a state party, it becomes rather clear that the impact of uncertainties and vagueness in evidentiary assessment cannot be negative for the individual.[118]

Hence, also when determining the standard of proof for the appellate asylum procedure a starting point can be taken in a standard of proof that lies at the general level for administrative judicial procedure. We can also determine that the uncertainties of asylum procedure are greater than the general level of uncertainties in administrative procedure, primarily because of the nature of persecution and the difficult practical evidentiary situation. Thus, the effect of uncertainties and challenges is that the doors must be opened wider than usual for the appellant so that the required standard of proof in asylum procedure is also lowered in view of the general threshold in appellate administrative procedure.[119] This is also recognised in international legal practice, where the standard of proof in matters of international protection is set at a comparably low level.

Also, there is the risk calculation connected to the possible outcomes of wrong decisions. As the stakes in appellate asylum procedure can be high in relation both to parties and risks and thus weighty on both sides, the calculation is not easily carried out. On the one hand, the state has an interest in providing protection to a foreigner and opening up the treasures of its society to a stranger. On the other hand, possible interests of the applicant range from

---

[118] Mäenpää (2007a) 33–37. Nevertheless, it is not self-evident that uncertainties in the evidentiary environment have any effect on the standard at all. Lindell is of the view that uncertainties that lead to a weakened standard of robustness, either quantitatively or qualitatively, cannot be allowed to affect the level of the threshold. Lindell (1987) 348–360. Heuman, again, shows examples of why the level of the applicable threshold must be addressed individually and that practice often is to allow for the standard of proof to be affected by robustness. Heuman (2005) 161–163. However, inclusion of evidentiary uncertainties in the framework relevant to the standard of proof is justifiable, keeping in mind that subsuming elements relating to robustness of investigations under the standard of proof and also adjusting the required standard to uncertainties in the evidentiary framework in administrative judicial procedure is clearly not a case-by-case study but establishing a threshold for different case-types and that question is often not about the availability of information but about the reliability of information.

[119] For general comments on the threshold in asylum matters see Gorlick (2003) 357–376.

hope for a small economic benefit to his or her life. Ultimately, the question is about calculating what is preferred: The risk of wrong positive decisions and the risk of granting protection and entry into the society to persons outside the scope of refugee *or* the risk of wrong negative decisions and the risk of denying refugees the protection they are afforded under international law.

This calculation is made even more difficult by the fact that the results of wrong decisions do not always correspond with the interests vested by the parties in the procedure and that the risk calculation does not always apply. For instance, even if a wrong decision is made in denying a refugee asylum, the risk that this decision would lead to persecution of the person in question is not to be overestimated. For instance, a large middle-ground exists with other forms of residence permits to be granted.[120] In the same way, the result of granting asylum to someone that is not a refugee does not necessarily mean that this person automatically becomes a full member of the society for eternity. The middle ground here encompasses the possibility for time-restricted protection, for instance.[121] The other side of the coin is the international obligations that states have bound themselves to. Another risk to be taken into consideration is thus the risk of breaching at an abstract level the obligations arising from international law through not granting refugees asylum. In the European context, the risk of infringing EC law is also clearly relevant to the calculations. Thus, bearing in mind what has been said about the risks *in abstracto, in concreto* and in relation to international law and EU legal standards, the risk calculation has to be reformulated.

It is commonly agreed that in asylum procedure the legal certainty of the individual must be honoured. In the light of the risk calculation it also seems that the effects of a wrong negative decision for the individual may have graver consequences than the effects for the state of a wrong positive decision – this said when considering the parties as the entities they are, namely an individual and the state and keeping in mind the large middle ground that to a greater extent than for the applicant allows the state possibilities to avoid or limit 'damage'. It has been argued that the risks for the individual are so great that a standard of proof well under the balance of probabilities is called for.[122] This argument has, however, been proposed as a result of risk calculation not taking into consideration the middle ground as presented above and referring to

---

[120] These include both time restricted residence permits and permanent residence permits.

[121] The possibility for time restricted protection is today also open in terms of international protection. In practice, the question is often about whether states have made it possible after granting asylum to restrict the rights of those protected. Further, cessation and exclusion may affect the evidentiary field.

[122] Gorlick (2003) 367–370.

administrative procedure, not to review procedure. Possible alternatives to the ultimate consequences of risks, and a re-evaluated risk assessment, must also affect the level of standard of proof. Additionally, the risk for the state, even if not as great as the risk for the individual, cannot be neglected.

Following the logic of not allowing the appellant to carry the negative consequences of the troublesome nature of the procedure, all these factors imply a lowering of the standard compared to the standard used generally in administrative judicial procedure. Thus, the standard of proof in asylum procedure should be lower than the general 75 % standard presented in relation to administrative procedure in general. Nevertheless, keeping in mind that the question is about appeal procedures, that the risks for the individual cannot be exaggerated, and that the state's interests in the procedure are also considerable, a standard as low as a possibility of around 10 % does not seem appropriate.

Taking into account the particular features of asylum procedure and the general thresholds presented for the administrative environment, the procedure-specific standard of proof should be placed at a rather low level which nevertheless is higher than a mere 1/10 probability. Thus, probability as such is not required, but, following international jurisprudence, a risk or possibility must nevertheless be shown. The standard of proof in asylum procedures thus lands at a level that is clearly lower than the general standard for administrative procedure but nevertheless higher than the very low standards proposed for asylum conduct. This standard could be referred to semantically as 'plausible'.[123]

7. *Evidence As a Procedural Instrument in Asylum Procedure*

Evidence in judicial procedures is used as a means of grasping and understanding reality to the extent that the reality is of interest in the procedure and the matter at hand. The way in which evidence is used as an instrument for comprehending realities very much depends on the structures around the judicial procedure and the more specific target of the procedure. Additionally, the formal requirements placed with evidentiary factors of the procedure vary depending on the procedural and factual framework.

In the asylum environment, use of evidence is steered and affected by several elements. On the one hand, the administrative nature of the procedure

---

[123] There is no approved list for transfer of the standard from mathematics to semantics, but "plausible" here refers to a term expressing lesser certainty than probability, but still more than possible.

gives a special structure for the evidentiary framework. Also the more partic-ular framework of asylum procedure has implications for how evidentiary standards are to be placed and evidence used in the procedure. High stakes, unequal positions, prognostic decision-making and the rather problematic pragmatic evidentiary situation all have an impact on how evidence is used in the procedure.

Nevertheless, through analysing the impact of the administrative environ-ment and the challenges posed by the asylum procedure itself, conclusions can be drawn regarding solutions for the evidentiary elements included in this study. Thus, by juxtaposing the object of evidentiary exercises undertaken in asylum procedure, the aim of the procedure, with the frameworks and chal-lenges presented in the procedure, inferences can be drawn regarding the bur-den and standard of proof, investigatory burdens and requirements for robustness in procedures, as well as regarding use of methods for evidentiary assessment.

Chapter V

Use of Evidence in German Appellate Asylum Procedure

1. Aims, Method and Material

The following chapter concerns German appellate asylum procedure and the solutions found in respect of evidentiary issues within the German procedure for refugee status recognition. The chapter will firstly provide background and framework to the German appellate asylum procedure and, secondly, examine the position of presented keys of comparison in the German appellate asylum procedure. The aim is to provide a functional understanding of how evidence and information is treated in German asylum procedure together with the reasons for and consequences of the solutions found.

A limitation to the scope of the study is that assessment of evidentiary factors in German asylum procedure will not take special note of the so called airport procedures, border procedures in place for safe third country applications, or other accelerated procedures. The assessment will follow the general lines of the dissertation and focus on the regular procedure with full evidentiary assessment.[1]

The material on which the examination bases itself consists firstly of traditional legal doctrine on German asylum procedure, both from German and other sources. Doctrine is taken into account from various fields of legal science, but works relating to administrative procedure and asylum procedure are used in particular.[2] At times also rather old doctrine is taken account of, particularly in direct relation to the appellate asylum procedure. The motivation for the inclusion of such doctrine is linked to their

---

[1] Further, this study does not refer to the different forms of procedure in the determining authority or to the possibilities for internal review of some decisions within this authority.

[2] See for instance Kay Hailbronner, *Ausländerrecht Losblatkommentar* (Heidelberg 2007); Ferdinand O. Kopp & Wolf-Rüdiger Schenke, *Verwaltungsgerichtsordnung Kommentar* (München 2007), Marx (2007); Andreas Zimmermann, *Das neue Grundrecht auf Asyl* (Berlin – Heidelberg 1994); Kokott (1993) and Julia Dürig, *Beweismass und Beweislast im Asylrecht* (München 1990).

importance and continued use by decision-makers in the German appellate asylum procedure.[3]

Secondly, as judgments and decisions occupy an important position as sources of normative guidance on procedural and evidentiary issues in German asylum procedure, case law is also included in the materials. As the comparative examination of this study is limited to the practices of the first Administrative Court of appeal, decisions are taken into account on the one hand specifically from this instance in the procedure, and on the other hand from the higher Administrative Courts whose decisions have a bearing on the practice in the first Administrative Courts of appeal.

Lastly, material was gathered during a lengthy stay in Germany in 2007. This material consists of interviews and discussions with judges, immigration lawyers and other stakeholders in the asylum procedure.[4] Also, German Administrative Courts kindly provided possibilities for observations of oral hearings.

2. *Frameworks of German Asylum Procedure*

2.1. *General Framework*

The general framework in which German asylum procedure operates is a framework of strong civil law tradition, including a highly inquisitorial procedural approach to both civil and administrative judicial procedures.[5] Thus, embedded in German administrative justice procedures is a conscious tension between the judicial independence of the judge and the responsibilities of the judge towards evidentiary assessment. The judge must at the same time ensure sufficiency of the investigation while remaining independent and impartial.

---

[3] Paul Tiedemann, "Foreign Asylum Jurisprudence in German Courts" in *The Limits of Transnational Law* eds. Guy S. Goodwin-Gill & Hélène Lambert (Cambridge 2010) 57–84 at 63 argues that doctrine has a particularly strong position as source of law in the German asylum procedure.

[4] Annex I.

[5] On the framework of judicial procedures in administrative matters in Germany see Michael Nierhaus, "Administrative Law", in *Introduction to German Law*, eds. Werner F. Ebke & Matthew W. Finkin (The Hague – London – Boston 1996) 96–100. For an overview of how administrative law in Germany has been adapted to European standards, see also Mariolina Eliantonio, *Europeanisation of Administrative Justice? The Influence of the Ecj's Case Law in Italy, Germany and England* (The Netherlands 2009) 197–202.

Further, another characteristic element in the German legal environment is a strong reliance on legal doctrine, which is also evident in the practical work of administrative courts and judges. Legal scholarship and doctrine is highly appreciated as guidance and is to a comparably large extent used as references in rulings. It is clear that this factor mainly improves the quality of argumentation in decision-making. However, reliance on opinions of legal scholars also has the effect of mainstreaming certain arguments and lines of reasoning in a country with a great number of administrative courts and legal decision-making organs.

Also, it must be acknowledged that considerations relating to procedural efficiency and economy are of key importance to asylum procedure in Germany.[6] Thus, in relation to the procedure the judge is inquisitorially responsible for evidentiary standards but is also responsible for efficiency and procedural economy. Hence, in practice the judge must weigh considerations relating to evidentiary standards and procedural efficiency against each other when making decisions in the procedure.

However, apart from these notions of rather traditional principles and customs that influence the system, two distinct features of a historical character in the framework set the table for all legislative and judicial work in German asylum procedure: The heritage of the Second World War (WW II) and the lessons learned from the 1980s and early 1990s in German immigration policy. It is also clear that the emphasis placed on, for instance, economy and efficiency, is at least partly a product of these factors.

2.1.1. *World War II and German Asylum Procedure*

After WW II the development of an expansive protection scheme for refugees was seen in Germany as a means of reconciliation.[7] Thus, Germany is still the only European country to date to include a fundamental right to asylum for the politically persecuted, as occurred in its constitution in 1949.[8] However, the German Basic Law (*"Grundgesetz"* / "GG") did not include any exact definition

---

[6] See for instance Kopp (*et al.*) (2007) 1064–1090 especially 1077, where the efficiency and economy of administrative procedure is given an important role when establishing the limits of the *Offizialmaxim*.

[7] For comments on the history of German asylum procedure see Zimmermann (1994) 5–38, who places asylum procedure in the light of political developments at the time, and Helmut Quaritsch, *Recht auf Asyl* (Berlin 1984) 27 ff. On the background to the German asylum practice of today see also Tiedemann (2010) 57–62.

[8] This provision provided the politically persecuted with a claim-right to asylum and was thus stronger than the mere service-right provided to refugees by international law. Dürig (1990) 33–39, considers the relationship between the constitutional character of the right to asylum and the procedures for granting this right from the standpoint of duties and obligations.

of the protected group of people, but referred only to the "politically persecuted".[9] The frames of interpretation for this concept were developed in national
legal practice without further links to international law or practice. This resulted
in an interpretation of "politically persecuted" which came to differ from the
general, international law-based interpretation of the refugee concept.
Nevertheless, as Germany had also signed the 1951 Convention, the divergences
in interpretation forced the German legislator to adopt a secondary protection
norm, 'small asylum' in the Aliens Act (*"Ausländergesetz"* / "AusländerG").[10]
Linking protection under 'small asylum' to the 1951 Convention ensured that
Germany provided protection for all those falling under the 1951 definition.[11]

Despite the fundamental claim right to asylum included in the GG, numbers of asylum seekers were kept fairly low through a practice of concluding
bilateral agreements on immigration for work purposes with states that otherwise would have produced asylum seekers.[12] However, immigration through
these agreements came to an end in the early 1970s, resulting in rapidly
increasing numbers of irregular migrants, among them asylum seekers.[13]

During the 1980s and early 1990s German asylum procedure saw many
changes, mostly introduced as a means of coming to terms with increasing
numbers of asylum seekers.[14] Despite an increasingly restrictive approach to
the fundamental right of asylum, Germany annually received high numbers of
asylum seekers throughout the 1980s and early 1990s. When the Maastricht

---

[9] Grundgesetz (BGBl. I 1949, S. 1), Art 16 A. The Article was changed through the Act
  Amending the Constitution (BGBl. I 1993, S. 1002), and was previously included in
  Article 16.

[10] Ausländergesetz (BGBl I 1990, 1354–1356), section 52; today included in Aufenthaltsgesetz
  (BGBl I 2004, S. 1950) section 60.

[11] The norms of eligibility under the GG and the AusländerG were supported by norms of procedure. As of 1953 asylum procedure was regulated by a special regulation, the Asylum
  Decree (Asylverordnung 1953 BGBk. 1. 1953, S. 3) and in 1965, a special Aliens Act was
  issued, concerning issues on a broader spectrum of aliens law (Ausländergesetz BGBl. 1.
  1965, S. 353).

[12] Marc Beckmann, *Europäische Harmonisierung des Asylrechts* (Münster 2001) 5 ff.

[13] *Ibid.* In 1974 8183 persons applied for asylum in Germany. In 1980 the number was 92 918,
  in 1983 197 000 and in 1992 440 000.

[14] In 1982, the procedural rules on asylum procedure were transferred from the AusländerG to
  the AsylverfG (BGB1. I 1982, S. 946). See also Beckmann (2001) 5 ff, for accounts of how the
  AsylverfG at this time only applied to applications assessed under the GG and applications
  assessed under the "small asylum" included in the AusländerG were thus left without this
  procedural support. This was later revised, and today the provisions of the AsylverfG apply to
  the entire asylum procedure, with both norms of eligibility. In 1987 far-reaching restrictions
  on the fundamental right to asylum for the politically persecuted were for the first time introduced through amendments to the GG (BGBl 1987 I, S 89).

Treaty changed the position of immigration matters from purely national to European, Germany alone hosted 78% of all asylum seekers in Europe.[15]

2.1.2. *Germany and Europe*

In 1993, the GG article on asylum was fundamentally reformed.[16] From being an open article giving the politically persecuted the right to asylum, new Article 16 a introduced far reaching restrictions and derogations to the basic right to asylum. Most famously, the reform introduced the concept of 'safe third country' as a ground for refusing asylum.[17]

The 1993 reform did not bring the definition of "politically persecuted" in the GG any closer to the 1951 Convention's refugee definition since the backup norm, "small asylum", was left untouched. In fact, the importance of this back-door to international law has increased ever since the 1993 reform of the Constitution, as means outside the Constitution are needed to ensure that obligations arising from international law are respected. Today, it is through 'small asylum' that EU legislation is implemented, lending 'small asylum' greater practical importance.[18]

---

[15] Beckmann (2001) 12.

[16] For an analysis of the reasons for the changes and their effect on European asylum policy see Fleur Alink, "Reforming Germany's Constitutional Right to Asylum: A Shifting Paradigm", in *Reform in Europe Breaking the Barriers in Government*, eds. Lisbet Heyse, Sandra Resodihardjo, Tineke Lantink & Berber Lettinga (Cornwall 2008) 73–87 and Dorothee Post & Arne Niemann, *The Europeanisation of German asylum policy and the "Germanisation" of Europan asylum policy: The case of the "safe third country" concept* (Paper prepared for the conference of the European Union Studies Association EUSA Montreal May 2007) 11 ff. See also Philip L. Martin, "Germany: Reluctant Land of Immigration", in *Controlling Immigration A Global Perspective*, eds. Wayne A. Cornelius, Philip L. Martin & James F. Hollifield (Stanford 1994) 189–215, where the author places the amendments of 1993 in a broader perspective.

[17] The reform was implemented by the Gesetz zur Änderung des Grundgesetzes (BGBl 1993 I, S 1002).

[18] The GG asylum differs in nature from most norms on asylum in Europe and it would hence be difficult for the German legislator to implement common norms through the GG. The "small asylum", on the other hand, takes its starting point in common definitions in international law and can thus more easily be adapted to demands on commonality. For an overview of imple-mentation of the QD in German law in which attention is also drawn to tensions between the national and the regional, see Roland Bank, "Transposition of the Qualification Directive in Germany", in *The Qualification Directive: Central Themes, Problem Issues, and Implementation in Selected Member States*, ed. Karin Zwaan (Nijmegen 2007) 109–126. There has been some discussion regarding the impact of the new, European, norms on German practice. Reinhard Marx is of the opinion that all prior practice and guidance from the GG will become obsolete with the transposition of EU norms. However, Administrative Court practice today shows that this is not the case, and that the parallel themes of proof are indeed still used and that Europeanised norms affect, but do not replace, national practice. Marx (2007) 1079.

The legal framework of 'small asylum' changed in 2005 from the AusländerG to the Act on Residence Permits (*Aufenthaltsgesetz* "AufenthG") as changes to immigration legislation were introduced as a result of developments on the EU level.[19] Nowadays, the 'small asylum' of the AufenthG refers directly to the 1951 Convention. However, the norm also provides *non-refoulement* for persons that receive their status under the GG.[20]

2.2. *Legal Framework for German Asylum Procedure*

2.2.1. *Definitions and Eligibility*

Grundgesetz
As we have seen, the first norm of interest when assessing eligibility for asylum under German asylum procedure is Article 16 (a) of the GG, which states that the politically persecuted have the right to asylum.[21] This norm gives the politically persecuted a fundamental claim-right to asylum pending eligibility under the interpretation developed for the concept "politically persecuted" and refers to as well the 1951 Convention as to the European Convention of Human Rights as sources of interpretation. However, the Article also includes rather extensive derogations from the right to have an application for asylum heard according to the procedural rules prescribed for assessing claims under the GG.[22] Amongst others, persons arriving from or through safe third countries and applicants and persons whose applications are seen as manifestly unfounded are excluded from the scope of the article. The wording of Article 16 a reads:

(1) Persons persecuted on political grounds shall have the right of asylum.
(2) Paragraph (1) of this Article may not be invoked by a person who enters the federal territory from a member state of the European Communities or from another third state in which application of the Convention Relating to the Status of Refugees and of the Convention for the Protection of Human Rights and Fundamental Freedoms is assured. (...)

---

[19] The amendments were implemented via the Zuwanderungsgesetz (BGBl. 2004 I, S. 1950), consisting of the Aufenthaltsgesetz (the Residence Act), and the Freizügigkeitsgesetz (the Act on Free Movement).

[20] Gesetz zur Umsetzung aufenthalts- und asylrechlicher Richtlinier der Europäischer Union (BGBl 2007 I, S 1970).

[21] For comments on eligibility under Art 16 a of the GG see BVerfG (10.10.1989) 80, 315f, BVerfG (1.7.1987) 76, 143 f and Hailbronner (2007) GG Art 16 a. Cpr, however, Marx (2007) 1079, who clearly takes the standpoint that the interpretation developed for GG Article 16 a loses all its importance with the entry into force of the Qualification Directive.

[22] See Hailbronner (2007) GG Art 16 a 170–243, 302–459 for analysis of the restrictions.

(3) By a law requiring the consent of the Bundesrat, states may be specified in which, on the basis of their laws, enforcement practices, and general political conditions, it can be safely concluded that neither political persecution nor inhuman or degrading punishment or treatment exists. It shall be presumed that a foreigner from such a state is not persecuted, unless he presents evidence justifying the conclusion that, contrary to this presumption, he is persecuted on political grounds.

A result of the choice to diverge from international concepts in eligibility criteria for asylum in the GG and of nationally confined definitions and developments of the concept is that the meaning of "politically persecuted" today does not by all standards meet the refugee concept as derived from the 1951 Convention.[23] Thus, restrictions on the claim-right to asylum are clear on the one hand, in cases excluded from asylum procedure via the grounds in the Article itself, but also on the other hand, for persons not eligible as politically persecuted even though refugees according to international law.

Aufenthaltsgesetz
Turning to the second norm of importance for asylum procedure in Germany, focus now shifts to the AufenthG.[24] Section 60 of that Act provides the means for recognition as refugees of persons that fall outside the scope of Article 16 (a) GG but that are still eligible for refugee status according to interpretation of the 1951 Convention or the QD.[25] The norm is construed as a norm of *non-refoulement* and states that no-one can be returned to a state where he fears for

---

[23] Hubert Heinhold, *Legal Handbook for Refugees – A Practical Guide Through German Asylum and Alien Law* (Karlsruhe 2000) 58 ff.

[24] Aufenthaltsgesetz (BGBl 2004 I, 1950). Semantically, persons eligible for asylum under the GG are in German legal text referred to as "persons entitled to asylum" ("Asylberechtigten"), whereas persons eligible for asylum under the Aufenthaltsgesetz are referred to as "Convention refugees" ("Flüchtlingen nach der Genfer Flüchtlingskonvention").

[25] For general comments on eligibility under the AufenthG, see Hailbronner (2007) AufenthG § 60, paras 14–76. There are clearly instances when German national interpretation of eligibility for international protection, also when both the GG and the AufenthG are read together, challenges the international interpretation. See for instance the case of *Regina v Secretary of State for the Home Department Ex p Thangarasa and Regina v Secretary of State for the Home Department Ex p Yogathas,* House of Lords 17.10.2002, where German asylum practice is discussed in the light of chain-refoulements from the UK. See also cases BVerfG (10.8.2000) 2 BvR 260/98 und 1353/98 - NVwZ 2000, 1165 and BVerwG (20.2.2001) 9 C 20.00 where German doctrine on agents of protection is discussed in the light of international norms and differences between the two frameworks are emphasised. Many of these problems have been addressed through implementation of the QD, but observers report that changes to legislation have in fact done little to change practice. See UNHCR, *Asylum in the European Union: A Study on the Implementation of the EC Qualification Directive* 7.11.2007 (Geneva 2007).

his life or freedom on grounds of race, religion, nationality, belonging to a particular social group or political opinion.

Persons protected under 'small asylum' but not under 16 a GG include, for instance, refugees *sur place* and refugees without clear causality between flight and persecution. Also, some of the nexus criteria have certainly been interpreted more broadly in relation to 'small asylum' than under the GG, while implementation of the QD has opened up interpretation of certain details in the definitions.[26] However, persons protected under 'small asylum' do not have a right *per se* to asylum – the Article extends only to provide them with an absolute right to *non-refoulement.*

While Article 16 (a) of the GG has traditionally been the prime norm of eligibility in German asylum procedure, if importance is measured only in numbers, then recent changes to legislation, applicant patterns and especially the introduction of EU norms to German legislation have also rendered the AufenthG increasingly important.[27] The increase is felt both in numbers of residence permits granted on grounds of protection and in theoretical and practical interest. Today, the AufenthG, incorporating the EU definition of a refugee, is the primary norm of protection in German asylum procedure.[28]

2.2.2. *General Procedural Framework*

The German Constitution, the GG, in Article 19 (4) provides for a general right to challenge decisions from the administration via the judiciary. The German administrative justice procedure in asylum matters is an Administrative Court procedure, bound by the general norms of the Administrative Court Statute (*Gerichtsverfassungsgesetz* "GFG").[29]

Further, as asylum procedure is an administrative justice procedure, it adheres to the general procedural rules for administrative matters. Most important is the Act on Administrative Judicial Procedure (*Verwaltungsgerichtsordnung* "VwGO").[30] Where the GFG provides the very fundamental points of departure

---

[26] Bank (2007) 111–112, 114–116 and UNHCR (2007) for comments on implementation of the QD.

[27] It should, however, be noted, that Germany has opposed many of the norms introduced at EU level and also implementation has been carried out at a minimum level. See Groenendijk (2007) 433.

[28] In practice, both eligibility under the GG and the AufenthG are tried under the same, integrated procedure. On differences between eligibility norms prior to changes to the GG, see BVerfG (26.11.1986) 74, 51 [64].

[29] Gerichtsverfassungsgesetz (BGBl. I 1975, S. 1077).

[30] Verwaltunggeritchtsordnung (BGBl. I 1991, S. 686).

for the procedure, the VwGO in turn gives somewhat more detailed rules on issues particular to the administrative framework – such as the duty of the Administrative Court to investigate.[31]

2.2.3. *Particular Procedural Frameworks*

Aside from the general rules of the VwGO, specific procedural rules specifically govern asylum procedure in appellate Administrative Courts. These particular norms apply to the 'single procedure' in which appeals in matters of international protection are decided but not, for instance, to appeals regarding other forms of residence permits.

The relevant procedural norms for the appellate Administrative Court are found in the Act on Asylum Procedures (*Asylverfahrensgesetz*: "AsylverfG").[32] This Act controls in detail the procedural, procedural-technical and evidentiary issues at both first and appellate levels of procedure.[33] The rules in the AsylverfG are adapted to the requirements of EU law and requirements at EU level are implemented frequently. However, as to appellate procedure specifically, the Act is not very detailed and includes very little guidance in relation to evidentiary assessment and evidentiary standards. The norms that are also relevant to appellate stages of the procedure are mainly addressed to the appellant as a guide regarding deadlines for filing claims and evidence or the like. Normative guidance for the Administrative Court is scarce and the importance of the general legal-procedural framework thus weighty. Hence, few normative sources can generally be found in support of evidentiary solutions at the appellate level of the German asylum procedure.

2.3. *Institutional Framework and Judicial Review*

2.3.1. *Institutional Framework*

The authority responsible for first instance decision-making in German asylum procedure is the *Bundesamt für Migration und Flüchtlinge* (BAMF).[34] BAMF is a federal authority with a central unit in Nuremberg and which deploys side-offices across the country. BAMF is obliged under the AsylverfG and the AufenthG to assess eligibility both under the GG and 'small asylum'.[35]

---

[31] *Ibid* at section 86.
[32] *Supra* at 14.
[33] AsylverfG, Chapter 7.
[34] Previously "Bundesdienststelle für die Anerkennung ausländischer Flüchtlinge"; today, "Bundesamt für die Anerkennung ausländischer Flüchtlinge". www.bamf.de (visited 23.11.2011).
[35] On procedure and decision in the BAMF see Heinhold (2000) 93–105.

BAMF employs its own fact-finding unit, librarians, and other researchers to gather information to be used as evidence in procedures.

Germany opted from the very start for a review system allowing general administrative courts instead of specialised organs or tribunals to review decisions made by BAMF. At the start, competence was confined to only two courts.[36] However, as of 1978 all administrative courts are also competent decision-making organs in asylum and immigration matters.[37]

The first appellate instance in German asylum procedure is the *Verwaltungsgericht* (Administrative Court), with regional competence over the case in question.[38] The *Verwaltungsgericht* does not employ any admissibility procedures when reviewing asylum decisions.[39]

From the *Verwaltungsgericht* the parties have the right of appeal to the regionally competent *Oberverwaltungsgericht/Verwaltungsgerichtshof* (High Administrative Court).[40] However, appeals are not allowed if the *Verwaltungsgericht* has upheld decisions stating that an application for asylum is manifestly unfounded or that the applicant arrived from a safe third country.[41] Moreover, all other appeals from the *Verwaltungsgericht* to the *Oberverwaltungsgericht/Verwaltungsgerichtshof* depend on decisions on admissibility taken *in casu*. Grounds for admissibility include the profound importance of the question raised, basic formal errors in the decision of the Administrative Court and interdependence between the matter in question and a case pending before the *Bundesverfassungsgericht* (Federal Constitutional Court) or the *Bundesverwaltungsgericht* (Federal Administrative Court).[42] If an appeal from the *Verwaltungsgericht* to the *Oberverwaltungsgericht/Verwaltungsgerichtshof* fails on admissibility, a complaint against the negative decision on admissibility can be brought before the *Bundesverfassungsgericht*.

---

[36] Verwaltungsgericht Ansbach and Verwaltungsgerichtshof München. For an overview and history of the German institutional solutions in asylum procedure see Tiedemann (2010) 59 ff.

[37] The legal changes were enforced through amendments to the AsylverfG (BGBl 1978 I, s. 1107). However, many still consider the Ansbach and Munich Administrative Courts as most substantially competent in the area of asylum, partly due to their history and partly due to their geographical position close to the BAMF, which in turn refers to them a large volume of applications for review.

[38] On regional competence in asylum procedure see Marx (2007) 1276 ff and Tiedemann (2010) 59.

[39] AsylverfG, section 74 and *ibid.*

[40] AsylverfG, section 78 (2).

[41] AsylverfG section 78 (1).

[42] AsylverfG 78 (3).

However, this complaint in itself also depends on a declaration of admissibility by the *Bundesverfassungsgericht*.[43]

Regional competence over asylum procedure stops with the *Oberverwaltungsgericht/Verwaltungsgerichtshof* of the *Länder*, as the next instance is the federal *Bundesverwaltungsgericht*, access to which is nevertheless strict, as only questions of law are tried and only then after the appeal has been declared admissible.

Thus, German appellate asylum procedure is confined *per se* to the administrative courts. However, after exhaustion of other possibilities to review within administrative judicial procedure, the *Bundesverfassungsgericht* also has competence to review matters from asylum procedure if the matter is of constitutional importance and the complaint presented before the Court is admissible.

2.3.2. *Judicial Review of Asylum Decisions*

The AsulverfG stipulates, firstly, a two-week deadline for filing an appeal to the *Verwaltungsgericht*.[44] Additionally, the AsylverfG stipulates a second deadline by requiring the appellant to submit all evidence and facts on which he relies in his claims within one month of notice of the BAMF decision.[45] However, this norm is in no manner absolute and AsylverfG section 74 enables the judge to allow evidence also to be presented at later stages of the procedure and therefore adopt a dynamic approach to the gathering of evidence. Aside from this, previously unknown new evidence and facts can be presented at any stage of the procedure.

Flexibility in terms of deadlines is a sign of the important position of procedural efficiency in German asylum procedure. Despite reliance on the *Offizialmaxim*, a highly inquisitorial approach and a clear striving towards opening up procedural possibilities to the parties at all stages of the procedure, the 'counter argument' relating to procedural economy and efficiency seems to play a great role in both legislative solutions and practice.

Review of asylum decisions in the *Verwaltungsgericht* is usually carried out by a single judge. The review is carried out by a chamber only when the matter touches on constitutional issues or if questions of either law or fact raised are complex.[46]

---

[43] GG Article 93 empowers the Bundesverfassungsgericht also to decide on matters between private persons and the state. The Gesetz über das Bundesverfassungsgericht 11.11.1993 (BGBl. I S. 1473) provides detailed rules for proceedings in the Court.

[44] AsylverfG section 74 (1).

[45] AsylverfG section 74 (2). For comments see Hailbronner (2007) AsylverfG § 74, paras 37–48.

[46] AsylverfG section 76.

A procedural requirement of importance at the stage of review by the *Verwaltungsgericht* is the requirement to arrange an oral hearing to which the parties to the procedure are summoned.[47] The *Verwaltungsgericht* is, as a starting point, obliged to arrange oral hearings in all asylum matters before it.[48] However, the parties can renounce their right to an oral hearing so that if all involved in the matter are of the opinion that oral hearings are not necessary, these need not be held. In order for the parties to make informed decisions about their need for oral hearings, the *Verwaltungsgericht* can issue a summary decision, the so called *Gerichtsbescheid*, a decision without a hearing based on how the *Verwaltungsgericht* sees the matter on the basis of the written material, and pursuant to which the parties then can decide about the need for oral hearings.

The oral hearing is interesting in the sense that in German administrative justice procedure the oral hearing presents an exception to the highly inquisitorial procedural approach. The judge at the oral hearing often takes on the role of an adversarial procedural leader, especially if both the private party and the first instance authority are present.[49]

The oral hearing is also the 'home' for the *Beweisantrag* (motion to take evidence), an evidentiary instrument stemming from German criminal law, which is of importance to practical evidentiary work in German asylum procedure.[50] In essence, the *Beweisantrag* entails the possibility for the appellant to request the judge to make special evidentiary enquiries regarding a particular sub-theme of proof, defined by the appellant in the *Antrag*. The purpose of the *Beweisantrag* is to structure the evidentiary scene in the individual case, and to provide the judge with means to clarify and assess the need for information. At the same time the *Beweisantrag* gives the parties to the procedure means to request separate decisions on the need for information and evidence regarding narrowly defined sub-themes of proof. Chapter 3.3 below looks more closely at this instrument.

Appeal from an asylum decision is cost-free for the applicant. The applicant may be granted legal aid to fund a representative. However, legal aid is only

---

[47] AsylverfG section 77 states that the Administrative Court must base its decision on the legal situation at the time of the latest oral hearing.

[48] Oral hearings are not arranged in procedures for interim measures against enforceable negative decisions taken in accelerated procedures.

[49] In asylum procedure this becomes evident especially at hearings where both the BAMF and the appellant are present, where the judge takes a minor role in the proceedings.

[50] The Beweisantrag is provided for in VwGO section 86. See Kopp (*et al.*) (2007) 1064 ff. Also Rainer Hassemer, Winfried Hamm & Jürgen Pauly, *Beweisantragsrecht* (Heidelberg 2007). Marx (2007) 1355 ff analyses the instrument in the direct light of asylum procedure.

granted post-procedure and only in cases where the appellant had a clear possibility of success.[51]

3. Salient Features of German Asylum Procedure

3.1. Responsibility for Establishing Facts

German asylum procedure is above all an inquisitorial administrative justice procedure. Section 86 of the VwGO states that it is for the court to investigate the facts of the case.[52] The inquisitorial nature is also evident at appellate stages of the procedure and the Courts involved have a rather clear dual competence in cases as they function as both decision-makers and fact-finders.

The impact and effects of this dual nature of decision-making are several: On the one hand, the fact that the *Verwaltungsgericht* is entrusted with the responsibility for establishing facts ensures that the decision-maker is at all times aware of the information available and can continuously assess the evidence. Clearly, this also implies that the judge can effectively determine what is needed in terms of information and knowledge, and where best to get this.

However, challenges are also involved, not least with reference to the judicial independence of the decision-maker. It is clear that fact-finding must be carried out on the terms of the individual judge or *Verwaltungsgericht*, and cannot be steered politically for instance in relation to the sources used. However, as the Courts involved in asylum procedure are general

---

[51] Norms on legal aid in asylum matters follow general norms laid down in the Beratungshilfegesetz (BGBl I 1999, S. 2400). See also VGH Baden-Württemberg 26.10.2006 13 S 1799/06, in which the Court clearly spells out and applies the requirements for legal aid to be granted. In negotiations for amendments to the APD abolishing the possibility to connect the grant of legal aid to the chance of success, Germany has clearly stated that these amendments will not be accepted. Council directive 2005/85, OJ 1.12.2005, (L 326) 13 on Minimum Standards on Procedures in Member States for Granting and Withdrawing Refugee Status andProposal for a Directive of the European Parliament and of the Council on minimum standards of procedures in Member States for the granting and withdrawing of international protection COM (2009) 554/4 and Amended proposal for a Directive of the European Parliament and of the Council on common procedures for granting and withdrawing international protection status (Recast), COM(2011) 319 final.

[52] See Dürig (1990) 41 ff for specific debate on the impact on standards of evidence of the inquisitorial duties of the court in asylum matters and Hailbronner (2007) AsylverfG vor § 74, paras 33 f, examining the content of inquisitorial responsibilities. On inquisitorial solutions in asylum, as opposed to adversarial, procedures see Ida Staffans (2008) 149–166.

Verwaltungsgerichte, without any special resources for fact-finding, they cannot make use of any own fact-finding or research-orientated services and thus in practice are often confined to the resources provided by the government.[53]

Further, the workload produced for the judge by duties linked to the inquisitorial nature is bound to have an impact on the requirement for procedural effectiveness and procedural economy, which in German asylum procedure are features of key importance. One of the central contradictions of German asylum procedure is clearly the requirement for evidentiary robustness versus the requirement for procedural economy. The judge is ultimately responsible for both of these and is thus obliged to weigh these interests against each other continuously.

Lastly, it must be noted that inclusion of establishing the facts in the *ex officio* obligations of the judge is bound to increase attention paid to these questions both by the parties and by the judge. For the parties, the judge's responsibility for fact-finding may offer practical means of addressing questions of evidence as questions of law, in order to gain access to further appeals. For the judge, responsibility for fact-finding combined with the threat of providing the parties with an opening for appeal clearly gives incentives for proper attention to issues of evidence.

3.2. *National Environment*

German asylum procedure is characterised by confinement to the national and domestic environment. This is evident both from the sources and argumentation that feed the procedure, such as doctrine, case law and public debates, and from internal argumentation and discussions within the procedure.[54]

---

[53] See for instance the databases of country of origin information provided by the BAMF at https://milo.bamf.de (visited 23.11.2011).

[54] National orientation is also evident e.g. from the lack of international Administrative Court practice and international recommendations on interpretation in German practice on asylum and immigration. For instance, comparison of decisions from the Bundesverwaltungsgericht with decisions from the English High Administrative Court makes national orientation abundantly clear. See for example Wilhelm Treiber, "Politische Verfolgung im Kontext eines Bürgerkrieges: Anmerkungen zur deutschen Entscheidungspraxis", in *Aktuelle asylrechtliche Probleme der gerichtlichen Entscheidungspraxis in Deutschland, Österreich und der Schweiz*, eds. Klaus Barwig & Aalter Brill (Baden-Baden 1996) 33–60 and Kay Hailbronner, *Asyl- und Ausländerrecht* (Stuttgart 2008) 317–319. See also Patrick Birkinshaw, *European Public Law* (Beccles – London 2003) 135–148, for analysis of the particularities of the German system of administrative law, its background and framework. For analysis of domestic orientation, particularly of appellate asylum procedure, see Tiedemann (2010) 57–84. Teidemann has conducted a survey of the use of foreign law in German asylum procedure and came to the conclusion that 52 % of judges that answered his call had never used foreign case law for a factual investigation.

As we have seen, German asylum procedure is the product of a very particular past. Due to inclusion of the basic right to asylum in the GG, for many years the procedure did not match other asylum procedures in Europe. As a result, commentary on, interpretation and explanation of the procedure has necessarily had to be carried out in a nationally confined environment.[55] Even if procedural differences today are clearly less than before, the tradition of nationally confined support is still very strong.

The importance of the national environment is also evident from the argumentation in asylum procedure, both as presented by the parties and the Courts themselves in their rulings. References to sources outside the German legal system are rare whether in form of doctrine or case-law. Further, the choice of sources for fact-finding effectively favours domestic sources at almost all costs. Pragmatic reasons for this exist, as linguistic accessibility to other sources is not always self-evident in German asylum procedure.

When these facts are put together, it becomes clear that the domestically oriented nature of the procedure also leaves its mark on evidentiary and procedural solutions found in German asylum procedure. Solutions are found in an utterly particular environment without greater ties to regional or international practice in the relevant field. Rather, attention is paid to issues raised internationally through legislative action.[56] Nevertheless, the closed circle of argumentation – reaching as high as the German GG, but not beyond in any respect – makes the procedure difficult for the outsider to penetrate.

A subsequent and unavoidable question in this respect refers to the impact of domestic tradition on the role of German asylum procedure in the European environment.[57] It is abundantly clear that the importance placed by national tradition on, for example, interpretation has been a matter of importance when at the European level Germany has successfully transported some of its national solutions to EU legislation.[58] However, it remains to be seen how well

---

[55] A requirement for national orientation has been that facilities and possibilities for internal debate, discussion and development have been available in Germany. As the German federation is a big country involving many actors in discussions on asylum procedure, national orientation has had good grounds.

[56] In Birkinshaw (2003) 149, the author considers the implementation of EC law in German administrative law.

[57] Paul Kirchhof, "Europäische Integration", in *Handbuch des Staatsrechts*, eds. Josef Isensee & Paul Kirchhof (Heidelberg 1992) 857 ff. considers the relationship between European integration and Germany as a state.

[58] See for instance QD Art 4 (4), relating to the shifted burden of proof in cases of prior persecution, which is a direct transplant from German asylum practice to European norms on international protection.

its nationally confined procedure is able to receive legislative and procedural-argumentative incentives from the European level.[59]

3.3. *Procedural Efficiency and the Motion to Take Evidence* (Beweisantrag)

Thirdly, and last to be mentioned among the defining characteristics of German asylum procedure is the heavy demand for procedural efficiency and the solution presented for this in the instrument referred to as the *Beweisantrag* (motion to take evidence).

German appellate asylum procedure is organically constructed to support and advocate efficiency, especially time-wise, and the demand for efficiency is recognisable as an issue of importance within the review mechanisms of German appellate asylum procedure. Aside from the argumentative weight of considerations regarding procedural economy, at least one pragmatic solution or result of this thinking is clearly visible: the *Beweisantrag*.

The *Beweisantrag* is a procedural instrument imported to administrative judicial procedures but originating from German criminal procedure via civil procedure. It is used as a formal means of deciding on the need for further fact-finding in the procedure. There are no separate rules on the *Beweisantrag* in the AsylverfG, but reference is made in doctrine to general rules on the matter in the German Criminal Procedure Code (*Strafprozessordnung*).[60] In practice, a party in the oral hearing presents a *Beweisantrag* (motion) before the judge asking the judge to further investigate a specific issue or to obtain specific information of relevance to the case.[61] The judge then decides whether to accept the *Antrag*, whether to acquire the additional information and, if the decision is positive, on the sources to be used. The decision is separately appealable, pending leave to appeal.

Not all evidence that appears before the *Verwaltungsgericht* is presented with the aid of this instrument. Evidence is presented also outside the time-frame provided by the AsylverfG, and evidence regarding new facts can be produced at any time. However, the *Beweisantrag* enables the parties to test the judge's opinion on certain matters, as the judge would only allow further investigation into matters about which he or she is not certain.

---

[59] Even if the standards are implemented in legislation, practice may have a hard time keeping up the pace. See UNHCR (2007) in which Germany is criticised for lacking practical implementation of European norms. For a general account of the possibilities for implementation of unified norms, see also Staffans (2008) 149–166.

[60] Strafprozessordnung (RGBl. I 1877, S. 253) section 244.

[61] The formal requirements for the Beweisantrag are in the asylum context derived from criminal and civil procedures. Hailbronner (2007) AsylverfG vor § 74, paras 156 ff.

Further, the *Beweisantrag* offers the party a separate decision on which to file an appeal, a possibility that may be attractive for several reasons.[62]

In respect of procedural economy, the *Beweisantrag* ideally functions to clarify and simplify the factual basis for decisions in asylum procedure, and allows for structured approaches to the facts of the case. It is also an effective means for turning the attention of agents in the procedure to various issues of importance. However, in practice the *Beweisantrag* is often used as a tactical means for steering or for prolonging the procedure.[63] On the one hand, awareness of the added workload and negative impact on the procedural efficiency of complicated fact-finding measures may compel judges, under threat of a *Beweisantrag* – or even several of these – more easily to accept some fact as certain in evidentiary assessment. Thus, in the battle between evidentiary standards and procedural efficiency, the *Beweisantrag* can also be used at the cost of evidentiary robustness. On the other hand, the *Beweisantrag* may also be used for the sole purpose of buying time in the procedure as the judge is obliged irrespective of the outcome to make a separate decision to allow or reject the *Beweisantrag*, which in turn is separately appealable. Even if this appeal depends on leave, the additional time bought by presentation of a *Beweisantrag* may be as good an incentive as any for the individual applicant to file such a motion.

4. *Evidence in German Appellate Asylum Procedure*

The following chapter will examine the use of keys of comparison in the context of the German appellate asylum procedure. Burden of proof, evidentiary robustness, methods for evidentiary assessment and standard of proof will be pin-pointed in the particular context of the German appellate asylum procedure. Focus is on the empirical or, so to speak, factual use of the keys of comparison, however, taking account of the relationship between normative and empirical findings. The comparison between findings in the German context and other legal systems is undertaken in chapters VIII–IX.

---

[62] In BVerwG (24.6.2008) 10 C 43.07, albeit not concerning the Beweisantrag, the procedural importance of separately appealable decisions on procedural matters becomes apparent.

[63] See for instance BGH 14.6.2005–5 StR 129/05, where the Bundesgerichtshof had to decide on the feasibility of giving time limits for requesting Beweisanträge in the name of general procedural efficiency.

4.1. *Burden of Proof*

We can remember that the burden of proof concerns the suffering of negative consequences for not being able to prove the theme of proof. Who in the German asylum procedure carries this burden and which duties follow with the burden?

Conceptual Issues

To begin with, and in terms of the burden of proof in German appellate asylum procedure, the conceptual framework must be clarified as German evidentiary doctrine draws a distinct line between the material and formal burden of proof.[64] As the position of the doctrine is strong and as it clearly also influences judicial practice, these conceptual characteristics in turn pragmatically affect distribution of obligations and rights.

The formal (objective) burden of proof equals the abstract notion of the burden carried by the party who needs to prove their claims before the *Verwaltungsgericht* and who has to carry the negative consequences if the theme of proof cannot be proven to the level of the standard of proof. In other words, it determines the placement of ground zero in the procedure. The material (subjective) burden of proof, on the other hand, refers to the practical burden of actually leading the claims in proof by presenting evidence before the *Verwaltungsgericht*, or at least through pointing out the issues of importance for the claims. The material burden of proof could be described as a burden of investigation and presentation of evidence. Thus, the German understanding of the burden of proof is that the concept clearly embraces both the abstract risk of facing the negative consequences of unsuccessful claims and the obligation to produce evidence before the *Verwaltungsgericht*.[65] This outspoken dichotomy is not merely of importance to doctrinal discourse on issues of evidence but also to the very pragmatic solutions found within the procedure, as rules and guidelines are generally not understood as self-evidently encompassing both forms of the burden of proof.[66]

---

[64] Kokott (1993) at 324–325 explains how the dichotomy between material and formal burden of proof is construed in the German asylum context, as opposed to the general public legal framework, where only formal burden of proof is used.

[65] Kokott (1993) 324–325. This study does not distinguish between material and formal burdens of proof in general, but uses an integrated approach to burden of proof.

[66] The distinction between material and formal burden of proof can of course be drawn for any procedure involving burden of proof. However, the dichotomy is placed in the forefront of German asylum procedure.

The Fundamental Nature of the Right to Asylum

Further, the fundamental nature of the right to asylum interferes with general interpretation of placement of the burden of proof as presented by international doctrine.[67] Through granting the politically persecuted a fundamental claim-right to asylum, it could and has been claimed that the state in fact also has a responsibility to procedurally ensure that the state meets its obligation to grant asylum to all who are eligible.[68] Partly, the German discussion reflects the internationally recognized possibility to view the asylum procedure either as an international procedure for the assessment of *non-refoulement* or as a national procedure for the granting of the benefits of asylum.[69] The obligation of the state to ensure *non-refoulement* could be seen as including the formal burden of proof. However, it has been acknowledged that aside from the fundamental nature of the right to asylum, other considerations of both a political and judicial nature must also be taken into account when establishing distribution.[70] In doctrine as well as practice, the result of juxtaposing the fundamental rights character of the right to asylum with these other political and judicial concerns has been the prevalence of the latter mentioned factors. It is thus regarded that the starting point in the procedure is that the applicant or appellant is not a refugee, and that the contrary must be proven.[71]

There is no general rule in written German law regarding the burden of proof. Normatively, section 15 of the AsylverfG, placing a general duty of cooperation with the applicant, at least partly regulates the material burden of proof.[72] This rule corresponds with the requirements for cooperation as posed in international doctrine and by EU law. According to the norm, the applicant in the asylum procedure must provide relevant documents and other evidence,

---

[67] See Kokott (1993) 335–343, on the fundamental status of the right to asylum and its possible impacts on the burden of proof. Also Dürig (1990) 125 ff.

[68] *Ibid.*

[69] *Supra* at Chapter IV 3.2.

[70] See BVerfG, (26.11.1986) 74, 51 f concerning *sur place* refugeehood, where the Bundesverfassungsgericht spells out the basis of state responsibility in asylum procedure. The court takes into account the relationship between refugee status and a right of residence and participation in society in the particular framework of *sur place* refugeehood.

[71] BVerwG (21.4.2009) 10 C 11.08 provides a good example of how the formal burden of proof is placed with the applicant throughout all possible stages of appeal in German asylum procedure. However, since burden of proof as a concept encompasses both formal and material burden of proof, merely placing the formal burden of proof on the applicant does not mean the entire burden of proof being borne by the same party. Rather, it must be acknowledged that where the starting point is that the applicant must prove entitlement to benefit, the applicant shares the burden of investigation with the state.

[72] AsylverfG, section 15.

including all documents at his disposal of relevance for the application for asy-lum. However, section 24 of the same Act also requires the authority in admin-istrative conduct to produce evidence where necessary.[73] Hence, normatively a material burden of proof is placed with the applicant, but the limits of this bur-den are drawn at the level of evidence at the disposal of the applicant.

In doctrine and practice the material burden of proof relating to investiga-tions and production of evidence between is seen as divided between the state and the applicant.[74] Due to the weak evidentiary position of the asylum appli-cant, German asylum procedure has namely also in practice seen fit to 'ease the burden' on the applicant and place part of the responsibility for fact-finding with the authorities. Thus, even at the appellate stages of asylum procedure one can see an obligation to present evidence divided between the appellant and the representatives of BAMF.[75] Further, as asylum procedure is an administrative justice procedure, the *Verwaltungsgericht* also has a responsibility *ex officio* for production of evidence via the responsibility for establishing facts in the VwGO section 86. Hence, in addition to the division between the applicant and the BAMF, a division also exists between the appellant and the *Verwaltungsgericht*. Nevertheless, the applicant holds part of the material burden and must discharge this in order to discharge the burden of proof in general.

Shifted Burdens of Proof
A third factor that influences distribution of the burden of proof in German appellate asylum procedure is the evident and common use of shifted burdens of proof. This feature can clearly be seen as a result of the doctrine behind the fundamental status of the right to asylum, as a shifted burden of proof is an evidentiary indicator of more responsibility moved towards the state and away from the asylum seeker or appellant.

A shifted burden of proof is used firstly in cases where prior persecution can be established by the asylum applicant, after which it is for the state to show that persecution will not occur in the future.[76] As we have seen, this

---

[73] AsylverfG, section 24.

[74] Kokott (1993) 332 ff. See, however, also Wilfried Berg, *Die verwaltungsrechtliche Entscheidung bei ungewissem Sachverhalt* (Berlin 1980) 178–218, where the author examines numerous solutions to division of the formal burden of proof in the light of the German procedure of administrative justice. Berg's assessment clearly shows that placing of the burden is not self-evident by any means.

[75] This obligation for the BAMF is rather theoretical and in practice often carried out through submission of evidentiary assessment included in the decision under appeal.

[76] BVerfG (2.7.1980) 54, 341 where the Constitutional court refers to standards implying that it is for the state to "rule out" possibilities of future persecution, and Kokott (1993) 362–363. See also Marx (2007) 1120–1122, examining the implications of German practice for EU legisla-tion in this respect.

practice has been codified and lifted to EU level.[77] Secondly, use of some empirical facts or presumptions as evidentiary facts may also lead to over-thrown burdens according to German practice.[78] In these cases, empirical facts are used to *prima facie* establish the refugee status of the applicant, an assumption that the state then can overthrow by producing enough evidence in support of the contrary claim.

4.2. *Evidentiary Robustness*

Evidentiary robustness concerns the qualitative and quantitative robustness of the material basis on which decisions are made, and the means and duties employed for reaching this robustness. We have seen that different strategies can be employed to reach optimal robustness and that different national customs and practices also impact on the matter.

German asylum procedure functions in an environment with institutional settings that impact on evidentiary robustness. Most influential is the inquisitorial maxim guiding the *Verwaltungsgericht* proceedings[79], which makes the court *ex officio* responsible for the general robustness and the choice of means for acquiring an adequate evidentiary base for the decision. VwGO section 86 states that the court will examine the facts of the matter *ex officio* and that the court in doing this is not bound by the presentations or *Beweisanträge* by the parties to the procedure.

Further, the importance given to procedural efficiency in the German judicial system must be recognised as a decisive feature when establishing investigative standards. Often, the pragmatic investigatory standard used in a particular case is indeed determined by the balance between inquisitorial responsibilities and procedural economy.

---

[77] Juliane Kokott, *Beweislastverteilung und Prognoseentscheidungen bei der Inanspruchnahme von Grundrechten und internationalen Menschenrechten*, Beiträge zum ausländischen öffentlichen Recht und Völkerrecht (Berlin – Heidelberg – New York 1993) 362–363, BVerfG (2.7.1980) 54, 341 (361) 1980 and Reinhard Marx, *Aufenthalts-, Asyl- und Flüchtlingsrecht in der anwaltlichen Praxis* (Frankfurt a M 2007) 1120–1122, examining the implications of German practice for EU legislation in this respect. It is interesting that in BVerwGE (27.4.2010) 10 C 5.09, the Court broadens the scope of application of this particular form of shifted burden as a result of implementation of EU legislation. Even if the rule has its source in German law, German practice must adapt to its own rules as a result of the transposition.

[78] Dürig (1990) 52–53 refers to instances where issues empirically proved to be probable shift the burden of proof regarding those issues. See also Kokott (1993) 367–368, referring to claims that on grounds of general experience are held to be true.

[79] VwGO section 86 and AsylverfG section 77. See Dürig (1990) 41–47, considering the impact of boundaries for the duty to investigate on the robustness of the evidentiary base. Also Hailbronner (2007) AsylverfG vor § 74, paras 33 ff.

4.2.1. *Quantitative Robustness*

Let us briefly consider the distribution of responsibilities for robustness between the appellant, the representatives from the home office, and the judge of the competent *Verwaltungsgericht*. The starting point is a statement in VwGO section 86, which places the final responsibility for evidentiary enquiries with the *Verwaltungsgericht*.

The Responsibility of the Appellant for Quantitative Robustness

As we have seen, section 15 of the AsylverfG places an obligation to present documentary evidence at his disposal with the applicant in relation to administrative conduct. Written law does not include any lists of relevant evidence corresponding with the lists presented by EU law, but leaves the obligation at a fairly general level. The implication of this norm is that even if the *Verwaltungsgericht* has the final responsibility for establishing facts, a burden of cooperation including an obligation to present also documentary evidence at his disposal is placed with the applicant.[80] This duty of cooperation is used extensively to motivate the obligation of any asylum seeker to present information to the administrative authorities regarding reasons for persecution, the journey to Germany, and other information. Even if the main implication of this duty refers to the need for the applicant to inform the decision-maker about circumstances of relevance to the claim, the requirement for cooperation also includes a limited obligation for the applicant to present evidence.[81] Accordingly, it may be stated that the burden of cooperation in administrative judicial procedure is effectively implemented in the form of the material burden of proof.

However, aside from the impact on the burden of proof, the duty of cooperation assigned to the appellant also effectively determines the frames for the inquisitorial duties of the *Verwaltungsgericht* in asylum procedure as the duty of cooperation requires the appellant through his or her claims to inform the court about circumstances of importance to the case.[82] Doctrine has argued that any distinct 'burden of allegation' cannot be established in German appellate asylum procedure but that the requirement of cooperation effectively obliges the appellant to lead the *Verwaltungsgericht* and the individual judge on the right track regarding the individual matter.[83] Moreover, German asylum

---

[80] AsylverfG section 15. See also Kokott (1993) 329–331, for a pragmatic approach to the role of the duty to cooperate in German asylum procedure by tying the duty closely to the court's possibilities to investigate.

[81] Clearly, the limits of this burden must be drawn with factual possibilities for the appellant to present evidence. See also Berg (1980) 51–56, for consideration of the implications of the duty to cooperate for the inquisitorial maxim.

[82] Hailbronner (2007) AsylverfG vor §74, para 40 and Dürig (1990) 41–47.

[83] Dürig (1990) 41.

practice has embraced the view that the court's duties under the inquisitorial maxim cannot reach beyond what is presented under the duty of cooperation by the appellant.[84]

Thus, in relation to evidence and knowledge regarding circumstances connected individually with the applicant, the *Verwaltungsgericht* has no obligation to use its powers to establish matters and investigate issues not presented by the applicant. However, the matter is otherwise when it comes to issues that are independent of the applicant's person and on which the *Verwaltungsgericht* does not need guidance *per se*: as to general issues such as political and social circumstances in the home country of the applicant, the responsibility of the *Verwaltungsgericht* for fact-finding is independent of the appellant's duty to cooperate. The duty of cooperation also depends on the health and other personal elements in relation to the appellant.[85]

Beyond the pure obligation to cooperate, appellants are free to present all evidence in support of their claims that they deem necessary, within the limits of the procedural rules. Thus, the appellant often presents at least some documentary evidence, either relating to specific and personal issues in the claims, or relating to the general situation in the home country. The German asylum system additionally features frequent use of other forms of evidence, so that for instance witnesses and expert-commentaries are common. Lastly, if the appellant wishes to present evidence or investigate matters outside his or her reach, a *Beweisantrag* can always be filed, asking the *Verwaltungsgericht* itself to take responsibility.

The Responsibility of BAMF for Quantitative Robustness
Secondly, requirements are placed with the representative from BAMF in relation to the quantitative robustness of the evidentiary base. In section 24 of the *AsylverfG* an obligation is placed with BAMF to investigate and produce evidence within the frames of the administrative conduct in the asylum procedure.[86] Hence, in fist-instance proceedings, BAMF carries the responsibilities of the *Offixialmaxime* for the investigations of the matter. Representatives from the first instance authority, however, only seldom participate actively in appellate proceedings, so that the impact from this agent on the material basis

---

[84] See Dürig (1990) 44–46. Berg (1980) 51–56 spells out the boundaries for inquisitorial duties in terms of cooperation of the appellant and determines that limits of these features closely follow each other.

[85] Dürig (1990) 46–47, where the author is of the opinion that the inquisitorial duty to investigate is interrupted by the need for the applicant to personally give an account and evidence of circumstances of a personal character. However, interruption of the inquisitorial duty to investigate does not imply that the inquisitorial duty disappears, as the obligation remains to give the applicant the chance to give evidence.

[86] AsylverfG, section 24.

for decisions at this level is mainly composed of material gathered for the decision made at first instance level.[87] This material is usually communicated and brought to appellate procedure through a decision by BAMF.

The Responsibility of the Court for Quantitative Robustness
Thirdly, there is the court, whose role in reaching optimal robustness in the individual case is vital. As we have seen, section 86 of the VwGO requires the court to investigate the matter before it. The inquisitorial maxim obliges the court to ensure sufficient investigations in each case – a responsibility that the judge can nevertheless exercise rather freely as no particular norms stating the means for addressing this control are available and as also the VwGO emphasises the independence of the court *vis a vis* claims of the parties to the procedure.[88] This particular combination of heavy obligations under great freedom could be seen as a result of general emphasis placed on judicial independence in all German judicial procedures, and the need for inquisitorial standards.[89] Inquisitorial standards are inherent to administrative judicial procedures but it has been impossible to provide more precise guidance on how inquisitorial responsibility is to be carried out as this would have endangered the judicial independence of the addressees.

The compulsory nature of the oral hearing clearly also functions as a measure in order to increase quantitative robustness in asylum procedure.[90] The oral hearing is clearly the prime channel for the appellant to meet obligations of cooperation. At the same time, it is nevertheless also the most important possibility for the judge and the *Verwaltungsgericht* to determine the boundaries of their inquisitorial responsibilities and to gather knowledge for future investigations in the matter. Additionally, it is clear that the oral hearing itself is a means of fact-finding and that the testimony of the applicant is important, not only as guidance for future investigations but also as independent evidence produced before the *Verwaltungsgericht* and thus as an addition to the quantity of evidence available.

---

[87] BAMF is by law responsible for investigations and production of evidence at the first instance level of asylum procedure. AsylverfG, section 24.

[88] VwGO, section 86 simply refers to the obligation for the Administrative Court to investigate the matter.

[89] Thus in comparison to English tribunal justice in asylum matters, the position is here the opposite. UK procedure, as we will see, presents judges with no obligations towards robustness and heavy formal restrictions in their work with the material basis for decisions.

[90] See VGH Baden-Württemberg 17.6.1998 A 14 S 1178/98, in which the court points to the basic nature of the right to an oral hearing in asylum procedure. The Verwaltungsgerichtshof in this decision further explains the central position of the oral hearing with references to the inquisitorial maxim and the need to ensure sufficient robustness of evidence.

4.2.2. Qualitative Robustness

We have seen that theoretically, sufficient investigation requires qualitatively defendable investigations into all claims presented. Also EU law presents direct requirements on the quality of evidence in the asylum procedure. German asylum has clear procedural mechanisms for transposing these requirements into practice, even if the precise wording of EU norms is not included in German written law. The normative starting point is section 86 of the VwGO, stating that it is for the court to investigate the facts of the case and to produce evidence, but also that the court is not bound by the claims and *Beweisanträge* presented by the parties.

Elements of Importance for Qualitative Robustness
The environment in which investigations are carried out is of direct importance to qualitative standards. As German asylum procedure is confined to general courts, generally no additional asylum-oriented means for fact-finding outside the general tools are available for the judges. Thence, the resources of the *Verwaltungsgericht* to do actual fact-finding are limited and that the information used in the appellate procedure is thus often inevitably either directly or indirectly acquired from the BAMF research department.

The general lack of special facilities for fact-finding at the *Verwaltungsgericht* also implies that the individual judge is of key importance for robustness. The skill, perhaps also the motivation, of the judge to carry out qualitatively well motivated research and fact-finding becomes a cornerstone for evidentiary standards in this respect.

Secondly, qualitative robustness of evidence is also affected by choice of sources of information. While databanks, the internet and other 'general' sources of information are indeed available for information on a general level about circumstances of a social, political or economic nature in the country of origin, the *Verwaltungsgericht* in most cases refers more specified requests to the *Auswärtigesamt*, the Federal Foreign Office. Other sources are also used but the *Auswärtigesamt* has a clear leading position as the authority on detailed information on foreign countries. Judges see the information as immediately and economically available and reliable.[91] However, use of the *Auswärtigesamt* also means that a vast part of the information acquired and used in the procedure is processed and presented by a governmental organ – a representative of the same entity as one of the parties to the procedure, which additionally has

---

[91] Aside from direct requests for information directed to the Auswärtigesamt the judges also often make use of information from the Auswärtigesamt produced for other procedures in other courts around Germany.

very strong interests in the procedure.[92] Clearly, frequent and systematic use of this kind of evidence can do little to support qualitative robustness in the procedure.[93]

Thirdly, practice relating to legal aid and legal representation is also of importance when considering the quantitative robustness of investigation.[94] We have seen that despite little direct input on evidentiary robustness, the applicant may promote quantitative robustness through the use of the *Beweisantrag*. However, in order for the appellant to use this possibility and hence for the procedure to benefit from this option, the appellant must in most cases be represented by a legal representative. The appellant, though, often has limited financial possibilities to employ legal representatives, which in turn means that norms concerning legal aid are also of vital importance for evidentiary robustness.

In German procedure, legal aid can be granted post procedure to asylum seekers appealing their BAMF decisions to the *Verwaltungsgericht* where sufficient prospects existed for the success of claims and the need for a legal representative was thus called for.[95] In practice, however, judges are restrictive in granting legal aid and most appellants have to finance their appeals themselves. This implies firstly that only few appellants have legal representatives, so that effective access to use of the *Beweisantrag* is limited accordingly. Secondly, legal representatives involved in the procedure are often poorly prepared, as they cannot be sure of gaining financially from their work until they receive a decision in the matter, post-procedure. Clearly, this is not optimal for qualitative or quantitative standards of robustness.

Lastly, the inquisitorial system with its 'concentration of power' in the hands of the court, together with the importance placed on judicial independence, emphasises the importance of judicial knowledge and expertise held by the individual judge. The tensions between these interests are clearly shown in the example of the *Beweisantrag*, where the judge is directly asked to Act according

---

[92] However, see BVerwG (22.1.1985) 9 C 52.83 where use of the Auswärtigesamt as the sole source of evidence is defended for reasons of robustness, and where the duty for the Auswärtigesamt to disclose its sources is restricted.

[93] See also Tiedemann (2010) 66, who states that the Federal Office at times "is prone to stress the evidence against the applicant" and that Federal Office argues mostly based on the diplomatic state interest and not on protection issues.

[94] The general rules on legal aid in the Beratungshilfegesetz (BGBL. I 1980, 689) also apply to asylum seekers.

[95] VwGO section 166 and Zivilprozessordnung (BGBl. I S. 3202; 2006 I S. 431; 2007 I S. 1781) section 114. On legal aid in asylum procedure see VGH Baden-Württemberg 26.10.2006, 13 S 1799/06, where the VGH examines the criteria for legal aid.

to the obligation to ensure sufficient investigations, but on the other hand is left the freedom to decide whether and if so how this is to be done.[96]

In German appellate asylum procedure, sufficient knowledge and expertise (and through this, procedural economy) is supported by a system where judges are assigned special types of cases, or cases from particular countries of origin, for long periods. However, encouraging use of judicial knowledge in the procedure places restraints on qualitative robustness as tacit knowledge is difficult to verify and legitimise.[97] In this respect, communication of evidence plays a key role.[98]

Aside from these general elements that affect qualitative evidentiary robustness in German asylum procedure, some very distinct mechanisms clearly impact on the qualitative robustness of evidentiary standards: Striving in the name of procedural efficiency not to present the appellant with any 'free' possibilities to gain access to higher levels of appeal beyond the *Verwaltungsgericht* effectively gives the judge a reason to include a broad spectrum of information in the basis for the decision.[99] That is, appeals are allowed if the *Verwaltungsgericht* fails to investigate circumstances relevant to the case under its inquisitorial obligations. The procedural norms and rules of appeal thus create an incentive for the judge to scrutinise the implications of the inquisitorial obligation to investigate each and every claim in the procedure.

Further, use of the *Beweisantrag* inevitably makes the judge aware of the opinion of the appellant regarding the importance of some particular matters in the procedure, thus creating a space for communication between the appellant and the *Verwaltungsgericht* regarding optimal robustness. However, the court is also responsible for procedural economy and is hence free to decline

---

[96] VwGO, section 86. Clearly, however, sources must be reliable and a certain amount of source criticism must be involved in assessing the facts.

[97] On judicial knowledge in German asylum procedure see Dürig (1990) 57.

[98] The need for proper communication is recognised in German practice, and four general routines are in place for the quality-enhancing mechanism: The first and most common procedure is that the Administrative Court for each country of origin lists all available information that the judge may use, and communicates these lists to the parties. The parties can then decide if the list includes material that they want to search out either using the internet or the court archives. A second method is to invite the parties to the court archives to inform themselves of the materials used. Thirdly, copies of relevant evidentiary material can be sent to the parties: and fourthly, communication can also take place during oral hearings at the Administrative Court. Of these strategies, the first seems to be the most popular.

[99] As we have seen, efficiency is of great importance in German asylum procedure. See also OVG Nordheim-Westfalen 27.7.2007 13 A 2745/04.A, where the Court makes explicit that in the name of free assessment of evidence an obligation exists to take as much evidence as possible, with natural limits for incorrect or otherwise false evidence.

or accept the *Antrag* as it sees fit.[100] Thus, it is clear that the impact of procedural economy on quantitative standards can go both ways and that the role of the court is often to find the right balance between robustness and efficiency.

Procedural Economy and Beweismittelfreiheit
It is clear from comments in German doctrine that the general concern is not about any lack of robustness in appellate asylum procedure.[101] On the contrary, the concern of Hailbronner amongst others seems to be that the inquisitorial maxim intrudes too much on the territory of procedural economy by obliging the *Verwaltungsgericht* to allow for vast amounts of evidentiary presentations and that judges in fact are misled by being obliged to accept too much data and information. Hailbronner argues for more extensive use of judicial knowledge and the possibility for judges to decline information on the grounds of tacit knowledge.

This argument is easily understood when analysed together with the weight placed on free production of evidence in German administrative justice procedures, including asylum procedure, and striving towards procedural efficiency. The *Beweismittelfreiheit* means that witnesses, expert witnesses and other forms of evidentiary production aside from the documentary basis for decisions are frequently used when the appellant presents information. This practice clearly leads to growing costs as procedures become more time-consuming. Again, the tension between robustness and procedural economy as well as between robustness and unnecessary evidence becomes apparent.

4.3. *Standard of Proof*

The standard of proof concerns the applicable threshold for determining refugee status in appellate asylum procedure. In the German context, it is clearly more accurate to speak about thresholds and standards in the plural as many different standards are applied to the asylum context. Clear attachment of the standard of proof to the models used for evidentiary assessment is also particular for German procedure. It should, however, be kept in mind that neither the AsylverfG nor other applicable norms include any specific rule regarding the standard of proof.[102]

---

[100] See OVG Nordheim-Westfalen 27.7.2007 13 A 2745/04.A for indications of the limits of the obligation to include evidence.
[101] Hailbronner (2007) AsylverfG vor § 74, paras 69 ff.
[102] When assessing the applicable standard of proof one must also keep in mind the divided theme of proof. Even if eligibility both under the GG and the AuslG today are assessed in the same procedure, elements of the individual application or appeal may render either one or the other of the eligibility norms more important and, thus, the object of the standard of proof.

Standards of Proof and Evidentiary Assessment
In German appellate asylum procedure, a clear interrelation exists between standard of proof and evidentiary assessment. Both are clearly divided into two phases and the need for detachment of these two phases is made clear by both doctrine and practice:[103]

The first stage of evidentiary assessment in the procedure involves establishing facts. At this stage of the assessment, all evidence gathered is assessed and conclusions are drawn regarding individual facts and claims presented by the parties and regarding the general situation in the country of origin of the applicant.[104] In the second stage, the assessment moves on to making a prognosis on the basis of the facts established. At this stage all the facts that have been established in the first round are assessed together (which implies that some facts, i.e. those which have not been established, are left outside the assessment) and a conclusion is drawn regarding the theme of proof.

This division in the assessment is of importance to the standard of proof as German appellate asylum procedure is outspoken in its use of two diverging standards depending on the stage of assessment. Indeed, use of two diverging standards and divided assessment has a clear effect on the outcome of the procedure as the practice very distinctly governs what information is used in the final assessment. This impact will be analysed further in the chapter on evidentiary assessment below.

In the context of the standard of proof used, let us firstly look at establishing facts, that is, the first step in assessment of evidence. German doctrine and practice from the *Bundesverwaltungsgericht* refers in this respect to a standard at the level of *voll richterliche Überzeugung* (fully convinced, evidence beyond a reasonable doubt), and actors in the procedure generally refer to a standard at the level of *überzeugungsgewissheit* (certainty at the level of conviction, evidence beyond a reasonable doubt).[105] By requiring the judge

---

[103] Kokott (1993) 318–319, where the author examines the impact of the prognostic element in asylum assessment and in this context refers to the divided assessment. Also Hailbronner (2007) AsylverfG vor § 74, paras 32 ff.

[104] On establishing facts in German asylum procedure see Hailbronner (2007) AsylverfG vor § 74, paras 33 ff and Kokott (1993) 324 ff.

[105] Kokott (1993) 319. The standard is not separately referred to in court decisions on asylum as these tend to be concerned only with the general standard of proof. However, the courts make use of the standard when including or excluding facts. See, however, VG Karlsruhe 6.2.2009 A 1 K 2018/08, where the Court makes it clear that evidence is accepted into general evidentiary assessment when they present an "überzeugende Schilderung" of the facts concerned. See also BVerwG (21.4.2009) 10 C 11.08, where the Court lists the facts that form part of the general assessment, but does not refer to evidentiary standards or to how these facts have been established and if any facts are left outside the assessment.

to be fully convinced, the standard is placed at the level of proof beyond reasonable doubt.[106]

However, in the practice of the *Verwaltungsgericht* the standard of establishing facts is also referred to by expressions such as "Der Kläger hat nicht *glaubhaft macht,* das ser wegen bereits erlittener oder unmittelbar drohender politische Verfolgung aus Kamerun ausgereist ist", in English translation that the appellant has not made certain issues 'credible'.[107] The use of divergent semantics does not, however, necessarily mean that divergent standards are used. A reference to *glaubhaft gemacht* can also be understood as not being a direct reference to a standard of proof but rather an expression of that the standard of *Überzeugung* either is or is not met. Hence, the standard of *voll richterliche Überzeugung* can be taken as point of reference for the standard of proof in establishing facts.

Then, the second step of the assessment – making a prognosis. The standard of proof used for establishing the prognosis (and hence the theme of proof) is lower than the standard used for establishing facts. The general standard is explicitly referred to by the expression: *"...den allgemeinen (Prognose-)Masstab der beachtlichen Wahrscheinlichkeit"*[108], in English "the general standard at the level of considerable probability".[109]

The standard of considerable probability is used when assessing whether the facts established do indeed imply a risk of future persecution. It is a standard considerably lower than qualification of facts to the assessment and refers to a probability that would leave the average objective person in fear of persecution.[110] It must, though, be noted that the practical implications of this standard are not in all instances clear. Whereas "reasonable likelihood" has internationally been considered to reflect a rather lower standard than overweight but still higher than a mere possibility, the German Administrative

---

[106] For idiomatic translations to English see Michael Duchstein, *Das Internationale Benchmarkingverfahren and seine Bedeutung für den gewerbliche Rechtsschutz* (Heidelberg 2010), 67–68 and specifically in the asylum environment BVerwG (24.11.2009) 10 C 11.08 para 35 where the English translation explicitly refers to "proof beyond a reasonable doubt". English translation available at http://www.bverwg.de/ (visited 28.11.2011).

[107] VG Karlsruhe 22.4.2002 A8 K 12204/00. See also Dora von Beseler, Barbara Jacobs, *Law Dictionary* (Berlin 1971), according to which glaubhaft machen: establishing the credibility, making credible, prima facie evidence, satisfactory proof, substantiation.

[108] BVerwG (18.7.2006) 1 C 15.05.

[109] For translations see BVerwG (1.6.2011) 10 C 25.10 para 9, where the English translation refers explicitly to "considerable probability". English translation available at http://www.bverwg.de/ (visited 28.11.2011).

[110] See Bayerischer VGH 14.11.2007, 23 B 07.30496, 8, where the Court refers to the implications of the standard.

Courts are not consistent in applying a threshold at this particular level. For instance, the Karlsruhe *Verwaltungsgericht* in a decision from 2007 refers to the applicable standard of proof as a standard requiring at least overweight.[111] This does not go hand in hand with what on a general international level is considered the implications of a standard of "reasonable likelihood".

The Standard Relating to Former Persecution
Furthermore, the general standard of reasonable likelihood is not the only standard used by German asylum procedure in establishing the prognosis for persecution: In cases where prior persecution can be established, using the *Überzeugung* standard for establishing prior persecution as a matter of fact, the burden of proof is shifted, as we have seen. Use of the shifted burden is explained through an argument based on the need to address the traumatisation caused by prior persecution.[112] However, the same decision concludes that the privilege of the overthrown burden of proof will only be granted if persecution that may occur in future is a continuum of prior persecution – e.g., carried out by the same actors.[113]

Practice suggests that it is for the state to show with *hinreichenden Sicherheit* (sufficient certainty) that new persecution will not occur.[114] This standard is explained as requiring more than just overweight regarding the fact that a person will not be persecuted in their home country.[115] In practice, the standard is even higher than the threshold of 'what can be expected'. Even if future persecution cannot according to the evidence be expected, the shifted burden of proof is still not discharged (and the applicant is to be granted asylum). The standard required for discharging the shifted burden of proof is higher than this and for the state to fulfil the burden of proof a very high degree of certainty is required that persecution will not be repeated.

Evaluation
Both the strictly divided approach to the standard of proof and the factual standards used in the procedure has been criticised. It is, as Hailbronner has

---

[111] Verwaltungsgericht Karlsruhe, A 11 K 11438/05, 13.2.2007: "... wenn bei qualifizierender Betrachtungsweise die für eine Verfolgung sprechenden Umstände ein grösseres Gewicht besitzen und deshalb gegenüber den dagegen sprechenden Tatsachen überwiegen", with reference to BVerwG (14.12.1993) 9 C 45.92.

[112] VG Karlsruhe A 11 K 11438/05 (13.2.2007).

[113] BVerwG (18.6.2006) 1 C 15.05 and BVerfG (26.11.1986) 74, 51 f.

[114] For an explanation of the implications of this standard see Marx (2007) 1210 and VGH Baden-Württemberg 11.12.2008 A 5 S 1251/06, where the Court scrutinises the standard and applies it at a high threshold.

[115] Hailbronner (2007) GG Art 16 a, paras 269 ff.

noted, not self-evident that an equally high standard relating to establishing facts can be used in asylum procedure as for instance in civil procedure. Hailbronner refers to the impossibility of treating political systems and societal circumstances as matters of fact, especially considering the obstacles for understanding that are created by e.g. divergences in culture and language.[116]

The German model used for the standard of proof may be influenced by confinement to the national environment as described earlier. Firstly, the solutions found in respect of standards used have taken very little influence from models or methods advocated on a regional or international level. German appellate asylum procedure rarely refers to standards used by international organs.[117] Secondly, it seems as if the requirement for a high standard of proof for establishing facts does little to increase the impact of the parties' actions on establishing the prognosis in the procedure: As only facts passing the relatively high threshold for establishing facts are relevant for considerations relating to future persecution, possibilities for the parties (more exactly, the possibility for the appellant) to directly impact on the prognostic decision are diminished. Some of the claims presented by the appellant may, in establishing facts, be completely ruled out of the prognostic equation.

Since establishing facts is so differentiated from making a prognosis, this effectively implies that even evidence that makes it through the first selection and on to assessment of future risk is used in a particular way. When evidence passes the first hurdle, the evidence as such is no longer important but rather the facts that are established. Thus, during assessment of the prognosis evidence is no longer evidence in its own right but evidence about facts that the judge has already assessed, scrutinised and approved. Thus, it will have the meaning that the judge has given it even before assessment of future risk begins.

This is evidently partly an issue relating to methods of evidentiary assessment, which we will consider in the next chapter. Partly, however, it is a result of using a comparatively high standard of proof at the first stage of evidentiary assessment and the strict requirement for a prognosis based only on the facts that have passed the threshold. Clearly, the impact of a lowered standard of proof regarding prognostic assessment at least partly loses its significance through the much higher threshold used for establishing facts.

---

[116] Hailbronner (2007) GG Art 16 a, paras 262 ff.

[117] German practice does not, for instance, refer to cases in the European Administrative Court of Human Rights, in which standards of proof for international protection are discussed. Cpr *Kajac v Secretary of State for the Home Department* [2001] UKIAT 00018, 19.7.2001 from the UK AIT where English practice is discussed in the light of relevant international case law.

4.4. *Methods of Evidentiary Assessment*

The methods of evidentiary assessment concerns strategies of assessment for coming to conclusions regarding the theme of proof based on the evidence presented. Are there inherent strategies in the German appellate asylum procedures? As we may remember, EU and international law only pose requirements for individuality, objectivity and impartiality of assessment.

Evidentiary assessment in German appellate asylum procedure is a divided process, as we saw when examining the standard of evidence. Perhaps more than with any form of method or abstract model, evidentiary assessment is characterised by systematic division into assessment of the facts of the case and assessment resulting in a prognosis. This division is rigid to the extent that diverging standards of proof are used. It is clear that this two-phased model contributes to the systematic character of evidentiary assessment.

In the first stage of evidentiary assessment, the assessment of facts, the judge takes into consideration all evidence, information and knowledge available in the case. The aim is to establish the facts of the matter according to the claims, a task carried out through systematic analysis of firstly the evidence itself and secondly the relationship between the evidence and the claims of the parties. Through analysing the evidence as such, the judge decides on which evidence will be allowed to influence establishing the facts.

As we have seen, the standard of proof applied to this process is a standard at the level used in civil procedures, implying that the judge needs to be convinced about the correctness of the facts. However, not much theoretical or practical back-up is available for interpretation of this standard, which may lead to variations in the interpretation of the threshold.[118]

The second part of evidentiary assessment in German appellate asylum procedure includes risk assessment, in other words establishing a prognosis of risk of future persecution.[119] This prognosis is made on the basis of the facts established in the first part of the assessment. Practical assessment of risk is

---

[118] The possibility for divergent practices entails a possibility for variation in the end result of establishing evidentiary facts: If judges use only evidence about which they are convinced they are correct, the inevitable result will be that the authenticity and correctness of the evidence determines the possibility to establish the facts. If, on the other hand, the judge also opens up the evidentiary base for "weaker" evidence, establishing the facts depends on a more general view of the background and framework. However, even in these cases the decision-maker clearly needs to be convinced of the correctness of the facts in order to find them established. However, in this case correctness of evidence does not equal correctness of facts.

[119] The nature of future persecution is, of course, dependent on the applicable theme of proof.

thus in practice evaluation of what the facts of which the judge is convinced say regarding future risk of persecution for the individual.[120]

We have seen that German appellate asylum procedure uses a standard similar to that of reasonable likelihood when making a prognosis. Thus, in order for asylum to be granted, the risk, assessed on the basis of the facts available, needs to be at the level of reasonable likelihood or above. Assessment is general and there are no direct requirements on how to assess the interrelation and inter-operability of the evidence. However, as German appellate asylum procedure seems on a general level to advocate a systematic approach to evidence and since great weight is placed on the requirement to give reasons in the decision, clearly the assessment leading up to prognosis must be carried out carefully and methodically.[121]

However, in evidentiary assessment the special rules regarding shifted burden of proof must again be taken into account. Basically, the elements of assessment are the same as in all other asylum cases: The first stage concentrates on establishing the facts – which in these particular cases leads to establishing the fact of prior persecution, with the legal consequences of shifting the burden. The second stage concentrates on risk assessment, and more precisely on the likelihood of repetition of persecution if the appellant is sent back. However, the interrelation between these stages is different in cases where prior persecution can be established compared to other asylum cases, since the second phase is not a direct continuum of the first phase but rather an assessment of the opposite theme. Thus, special care must be taken to ensuring that all facts, including those not directly linked to the theme of prior persecution, are allowed to influence risk assessment in the second stage of assessment.

Evidentiary assessment is often spelled out rather exhaustively in German decisions on refugee status.[122] This has to do with the general requirement of accountability even in relation to evidentiary assessment, a factor important in the German judicial system.[123] Clearly, the emphasis on judicial efficiency

---

[120] If one wanted to speak in Scandinavian terms of evidentiary theory, this second step would be establishing the legal facts of the case, especially in terms of well founded fear for future persecution. For an explanation of concepts see Bengt Lindell, *Civil Procedure in Sweden* (Uppsala 2004) 173 ff.

[121] Hailbronner (2007) AsylverfG vor § 74, para 32. See however also the AsylverfG, section 77, which states that the Administrative Courts do not in all instances need to spell out the facts of the case in the decision. Primarily this is the case if the Administrative Court relies on earlier establishment of facts, in which case the Administrative Court must still refer to this earlier establishment.

[122] Hailbronner (2007) AsylverfG vor § 74, para 32 on the need to communicate evidentiary assessment through the decision.

[123] Hailbronner (2007) GG Art 16 a, paras 285 ff.

and the striving to diminish possibilities for 'free' possibilities to appeal play a role in this context: the tradition of rigorous motivations and scrutinised argumentation is a useful tool in striving for systematic, clear and methodical evidentiary assessment.

5. *Conclusions*

German appellate asylum procedure has distinct features which clearly affect evidentiary standards and solutions used in the appellate stages of procedure. This is a procedure of traditionalist inquisitorial justice where the responsibilities of the state are even further emphasised through particular elements – the fundamental rights character of the right to asylum, to name one. Also, as solutions in the procedure have been refined quite far in a predominantly closed, domestic environment, lines of development and definitions of manifest concepts in the asylum environment in Germany have had little impact from the international scene or from other legal frameworks.

German appellate asylum procedure is also in terms of evidentiary assessment and evidentiary solutions a distinct procedure with characteristic features. The *Beweisantrag*, the shifted burden of proof and separate evidentiary assessment all constitute unique features in the procedure. Evidentiary assessment in German appellate asylum procedure builds on a logical and rather clear structure tied together by the *Offizialmaxime*. Evidentiary practice is based on national traditions and customs, and while in line with EU legal norms does not wholly conform to international standards.

Chapter VI

Evidence in Finnish Appellate Asylum Procedure

1. *Aims and Method*

This chapter concerns Finnish appellate asylum procedure and the methods and means used for evidentiary assessment in this particular procedure. The aim is to give a view of the system and to provide the basis needed for a comparative analysis of featured asylum procedures from a European perspective. Firstly, frameworks and background impacting on evidentiary solutions are analyzed. Secondly, the positions of the keys of comparison are examined.

The analysis is on the one hand based on traditional legal materials such as doctrine and case law. As very little has been written specifically regarding asylum procedure in Finland, much of what is presented relies more on general literature on administrative justice and administrative procedure.[1] Further, use of case law is somewhat particular in relation to Finland: Only very few cases are published and thus open to public access. The published cases have all been decided by the Supreme Administrative Court. No other cases are publicly available and special leave must be granted in order to gain access to other cases for research purposes.[2] Consequently, and as case law inevitably forms part of the basis for the study, some of the case law included in the material is only accessible to readers and others with leave from the courts concerned.

---

[1] See Tapio Kuosma, *Ulkomaalainen, pakolainen, turvapaikanhakija* (Helsinki 1999); Matti Saarelainen, *Perusteltu pelko* (Helsinki 1996) and Niemi-Kiesiläinen (1989) for direct references to Finnish asylum procedure. See Olli Mäenpää, *Hallintolaki ja hyvän hallinnon takeet* (Helsinki 2008a); Olli Mäenpää, *Julkisuusperiaate* (Helsinki 2008b); Mäenpää (2007a); Kaarlo Tuori, *Sosiaalioikeus* (Helsinki 2004); Heuru (2003); Halila (2000); Heikki Kulla, *Hallintomenettelyn perusteet* (Helsinki 2008). Also Matti Haapaniemi, *Virallisperiaate tuloverotuksessa ja tuloveroprosessissa* (Helsinki 2001) and Ryynänen (2000) are of interest as they refer to evidentiary structures in the administrative context. Janne Aer did in 2001 publish an Article on the subject of residence and expulsion in the light of EU law, which, however, do not particularly feature questions regarding international protection. Janne Aer, Maassa oleskelu ja maasta poistaminen EY-oikeuden välissä in (2001/5) *Defensor Legis*, 879–888.

[2] Act on the Openness of Government Activities (Laki viranomaisten toiminnan julkisuudesta 621/1999) section 24 (24); Act on Administrative Courts (Hallinto-oikeuslaki 430/1999) section 22 and Act on the Publicity of Administrative Court Proceedings (Laki oikeudenkäynnin julkisuudesta hallinto-tuomioistuimissa 381/2007) sections 5 and 11.

Further, interviews and observations of oral hearings regarding Finland have also been included in the materials.[3]

Why Finland?

In contrast to the other countries involved, Finland is not a country with high numbers of asylum seekers, nor is the impact of Finnish policies extraordinarily significant on the European level. Among the Nordic countries, there are examples of asylum procedures with far greater importance at least in terms of numbers measured.

However, inclusion of Finland in the study is still called for: Finland represents a middle way between the rather clear-cut common/adversarial and civil/inquisitorial procedures so far included in the study. Whereas the Finnish procedural system of administrative justice, as we will see, is imported from German administrative procedure, it has been the object of a 'functionalist' approach which has distorted some of the clear civil law features at play. Finland is also a representative of the Nordic legal family, which has been described by many comparative lawyers as a hybrid or mixed legal tradition.[4] Lastly, very little research has been carried out regarding Finnish asylum procedure so that inclusion of the procedure in this comparative study is thus also called for on the grounds of access to information about Finnish asylum procedure.

2. *Frameworks of Finnish Asylum Procedure*

2.1. *Legislative Framework*

Asylum procedure in Finland is an administrative justice procedure. Institutionally it is confined to the Finnish Immigration Service as a first instance and to the Helsinki District Administrative Court and the Supreme Administrative Court as appeal bodies. Thus, the procedure is governed on a general

---

[3] Annex I. The interviews for Finland were not as many as for the other countries included in the study, as Finland represents the home country of the writer and the need for basic knowledge was not as immediate. The work on Finnish asylum procedure has also benefited from research conducted within the UNHCR-funded project "Improving Asylum Procedures", an implementation study carried out in 2008–2009 in Finland and for which the writer was the National Project Officer. See UNHCR 2010.

[4] In 1977, Konrad Zweigert and Hein Kötz referred to the Nordic Legal Family as a distinct group of legal systems clearly not derived from the common law family but not direct representatives of the civil law family. See Konrad Zweigert & Hein Kötz, *An Introduction to Comparative Law* (Amsterdam – New York 1977) 284 ff.

level by general acts relating to administrative conduct and administrative procedural justice. Fine-tuning is provided by specialised acts either focusing on immigration as a subject or the institution or court involved in decision-making.

The Finnish Constitution includes provisions on the equality of legal subjects. It states that no one shall be discriminated against on grounds of their ethnicity.[5] This provision is of importance when interpreting procedural provisions regarding asylum procedure and when considering Finnish asylum procedure in the light of other administrative justice procedures.

The Constitution further includes a specific reference to *non-refoulement*, stating that an alien in Finland cannot be sent back to an area where there is a risk of death sentence, torture or other inhuman or degrading treatment.[6] In addition, the Constitution safeguards the right to a fair trial for all whose matters are dealt with in Finnish administrative authorities or courts, thus embracing also the requirements presented in the EU Charter of Fundamental Rights.[7]

2.1.1. *General Administrative Framework*

Procedures of administrative conduct in Finland are regulated by the Act on Administrative Conduct, which includes norms on matters of both competence and procedure.[8] The present Act is relatively new and to a great extent reflects modern requirements for good governance in administration.[9]

Appeals procedures of an administrative character are governed by the Act on Administrative Justice.[10] This Act is also relatively new, and in particular the constitutional right to a fair trial was highlighted in preparations for the act. Nevertheless, the Act is general in nature and does not include detailed norms on procedural or evidentiary matters.[11] The Act provides general rules regarding the filing of appeals and competences of administrative court and, in relation to

---

[5] The Constitution (Perustuslaki 731/1999) section 6.
[6] *Ibid* at section 9 (4).
[7] *Ibid* at section 21.
[8] Administrative Procedure Act (Hallintolaki 434/2003).
[9] For general comments on the Administrative Procedure Act see Niemivuoto (*et al.*) (2003) and Mäenpää (2008a). The individual authorities may then have separate legislation or administrative guidelines to guide their work. The Immigration Service has the Administrative Asylum Guidelines produced by the Ministry of the Interior with regard to treatment of asylum seekers in Finland. Turvapaikkaohje SM 109/032/2008.
[10] Act on Administrative Judiciary Procedures (Hallintolainkäyttölaki 586/1996).
[11] For general comments see Mäenpää (2007a). Again, courts have their own procedural legislation, such as the Act on Administrative Courts (Hallinto-oikeuslaki 430/1999) and the Act on the Supreme Administrative Court (Laki korkeimmasta hallinto-oikeudesta 1265/2006).

evidence, presents the court of appeal with a responsibility for investigating the matter at hand.[12] Section 33 of the Act on Administrative Judiciary Procedures states that the court must guide the parties to the procedure regarding which information must be presented, and that the court, further, if called for by considerations regarding equality of arms also may present evidence *ex officio*. The Act provides for an obligation to hear the appellant, and states that oral hearings must be arranged in all cases where this is not evidently unnecessary.[13]

As Finnish administrative justice procedures stem from and to a certain degree rely on general civil procedure norms – perhaps especially true of solutions relating to evidence, proof and evidentiary assessment – the general procedural act relating to civil justice and judicial proceedings in civil matters is also of importance to the administrative environment and hence to asylum procedure.[14] Legislation in the field of administrative judicial procedure refers to civil law norms at times but the connection is also important without explicit references as the impact of civil procedures as sources of interpretation for the administrative environment is evident.

2.1.2. *Special Legislation*

In Finland, targeted legislation relating to immigration and asylum is by tradition gathered mainly in the Aliens Act.[15] This Act includes provisions both on eligibility and procedure for purposes of asylum procedure. In the Aliens Act also requirements from EU level are implemented.

Provisions regarding asylum were first introduced to Finnish legislation in 1930, through a provision in the Aliens Decree stating that persons who claim asylum cannot be refouled until the Foreign Ministry had made a decision in the matter.[16] The first Aliens Act was put in place in 1983.[17] This act, in section 12, stated that asylum can be granted to persons with probable reasons for status as refugees. The norm also referred to the refugee-definition of the 1951 Convention. It is clear, on examining the norm, that Finland had at this stage already chosen its policies on immigration by concluding in the legislation only that asylum *can be granted* to refugees, thus emphasising that the right

---

[12] Act on Administrative Judiciary Procedures, section 33.
[13] *Ibid* at sections 37–39.
[14] Code on Judicial Procedures (Oikeudenkäymiskaari 4/1734).
[15] Aliens Act (Ulkomaalaislaki 301/2004).
[16] Aliens Decree (27/7.2.1930) section 11. Similar norms were included in successive decrees even if the power to make decisions eventually shifted to the Ministry of the Interior. See for instance the Aliens Decree 182/1958 section 24, according to which decisions on asylum were made by the Ministry of the Interior after the Ministry of External Affairs had delivered their opinion in the matter.
[17] Aliens Act (400/1983).

to asylum is by no means a claim-right for the applicant. The subsequent Aliens Act of 1991 included similar norms, stating that asylum can be granted to persons with a well founded fear of being persecuted.[18]

Present legislation yet again specifies the theme of proof in Finnish asylum procedure as the refugee definition from the 1951 Convention. Section 87 (1) of the Aliens Act states:

> Aliens residing in the country are granted asylum if they reside outside their home country or country of permanent residence owing to a well-founded fear of being persecuted for reasons of ethnic origin, religion, nationality, membership in a particular social group or political opinion and if they, because of this fear, are unwilling to avail themselves of the protection of that country.

The Aliens Act does, further, provide normative guidance in relation to some evidentiary features of the asylum procedure: Section 7 of the Aliens Act takes a stand on the material burden of proof stating that the applicant must provide information in support of the claims made. The same section also places a general duty of cooperation with the applicant, without further detail about what this entails. Section 97 of the Aliens Act provides for the asylum interview as the most central form of investigation in the procedure and section 98 requires any decision in the procedure to be based on an individual assessment of the application taking into account the evidence presented by the applicant and evidence acquired *ex officio* from various and up-to-date sources.[19] Further, the same section provides for the granting of the benefit of the doubt if the applicant has dispatched of his burden of cooperation.

The targeted legislation, the Aliens Act, indeed, thus, provides guidance in matters of evidence. Rules are, however, primarily concentrating on how to bring about information in the procedure, and more abstract questions of evidence are not included.

2.2. *Institutional Framework*

As we have seen, Finnish asylum procedure is an administrative justice procedure and hence confined to institutions of an administrative nature. Today, the appellate stages of the procedure are governed by independent administrative courts.

---

[18] Aliens Act (378/1991). Niemi-Kiesiläinen (1989) 121 ff describes the work towards this act, although without the Nordic dimension found in Klaus Törnudd, *Finland and the International Norms of Human Rights* (Leiden 1986).

[19] The norm regarding the quality of the evidence was enacted as a result of implementation of the APD in 2009.

2.3.1. *Historical Development and Present Status*
Distinctive provisions regarding treatment of persons claiming asylum from persecution have been included in Finnish legislation since the 1930s. However, over more than 50 years asylum procedure implied merely that foreigners in Finland claiming asylum could not be extradited but that their cases had to be subordinated to political decision-making.[20] A more modern and institutionalised form of asylum procedure was created by the 1983 Aliens Act, putting in place an informal body consisting of representatives from various ministries, the police and other relevant organisations with the task of considering applications for asylum brought before them by foreigners in Finland via the police.[21] However, the Aliens Act, which entered into force in 1993, created a new model for decision-making in matters concerning international protection. Initial decision-making was transferred from the police to a self-managed but certainly not independent section of the Ministry of the Interior called the Centre for Foreigners (*Ulkomaalaiskeskus*). Further, a new organ was founded to review decisions by this centre. This appellate organ (Asylum Board, *Turvapaikkalautakunta*) was created as a board consisting of independent experts from the field, including persons from the NGO sector, from ministries and from the judiciary.[22]

In 1995 the structure changed anew as the Directorate of Immigration, which in 2008 changed its name to the Finnish Immigration Service, gaining competence over first level asylum decision-making, while all appeals over decisions from this authority were directed to general administrative courts. However, asylum matters were confined to one administrative court only, the Helsinki District Administrative Court. The decisions of this court can be appealed pending leave to the Supreme Administrative Court of Finland.[23]

2.2.2. *Current Structure of the Procedure*
Asylum claims in Finland can be lodged either at the border or at police stations. The police and border guards have the competence to investigate

---

[20] The 1958 Aliens Decree states (section 24): "If an alien shortly after entry into the country requests asylum on grounds of status as political refugee and presents probable reasons for this claim, the Ministry of the Interior, after having had the opinion of the Ministry of Foreign Affairs, can decide to grant this person a residence permit".

[21] Saarelainen (1996) 31.

[22] On discussions relevant for the decision to renew the legislation see Government Bill for the Aliens Act 47/1990, 3 ff. See also the Decree on the Asylum Board (448/1991) and the Decree imposing Changes to the Ministry of the Interior (78/1989). Saarelainen (1996) 31, states that the most important novelty was the right of appeal for rejected asylum seekers.

[23] Aliens Act (301/2004), section 193.

the travel route and identity of the applicant.[24] The claim for international protection is forwarded to the Finnish Immigration Service (FIS), which arranges the asylum interview, carries out assessment of the claim and functions as the determining authority in matters of international protection.

General information of concern to the application is gathered by the FIS both prior to and after the asylum interview, mostly using sources gathered by the research department within the FIS.[25] The sources include both general Country of Origin Information (COI) as well as more specific information such as answers to specific questions and reports with reference to particular issues addressed, e.g. to research institutes and embassies, and reports from fact-finding missions carried out by the FIS.

Assessment of applications can be carried out either in the accelerated or regular procedure. The main difference between these procedures concerns enforceability of decisions that in due time are taken by the Immigration Service and served on the applicant. Regardless of the procedure, decisions include reasoning and references to material used as evidence and sources of information.[26]

The first appellate organ of the Finnish asylum procedure is the Helsinki District Administrative Court (*Helsingin hallinto-oikeus*).[27] This is a general administrative court, of which there are a total of eight in Finland, with special competence in matters concerning international protection. Asylum matters are dealt with by two sections of the court. However, these sections also assess other forms of administrative appeal such as environmental issues and child protection matters.[28]

Legal clerks at the District Court prepare cases for the judges. At the stage when the file arrives at the court it will include the material that the

---

[24] Finnish asylum procedure applies a number of accelerated procedures, for instance in relation to safe countries of origin, manifestly unfounded applications and subsequent applications. Aliens Act (301/2004), sections 99, 100 and 103.

[25] The Immigration Service hosts their own research department and also conducts field trips to countries that produce asylum seekers to Finland. Additionally, traditional sources such as various databanks are of course used. See Finnish Immigration Service: Annual Report 2008 (Helsinki 2009).

[26] Both the determining authority and the appellate court have been criticised for not disclosing sufficiently precisely the basis of information on which their decision is made. See for instance the decision in case 07/0043/1 based on "information available to the Administrative Court" ("Hallinto-oikeuden käytettävissä olevien tietojen mukaan...") without accounting further for sources.

[27] Aliens Act (301/2004), section 193.

[28] On the competences of Finnish administrative courts see Mäenpää (2007a) 97 ff.

Immigration Services has based their decision on, the appeal, and possible additional documentary evidence filed by the appellant. It is the task of the clerk to assess whether further investigations are needed and how to go about these. If additional information is required the District Court has several possibilities. It is possible to ask either party (the appellant or the FIS) to file additional information with the court. It is also possible that the court itself investigates the matter. However, resources for this are not vast – internet is widely used, while the small library contains country information and reports by various national and international organs.

Additionally, the Administrative Court is competent but not obligated to facilitate oral hearings in asylum matters brought before it.[29] In practice, only a small amount of cases brought before the court benefit from this opportunity.[30] The decision to arrange a hearing is made by the judge or judges assigned to the case. If an oral hearing is arranged, the appellant, their representative and a representative from the FIS will be present. The court is usually represented by three judges and a legal secretary. During the hearing, an inquisitorial approach is used and the main attention is given to the account of the appellant.

Evidence can be filed with the Court at any stage of the appeals procedure, irrespective of a possible hearing, until a decision is made. For example, it is not uncommon for the District Court during the oral hearing to ask the parties to further clarify certain issues by means of documentary evidence.[31]

The general rule is that the Administrative Court makes its decisions in a composition of three judges. However, in asylum matters handled under the accelerated procedure decisions are also made by a single judge representing the Court.[32] Plenary compositions, including all the members of the section, are only used in matters of particular weight for the jurisprudence of the court.

The final appellate organ in Finnish asylum procedure is the Supreme Administrative Court (*Korkein hallinto-oikeus*).[33] Most decisions taken by an Administrative Court can be appealed to the Supreme Administrative Court.

---

[29] The Act on Administrative Judicial Procedure (586/1996), section 37 states that oral hearings can if necessary be arranged and that parties, experts, authorities and witnesses can be heard. Section 38 of the Act concerns oral hearings at the request of the parties to the procedure and states that an oral hearing must be arranged at the request of a private party to the procedure unless the oral hearing is manifestly unnecessary.

[30] Representatives from the Administrative Court nevertheless state that the Administrative Court has tried to increase the number of interviews during recent years.

[31] This was the case during the oral hearing observed 7.5.2008.

[32] Aliens Act (301/2004), section 193.

[33] *Ibid* at section 196.

However, all matters are subject to leave to appeal, regardless of the reason for the appeal or whether the decision belongs to the accelerated or normal procedure, so that only some are assessed on their merits by the Supreme Administrative Court.

Legal aid

Asylum applicants in Finland are entitled to legal aid under general rules in the Act on Legal Aid (*Oikeusapulaki*).[34] Some specifications to the general provisions of the Act appear within the framework of the Aliens Act.[35] Legal aid at the appellate level of asylum procedure is available for all asylum seekers. However, aid is not automatic and financial requirements are laid down.[36] The grant of legal aid does not, though, depend on the chances of success in the appellate body and is often granted pre-trial. Legal aid can in special cases also be granted to assist asylum seekers at the first level of asylum procedure.

3. Salient Features of Finnish Asylum Procedure

3.1. Institutional Solutions

As we have seen, asylum procedure is confined at appellate level to the Helsinki District Administrative Court and to the Supreme Administrative Court. The District Administrative Court is one of eight general administrative courts in the country and has general competence in all administrative matters.[37] The Helsinki Administrative Court has, however, also been given exclusive competence in asylum matters – implying that whereas most other appeals concerning issues arising from the Aliens Act are distributed between the eight district administrative courts according to the residence of the appellant, all asylum appeals are handled by the Helsinki District Court.[38]

This solution represents middle ground between either having the procedure located to general administrative courts under general administrative rules on the competences of courts or locating the procedure to a specialized

---

[34] Act on Legal Aid (Oikeusapulaki 257/2002).
[35] Also Mäenpää (2007a) 475 sees legal aid as a natural part of the system of administrative justice.
[36] Act on Legal Aid (257/2002), sections 2 and 3.
[37] Generally on procedures in administrative courts in Finland see Veijo Tarukannel & Heikki Jukarainen, *Oikeudenkäynti hallintotuomioistuimessa* (Helsinki 1999), 188–301.
[38] The Helsinki District Administrative Court also has exclusive competence in a number of issues concerning customs and taxation. Asylum matters are confined to two sections of the Administrative Court.

organ such as a board, tribunal, or the like.[39] Placing the appellate stages of asylum procedure in the District Administrative Court was a conscious choice in terms of steering asylum procedure closer to 'general administrative justice' and of emphasising that the question is of a procedure within the frameworks of general administrative law. On the other hand, the special competence signals that this particular type of administrative matter may require special attention both legislatively-procedurally and practically-procedurally from the judges of the court.

In terms of resources for investigation, clearly confinement to a general administrative court implies fewer possibilities for special forms of fact-finding.[40] The District Administrative Court hosts a small asylum-related library, including country of origin information and other sources. One person also works full time with information services for the staff. However, this person carries the responsibility for information on all areas of administrative law and is also entrusted with the task of administering a number of other libraries within the court. Court staff also have access to the COI databases provided by the FIS research department. In practice, information provided by FIS is also often used as a source. This is bound to have implications for evidentiary standards of the procedure.

Further, confinement to a general court also places restraints on resources time-wise for appellate asylum procedure. As asylum matters are integrated in general decision-making in the court, backlogs in appellate asylum procedure also affect decision-making in other matters before the court. Then again, this is also true vice versa: If for legislative or other reasons the need arises to invest energy and resources in decision-making in other types of case than asylum, then asylum cases brought before the court will have to wait so that delays will be created in asylum procedure.[41]

3.2. *Low Levels of Applications*

In relation to its neighbouring Nordic countries and to most other European countries, levels of asylum seekers in Finland are low.[42] This means that only a few decisions are made each year and that asylum decisions are not mainstreamed to the same extent as in many other European countries and

---

[39] On institutional solutions for appellate asylum procedures see Staffans (2006a).

[40] *Ibid* at 114–116.

[41] A backlog in Finnish asylum procedure was, for instance, created when legislation on car taxation changed and the Helsinki District Administrative Court was faced with a large number of appeals in this type of matter.

[42] In 2010 4018 persons applied for asylum in Finland.

relatively little attention is paid to Finnish asylum procedure in terms of resources for special or tailored procedural or practical support.

No independent studies have been carried out on the reasons for low levels of applications, so that one can only speculate as to the reasons: Finland has traditionally been perceived not as a country of immigration but as a country of emigration.[43] Hence, no large foreign population in the country exists that would attract fellow foreigners. Finland has not led any active 'recruitment work' regarding foreign workers, for example, but rather in the international field has emphasised that Finnish language and culture are not easily mastered. Finland is a country with a geographic location that, especially in the light of relevant EU legislation on burden sharing, keeps levels of asylum seekers low.[44]

However, aside from low applicant numbers, it is also a statistical fact that Finnish asylum procedure represents a procedure with comparably low recognition rates in terms of asylum and refugee status. If considering only decisions where refugee status was granted, 2010 represents a recognition rate of 3,1 %.[45] A clear movement towards higher rates can clearly be seen, but the rates are still in general low. Additionally, it should be noted that processing times for decision-making in Finland both at first and appellate instances are lengthy – decisions in first instance take up to over a year.[46]

One explanation for low recognition rates in Finland may be the frequent use of subsidiary protection. If positive decisions on subsidiary and humanitarian protection are added to refugee status, the percentage of positive protection decisions reaches almost 30 %.

---

[43] During wars and famine people left Finland for countries such as Sweden, Denmark and the USA. At the same time, however, Finland also received relatively large groups of immigrants from neighbouring countries as a result of shifted borders and international agreements. For an overview of immigration to Finland during recent centuries see Antero Leitzinger, *Ulkomaalaiset Suomessa 1812–1972* (Helsinki 2008a) and Eeva Nykänen, Elina Pirjatanniemi, Ida Staffans & Olli Sorainen, *International Encyclopeadia of Migration Law Finland* (The Netherlands 2010) 15 ff.

[44] According to statistics available from the Immigration Service, 19,1 % of all decisions made at first level in asylum procedure in 2010 were decisions to deport asylum seekers on the basis of the Dublin rules.

[45] The recognition rate here is calculated in relation to decisions on the merits of the cases, not in relation to all decisions made. Niemi-Kiesiläinen (1989) 122–123 argues in relation to recognition rates and the position of refugees in Finnish immigration related procedures that Finnish policies on immigration do not include considerations relating to asylum seekers *per se* but rather purport to facilitate immigration for other reasons. Statistics available at www. migri.fi (visisted 23.11.2011).

[46] In 2010 the average time for a decision in the regular procedure at first instance was 343 days. Appellate procedure in the first appellate organ in a regular procedure lasts around one year.

Low recognition rates and the importance of subsidiary and humanitarian protection should be kept in mind when exploring the evidentiary field around Finnish asylum procedure. The implications of these facts can be divided into those of a procedural-evidentiary nature, and those of a more practical nature:

Firstly, the position of subsidiary and humanitarian protection and the low number of recognised refugees may say something about the importance of the theme of proof in Finnish asylum procedure.[47] Since, in the light of the above statistics, the conclusion has to be that the practical weight of the theme of proof relating to refugee status in particular is small, one may be inclined to conclude that solutions found in terms of practical evidentiary and procedural issues within Finnish appellate asylum procedure may not have had serving fact-finding as to refugee status as their primary target but rather as to subsidiary protection or some form of 'general need for protection'.[48] Thus, the procedural solutions found in respect of the procedure are often based on a general view of decision-making relating to aliens and are hence not only inspired by asylum law and practice.

4. *Evidence in Finnish Appellate Asylum Procedure*

Both administrative doctrine and judicial practice in administrative justice matters in Finland have been reluctant to acknowledge any position of evidentiary theories or models in the procedural framework. Hence, national discussions have not in general referred to abstract positions or contents of burdens or standards of proof in procedures. The reason for considering evidentiary theories to be non-applicable in these types of procedures relates to the duty to investigate, which is strongly present in Finnish administrative justice procedures.[49] The duty to investigate has been perceived as altering the procedural environment to the degree making it unnecessary to apply general evidentiary frameworks either on a general or a particular level.

Further, as Mäenpää points out in one of the few books on Finnish administrative justice procedures, no need arises to use the concept of evidence in administrative justice procedures as it suffices to speak of information and knowledge. Mäenpää points out that this custom of not taking the procedural

---

[47] The theme of proof of refugee status being the definition of refugee in the Aliens Act (301/2004), section 87, which is directly transposed from the 1951 Convention.

[48] See for instance the Government Bill for the present Aliens Act, which clearly states that emphasis in legislative work was placed on general issues of procedures relating to aliens in Finland. Government Bill proposing the Aliens Act 28/2003, 1.

[49] Mäenpää (2007a) 374–375.

position of information or knowledge into account renders evidentiary theories and standards substantially non-applicable.[50] Thus, judicial practice in Finland has no custom of examining information using evidentiary concepts.

For the purpose of this examination, it has already been established that this view is not embraced.[51] Whereas it is evident that all information and knowledge related to a procedural environment cannot be evidence, sufficient space also exists for elements that can be classified as 'traditional' evidence in administrative justice procedures in general and asylum procedure in particular in order to analyse the procedure using evidentiary frameworks usefully.

However, in appellate asylum procedure the situation differs somewhat due to evident reliance on international law and international practice. Many of the guidelines applicable to Finnish asylum procedure through international and EU law stem from common law traditions, with a highlighted position for evidentiary standards.[52] This emphasis leads to evidentiary theories in Finnish asylum procedure being applied at least to the extent needed to invoke what is conceived to be international practice and guidelines, thus indicating a certain 'distinctiveness' of asylum procedure among administrative justice procedures.

4.1. *Burden of Proof*

Turning to the first key of comparison, the burden of proof, let us examine how the burden of proof is distributed in the Finnish asylum procedure and what is required in order to dispatch of this burden.

There are, in Finnish legislation, no direct normative references to the placement of the formal burden of proof in asylum procedure. However, the Aliens Act states, in section 7 (2) that the party to the procedure must present evidence in support of claims made and must also cooperate with the authorities in the investigation of the matter. Further, the Aliens Act emphasises that question is of an application for asylum, and, hence, emphasises the view of the procedure as relating to the granting of a benefit as opposite of a procedure for adherence to *non-refoulement*. The starting point taken in legislation is, thus, that the applicant asks for a benefit and must prove the existence of the pre-requisites for this benefit – a starting point which conforms with as well international as European practice.

---

[50] *Ibid.*
[51] *Supra* at Chapter III.
[52] See for instance the UNHCR Handbook, which gives guidance for asylum assessment using reasoning around evidentiary standards from the common law tradition. The handbook has been translated into Finnish and is used as a source by the Administrative Court. UNHCR (1992) 51. See for instance the decision by the Supreme Administrative Court 1872/11.8.2006 in which the handbook was referred to as a direct source.

Guidance as to the content of the burden of proof is also scarce. However, in section 98, the Aliens Act states that asylum applications are decided on individually and taking into account the information provided by the applicant and information acquired *ex officio*.[53] The same section refers to the benefit of the doubt, which is granted if the applicant has co-operated in the fact-finding.

A formal burden of proof is, however, clearly used in Finnish appellate asylum procedure. Decisions generally refer to the burden through argumentation and reasoning on the burden as a form of 'status quo' or starting point in the procedure.[54] Decisions make it evident that the applicant is considered not to be a refugee until otherwise proven so that a negative decision by the determining authority is correct as a starting point until otherwise proven. Appellate asylum procedure is initiated by a claim by the appellant regarding the wrongfulness of an act of the determining authority. Many decisions refer to this 'triggering point' in determining the burden of proof.[55] Thus, if the burden is understood narrowly as implying only the burden of suffering negative consequences if the theme of proof is not proved to the degree necessary, it is easily established that the burden of proof lies with the appellant in Finnish appellate asylum procedure. However, placing the burden of proof becomes more complicated if expanding the concept to include elements of a burden of allegation or a burden to produce evidence.

The Administrative Court requires the theme of proof to be established and presented via claims by the appellant.[56] Thus, in accordance with placement of the formal burden of proof, and in order to identify the theme of proof, the burden of allegation –the burden of presenting claims –

---

[53] Aliens Act, section 98.

[54] This is clear from the standardised formulation in the conclusions of negative decisions stating that "The appellant has not made it probable that he or she would have a well-founded fear of being persecuted in the meaning of section 87 of the Aliens Act (301/2004)" (Valittajalla ei ole tehnyt todennäköiseksi, että hänellä olisi ulkomaalaislain 87 §:ssa tarkoitetulla tavalla perustellusta aihetta pelätä joutuvansa vainotuksi kotimaassaan.) See for instance decisions 05/892/1 (21.6.2005), 07/0161/1 (13.2.2007) and 08/0274/1 (18.2.2008).

[55] The reasoning of the Helsinki District Administrative Court is generally that the theme of proof either has or has not been established and that the earlier decision in this respect is therefore either overturned or upheld. See for instance decisions 07/0161/1 (13.2.2007) or 05/1924/1 (8.12.2005) where this type of reasoning is very clear.

[56] See for instance decision 07/0779/3 (23.5.2007), where a possible scenario was dismissed by the Administrative Court as the applicant had failed to present relevant circumstances for a claim for this scenario.

is placed with the appellant. This burden and obligation is first and foremost discharged through the act of appealing in itself and through the claims that are inevitably presented in connection with the appeal.[57] But it is also supported by the asylum interview carried out by the determining authority, transferred to the appellate stage via the record of the interview, and possible oral hearings in appellate institutions, and additionally by documentary evidence presented before the appellate court.

Hence, information retrieved as part of triggering the procedure and allocation of the burden of proof acts as the point of departure for the responsibility to establish facts that is carried both by the courts and the determining authority.[58] At the same time, however, information retrieved is in fact also used as direct evidence and is included as such in the evidentiary assessment carried out by the court. The task of the information is thus two-fold: To function as a procedural mechanism and to function as evidence.

Despite the fact that Finnish asylum procedure is scarcely populated and relatively slow, it is by no means self-evident that an oral hearing will be arranged. Thus, the obligation for the applicant to 'lead the court on' and present claims is most often discharged by the act of appealing and transfer of the interview records from the determining authority alone.

So, what about the duty to present evidence as part of the material burden of proof? Do the Helsinki District Administrative Court and the Supreme Administrative Court include a burden for the applicant to present evidence in support of their claims in the burden of proof?

The record of the interview at the determining authority is transferred automatically to the appeal level. Thus at least one piece of evidence is always produced by the applicant. However, oral hearings are not arranged in all cases where the applicant asks for them. In most cases where the appellant asks for an oral hearing, the Appellate Court would deny the

---

[57] Through the chain of responsibility and duties created via the burden of allegation and the burden of proof it is important for appellants to be able to state their claims and thus "lead the court on" in order also to discharge their burden of proof. In asylum procedure, the position of the appellant in relation to these duties is particular, as he or she is not likely to be acquainted with the procedural system or with the judicial culture of obligations. Thus, on the one hand, the responsibility of the Administrative Court for correctly interpreting the actions of the appellant is increased. On the other hand, the role of legal representatives also increases in the procedure. See also Staffans (2006a).

[58] Halila (2000) 278–294, points to demands and solutions for impartiality of the Administrative Court in situations with unequal balance of powers between the parties and a strong role for the Administrative Court in the proceedings.

request.[59] Hence, it cannot be considered that there would indeed be a burden for the applicant to present evidence orally aside from what the record from the interview by the determining authority brings to the procedure. This in turn indicates strongly that in Finnish appellate asylum procedure there is no duty to present evidence aside from the claims and the record of the interview by the determining authority.[60] Again, this must be seen in the light of the responsibility for fact-finding placed with the appellate organ and the particularities of the procedure such as low numbers of applicants, which enables the Administrative Court to actually meet this responsibility.

Even if some structure for the material burden of proof can thus also be established, it is further clear that the precise contents of the burden are not always apparent in the procedure. Unsurprisingly, the narrowly interpreted burden of proof (as only encompassing suffering negative consequences) is easy to implement, and the court is indeed consistent in use of this concept. However, when it comes to defining the scope of the burden of allegation and presenting evidence, the concepts are no longer clear. On the one hand, decisions are not reasoned in lines of evidentiary burdens or standards. On the other hand, even if read abstractly the different layers of burden of proof are not applied sufficiently systematically in order to enable an analytical approach to individual decisions.

An example can be found in a judgment from the Helsinki District Administrative Court, where the appellant as a relevant fact included in his appeal presented his activities *sur place* within a certain political party in the country of origin, whose government was aware of this activity.[61] The appeal was rejected by the Administrative Court; in the motivations the court states that the appellant did not present evidence in support of his actions being

---

[59] See for instance case 07/0163/1 (14.2.2007), where a request for an oral hearing was denied even though questions of credibility were at the core of the claim. Also, in case 06/1689/1 (5.12.2006) the Administrative Court motivated its decision not to arrange an oral hearing by stating that taking into account the documentary evidence, an oral hearing would not add any new information to the case. The practice of not arranging oral hearings is not new. In case 03/0027/7 (decision 20.1.2003), the Administrative Court denied a request by the appellant to arrange an oral hearing. In the case, the appellant stated that the initial interview with the Immigration Services had been very challenging and that the protocol was not clear. The Court, however, stated that as the appellant had a legal representative, amendments to the protocol could have been made in writing.

[60] It could here be noted that interviews conducted by the determining authority are often extensive and inclusive. In the regular procedure an interview may last from 3–4 hours to several days.

[61] Helsinki District Administrative Court 06/0761/1 (30.5.2006).

known to the government so that this activity cannot be taken as a reason for persecution. The court made no effort to establish the matter itself, nor did the court ask the determining authority or the appellant for additional information.

The court is here clear that the burden of proof in a narrow sense is placed with the appellant – if the theme of proof is not proved, the earlier decision remains in force, so that negative consequences are suffered by the appellant. Further, the court requires the appellant to substantiate the appeal by allegations – the appellant must, so to speak, lead the court on to the relevant circumstances. This duty was successfully carried out by the applicant at least regarding the isolated fact of political activity, as the Administrative Court indeed found this claim to be of material importance to the matter. However, the court, in this case, additionally seems to place responsibility for establishing facts with the appellant at both a theoretical and practical level.[62]

4.2. Evidentiary Robustness

Responsibility for Establishing Facts
Under the Act on Administrative Judicial Procedures governing Finnish appellate asylum procedure, the Administrative Court is responsible for establishing facts in all matters.[63] The Act states in section 33 that it is the task of the Administrative Court to ensure adequate investigation and if necessary request the parties to produce additional information. When requesting information from the parties the Administrative Court must also include considerations as to the procedural strength of the parties and their possibilities to obtain further evidence. The Act further states that the court is responsible *ex officio* for obtaining necessary information that cannot be obtained from the parties. It can thus be said that the Act on Administrative Judiciary Procedures refers to an "*Offizialmaxime*", albeit in the Finnish setting.[64]

The Aliens Act provides particular guidance regarding how this responsibility is to be carried out. In section 97 a, the Aliens Act requires first instance authorities to carry out an interview. Section 98 states that the decision must

---

[62] The end result regarding the claims presented in the matter is that the appellant's claim regarding his political activity was not investigated nor was any evidence presented regarding the claim.

[63] Administrative Judicial Procedures Act 586/1996, section 33. See also Pekka Hallberg, *Perusoikeudet ja oikeusvaltion periaatteet*, speech given at a Seminar for Leading Prosecutors in Turku 22.9.2000, in which the president of the Supreme Administrative Court of Finland highlights the role of the obligation to investigate as a support for the fundamental rights of the person placed against a governmental body in the administrative courts.

[64] See Halila (2000) 273 ff.

take into account information provided by the applicant and information acquired *ex officio* from various and up-to-date sources, and, thus, codifies in national legislation the requirements of the APD on qualitative robustness. European Union requirements on qualitative robustness have been elaborated on in section 97 b, which states that investigations made under the duty to investigate may not be undertaken in a manner placing the applicant in danger. However, Finnish law does not include any listing or alike of elements to be presented, such as the list provided for in Artice 4 of the QD.

Responsibility for establishing facts and investigative standards thus lies with the appellate organ – the Helsinki District Administrative Court. The duty is two-fold: Firstly, an obligation exists as to the need to determine whether fact-finding is qualitatively and quantitatively sufficient. Secondly, a responsibility arises for practical measures in order to achieve desired robustness. The latter responsibility can as we have seen be exercised either by requesting the parties to file additional information or by investigations *ex officio* by the court.[65]

It is noteworthy in this context that the Administrative Court only seldom allows oral hearings to be arranged.[66] When oral hearings are arranged, it is most often based on the need to clarify the credibility of the appellant or due to poor quality of the interview with the determining authority. Oral hearings with the purpose of hearing witnesses or external experts are extremely rare in the Finnish context.[67] This partly implies that the Administrative Court has abandoned oral hearings as a systematic means for increasing the quality or quantity of evidence in favour of a case-by-case approach to sufficiency of evidence both qualitatively and quantitatively. This situation surely reflects the low numbers of applicants and thus appellants in Finnish procedure: With higher numbers more institutionalised and 'automatised' methods would have to be used. On the other hand, lack of oral evidence at appellate stages of the procedure increases the relevance of documentary evidence.

---

[65] See decisions in matters 07/0201/1 (27.2.2007) and 07/0700/1 (4.6.2007) for examples of cases where the Helsinki District Administrative Court has asked the parties to add information to the case. In the decision in case 07/0201/1 (27.2.2007) the Administrative Court asked the applicant to add more information about the actions and positions of certain family members in the country of origin.

[66] No statistics are available to pinpoint the actual frequency of oral hearings. However, a rough estimate is that less than 10 % of cases dealt with within the limits of the regular procedure in the District Administrative Court benefit from oral hearings. The court, however, states that it has a clear ambition to increase the amount of oral hearings within the future.

[67] It should be noted that any expert evidence is also exceptional in written form.

Another issue is that of responsibility for establishing facts in relation to the burden of proof. Whereas it is clear that there indeed is an *Offizialmaxim* and a responsibility of the Administrative Court over fact-finding, a duty of cooperation is also tied to the appellant through the burden of proof. We have seen that the burden of proof in practice indeed includes a burden of allegation, which takes its form in a duty of 'leading the Administrative Court on'. However, it is not completely clear whether this burden – aside from the abstract duty to lead the court on – would also include the burden for the appellant of producing evidence and responsibility for investigative standards. Many decisions seem to indicate that such a burden is indeed present.[68]

When analysing the practice of the Helsinki District Administrative Court it becomes clear that the court indeed uses the *ex officio* possibility to carry out fact-finding as a last resort, in accordance with the legal norms on the matter.[69] It appears as if most of the knowledge and information available in cases before the Administrative Court has been produced by the parties – either voluntarily or on request by the court.

General Robustness
Finnish appellate asylum procedure does not uphold rigid time frames for producing, presenting or collecting evidence. Evidence can be presented by the parties at any time during the procedure, also after a possible oral hearing. The court can also *ex officio* further investigate relevant circumstances at any stage of the procedure or ask the parties to add information and evidence.[70] This flexibility is possible partly due to the relatively low number of appellants in Finnish asylum procedure combined with lengthy procedures, allowing the Administrative Court to deal with each matter thoroughly. It is also clear that

---

[68] Helsinki District Administrative Court 06/0761/1 (30.5.2006), cited *supra* at 61, where the political actions of the applicant had not been investigated and could not be seen as reasons for persecution. Cpr German practice according to which doctrine and practice regarding limits of the burden of proof and the duty to investigate are far more elaborate.

[69] It is a clear problem when analysing the origins of evidence used by the District Administrative Court that in its decisions the court does not always state the origins of the information or the sources used. However, see for instance cases 07/0401/3 (15.3.2007) and 07/0402/3 (15.3.2007) in which the identity of the applicant had not been established in first instance proceedings and in which the Helsinki District Administrative Court subsequently did not investigate the matter at all of its own motion nor did it ask the parties for further information about identity, but was content to state in the decision that identity remained unclear. Questions relating to the identity of the applicant also become material for an application for asylum as the Administrative Court, as evidence from these cases shows, sees difficulties in verifying identity as an indication of the level of credibility of the applicant.

[70] Often the court uses the chance during oral hearings to ask for further documentary evidence which is then submitted at a later stage of the proceedings.

the relatively long time for processing claims in the Administrative Court requires certain flexibility from the procedure. It is clear that flexibility is an advantage for both qualitative and quantitative evidentiary robustness in the procedure.

Flexibility nevertheless places certain demands on the actions of the court. As information can be added at all stages of the procedure, communication of any new information becomes vital in order to secure quality of evidence.[71] The parties to the procedure must be allowed to comment on all information, regardless of whether information arises from the actions of the appellant, the determining authority, or from investigations *ex officio* by the Administrative Court.[72] It is further clear that in a procedure where information and evidence can be added to the case at all stages, it is important for the court in its decision to clearly state the facts and information on which the decision is based.

The principle of hearing the parties and communicating evidence has been well embraced by the Helsinki District Administrative Court in relation to evidence presented by the parties to the procedure. Representatives from the court see it as self-evident that all such information is communicated to the other party and that a possibility for comments or critique is given – regardless of when the information is presented before the court, and practice also show that this is done.[73] This principle is also important in the practice of the Administrative Court, where lengthy procedural times occasionally result precisely from the requirement for hearing.

Then again, the Administrative Court is hesitant in communicating evidence that has been obtained *ex officio*, such as general COI or individual answers to questions obtained from specific sources or the like. In a decision from 2008, the court motivates the practice to not hear the parties regarding such evidence

---

[71] Administrative Judicial Procedure Act (586/1996), section 34, requires the Administrative Court to hear parties on all issues that "may have an effect on the outcome of the matter". Halila (2000) 295–302, considers exceptions to this rule, but concludes that the general rule on communication, and thus the hearing, is strong.

[72] See Olli Mäenpää, *Oikeudenkäynnin julkisuus hallintotuomioistuimissa* (Helsinki 2007b) 124 ff and 144–149, the latter particularly on communication in written procedures.

[73] In practice, it is often settled that the parties at the same time as filing evidence before the court must communicate copies to each other, especially if evidence is requested by the Administrative Court during oral hearings when it is easy for the parties both present to agree on forms of communication. Mäenpää (Helsinki 2007b) 146–149, firstly states that written procedures are, as a starting point, not possible in matters that require presentation of evidence. He further does not consider communication of evidence obtained by the court *ex officio*. Asylum appeals, where the procedure is often written and still requires evidence, thus fall outside the framework considered customary by this author.

by stating that the information is of a general nature and that the legal representative of the appellant has had the opportunity to read earlier decisions concerning the country and thus become acquainted with the information used by the Administrative Court.[74] Taking into account the importance of preserving a balance of powers between the parties and the fact that much of the COI used by the Administrative Court indeed stems from the research department of the determining authority, the practice not to communicate COI does seem unmotivated. While the court cannot be expected to hand over to the parties copies of all material used as evidence, it cannot be seen as feasible that the court discharges the responsibility for correct communication to the legal representative available, especially since not all appellants are represented. Also from the point of view of quality-enhancement through communication, non-communication is clearly an issue.[75]

It should also be noted that references to evidence in decisions of the Administrative Court are often unclear and that the precise sources of information in the individual case are often not revealed. For instance, common expressions in decisions are "as international COI reports state that..."[76], or "according to information that the court has obtained..."[77]. In combination with difficulties in communicating all evidence, unclear references make it very difficult for anyone other than the decision-maker to gain a full picture of how evidentiary assessment has been undertaken.[78]

Quantitative Robustness
Looking specifically at quantitative standards of investigation, the low number of oral hearings again arises as a factor of importance. In most cases before the Administrative Court, oral hearings are not arranged. When estimating the quantity of evidence, one can thus differentiate between two categories of cases:

Firstly, there are cases in which oral hearings are arranged by the District Administrative Court.[79] In these matters the bulk of evidence includes records of interview at the determining authority and other possible evidence transferred from first level to second, evidence that has possibly been presented before the Administrative Court by either party and of possible evidence obtained *ex officio*

---

[74] 07/0274/1 (14.3.2007).
[75] Cpr, again, the German practice of submitting lists of information available.
[76] For instance 07/0716/1 (5.6.2007) ("Kansainvälisistä maaraporteista ilmenee...")
[77] 05/1940/1 (13.12.2005) ("Saadun selvityksen mukaan...")
[78] The practice of not revealing sources of information and evidence is not exclusive to the Administrative Court as the determining authority also often does not include sources in its decisions.
[79] These cases constitute less than 10 % of all cases dealt with under the normal asylum procedure in the Helsinki District Administrative Court.

by the Administrative Court. And in these cases there is an oral hearing. Considering that the time limits for presenting evidence are flexible and that procedures are often lengthy, each case will usually include at least some additional evidence aside from the record from the determining authority. Also, the *in casu* approach to evidence implies that the material will often include COI acquired *ex officio* by the Administrative Court.

The oral hearing of the appellant is evidence in itself and thus adds to the quantity of the evidence in the case. However, the oral hearing often gives rise to additional questions and issues about which documentary evidence is produced after the hearing – either by the parties or by the Administrative Court. Thus, aside from the immediate effect on the quantity of evidence in the procedure, the oral hearing also has an indirect effect through producing additional evidence.

Secondly, there are cases in which no oral hearings are organised. In these cases the court has to rely on written evidence produced and transferred at first instance and on information produced at appellate level. In the absence of oral hearings, the weight placed on documentary evidence inevitably increases – both in relation to quantitative and qualitative robustness. In terms of quantitative standards, absence of an oral hearing has both a direct and an indirect effect: It diminishes the amount of evidence both directly, as it is not included in the evidentiary basis, and indirectly as there is no opportunity to use the oral hearing as a bridge to obtaining new evidence.

Aside from the issue of the oral hearing, the Finnish procedural institutional framework also affects quantitative robustness. Keeping in mind that the competent appellate instance is a general administrative court without special facilities for fact-finding, it is clear that the possibilities for investigations *ex officio* are limited. Fact-finding with limited resources is demanding and requires thorough knowledge of both the questions at issue and available sources. In Finnish appellate asylum procedure the situation has led to heavy reliance on the research department of the determining authority by the Administrative Court, too. This may as we have seen distort the balance of powers between the parties.[80]

Qualitative Robustness
Turning to the qualitative robustness of the evidentiary base, questions regarding sources, source criticism, and quality-enhancing mechanisms become apparent. We have seen that the Aliens Act requires the investigator to ensure

---

[80] However, a report by the working group of the Ministry of the Interior in 2009 concludes that asylum procedure would benefit from more than one administrative court being involved as appeals instances in the procedure. Ministry of the Interior: *Näkökulmia turvapaikkapolitiikkaan* (Helsinki 2009) 465.

that information from as well various as up-to-date sources are included in the assessment.[81] The rule was included in national legislation as a step in the implementation of the APD.

However, also in relation to quality, one must consider the impact of the fact that very few cases benefit from oral hearings: Cases determined without oral hearings include mostly documentary evidence. The oral evidence available, indirectly and in this procedure in written form, stems from the asylum interview conducted by the determining authority, which is procedurally very far from the Administrative Court.[82] Not only the rules but also the practices and the institutional setting around acquisition of information from the applicant are in first level proceedings distant from the Administrative Court framework. Procedural distance adds to the risk of misconceptions and misunderstandings. Further, if no oral hearing is conducted the demand for high quality documentary evidence clearly increases. We have seen that the oral hearing can often be used as a portal to acquiring more evidence and clearly opposing larger volumes of information against each other enhances the quality of evidence.[83]

Another distinct character of the procedure with an apparent effect on quality of evidence is lack of communication and hearing the parties regarding some forms of evidence. It is evident that communication increases quality, as opinions are given on the information contained in the evidence so that there is more support for interpretation of the information. This quality-enhancing mechanism is lacking in relation to a great deal of evidence obtained *ex officio* by the Administrative Court. Keeping in mind the limited resources for fact-finding and the relatively one-sided use of sources of information, circumvention of this quality-enhancing mechanism must be seen as unfortunate. On the other hand, flexibility and case-by-case approaches to evidence clearly work in favour of qualitative standards as they *per se* give both the parties and the Administrative Court the time and possibility to make an effort in fact-finding.

---

[81] Council directive 2005/85, OJ 1.12.2005, (L 326) 13 on Minimum Standards on Procedures in Member States for Granting and Withdrawing Refugee Status andProposal for a Directive of the European Parliament and of the Council on minimum standards of procedures in Member States for the granting and withdrawing of international protection COM (2009) 554/4 and Amended proposal for a Directive of the European Parliament and of the Council on common procedures for granting and withdrawing international protection status (Recast), COM(2011) 319 final, Art 8.

[82] See also Smith (1990) 89–101, for a study of quality of evidence through forms of procedural distance.

[83] Further, according to the Aliens Act (301/2004), in some accelerated procedures oral hearings are not compulsory. This concerns Dublin issues and subsequent applications. This is not considered to be a problem as the appeal does not, in these cases, concern grounds for protection, but the formal requirements for assessment on the merits of the case.

As stated earlier, it is not easy to determine how the Administrative Court in practice ensures the highest possible qualitative standard of evidence as often no references to the evidence are available in decisions. However, it is clear that appellate asylum procedure in Finland relies on the skills of the individual judge in terms of quality of evidence available. Thus, it is vital for the procedure that the judge and the assessor of evidence is not only aware of the limitations in the procedure but also that he or she is capable of conducting the best possible fact-finding despite these obstructions. Further, it is also vital that the assessor of evidence is able to grasp the consequences of the different procedural limitations on the information provided by the evidence.

4.3. *Standard of Proof*

There is no normative guidance regarding the standard of proof in the Finnish asylum procedure aside of the determination of the theme of proof, where the pre-requisite for asylum is defined as *well-founded fear*.[84] We have seen that the well-foundedness is not a measure of the general standard of proof in the asylum procedure, but a measure of the intensity or sufficiency of the fear.

Nevertheless, in practice and on the surface, use of the standard of proof in Finnish appellate asylum procedure is straightforward, almost simplistic. Motivations to the decisions of the Court always include a phrase referring to the standard of proof and The Helsinki District Administrative Court is consistent in motivating its decision by referring to a common standard of proof at the level of 'probable'.[85] A common expression used is that the appellant has not made it probable that he or she would have a well-founded fear of being persecuted if returned home.

Also, references to burden of proof in connection to standard of proof are clear and exact. The reasoning emphasises that it is the responsibility of the appellant to ensure that the theme of proof is reached to the level of the standard of proof and that if the appellant has not been able to make the risk for persecution 'probable', then asylum is not granted.

The expressions used in referring to the standard of proof at a level of probability are highly standardised expressions in the decisions of the Court. Almost all references to the standard include the same wording, and variations on the

---

[84] Aliens Act, section 87.
[85] The Finnish term used is "todennäköistä". See for instance decisions 07/0253/1 (8.3.2007) and 07/0474/1 (20.4.2007): "Valittaja ei ole tehnyt todennäköiseksi, että hänellä olisi ulkomaalaislain 87 §:n 1 momentissa tarkoitetulla tavalla perustellusti aihetta pelätä joutuvansa vainotuksi kotimaassaan." (The appellant has not made it probable that in his country of origin he would have a well-founded fear of being persecuted in the meaning of the Aliens Act section 87 (1)).

theme are small.[86] Thus, it does seem as if the standard is, indeed, rigid and applied in a consistent and systematised manner.

Nevertheless, the broader context of decisions and of the motivations and argumentation relating to the standard of proof in decisions suggest that the semantic description of standard of proof used in Finnish appellate asylum procedure in fact refers to several divergent levels of the threshold. 'Probable' may, so to speak, imply different things depending on the context.[87]

This means that the standard of proof used in Finnish appellate asylum procedure is not a consistent concept and on the other hand that in any case it semantically diverges from the standard of reasonable likelihood as referred to by various international organs. However, it is not clear whether it has been the conscious intention of the Administrative Court to divert from international recommendations used in asylum law or if divergence has come about as an inherent result of differences in administrative environments, evidentiary discussions and languages between the Finnish and international contexts. Further, as the Finnish standard of proof is somewhat floating, a direct comparison between concepts cannot be made.

Tracing the meaning of expressions placing the standard of proof at the level of probability to the common Nordic discussion on evidence and proof, the threshold would imply a standard lower than that of criminal procedure, but higher than a balance of probabilities.[88] In relation to balance of probabilities, this standard of probability implies a clearly higher level, not only a minor step over the balance. Thus, even if direct comparison is impossible, both the wording of the concepts and the doctrine developed around, on the one hand, probability in the Nordic evidentiary context, and real risk or reasonable likelihood, on the other, suggest that the standard of probability is a standard clearly higher than that of real risk or reasonable likelihood.[89]

Finally, let us consider how the standard of proof is built up in Finnish appellate asylum procedure: Clearly, a general standard exists at the semantic level of probability, which concerns the threshold for the general theme of proof. This standard is referred to in all decisions through the standardised expressions mentioned earlier. We have also seen that the precise contents of this standard are somewhat unclear. Aside from this general standard, however, Finnish procedure also makes use of some even higher standards when it comes to admitting facts to evidentiary assessment.[90]

---

[86] *Ibid.*
[87] This is also confirmed by the judges interviewed.
[88] Ekelöf (*et al.*) (2009) 86 ff.
[89] For further references to the Nordic discussion see Lindell (1998) 463 ff and Diesen (1993) 379 ff.
[90] Cpr German practice of two clearly distinct standards of proof, Chapter V 4.4.3.

Again, the motivations of Finnish decisions make it difficult to see which facts are used in general assessment and on what grounds facts are included or excluded from general assessment. Nevertheless, decisions reveal that it is not uncommon that facts are excluded from general assessment on the grounds that "it has not been excluded" that the concerned facts are erroneous.[91] This would firstly imply that there indeed is a substandard to the general standard of proof which concerns admission of facts to general assessment of proof. Secondly, the reasoning implies that a very high standard of proof is used for proving the correctness of the facts, the passing of which in turn would be a prerequisite for inclusion in general assessment of the theme of proof. In analysis of decisions from the Administrative Court the sub-standard for admitting facts to evidentiary assessment often seems to be placed at a level very close to certainty about the correctness of the information. If the Administrative Court is at all unsure of evidence, it is not included in assessment. Further, analysis seems to point to assessment of reliability of evidence taken in isolation – evidence is not in general assessed together before being admitted or not admitted to assessment.

As with many other evidentiary features of Finnish procedure, the standard of proof is difficult to assess as the argumentation of decisions does not give clear accounts of evidentiary steps in assessment. However, it is clear that rather high standards are used, both in relation to the general theme of proof and the subthemes for individual case facts.

4.4. *Methods of Evidentiary Assessment*

It is difficult to clearly state how evidentiary assessment is undertaken in Finnish appellate asylum procedure. Partly, this is due to lack of references to evidentiary issues in decisions and doctrine. Partly, poorly reasoned decisions make it difficult to create a picture of the methods.[92] Normative guidance is

---

[91] See for instance case 07/0474/1 (20.4.2007) where scars on the body of the appellant were presented as evidence of past torture but were excluded from general assessment by the court on the basis that it had not been excluded that the scars could stem from sources other than torture. ("Valittajan arvista esitetty selvitys ei sulje pois sitä mahdollisuutta, että arvet ovat voineet syntyä myös muulla kuin valittajan kertomalla tavalla.")

[92] In Korkein hallinto-oikeus, *Päätösten perustelemisen kehittäminen* / Högsta förvaltningsdomstolen, *Utvecklande av beslutens motivering* (Helsinki 1996), the Supreme Administrative Court expressed its view on how to develop the reasoning of decisions in Finnish administrative judicial procedure. In relation to evidentiary assessment the court stated, pages 20–21, that it must be clear for the reader how conclusions in relation to the facts of the case have been reached, and that at times it may be necessary to state why a fact has been regarded as proved and others not. While the paper indeed shows that in 1996 the Supreme Administrative Court was aware of problems in regard to reasoning, developments in reasoning around evidentiary assessment have since been scarce.

given only to the extent that the Aliens Act requires decision-making to be undertaken individually and taking into account both evidence presented by the asylum-seeker and acquired *ex officio*.[93]

Some elements can, however, be verified: A two-step model is to some extent used in reference to use of facts in the procedure. Establishing the facts is clearly separated from assessing the facts in the light of the general theme of proof. This is evident from the way in which the Administrative Court at times, before general assessment, undertakes a separate assessment of facts.[94]

In many decisions, establishing facts seems to be based on little more than the opinion of the court. Thus, some decisions indicate a manner of discharging evidence on the basis of tacit knowledge or unrevealed evidence without further elaboration on the subject.[95] The court can, for instance, make claims about political or social circumstances in the home region of the appellant without *per se* giving sources or motivations for its views. On the basis of such claims, the court at times dismisses evidence that contradicts its opinions.

Further, the Administrative Court often refers to "international sources" or to "information acquired"[96] in its decisions without further specifying the sources. One must interpret these expressions as referring to internationally produced COI in the first place.[97] It seems rather clear, based on the decisions available, that the value attached to statements by the appellant directly depends on the possibilities of the court to verify the statements in the COI. Thus, if discrepancies are found the evidentiary value of statements by the applicant is decreased and if similarities are found, the evidentiary value of the applicant's statements is increased.[98]

---

[93] Aliens Act, section 98 (2).

[94] See for instance 06/1325/1 (21.9.2006), concerning an applicant from Ethiopia and resting mainly on COI and oral testimony in as well oral hearing before the court as in asylum interview. Claims and evidence were first accounted for and then analysed and assessed. In the assessment, some claims were dismissed and the court established the facts on which they rely. However, in a final general assessment of the theme of proof, all evidence was included.

[95] See for instance 07/1213/1 (28.9.2007), an otherwise well argued and clear decision with direct references to sources, where the Administrative Court gave its opinion on the possibilities for persons in different positions to run private businesses and to travel from the country without problems with the authorities. The Administrative Court did not give sources for its opinions on the matter even though they were central to the argumentation for a negative decision. Using these opinions as arguments, both oral and written evidence were dismissed and the evidentiary assessment was left with very little content.

[96] See decision 07/0716/1 (5.6.2007) which refers only to "international COI" and 05/1940/1 (13.12.2005), which refers to "information obtained" as examples.

[97] See for instance the well-argued decisions 07/0826/1 (26.6.2007) and 06/0076/1 (23.1.2006), where sources are spelled out and referred to correctly.

[98] See for instance decision 06/1325/1 (21.9.2006). It is noteworthy that the value of the COI does not seem to fluctuate in the court's opinion.

However, as the COI is only generally referred to, it is unclear how this procedure of verification is undertaken and what kinds of sources are used.

Credibility plays a central role in evidentiary assessment by the court.
Credibility assessment functions as an indicator of the quality of the evidence
presented by the appellant. As in all procedures, evidence or information that
is not credible cannot be taken into account in evidentiary assessment.
However, considering the strong reliance on credibility assessments together
with the low number of oral hearings, some questions arise: Can the court
effectively assess the credibility of the applicant without oral hearings? Such
arrangements would imply the use of a long 'procedural chain' from the interview with the determining authority to assessment of the statements and
claims made by the Administrative Court in order to establish credibility. And
also, what circumstances are allowed to impact on assessment of credibility by
the court? Aside from commonly acknowledged discrepancies in statements
and unawareness of key facts relating to claims as indicators of lack of credibility, a number of other indicators, such as behaviour during travel to Finland,
are also used by the court.[99]

Moving then from admission of facts to evidentiary assessment, to general
assessment of the evidence available in the case, very little is actually revealed
from the written decisions of the Helsinki District Administrative Court. Most
often the first step in assessment is establishing the facts of the case according
to the standards and routines referred to earlier, either admitting or dismissing evidence. After this, decisions include a standardised assessment of the
general theme of proof, including a comparison between the facts established
by the evidence admitted to assessment and the elements of the theme of
proof. Possibly, a general consideration of the facts also occurs without direct
links or references to the elements of the theme of proof.[100] However, comparison between the facts of the case and the elements of the theme of proof often
only extends to some of the elements – most commonly those questionable in
the light of the facts of the case.

---

[99] See for instance 06/1451/1 (13.10.2006), where the court stated that the fact that the appellant had travelled through several safe countries before arriving in Finland decreased the
credibility of the appellant with reference to the need for international protection.

[100] See for instance 06/1505/1 (25.10.2006), a case concerning alleged violations of basic human
rights in Russia. In its decision the court first assesses evidence presented before the court
and the claims by the appellant, regarding political activity and alleged inhuman punishment. The court accepts the majority of the claims made by the appellant. However, the
court continues by stating that the established facts of the case do not show that the appellant's problems had met the requirements for persecution, without further studying the
theme of proof or the impact on the theme of proof of established facts.

In all, the generality of evidentiary assessment seems at least to some degree to have given way to standardised cross-checking the facts of the case and the elements of the theme of proof. Decisions seldom show that any elaborate inclusive and general assessment of the facts put together takes place. Rather, resources are focused on individualised comparison. Decisions give the picture of a 'hurdle race' for the appellant where each established fact can either push the appellant further towards the goal or make him or her fail.

Thus, in terms of methods Finnish evidentiary assessment is clearly rather traditional. Risk-assessment is relevant only for establishing the standard of proof but not evident in the very assessment of the facts of the case. One must also consider the method used by the Helsinki District Administrative Court as relying heavily on investigations placed before the Court – the Court does not give space for the unknown or uncertain in its decisions. However, the 'method of comparison' used for establishing the theme of proof by matching the facts of the case with the refugee definition in the Aliens Act suggests that some form of method concentrating on inclusion of the theme of proof in the facts of the case is applied. This resembles the methods used for exclusion of hypothetical alternative scenarios: Requirements on conformity with a large amount of criteria minimise the possibility (or risk) that the facts can be explained by other scenarios than the theme of proof.

5. Conclusions

Finnish appellate asylum procedure is an example of asylum procedure in an environment with limited numbers of asylum seekers and involving a fairly controllable number of authorities and decision-makers. Throughout its history, the procedure has been affected by pragmatic reasoning both regarding the institutional format and the formal framework for the procedure, while the procedural legal framework and procedural customs have been adapted pragmatically in response to particular needs in the procedure. Hence, whereas Finnish appellate asylum procedure constitutes a part of the general administrative framework, the procedure has nevertheless developed into a procedure distinct from the common administrative framework, including in terms of evidentiary solutions.

Above all, Finnish evidentiary procedure is characterised by a strong sense of uncertainty. Pragmatic solutions, flexible approaches and good intentions place high demands on assessment of evidence and on clarity in reasoning. These demands are not always met. A gap is created between the factual basis for decisions and the evidence actually used in decision-making. On the other hand, a gap also exists between the possibilities for understanding the evidentiary basis for the decision and the formal requirements stemming from international or national law and practice.

Chapter VII

Evidence in English Appellate Asylum Procedure

1. *Aims and Method*

This part of the study, encompassing English appellate asylum procedure, will communicate an understanding of English appellate asylum procedure to the extent relevant for understanding the evidentiary solutions found within the procedure. This chapter also aims to explore the procedure's evidentiary standards. Thus, also this chapter will firstly provide background and framework to the procedure and, secondly, examine the position of the keys of comparison in the distinct procedure at hand. The aim is to reveal the function and position of the comparative keys as set out in chapter IV above.[1]

A limitation to the study is that any fast-track proceedings within the appellate structure of English asylum procedure will not be given attention. Nor are statutory appeals included. The study of English asylum procedure focuses solely on appeals in regular appellate asylum procedure.

Vast amendments to English appellate asylum procedure were introduced in 2008 and 2009, taking effect in early 2010.[2] The amendments concern a new order of appellate instances and transfer of first level appeals from the Asylum and Immigration Tribunal (AIT) to the First-Tier and Upper Tribunal (FTT and UT). These amendments have been incorporated in the study.

The findings presented in this chapter are based on a variety of materials and sources. Firstly, there is the traditional body of legal doctrine. This encompasses research carried out and documented particularly in immigration and asylum law and in more general fields such as tribunal justice, procedural law and evidentiary law by English scholars and others. Secondly, as England represents common law and as the outsets for asylum procedure to a high degree also rely on authoritative decisions, a number of decisions and judgments

---

[1] The comparative keys are: burden of proof, evidentiary assessment, methods for evidentiary assessment and the standard of proof.

[2] Statutory Instrument 2010 No.21 Tribunals and Inquiries: The Transfer of Functions of the Asylum and Immigration Tribunal Order 2010, in force 15.2.2010. For a comprehensive overview of the changes to the appellate system see Mark Symes & Peter Jorros, *Asylum Law and Practice* (Wiltshire 2010) 825 ff.

from English institutions with competence in the asylum field are included in the base material. Finally, the presentation also relies on pragmatic sources of information: interviews conducted with judges, solicitors and researchers affiliated with English appellate asylum procedure and observations made of the practice in relevant institutions during hearings.[3] This information was gathered during a stay in England in 2007.

2. *Frameworks for English Asylum Procedure*

2.1. *Defining Frameworks and History*

In order to understand how English appellate asylum procedure functions and where its limits are set, it important to understand the background of the procedure as an independent procedure of tribunal justice within the wider framework of judicial procedures in England. This is especially true considering the rather exceptional background to the procedure as it stands today – a procedure that during the last ten years has been the object of several fundamental institutional, procedural, and substantive revisions and thus a procedure very much in motion.[4] Recurring changes to the procedure have on the one hand allowed for dynamic procedural responses to issues and challenges raised by increasing numbers of applications and changing forms of argumentation, at times also affecting evidentiary practices.[5] Thus, the rules of asylum procedure have also in respect of evidentiary norms been created in a flexible environment designed to keep the procedure at pace with demands from changes around it.

An independent appellate procedure for matters relating to immigration and nationality was introduced in the United Kingdom through the Immigration Appeals Act of 1969[6], creating an appeals system including adjudicators and the Immigration Appeals Tribunal (IAT).[7] The appeals procedure

---

[3] Annex I.

[4] Robert Thomas describes the procedure as "continually reformed". Robert Thomas, "Evaluating tribunal adjudication: administrative justice and asylum appeals" (2005/3) *Legal Studies*, 462–463.

[5] Clearly, political pressure and demands for various concerns also to be raised in procedural and systematic structures of the procedure have also influenced changes to the procedure. See *ibid* at 462–498 and same, "Asylum Appeals Overhauled Again" (2003/summer) *Public Law*, 260–271.

[6] Immigration Appeals Act 1969, sections 2–7. See also B. A. Hepple, "Immigration Appeals Act 1969" (1969/3) *Modern Law Review*, 668–672.

[7] A comprehensive outline of the history of English asylum procedure up to 2002 can be found in Thomas (2003) 260–271 and from 2002 onwards in Thomas (2005) 462–470 and Robert Thomas, "After the Ouster: review and reconsideration in a single tier tribunal" (2006/4) *Public Law*, 674–686.

created was a two tier procedure with adjudicators of the Immigration Appeals Authority (IAA) reviewing decisions from Home Office authorities on their merits as the first stage of appellate justice. Asylum or international protection was not referred to in the Act.[8]

The possibility to appeal decisions specifically relating to asylum and refugee status was introduced in 1993.[9] The Asylum and Immigration Appeals Act of 1993 paved the way for the two-tier procedure of administrative justice following negative decisions on applications for asylum.[10] Appeals were heard on their merits before adjudicators within the IAA with a possibility of further appeals on errors of law to the IAT. From the IAT onwards the Administrative Court, the Court of Appeal and as final instance, the House of Lords, were competent to review earlier decisions in asylum procedure.

The system with a two-tier appeal structure was created in the midst of increasing flows of asylum seekers to England. As the number of applications for asylum increased steadily throughout the 1990s, it soon became apparent that the quite complicated procedural structure of the IAA and the IAT could not effectively deal with the increased workload.[11] It was also considered that aside from numerical changes in the amount of appeals to appellate bodies, the nature of asylum as a means of migration had also changed and that substantial changes to the appeals structure were needed.[12]

Changes brought about with the 1999 Immigration and Asylum Act introduced 'one-stop appeals'.[13] This implied that instead of several different appellate procedures that all in part reviewed previous decisions, all matters relating to one person were to be heard within one appellate procedure. Thus, all grounds for appeal were gathered in one procedure under one appeal. Further, human rights appeals were introduced as a form of safety net for applicants and as a way for decision-makers to include all relevant aspects of the matter at hand in their decisions. The changes made individual proceedings in each case far more complex. Decision-makers were now expected to investigate

---

[8] The 1969 Act refers to appeals against decisions made with support of the 1962 Commonwealth Immigrants Act, which exclusively concerned immigration rules for Commonwealth citizens.

[9] The Asylum and Immigration Appeals Act 1993.

[10] Sections 8 and 9 of the Asylum and Immigration Appeals Act 1993 (c. 23).

[11] In 1994, 32830 persons applied for asylum in the UK and a total of 825 persons were granted refugee status. In 1999 71160 persons applied for asylum and 7815 were granted status as refugees. Statistics are available from the Immigration Research and Statistics Service within the Home Office.

[12] One of the goals with the 1999 amendment was to decrease the possibilities for misuse of the system through faster and more efficient decision-making. Thomas (2003) 262.

[13] *Ibid* at 262–264.

and decide on broad entities of information and to rely on a vast amount of rules and practices under the heading of one single appeal. After some time up and running it became clear that the structure of this revised system did not function as effectively as expected and that the 'one-stop' procedure in fact clogged up appellate channels in immigration issues, especially between the IAA and the IAT.

Hence, procedural changes were again introduced in 2002 with the declared aim of making the procedure simpler for all parties involved and more efficient in terms of time and money.[14] One of the structural changes in this reform was introduction of so called "starred decisions", i.e. decisions that function as guidelines for similar cases.[15] However, despite numerous updates the procedure in 2003 was still seen as ineffective and financially too consuming so further substantial reforms were prepared.

In 2005 radical institutional and structural changes were introduced to the appellate asylum procedure in England.[16] Through these changes both the IAA and the IAT were abolished and replaced by a single tribunal, the Asylum and Immigration Tribunal (AIT). Thus, while the 'one stop'- procedure was maintained, with decisions on various issues in connection to one appellant taken in the same procedure, the two-tier structure with adjudicators and tribunal decision-making was brought to an end in favour of a one tier structure, with the AIT as the first appellate instance after decisions by the Home Office. Nevertheless, the role of initial appeals as bringing about review not only of questions of law but also on the merits of the case was upheld, making the Tribunal competent to review a case on its merits at the first stage of appeal.[17]

In 2008 new changes to the procedural environment of English appellate asylum procedure involved new rules proposed with the main objective of securing timely decision-making.[18] As a result of this proposal, deep cutting structural changes were implemented to English asylum procedure

---

[14] Nationality, Immigration and Asylum Act 2002.

[15] In the course of preparations for the 2002 legislation, the legislation in place since 1999 was often described as badly prepared and lacking in quality. Thomas (2003) 264–271.

[16] Asylum and Immigration (Treatment of Claimants, etc) Act 2005.

[17] See also Héléne Lambert & Raza Husain, "British Judiciary's Search for Reciprocal Relations" in Goodwin-Gill (*et al.*) (2010) 127–131.

[18] Statutory Instrument 2010 No.21 Tribunals and Inquiries: The Transfer of Functions of the Asylum and Immigration Tribunal Order 2010, in force 15.2.2010. See also the Consultation: *Immigration Appeals Fair Decisions; Faster Justice*, responses to this and the Government Response available at http://www.judiciary.gov.uk/publications-and-reports/judicial -views-and-responses/consultation-responses/2008/responses-immigrationi-appeals -fair-decisions-faster-justice (visited 23.11.2011).

in early 2010. The AIT was abolished in favour of First-Tier Asylum and its Immigration Chamber (the Chamber), a part of the First-Tier Tribunal established through the reforms together with the Upper Tribunal. Procedurally, many of the rules governing the AIT were transferred directly or slightly amended to the Chamber of the First-Tier Tribunal and, in the words of the Tribunals Service themselves: "The existing AIT judges and non-legal members will transfer into the new system and continue their vital work in the same way as at present".[19] The goal of the reform was to draw together the scattered Tribunals into one First-Tier and Upper Tribunal, thereby securing greater efficiency in their work.[20]

2.2. Institutional Framework

The agents involved in English asylum procedure are many and the institutional map of the procedure is far from simple. The actors in the procedure, aside from the asylum seeker and his possible representative, are: the Home Office, its Border & Immigration Agency, and the Department for Constitutional Affairs[21], the First-Tier and Upper Tribunal, the Civil Division of the Court of Appeal, and the Supreme Court. An application for asylum, the decision on this and possible subsequent appeals, are not pushed through these bodies in a linear manner but can be tossed back and forth between different instances.[22]

Initially, decisions on asylum applications are made by officials of the Border & Immigration Agency, falling under the Home Office, either in regular, fast track or border procedures. The Border & Immigration Agency carries out the interviews that form the basis for considerations on the grant of asylum, reviews the country of origin information relevant for the case, and

---

[19] See the Tribunal Service: Transferring asylum and immigration appeals into the unified tribunal structure Q&A available at http://www.jonathanmitchell.info/uploads/AIT%20 transfer%20q%20&%20a.pdf (visited 23.11.2011)

[20] Procedurally, the Asylum and Immigration Tribunal (Procedure) Rules 2005, Statutory Instrument 2005 No. 230 (L 1), which had governed the procedure in the AIT, were transferred directly, but in a consolidated version, to the procedure before the FTT. The UT also works in asylum matters under the main Tribunal Procedure (Upper Tribunal) Rules 2008, Statutory Instrument 2008 No. 2698 (L 15).

[21] The Border & Immigration Agency is responsible for initial decisions on applications for asylum and other decisions in immigration issues. The Department of Constitutional Affairs is the department responsible for the tribunal system in the UK.

[22] For graphic charts presenting the institutional structure of the English asylum procedure see Jonathan Lewis, *Immigration and Asylum Law Bench Book* (Court of Appeal Civil Division 2007), sections 3–1 to 3–2.

collects other relevant information. The Border & Immigration Agency is, as an authority, also compelled to actively pursue information and knowledge beneficial for the applicant and to review the information gathered in each case without prejudice.[23]

If the Border & Immigration Agency rejects an application for asylum, an appeal can be filed with the First-Tier Asylum and Immigration Chamber, which will review the case on its merits. When reviewing decisions from the Border & Immigration Agency, the Chamber's composition may vary according to the nature of the matter at hand. Most frequently 'regular' asylum appeals are dealt with in a composition of more than one judge.[24]

Review of a decision by the Border & Immigration Agency often includes two hearings: a case management hearing where practical issues surrounding the review are set out, such as length of proceedings, lists of witnesses and issues relating to funding of possible representatives, and a main hearing where the case is presented in its entirety before the tribunal.[25] Before the main hearing, the parties are required to file all necessary evidence with the Chamber and can also file evidence that was not presented before the first instance authority. The main hearing additionally includes hearing the appellant and possible witnesses, whereby oral evidence is given before the court.[26]

After reviewing the decision by the Border & Immigration Agency, the Chamber may either decide to dismiss or to allow the appeal. It is also possible that the appeal is party allowed, for instance dismissing it on grounds of asylum but allowing it on humanitarian grounds. The losing party, which can be either or both of the parties represented (the appellant and the Home Office) has a right of further review on points of law to the Upper Tribunal, pending permission. Upper-Tribunal decisions are appealable to the Court of Appeal, Civil Division.

---

[23] On administrative conduct in asylum matters within the Home Office see Symes (*et al*) 2010, 639–696.

[24] Section 2 of Practice Statements for the Immigration and Asylum Chambers of the First Tier and Upper Tribunals gives guidelines for the composition of the Chamber.

[25] Section 7 of Practice Directions for the Immigration and Asylum Chambers of the First Tier and Upper Tribunals.

[26] Statutory Instrument 2005 No. 230 L.1: The Asylum and Immigration Tribunal (Procedure) Rules, section 51, in force also in relation to the FTT by virtue of Statutory Instrument 2010 No.21 Tribunals and Inquiries: The Transfer of Functions of the Asylum and Immigration Tribunal Order 2010, in force 15.2.2010.

2.3. *The Nature of Tribunal Justice*

A feature in the context of English appellate asylum procedure that heavily influences the solutions found within the procedure is that the review procedure is an administrative tribunal justice procedure.[27]

The political sensitivity of administrative justice may open up the procedure for political pressure to a greater extent than many other forms of judicial procedure.[28] When the procedure additionally takes place in a tribunal supervised by the same administration that is heading the first instance authority, the possibilities for political influence over the procedure increase.[29] However, as has repeatedly been pointed out, the need for independent decision-making and the judicial, non-political, nature of the tribunal at their outsets require political influences to be carried out in some other context than in the decision-making of the tribunal, for instance in shaping the institutional or structural frameworks for the procedure.[30]

In relation especially to the Chamber and administrative justice in English appellate asylum procedure, the emphasis in decision-making often seems to be on the independence of the tribunal. Judges are aware of the pressures and tensions between politics and the judiciary but often seem to tackle these through leaning on the requirements for legal certainty, the rule of law and the independence of the tribunal as an organ in the judicial

---

[27] In 2001 an in-depth review of the system of tribunal justice in Britain was undertaken by Sir Andrew Leggatt. In his report, Sir Andrew emphasised the importance of independence and striving towards a more court-like environment in the tribunal justice system. See Andrew Leggatt, *Tribunals for Users One System, One Service* (London 2001). The Legatt report was very much the stepping stone for reforms to asylum procedure undertaken in 2008–2010. On the nature of tribunal justice in comparison to other forms of administrative justice see H.B. Jacobini, *An Introduction to Comparative Administrative Law* (New York – London – Rome 1991) 80–81.

[28] An example of this political sensitivity is seen in vast changes to asylum procedure during recent decades. On the development of judicial review in England within the administrative field see also Dimitra Nassimpian, "National legal tradition – United Kingdom" in *Judicial review A comparative analysis inside the European legal system* ed. Susana Galera (Council of Europe 2010) 157–172 at 162, where the author states that "The historical reluctance to challenge the lawfulness of Acts of Parliament and the notion of the absolute authority of the monarch have been readjusted in view of the need for accountability of public bodies."

[29] Thomas refers to the tribunal system as one comprising "part of the decision-making process in securing the implementation of policy goals". Thomas (2005) 493.

[30] See also Birkinshaw (2003) 327 ff., for a consideration of the guiding principles of English administrative review in the light of the background and framework of English administrative procedure. The possibility to actually contest and review administrative decisions within an institutionally "stable" context is considered to be a vast development in the English setting.

system.[31] This has implications for evidentiary assessment and the readiness of judges to accept argumentation and proof that has roots in the political deliberations of the supervising Home Office.[32]

On the other hand, tribunal decision-making allows for tailor-made procedures.[33] The legal requirements for tribunal justice *per se* allow for greater freedom in the procedural solutions found and the need to strictly follow the rules set out for courts is not without exceptions. The composition of the tribunal, inclusion of lay members and experts in decision-making, the evidentiary standards applied by the tribunal and the rules and practices surrounding review of individual matters are far from pre-determined and can be tailored to fit the nature of the tribunal and procedure.[34]

2.4. *Legislative Framework*

The procedure in the Asylum Chamber of the First-Tier Tribunal is primarily and in detail regulated by two written legal sources. The Rules of Procedure as amended in connection with the transfer from AIT to the First-Tier Chamber function as basic rules of procedure for the Chamber.[35] In relation to evidence, these Rules of Procedure include some normative guidance.

---

[31] Eliantonio (2009) 203 ff, refers to English administrative review procedures as distinct in their form as supervisory procedures, rather than review procedures. Partly, the emphasis on independence may indeed stem from the hierarchical structure of the review procedure. Nevertheless, review of asylum decisions does quite clearly present a form of administrative review in England where the particular review-function is also particularly important aside from and, partly, despite the supervisory function of the procedure.

[32] See also Anthony Good, *Anthropology and Expertise in the Asylum Court* (Oxford 2007) 233–237, on the nature of tribunal justice in asylum matters.

[33] For a still valid comparison between courts and tribunals in the British judicial system, see R.E. Wraith & P.G. Hutchesson, *Administrative Tribunals* (London 1974) 250–287.

[34] In English asylum procedure the procedural rules have been tailor-made in many respects. This is not least evident in the transfer of rules from the AIT to the First-Tier and Upper Tribunal, which has upheld the principle that the tribunal is allowed to neglect general rules of evidence, which as a result of the common law tradition are far from simple, in favour of an approach where the tribunal is able to consider all evidence it deems necessary. Another issue is then that the tribunal and higher courts themselves in authoritative decisions have laid down requirements for bringing evidence before the tribunal and for the tribunal to consider the information provided. See The Asylum and Immigration Tribunal (Procedural) Rules, section 51 and *Karanakaran v. Secretary of State for the Home Department*, [2000] EWCA Civ. 11, Court of Appeal (England and Wales), 25 January 2000. Also Birkingshaw (2003) 331 ff.

[35] Statutory Instrument 2005 No. 230 L.1: The Asylum and Immigration Tribunal (Procedure) Rules in force also in relation to the FTT by virtue of Statutory Instrument 2010 No.21 Tribunals and Inquiries: The Transfer of Functions of the Asylum and Immigration Tribunal Order 2010, in force 15.2.2010.

Firstly, the Rules of Procedure in section 53 take a direct stand on the question of burden of proof. Section 53 explicitly places the burden of proof with the appellant both in relation to the claim for refugee status and in relation to sub-themes of proof. This is noteworthy, as neither international law nor EU law *per se* include normatively binding rules on the burden of proof. Secondly, section 51 refers to several practical issues in relation to evidentiary assessment: According to the rules of procedure the Chamber may "allow oral, documentary or other evidence to given of any fact [...] even if that evidence would be inadmissible in a court of law." Hence, the Rules of Procedure opens up the evidentiary assessment in appellate asylum claims to evidence unfamiliar to the 'regular' common law court procedure. It must be considered that this is a step undertaken as a result of the difficult evidentiary environment in the asylum procedure. Further, section 51 of the Rules of Procedure also provides for the possibility for oral evidence and allows the court to require documentary evidence to be presented as original documents and not as copies. Section 51 also stresses that the Chamber cannot consider any evidence that has not been properly communicated to all parties.

The rules of procedure are accompanied and continued by Practice Directions for the Chamber.[36] Also the Practice Directions include detailed norms on evidence. However, these particular evidentiary rules are not in force in relation to appeals before the Chamber of the First-Tier Tribunal, but only in relation to onward appeals to the Chamber of the Upper Tribunal.[37] In relation to evidentiary issues in the Chamber of the First-Tier Tribunal the directions only contain rules on the rights of parties to present expert evidence before the Chamber.[38]

3. Salient Features of English Asylum Procedure

3.1. Argumentative Justice

One of the clear characteristics of common law judicial procedures is the emphasis and importance placed on individual assessment and the weight attached to requirements for thorough argumentation and comprehensive reasoning in decision-making.[39] These features are clearly linked to the role of the judiciary within this legal tradition.

---

[36] Practice Directions for the Immigration and Asylum Chambers of the First Tier and Upper Tribunals.

[37] *Ibid* at section 4.

[38] *Ibid* at section 10.

[39] See Good (2007) 248–251.

Thus, one can expect decisions in appellate asylum procedure that are well-reasoned and exhaustively considered and in which the argumentation is thorough and of high quality. These expectations are additionally fuelled by some distinctions of the environment that the asylum procedure operates in: Firstly, decision-making is neither purely bound by precedent nor by written law and the role of the Chamber, the Tribunal and the courts is to an extent both law-making and interpretative.[40] Secondly, since asylum as a field of law is also characterised in England by comparably weak academic attention, the role of decision-makers in interpreting acts and statutes is emphasised within this field of law.

Moreover, in addition to the interpretative character of decisions, their function as precedents is of undisputable importance for the nature of argumentation, as it places argumentation, clarity and thoroughness in the focus. Whereas all decisions may have effect as precedents in accordance with the traditional view of legal sources, the AIT in addition created a scheme of its own for internally binding precedents, which was transferred to the FTT in the latest reform. It may thus be decided that a matter is starred or that it is a country guideline determination.[41] Starred decisions are decisions that function as binding precedents in matters of procedure or regarding interpretation of certain issues of law. Country guideline decisions have the same function in relation to conditions in certain countries and risks for persons from that origin.[42] These determinations are treated with more scrutiny than others and

---

[40] There are statutes governing both the substantive issue of asylum procedure, and separate acts that deal with procedural issues in the Tribunal. However, the Chamber also follows precedents from higher courts regarding interpretation of written law, and also itself has a system for internally starred decision and specific country decisions that have binding effect as authoritative sources of law. Thomas (2003) 268–269.

[41] The initial rules stated that in order to be starred, a decision had to be taken by a panel of legally qualified vice-presidents of the AIT. The practice directions of the AIT stated that starred decisions are to be treated as "authoritative in respect of the matter to which the 'starring' relates, unless inconsistent with other authority that is binding on the Tribunal". Asylum and Immigration Tribunal Practice Directions, section 18, in the new Practice Directions for the Immigration and Asylum Chambers of the First Tier and Upper Tribunals section 12 spells out the importance of both starred and country guideline decisions. *Ali Haddad v Secretary of State for the Home Department* [2000] INLR 117 (IAT) and *Sepet and Bulbul v Secretary of State for the Home Department (UN High Commissioner for Refugees intervening)* [2001] Imm. A.R. 452 at 488. However, see also a critique of the system with country guideline cases presented by the Immigration Advisory Service in IAS, *Country Guidline cases: benign and practical?* 2005.

[42] Robert Thomas, *Administrative Justice and Asylum Appeals* (Cornwall 2011) 197–198 sees country guidance decisions as means for conform decision-making.

practice enables the tribunal to pinpoint and elaborate on specific issues at length in some decisions and then use these as references. Aside from the clear effect on argumentation in starred decisions, practice with internal precedents is also bound to influence reasoning in other decisions.[43]

Another typical characteristic of asylum procedures in general is that applicants usually attempt to stay within the procedure as long as possible. In English procedure, appellate levels beyond the Chamber are limited to errors of law, which for instance includes failure to assess all relevant aspects of the matter brought before the tribunal. Thus, in order to avoid appeals purely on the grounds that all relevant circumstances have not been taken into proper account or that the considerations are somehow lacking, the judges at first instance review tend to elaborate their decisions in detail and also include considerations and argumentation on rather peripheral matters. This also adds to the relative thoroughness of the reasoning in decisions on review.

3.2. *Adversarial Procedures*

English appellate asylum procedure is an adversarial justice procedure in contrast to most continental, inquisitorial asylum procedures. The implications of the adversarial nature are two-fold: On the one hand, adversarial procedures means increased emphasis on the independence and detachment of the Chamber from practical evidentiary work, as it itself is not involved with producing evidence or information.[44] On the other hand, the adversarial nature affects the position of the parties through making a clear two-party structure more identifiable in proceedings before the Chamber and through stressing the responsibilities of the parties towards the matter at hand. This has implications for the evidentiary structure of the procedure.[45]

---

[43] Robert Thomas, "Consistency in Asylum Adjudication: Country Guidance and the Asylum Process in the United Kingdom" (2008/4) *International Journal of Refugee Law*, 489–532.

[44] Section 51 of the Asylum and Immigration Tribunal (Procedure) Rules 2005 provides rules on presentation of evidence before the appellate body. These rules are also in force in relation to the FTT by virtue of Statutory Instrument 2010 No.21 Tribunals and Inquiries: The Transfer of Functions of the Asylum and Immigration Tribunal Order 2010, in force 15.2.2010. On distribution of tasks between the parties and the Tribunal see Ian A. Macdonald & Frances Webber, *Immigration Law and Practice in the United Kingdom* (London 2005) 776–781, which deals with the matter generally outside the Tribunal-setting.

[45] Thomas (2011), 83–87 studies the nature of tribunal justice in asylum matters and states that despite inquisitorial inclinations in other forms of tribunals, the asylum appellate procedure "has a strong preference toward the adversary process."

In relation to the parties particularly to the appellate asylum procedure, it can be questioned whether the uneven positions of strength between the parties in combination with the adversarial nature of the proceedings and the emphasis accordingly placed on the responsibility of the parties for the outcome of the procedure may lead to diminished possibilities for the Chamber to efficiently address the issues before it: The parties are responsible for bringing relevant facts and material to the attention of the decision-maker but often at the same time have different ambitions with these actions from the Chamber. Additionally, the parties rarely share ambitions and reasons for presenting certain information before the Chamber.[46] Thus, the inequality between the parties may mean that the view of the weaker party is given less attention in the evidence before the decision-maker, especially if the weakness is linked to the possibility to attain and present relevant facts, and that the entirety of the material before the decision-maker is unevenly concentrated on the ambitions and goals of the stronger party.

It must be noted that the adversarial nature of the procedure has given communication of information a highlighted position in the proceedings. As it is recognised within the procedure that the source of evidence provided is not objective but subjective, the possibility for the other party involved to comment on the evidence and if necessary to contest its subjectivity before the Chamber is seen as decisive.[47] Failure to meet the requirements on communication of evidence taints the decision with an error of law that can be used as a ground for reconsideration.

3.3. *The Parties to the Procedure*

The adversarial nature of the proceedings before the Chamber creates a rather clear cut two-party setting at the stage of first instance appeals.[48] On one side

---

[46] On the interests of the parties, Staffans (2006a).

[47] The ground rule on communication is included in the Asylum and Immigration Tribunal (Procedure Rules), section 51(7), which states that the Tribunal may not "take account of any evidence that has not been made available for all parties". The requirement for communication also requires the Tribunal to allow cross-examination of witnesses brought before it. The Asylum and Immigration Tribunal (Procedure) Rules are also in force in relation to the FTT by virtue of Statutory Instrument 2010 No.21 Tribunals and Inquiries: The Transfer of Functions of the Asylum and Immigration Tribunal Order 2010, in force 15.2.2010. See also Macdonald (*et al.*) (2005) 1267–1270.

[48] In the reconsideration stages of asylum procedure, the structure of the procedure is less clearly a two-party structure, as the object of the proceedings in the later stages is purely errors of law in previous decisions and not the matter as such.

stands the appellant, the asylum seeker, and on the other representatives of the first instance authority, the Directorate for Immigration and Asylum within the Home Office. Additionally, a representative of the UNHCR has the right to intervene in any matter.[49]

3.3.1. *The Home Office*
The Home Office is represented in the review procedure before the Chamber by a Presenting Officer. Presenting Officers appear regularly in asylum procedure and have vast experience in arguing immigration issues.

Despite representing an authority, it is not the task of the Presenting Officer to pursue any form of 'objective justice' in appellate asylum procedure but to advocate the view of the Home Office in the matter at hand.[50] Often this implies a defence of the decision made by the Home Office Department for Immigration and Asylum. However, if new circumstances or evidence are brought to the matter, the Home Office can also re-evaluate their view. It is also the task of the Home Office to present evidence before the Chamber in support of its view. In practice, presentation of evidence often implies that country of origin information provided by the Home Office research team is produced before the Chamber.

3.3.2. *The Appellant*
The appellant is the weaker party in appellate procedure and has the right to make use of the services of an interpreter and representative in the procedure.[51] The appellant is nevertheless also the most important source of information in the procedure and the possibilities for the judge to make accurate decisions largely depend on the possibilities of the appellant to provide the judge with relevant and accurate information. Hence the importance of the role of the representative of the appellant, who can

---

[49] Asylum and Immigration Tribunal (Procedure) Rules 2005, sections 2 and 49. The Asylum and Immigration Tribunal (Procedure) rules are also in force in relation to the FTT by virtue of Statutory Instrument 2010 No.21 Tribunals and Inquiries: The Transfer of Functions of the Asylum and Immigration Tribunal Order 2010, in force 15.2.2010.

[50] On the obligations of the Home Office towards asylum procedure *see Secreary of State for the Home Department v Abdi and Gawe* [1994] Imm AR 402, CA, affirmed as *Abdi v Secretary of State for the Home Department* [1996] 1All ER 641, [1996] 1 WLR 298 (HL).

[51] Section 49 A of the Asylum and Immigration Tribunal (Procedure) Rules 2005 gives the appellant the right of interpretation when giving evidence and in other circumstances as considered necessary by the Tribunal. These rules are also in force in relation to the FTT by virtue of Statutory Instrument 2010 No.21 Tribunals and Inquiries: The Transfer of Functions of the Asylum and Immigration Tribunal Order 2010, in force 15.2.2010.

constitute a link between the information that the appellant has and understanding what is needed and relevant for the judge to have.[52]

However, as most asylum seekers are not in a financial position to pay for legal representation, legal aid is a cornerstone for the quality of the procedure as a whole. Legal aid in English asylum procedure is granted according to the same norms as in other forms of judicial procedure and is thus subject to requirements of both means and merits.[53] Thus, only appellants of a particular financial situation are considered for legal aid and even if the financial requirements are met there is a requirement as to the merits of the case to be fulfilled.[54] This requirement stipulates legal aid to be granted only if the appeal has a fair possibility of success. Thus, many appellants are faced with proceedings before the Chamber without the possibility to have a legal representative funded by legal aid.

There are no requirements *per se* on the legal representative. However, if the legal representative is remunerated by public funding, either through legal aid or through a publicly funded organisation, the Legal Services Commission requires the representative to be accredited through the Immigration and Asylum Accreditation Scheme.[55] Through the Accreditation Scheme, knowledge of immigration law and asylum procedure is guaranteed and the quality of representation can be monitored. However, it is clearly a debatable question to what degree state-run training of representatives infringes on the independence of the procedure.

3.4. *Judicial Openness*

Lastly, it is in place to point out the very public nature of English appellate asylum procedure. The ground rule is that the review procedure before the Chamber is public.[56] Case management hearings and main hearings as well as

---

[52] See Louise Ellison, *The Adversarial Process and the Vulnerable Witness* (Oxford 2001) 19 ff on the role of testimony by persons with special "procedural disabilities" in the adversarial procedure. On the role of the representative in the asylum procedure see also Ida Staffans, "Biträdet i asylärenden – utsikter för en omorganisering" (2006b/3) *Defensor Legis*, 483–493.

[53] Thomas (2006) 680–682.

[54] The Legal Services Commission's Funding Code paras 13.3–13.5, state that legal representation according to the scheme will "be refused if the prospects of achieving a successful outcome for the client are: (i) unclear or borderline, save where the case has a significant wider public interest, is of overwhelming importance to the client or raises significant human rights issues; or (ii) poor."

[55] The Immigration and Asylum Accreditation Scheme is run by the Law Society and the Community Legal Service.

[56] The Asylum and Immigration Tribunal (Procedure) Rules, Section 54. The Asylum and Immigration Tribunal (Procedure) rules are also in force in relation to the FTT by virtue of Statutory Instrument 2010 No.21 Tribunals and Inquiries: The Transfer of Functions of the Asylum and Immigration Tribunal Order 2010, in force 15.2.2010.

hearings in the reconsideration stages of the procedure are in general open to the public. Restrictions on this can be invoked in the interests of public order or national security and if restrictions are necessary in order to protect the private life of a party or the interests of a minor.[57] Further, hearings can be closed to the public if it is considered that publicity may prejudice the interests of justice. Additionally, both public and parties are excluded from hearings when the Chamber considers whether documents brought before it are forged.[58]

Exceptions to the rule on open hearings are not interpreted by the Chamber in an expanding manner. Hearings are actually open to the public, lists of forthcoming hearings are regularly published in order to serve and invite the public and exceptions to the main rule are few.[59] However, it must be noted that most asylum cases that are closely linked to considerations of national security and the public interest are not heard at all before the First-Tier and Upper Tribunal but before the Special Immigration Appeals Commission (SIAC).[60] This gives the Chamber possibilities to work more openly.

Decisions made within appellate asylum procedure are, as a ground rule, public decisions. Under the AIT, a public database was opened which contained some of the written decisions of the tribunal. However, decisions are often written and published so as not to disclose the name or the identity of the applicant.

It is clear that the very public nature of the procedure has effects on judges, parties and the procedure itself. Openness implies greater awareness of decisions and may thus encourage judges to extra scrutiny in the procedure and when writing decisions. However, considering the nature of the theme of proof, openness may also imply that the appellant is modest in presenting his or her claim and evidence to support it. In relation to the procedure in a more general manner, the public nature of the proceedings may contribute to diminishing the aura of 'specialness' that often surrounds asylum procedures.

---

[57] *Ibid* at section 54 (2) to (4).
[58] Asylum and Immigration Tribunal (Procedure) Rules, Section 54 (2). The Asylum and Immigration Tribunal (Procedure) rules are also in force in relation to the FTT by virtue of Statutory Instrument 2010 No.21 Tribunals and Inquiries: The Transfer of Functions of the Asylum and Immigration Tribunal Order 2010, in force 15.2.2010.
[59] Daily court lists are available at http://www.tribunals.gov.uk/ImmigrationAsylum/ DailyCourtLists/dailyCourtLists.htm (visited 23.11.2011).
[60] The SIAC, created in 1997, has authority to hear appeals on decisions to deport a person or deprive a person of UK citizenship for reasons of national security or other grounds relating to the public interest. Hearings before the SIAC are as a ground rule also public. See The Special Immigration Appeals Commission Act 1997.

4. *Evidence in English Appellate Asylum Procedure*

The English asylum procedure operates in an environment distinct from as well the German as the Finnish asylum procedure. How does the English asylum procedure position the keys of comparison at the appellate level?

Evidence occupies a central position in English asylum procedure. Questions relating to evidentiary standards often bind together the traditional weight of procedural argumentation, reliance on questions of law and substantive issues in individual matters before the Chamber, hence their important position in argumentation in English asylum procedure. Both parties and the Chamber itself very often use evidentiary argumentation. The respect and 'seriousness' attached to evidentiary argumentation within the procedure is substantial.[61]

4.1. *Burden of Proof*

Allocation of the burden of proof in English appellate asylum procedure is quite clear both in theory and practice: The procedure as well in written law as in practice recognises the right to asylum as a service right and thus as a benefit to be awarded to the applicant.[62] The Rules of Procedure codifies the practice in relation to the burden of proof and states in section 53 explicitly that the burden of proof lies with the appellant.[63] The English administrative system hence recognises that the duty in procedures awarding applicants administrative benefits is for the person claiming these to show their eligibility, not for the state to show the opposite. In the review procedure of the First-Tier Tribunal, the applicant holds the burden of proof and the starting point of the procedure is that the decision under review was correct.[64]

---

[61] See for instance Ayan J. Stedman & Benjamin Hawkin, *A practical guide to presenting asylum and human rights claims* (UK 2003) 223, suggesting that "questions of evidence" is the first issue worth looking into when considering appealing an asylum decision.

[62] Good (2007) 242–243.

[63] The AIT rules of procedure included a specific section on distribution of the burden of proof, clearly stating that the burden lies with the appellant. Asylum and Immigration Tribunal (Procedure) Rules 2005, section 53. The Asylum and Immigration Tribunal (Procedure) Rules 2005 are also in force in relation to the FTT by virtue of Statutory Instrument 2010 No.21 Tribunals and Inquiries: The Transfer of Functions of the Asylum and Immigration Tribunal Order 2010, in force 15.2.2010.

[64] Macdonald *(et al.)* (2005) 687–688. See also *AA (Iran) -v- Secretary of State for the Home Department* [2006] EWCA Civ 1027, where the Court of Appeal elaborated on possible use of inverted burdens of proof on the applicant's side and *R v. Secretary of State for the Home Department, Ex parte Sivakumaran and Conjoined Appeals (UN High Commissioner for Refugees Intervening)*, [1988] AC 958, [1988] 1 All ER 193, [1988] 2 WLR 92, [1988] Imm AR 147, United Kingdom: House of Lords, 16 December 1987 which clearly spells out that it is for the appellant to establish a well-founded fear.

However, also the question regarding the contents of the burden of proof and its practical meaning must be raised. As we will see in the following chapters, investigative standards and the standard of proof define the parameters of what the applicant must do in order to 'win'. Thus, much of the practical content of the burden of proof is displayed through other theoretical tools. However, the burden of proof in its own right also shows some distinct features of relevance to the greater evidentiary picture:

English appellate asylum procedure is theoretically very strict in distributing procedural help to the asylum seeker. It is recognised both in literature and in practice that the situation of the asylum seeker requires some alteration of procedural standards in order for the pursuit of justice to be feasible.[65] However, instead of allowing the weaker situation of the applicant to influence decision-making in asylum procedure on a general level, the need is stressed for clear allocation of special solutions required through legislative action.

One of the evidentiary implications of strict distribution of procedural 'help' is the exclusion of procedural relief from the burden of proof and its clear inclusion within the standard of proof. In short, the applicant is not helped through any reduction of the content of the burden of proof itself. All procedural help relevant for the evidentiary field is concentrated and isolated to the standard of proof, which we will see is lowered to the benefit of the applicant.

Another feature of the burden of proof that is interesting in practice in English procedure relates to use of the benefit of the doubt. An integrated requirement of international refugee law accepted widely in national asylum procedures is that the applicant is granted the benefit of the doubt within the burden of proof. The implication of the benefit of the doubt is that oral evidence if credible is sufficient to fill the burden of proof from the applicant's side and is a response to lack of documentary evidence in asylum procedure.

Nevertheless, the benefit of the doubt in English appellate asylum procedure is given a rather complex and also contradictory position. On the one hand, the benefit of the doubt is recognised in the procedure as a requirement of international law. At the same time, it is accepted in the procedure that oral evidence, even if credible, is seldom enough to prove refugee status.[66] As solicitors themselves have noted, the practice during the 1980s and early 1990s of

---

[65] See *Karanakaran supra* at 34, in which Lord Justice Brooke concludes that the predictive element of determining refugee status requires "different techniques" to be employed in evidentiary assessment in asylum procedure. Also Robert Thomas, "Risk Legitimacy and Asylum Adjudication" (2007/1) *Northern Ireland Legal Quarterly*, 49–77 at 53 and Good (2007) 256.

[66] See Mark Henderson, *Best Practice Guide to Asylum and Human Rights Appeals* (ILPA Refugee Legal Group 2003) 157–158, where the author stresses the need for documentary evidence to support the oral witness for the appellant.

strengthening the oral testimony of the applicant with documentary evidence somewhat backfired, rendering oral testimony without supporting documentary evidence of very little value.[67] On the other hand, credibility is nevertheless one of the major issues debated in appellate level asylum procedures in England and the focus of a vast percentage of individual asylum procedures raised before the AIT during the past few years.[68]

4.2. Evidentiary Robustness

4.2.1. Robustness and Adversarial Justice

Through its adversarial nature, English appellate asylum procedure turns many presuppositions about robustness upside down. The adversarial nature implies that anything like the *Offizialmaxime* that gives the decision-maker powers over the material basis for the decision must be abandoned.[69] However, adversariality does not imply that striving towards material justice is completely abandoned or that the goal of investigations would be anything other than sufficient robustness.

English procedure clearly acknowledges that the goal of asylum procedure is to grant asylum to persons fulfilling the criteria for refugee status and to not grant asylum to persons who do not fall under these criteria.[70] The procedure also recognises that the exquisite evidentiary situation and perhaps foremost the position of the applicant requires the procedure to be amended so that the Chamber can reach the most accurate decisions possible. In written law the particular nature of the asylum environment and the importance of robustness has been taken into account in section 51 of the rules of procedure for the Chamber, where it is stated that "The Tribunal may allow oral, documentary or other evidence to be given of any fact which appears to be relevant to an appeal or an application for bail, even if that evidence would be

---

[67] Annex I.

[68] Thomas (2007) 51–61.

[69] Practice Directions for the Immigration and Asylum Chambers of the First Tier and Upper Tribunal, section 7, encourages the Chambers to accept a broad variety of evidence at all stages of the procedure. The Asylum and Immigration Tribunal (Procedure) Rules 2005 do not include any provision on the activity on the tribunal beyond what is stated regarding directions by the Tribunal. Section 45 of the Rules states that the Tribunal may give directions to the parties regarding the conduct of any appeal or application. The Asylum and Immigration Tribunal (Procedure) Rules2005 are in also force in relation to the FTT by virtue of Statutory Instrument 2010 No.21 Tribunals and Inquiries: The Transfer of Functions of the Asylum and Immigration Tribunal Order 2010, in force 15.2.2010.

[70] Karanakaran, *supra* at 34, where the reason for the lowered standards of proof applied was striving to correct decisions. Also Thomas (2007) 51–55.

inadmissible in a court of law." The appellate asylum procedure is, thus, in terms of evidence formally opened up to other material evidence than the for common law court procedures customary evidence.

However, and as stated earlier, English appellate asylum procedure is very strict in distributing procedural relief and has allocated the 'help' awarded to the applicant in evidentiary assessment of the standard of proof. Thus, the adversarial impact on the evidentiary basis for decisions is not *per se* affected by the position of the applicant or the need for special attention to evidentiary issues.

Let us look at how the powers in relation to the material basis for the decision are distributed between the stakeholders in the procedure:

The applicant holds the burden of proof and is thus obliged to prove his or her claims in order to succeed in the appeal. As we have seen, the benefit of the doubt in theory renders credible oral testimony sufficient to fulfil the burden of proof. In practice, however, the applicant is also required to present documentary evidence. Hence, what the applicant needs to do before the Chamber is to deliver oral testimony and supporting evidence, either oral or documentary.[71]

Firstly, there is the oral testimony of the appellant. A prerequisite for oral testimony by the applicant is clearly that the appellant is present at the hearing.[72] Further, as a result of the adversarial nature of the proceedings, it is for the appellant and his or her representative to decide whether to present oral testimony as evidence before the Chamber. In most cases the appellant's testimony is the backbone of the evidence presented by the appellant.

Oral evidence is given before the Chamber in a hearing generally following the rules of testimony in civil proceedings, including the right to cross-examination by the opposite party and the right for the decision-maker to pose questions.[73] During the oral hearing the applicant has the same right to an

---

[71] Henderson (2003) 146–175.

[72] The Asylum and Immigration Tribunal (Procedure) Rules 2005, section 19 require the Tribunal to hear an appeal in the absence of a party if the party has been called to the hearing correctly. The Asylum and Immigration Tribunal (Procedure) Rules 2005 are also in force in relation to the FTT by virtue of Statutory Instrument 2010 No.21 Tribunals and Inquiries: The Transfer of Functions of the Asylum and Immigration Tribunal Order 2010, in force 15.2.2010. Comparably, the Guidance Note on Unrepresented Appellants Who Do Not Understand English 12.8.2004, gives guidance on the proceedings when the appellant is present but not able to understand the procedure.

[73] However, The Asylum and Immigration Tribunal (Procedure) Rules 2005, section 51, allows the Tribunal to disembark from the evidentiary rules of civil procedure and to amend the hearing in order to suit asylum procedure better. The Asylum and Immigration Tribunal (Procedure) Rules 2005 are also in force in relation to the FTT by virtue of Statutory Instrument 2010 No.21 Tribunals and Inquiries: The Transfer of Functions of the Asylum and Immigration Tribunal Order 2010, in force 15.2.2010.

interpreter as in the rest of the procedure. The appellant may also decide not to present oral testimony but to rely on the written record of the oral testimony presented before the Home Office.

Aside from their own testimony, the appellant may also produce other oral evidence. Witness testimony is neither rare nor often presented and has received much attention both by academia and tribunals lately as the role of experts in various administrative justice procedures has been under debate.[74] Often, the witness is a country of origin expert, a medical expert or an expert representing some other branch. At times, though, the witness may be a family member, a fellow asylum seeker or someone else with a connection to the applicant. Hearing the witness is conducted according to civil procedure rules for oral evidence, with a main hearing, cross-examination and the possibility for the judge to ask questions.

It must be noted that the role of oral testimony in English appellate asylum procedure is important and that the use of oral evidence aside from testimony by applicants is also quite common. One explanation for the important role of oral testimony is certainly found in the overwhelmingly oral character of asylum proceedings in general – all matters in the review-stages of asylum procedure are indeed heard in oral proceedings.[75] The weight placed on oral statements also means that the routine and the parameters for conducting oral hearings are strong and reliable. It is also rather clear that the role and position of oral hearings also affect evidentiary assessment, as judges in asylum procedure have a source of information in oral hearings that differs in many respects from judging solely on the basis of written material.[76]

Aside from oral testimony, either presented before the Chamber or as retrieved from the Home Office hearings, and possible other oral evidence, the applicant also presents documentary evidence in support of his or her claims. The nature of the adversarial procedure means that the appellant cannot rely on any knowledge that the decision-maker may already have but needs to present all relevant documentary evidence both in relation to general considerations about the state of affairs in the home country and in relation to the specificities of the individual appeal. Thus, everything from country

---

[74] See Anthony Good, "'Undoubtedly an Expert?' Anthropologists in UK Asylum Courts" (2004a) *Journal of the Royal Anthropological Institute*, 113–133; same: "Expert evidence in Asylum and Human Rights Appeals: an Expert's View" (2004b) *International Journal of Refugee Law*, 358–380; Henderson (2003) 192–269; Thomas (2007) 64–70.

[75] Asylum and Immigration Tribunal (Procedure) Rules 2005, section 15 spells out the ground rules of oral hearings in review procedures and the exceptions to this.

[76] On the quality of information extracted from oral hearings see Ellison (2001) 19 ff.

reports by various organisations, newspaper articles, personal documents and certificates is presented. Additionally, the applicant must present all authoritative decisions from the Chamber, former tribunals or other, higher, courts or international tribunals or courts that he or she wishes to rely on.[77]

In all, the responsibility of the applicant towards robustness of investigations is significant. As the Chamber cannot contribute to the investigations and as the evidentiary input of the Home Office is limited, as we will soon see, the appellant holds the key to the material standards of the investigation. Additionally, as the appellant also has the right to decide which claims to bring before the Chamber, the appellant also has the power to decide on the circumstances that are of relevance to the proceedings.

How then is the responsibility for robustness met by the applicant? As it is in the interest of the applicant to meet the burden of proof, a natural incentive exists for the appellant to present solid material in the proceedings. This incentive is nevertheless restricted to issues that the appellant deems important and significant. However, it is eminent that the role of the representative of the appellant is also highlighted, as in most instances it is impossible to require that the appellant should both understand the rules of evidence according to which the appellate asylum procedure functions and additionally to be able personally to find resources enough to produce the evidence required to fulfil the burden of proof.[78]

In practice, prior to any oral hearing the appellant is expected to file a bundle with all documentary evidence and lists of oral evidence to be presented. In the event that a case management hearing is conducted, the appellant here also has the possibility to give the Chamber and the HO notice of material to be presented.[79] The role of trial bundles is central and even if material can be added to the evidence the bundle is still treated as the main source of information both by the parties themselves and by judges.[80]

---

[77] For comments on presentation of documentary evidence see Henderson (2003) 157–172 and 183–190.

[78] On representation in asylum appeals see Macdonald (*et al.*) (2005) 1258–1259. See also the answers by Mr Justice Hodge in oral evidence before the House of Commons Home Affairs Committee's inquiry, *Immigration Control* (2005–2006 HC 775-iv) January 24, 2006 (questions 373 and 374), in which Mr Justice Hodge acknowledges the importance of representation in asylum procedure.

[79] On the purpose of the case management review see Symes (*et al*) 2010, 896–897.

[80] Asylum and Immigration Tribunal (Procedure) Rules 2005, section 45 (e) concerns the right of the Chambers to require bundles to be served in due order. The Asylum and Immigration Tribunal (Procedure) Rules 2005 are also in force in relation to the FTT by virtue of Statutory Instrument 2010 No.21 Tribunals and Inquiries: The Transfer of Functions of the Asylum and Immigration Tribunal Order 2010, in force 15.2.2010.

Opposite the appellant stands the Home Office. The HO representative has as we have seen no particular obligations *per se* towards robustness stemming from its position as representative of an administrative authority.[81] Thus, and as a result of the procedure in fact being a product of diverging opinions between the parties, the role of the HO in appellate proceedings is often limited to revealing the reasons for the view of the HO and to relate this view to the evidence presented by the appellant.

The HO has the same right as the appellant to call oral witnesses. At times, this also occurs and the HO presents evidence before the court from various experts. However, it is not as usual for the HO to present oral evidence as it is for the appellant.

Often, the evidentiary presentation of the HO is limited to country of origin information. The HO has their own unit for production of such information and produces extensive country reports from the countries from which most asylum seekers in England originate.[82] In relation to other countries of origin, shorter reports are produced. Criticism has been directed towards country reports by solicitors and NGOs stating that the reports lack objectivity and integrity. As a response to this criticism the HO established a body of independent experts whose task is to guarantee correctness and objectivity in reports. The result has been that the quality of the reports is generally seen as improved.[83]

The HO may also want to present documentary evidence other than country reports. Specific information relating to the individual matter, authoritative decisions from other judicial bodies or from the AIT or other tribunals may be included. In the same manner as the appellant, the HO is also required to present their evidence in a bundle that is distributed to all agents in the procedure before the main hearing.

Lastly, there is the Chamber itself, represented in the individual case by the judge or judges. As we have seen, the adversarial nature of the proceedings forbids the Chamber from making use of information that does not stem from evidence presented by the parties.[84] Additionally, the ground rule

---

[81] See *Abdi and another v. Secretary of State for the Home Department and another*, [1996] 1 All ER 641, [1996] 1 WLR 298, [1996] Imm AR 288, United Kingdom: House of Lords, 15 February 1996. However, quite clearly the Home Office has obligations towards the robustness and the material correctness of the material that they present.

[82] Henderson (2003) 175–181.

[83] For both criticism and an overview of improvements made see Immigration Advisory Service: *Submission to APCI: An Analysis of Home Office Country Reports* (2005).

[84] For a concentrated outline of evidentiary rules and practises in adversarial procedures as opposed to inquisitorial procedures see Michael K. Block, Jeffrey S. Parker, Olga Vyborna & Libor Dusek, "An Experimental Comparison of Adversarial versus Inquisitorial Procedural Regimes" (2000/1) *American Law and Economics Review*, 170–173.

according to the adversarial tradition is that the Chamber must preserve a passive role in relation to acquisition of evidence in the procedure, letting the parties present the evidence they wish, as they wish. Thus, the Chamber must be careful in requesting or compelling the parties to present or produce certain evidence, even if it indeed has the right also to exercise these powers.[85]

A contested issue in relation to appellate procedures is use of judicial (tacit) knowledge as a basis for decision-making or for procedural decisions.[86] The outset, also in relation to tacit knowledge, is that the Chamber cannot make use of any information unless presented by the parties. However, at times this requirement seems to be bent to a rule stating that the Chamber can use any information it has, as long as it is communicated with the parties.[87] In these circumstances the judge may exercise activity through 'ventilating' views or information with the parties in order to give them the possibility to comment on and if necessary contest the information. Thus, also tacit knowledge can be added to the quantitative evidentiary base.

4.2.2. *Quantitative Robustness*

We may recall that the requirement for quantitative robustness implies that sufficient information must be presented about enough circumstances – that is, all circumstances relevant to the matter before the court. The starting point in any evaluation of how this requirement is met in English appellate asylum procedure must also take its starting point in the procedural rules that bind

---

[85] The Asylum and Immigration Tribunal (Procedure) Rules 2005, section 51(2) states that the Tribunal cannot compel a party to present evidence that he or she could not be compelled to present in a civil procedure. The Asylum and Immigration Tribunal (Procedure) Rules 2005 are also in force in relation to the FTT by virtue of Statutory Instrument 2010 No.21 Tribunals and Inquiries: The Transfer of Functions of the Asylum and Immigration Tribunal Order 2010, in force 15.2.2010. See also Symes (*et al*) 2010, 903 ff and 918 ff. for an overview of typical directions given by the Chamber and comments on the right for the judge to pose question to parties and cross-examination.

[86] On tacit knowledge in asylum procedures see Hendrik Wagenaar, " 'Knowing' the Rules: Administrative Work as Practice" (2004/6) *Public Administration Review*, 643–656. In Symes (*et al.*) (2010), 919, the author states that "The greatest care should be taken in relying on personal knowledge".

[87] The Asylum and Immigration Tribunal (Procedure) Rules 2005, section 51(7) compels the Chambers to communicate all evidence in the procedure, also tacit knowledge. The Asylum and Immigration Tribunal (Procedure) Rules 2005 are also in force in relation to the FTT by virtue of Statutory Instrument 2010 No.21 Tribunals and Inquiries: The Transfer of Functions of the Asylum and Immigration Tribunal Order 2010, in force 15.2.2010.

the tribunal to "allow oral, documentary or other evidence to be given of any fact which appears to be relevant to an appeal", implying that the scope of evidence must be broad.[88]

In English appellate asylum procedure both the claims that direct the procedure and most of the evidence are presented by the appellant. Thus, the robustness of the material basis for the decision to a large extent depends on the appellant and their possibilities and abilities to present evidence. However, as the burden of proof – in fact and as applied in English appellate asylum procedure – requires the appellant to present rather extensive evidence of the claims in the appeal, the incentive is also strong for the appellant to meet the criteria on robustness. Also, the two-party setting of the procedure, with the role of the HO as clearly in opposition to the appellant with a more or less clear role as contester of evidence presented by the appellant, is bound to increase incentives for both parties to produce solid evidence. However, if the traditional passive nature of the decision-maker is taken as the absolute norm, some doubt still lies with possibilities to pay evidentiary attention to issues of objective relevance to the matter before the Chamber that either by coincidence or as a result of evidentiary tactics fall outside the scope of what the appellant presents as relevant before the tribunal. In fact, robustness is indeed highly dependent on a working opposition by the HO to the claims, facts and information presented by the applicant.

4.2.3. *Qualitative Robustness*
The requirement for qualitative robustness implies a requirement for objectivity and quality in the information provided. Qualitative robustness is not a complement to the requirement for quantity but the two work together in parallel. One can also refer the criteria on communication to the requirements for qualitative robustness since communication emphasises the quality, good or bad, of any form of information.

Seen from the position of the Chamber and due to the adversarial nature of the procedure, clear difficulties arise in controlling qualitative standards of the material basis for a decision. As few possibilities occur to control the quality of the evidence as presented by the parties, the quality check must be made post presentation. Additionally, it is quite clear that one cannot expect the parties to be objective when presenting evidence in support of their claims, so that

---

[88] The Asylum and Immigration Tribunal (Procedure) Rules 2005, section 51 (1). The Asylum and Immigration Tribunal (Procedure) Rules 2005 are also in force in relation to the FTT by virtue of Statutory Instrument 2010 No.21 Tribunals and Inquiries: The Transfer of Functions of the Asylum and Immigration Tribunal Order 2010, in force 15.2.2010.

the Chamber has to face a material basis that is subjective both in relation to individual pieces of evidence and regarding the system, scheme and highlights of evidentiary material. This is also something that English appellate asylum procedure strives to correct post presentation.

It is clear that the two-party procedure and the clearly opposite roles of the parties in relation to the quality of the material basis for the decision is beneficial. As two subjective evidentiary entities meet, the Chamber may be able to draw some objective conclusions. On the other hand, three characteristics of English procedure are all bound to increase the quality of the material base: the role of credibility, the role of hearing and communication, and the position of expert evidence in the procedure.

Firstly, the central role that credibility plays in the procedure is clearly a counter-measure to the overweight on evidence subjectively produced by the appellant.[89] Through contesting the subjective nature of evidence in its most extreme form, its credibility, the quality of evidence is exhibited.

Secondly, strict rules on communication lead to all evidence becoming 'enhanced' through being contested.[90] This may be both negative and positive for the evidentiary value of each piece of evidence but is still bound to raise the awareness of the judge about the nature of the information provided and thus about the claims presented.

Finally, the role of expert evidence is also a clear reaction against the inability of the Chamber to acquire such evidence itself and a demonstration of objectivity by the parties. Expert evidence presented by the parties forms an important part of the basis for decisions either directly in the matter before the tribunal or indirectly through references to prior decisions. However, one must remember that the choice of presenting expert evidence and the theme for these testimonies are always subjectively made by the parties.

---

[89] On the role of credibility in English asylum procedure see Macdonald (*et al.*) (2005) 1270–1276; Thomas (2007) 56–61; Henderson (2003) 3–7 and 339–351, for comment on credibility in oral testimony. See also Catriona Jarvis, "The Judge as Juror Re-visited" (winter 2003) *Immigration Law Digest*, presenting a study of how IAT judges assess credibility especially in the light of asylum adjudication. Also *SY (Kurd – No Political Profile) Syria v. Secretary of State for the Home Department*, CG [2005] UKIAT 00039, where credibility assessment of oral evidence is thoroughly examined.

[90] The Asylum and Immigration Tribunal (Procedure) Rules 2005, section 51(7) forbids the tribunal to take account of any evidence that is not communicated to all parties. The Asylum and Immigration Tribunal (Procedure) Rules 2005 are also in force in relation to the FTT by virtue of Statutory Instrument 2010 No.21 Tribunals and Inquiries: The Transfer of Functions of the Asylum and Immigration Tribunal Order 2010, in force 15.2.2010.

4.3. *Standard of Proof*

The standard of proof is a central element to English appellate asylum procedure. On the one hand, the standard of proof is the central object of measures designed to even out differences in power and to remedy the evidentiary difficulties evident in review procedure. Hence, much attention has been paid to issues relating to the standard of proof when forming and analysing the procedure for refugee status determination.[91] On the other hand, the standard of proof is also much used and often referred to in the practice of the AIT, the First-Tier Tribunal and other immigration courts. The standard of proof in appellate asylum procedure is given vast practical significance both in relation to its possibilities to remedy the difficulties in the procedure and as an interesting and procedurally challenging purely evidentiary issue, and argumentation is common both as to the practical meaning of the standard in the individual case and as to the theoretical understanding of this by judges.

English asylum courts have also repeatedly referred to and elaborated on the applicable level of the standard of proof in appellate asylum procedure, quite in line with the central role of the standard of proof in the procedure.[92] In doing so, the courts have carefully kept asylum procedure separate from other forms of immigration procedures and emphasised that the special nature of the procedure calls for special attention.

As early as 1988 the House of Lords in *Sivakumaran*, referring to elaborations made in immigration matters in the 1970s, stated that the applicable standard of proof in asylum procedure is that of a *reasonable degree of likelihood* or real risk.[93] In the 2000 decision in *Karakanakaran*, the Court of Appeal reaffirmed this and elaborated at length on how the standard can be met.[94] In *Karanakaran*, the court did not solely consider the right standard of proof in

---

[91] For comments on the standard of proof in English asylum procedure see Macdonald (*et al.*) (2005) 1283–1287; Dallal Stevens, *UK Asylum Law and Policy: Historical and Contemporary Perspectives* (London 2003) 325–327 and Symes (*et al.*) (2010) 31 ff.

[92] Aside from authoritative decisions of higher courts, there are also starred decisions regarding standard of proof. See *Ahmed v. Secretary of State for the Home Department* [2002] UKIAT 00439, 19.2.2002.

[93] *Sivakumaran, supra* at 64 and *Reg. v. Governor of Pentonville Prison, Ex parte Fernandez* [1971] 1 W.L.R 987. The case of *Sivakumaran* initially concerned six Sri Lanka Tamils who applied for asylum in the UK, and in respect of whose appeal the Secretary of State considered the meaning of "well-founded fear".

[94] *Karanakaran supra* at 34. The case concerned Mr Karanakaran, a citizen of Sri Lanka, who had experienced problems as he did not want to be recruited to the Tamil Tiger movement. In the decision, the reasoning concerned the probability of continued problems if he returned and related evidentiary questions.

relation to the theme of proof in general but also considered the applicable standard in relation to historical facts and future events separately. Further, the court in *Karanakaran* elaborated extensively on correct methods of evidentiary assessment. Then in *Kajac* in 2001 the IAT held that the same standard that applies to asylum claims also applies to claims under Article 3 ECHR and that this standard may be referred to as a requirement of *real risk*.[95]

As apparent from these decisions, the theoretically applicable standard in English asylum procedure is a standard of reasonable likelihood or real risk, both expressions implying the same standard. This level refers to a standard clearly lower than both the criminal standard of proof and the civil standard of a balance of probabilities. Statistically speaking, standards may be placed at a level around 20–30 % certainty.

Theoretically the level and application of the standard of proof is thus fairly clear in English appellate asylum procedure. Even if there is no written law on the matter, authoritative decisions clearly establish the threshold. However, the standard becomes somewhat less clear when trying to establish the practical implications of the theoretical standard of reasonable likelihood. Thus, even if the applicable standard is clear and its application on paper coherent in line with authoritative decisions, it is also clear that all decision-makers interpret the meaning of semantically or statistically established standards subjectively and intuitively. In practice, 'reasonable' and 'likely' may simply mean different things to different people.

Some guidance in interpreting these expressions appears from case law. The House of Lords in *Sivakumaran* stated firstly that the test for reasonable likelihood refers to the need for objective support for an applicant's subjective fear.[96] Also, Lord Keith of Kinkel elaborated at length on the meaning of reasonable likelihood and referred to semantics such as "reasonable chance", "substantial grounds for thinking" and "a serious possibility".[97] Additionally, Lord Keith made apparent that the standard is lower than a balance of probabilities.[98] In *Karanakaran* it was emphasised that the test of the standard is a pragmatic test requiring common sense and sensible evaluation, rather than purely theoretical examination.[99]

---

[95] *Kajac v Secretary of State for the Home Department* [2001] UKIAT 00018, 19.7.2001. The approach was upheld by the Court of Appeal in *Klodiana Kacaj v. Secretary of State for the Home Department*, [2002] EWCA Civ 314, United Kingdom: Court of Appeal (England and Wales), 14 March 2002, reviewing *Kacaj* [2000] UKIAT 23044, in which the IAT took a position on the relationship between evidentiary standards in asylum matters versus other protection matters.

[96] *Supra* at 617 at 6.

[97] *Supra* at 617 at 10–13.

[98] *Ibid.*

[99] Lord Justice Sedley in *Karanakaran*, *supra* at 34, paras 15–16.

The most practical hints as to the meaning of the standard of proof come from persons involved in asylum procedure. The level of the threshold has been described by practitioners as a level met by "plausible oral testimonies with supporting sensible objective evidence".[100] This formulation also places great weight on pragmatic understanding and a 'common sense' approach to the applicable standard of proof. However, it is clear from commentators on English appellate asylum procedure that despite the coherent semantic application of the standard of proof, there are indeed differences in the pragmatic approach towards and intuitive understanding of the threshold.[101] Factors that may affect personal understanding and estimation of what in practice constitutes a "reasonable likelihood" are often linked to the background and experiences of the evaluator. Nevertheless, the threshold of a "reasonable likelihood" must be seen as the semantic expression of a commonly shared understanding of the standard of proof.

4.4. *Methods of Evidentiary Assessment*

Methods of evidentiary assessment encompass the models and strategies used both when assessing the evidence bit by bit and when evaluating the standard of the collected evidence in its entirety. Methods for evidentiary assessment are of help in the intellectual process of establishing the value and significance of information and knowledge and provide decision-makers with a map, an outline or a check-list for assessing their knowledge of circumstances relevant to the matter before them.

In reference to practical frames for use of these methods, we have established that the material before the decision-maker in English appellate asylum procedure is presented by the parties and that the decision-maker has little power over the material. Simultaneously, the decision-maker in evidentiary assessment is also restricted strictly to the evidence presented by and communicated to the parties. As English procedure cannot guarantee complete robustness of the evidentiary base, it is theoretically important that the method of evidentiary assessment used takes this weakness of the procedure into account.

On a general note it can further be established that the central position of evidence generally in English appellate asylum procedure implies that evidentiary assessment is given comparably considerable attention in the procedure.

---

[100] See Annex I.
[101] See also Dorothy K. Kagehiro & W. Clark Stanton, "Legal vs. Quantified Definitions of Standards of Proof" (1985/2) *Law and Human Behavior*, 159–178 in which the authors confront legal unquantified concepts in the standard of proof debate with quantifiable measures.

Thus, English procedure includes elaborate case law on the issue of how and why judges should assess the evidence before them.[102] Further, evidentiary assessment and correctly undertaking the assessment constitute questions of law. Therefore, errors in this respect may render a determination legally faulty, thus leading to procedures of reconsideration. Hence, aside from the attention generally given evidence in the procedure, a procedural incentive also exists for care in evidentiary assessment by the Chamber.

The most central case to evidentiary assessment is *Karanakaran*.[103] In this determination the Court of Appeal firstly acknowledged the importance of thorough evidentiary assessment, emphasising the need for both individual assessment of the pieces of evidence brought before the court and a subsequent gathered and unified assessment of all the evidence put together. The decision emphasised the importance of understanding elements of information both separately and together in order to be able to correctly assess their value and significance. It also stressed the need for awareness of the predictive element in refugee status determination when choosing a method of assessment and Lord Justice Brooke pondered long on the implications of the predictive element for assessing individual facts.[104] It was questioned whether the predictive element in fact means that evidentiary assessment in asylum matters is a two-stage operation, where establishing the historical facts and predictive risk assessment must be assessed separately and using separate standards of proof to establish reliability of information. Lord Brooke's outcome, still standing, was that the nature of refugee status determination requires a deliberate one-step approach and a holistic view of the evidence. Thus, both historical facts and future risk should be assessed according to the same standard of proof at the level of "reasonable likelihood" and assessment of the theme of proof must be made in relation to all evidence presented.

However, the emphasis on a one stage procedure and a holistic approach towards the evidence does not decrease the need for separate assessment firstly of the separate sections of evidence and secondly of the evidence in its entirety. In *Karanakaran* a model for individual assessment was presented:

According to Lord Brooke, referring to the determination in *Kaja*[105], evidence before the decision-maker should be collected under four headings: 1) evidence that the judge is certain about; 2) evidence that the judge thinks is probably true; 3) evidence which the judge considers to some degree credible,

---

[102] See Sivakumaran, *supra* at 64; Karanakaran, *supra* at 34 and *IN v Secretary of State for the Home Department* [2005] UKIAT 00106, 24.5.2005.

[103] *Supra* at 34.

[104] Lord Justice Brooke in *Karanakaran*, *supra* at 34 at 8 ff.

[105] *Kaja v Secretary of State for the Home Department* [1995] Imm AR 1.

even if the judge would not say that the evidence is probably true, and; 4) evidence which the judge does not consider credible. As a result of the low standard of proof both in relation to historical facts and future risk, all evidence from categories 1–3 should be included in evidentiary assessment.[106]

After categorising the available information, the interrelation between the evidence from categories 1–3 is examined. Ultimately, all evidence from these categories is assessed together, forming a unified standard of proof in the individual matter.[107]

The model presented by Lord Brooke does not *per se* present the court with the tools to decide on the value of the information before it. Nevertheless, the method gives evidentiary assessment a comprehensive structure and enables the decision-maker to encounter the information in an orderly manner.[108] Also, the availability of a key to assessment enables outsiders to understand and analyse evidentiary assessment rather thoroughly. This in turn enables argumentation about evidentiary assessment. Hence, it is not unusual for the appellate tribunal also to review evidentiary assessment and the tribunal is inherently elaborate on the issue in its own determinations.

However, in *MT, RB, U v. Secretary of State for the Home Department* from 2007, the Court of Appeal also held that in applying the *Karanakaran* categorisation common sense must be used. The court stated "It will be proper to exclude from consideration those matters which it can safely discard because it has no real doubt that they did not occur. The decision-maker should also take account of the absence of satisfactory information relating to matters of importance."[109]

Argumentation concerning evidentiary assessment may for instance concern failure to include all evidence either in the individual assessment or in the holistic assessment of all available information. Another issue that is sometimes brought up concerns judicial bias and prejudice towards the evidence in the assessment.[110]

---

[106] *Karanakaran, supra* at 34 at 10. The approach was upheld despite being contested in *MT (Algeria), RB (Algeria), U (Algeria) v. Secretary of State for the Home Department*, [2007] EWCA Civ 808, United Kingdom: Court of Appeal (England and Wales), 30 July 2007.

[107] *Karanakaran, supra* at 34 at 10–11.

[108] See for instance *IN, supra* at 102.

[109] *MT (Algeria), RB (Algeria), U (Algeria), supra* at 106, para 162.

[110] See for instance *Detamu v Secretary of State for the Home Department* [2006] EWCA Civ 604 in which the Court of Appeal took a stand on judicial bias in the assessment of expert evidence presented by the appellant.

An intriguing question in relation to the model presented internally within English appellate asylum procedure relates to choice of method of assessing the value of the evidence. It is quite clear that the model required by Lord Brooke invites the judge to calculate the reliability of individual pieces of evidence using measurements of probability. Thus, at least an element refers to assessment methods relying on calculations of probability. However, whereas mathematical and statistical references are made at times, the main focus in English procedure seems to be on a semantic and pragmatic understanding of probability as a measurement of the 'reasonability' of events.

Further, the emphasis on a comparably low standard of proof and a low requirement for probability in evidentiary assessment, and the argumentation surrounding both the existence and the implementation of these elements, hint at evidentiary assessment encompassing considerations on efficiency, acquisition of evidence and consequences. Thus, the judge is at least aware of these issues when assessing the information. In other words, the need for a pragmatic approach to evidentiary assessment keeping in mind the need for efficient implementation of the legislator's will, possible lack of robustness in the evidentiary background and the consequences of a wrong decision is highlighted in English appellate asylum procedure in order to overcome inevitable gaps in the procedure.

However, most striking in evidentiary assessment as carried out in appellate asylum procedure is the thoroughness with which assessment is undertaken. Judges seem to be just as at home in abstract argumentation on methods and probabilities as in very practical argumentation around credibility, implications of oral testimony and the interrelation between different and diverging information.[111]

Lastly, it must be noted that evidentiary assessment closely ties all evidentiary elements together. Doctrine on the standard of proof as applicable in general to appellate asylum procedure is transferred to a micro-level and used as support when assessing individual fragments of information. Further, a good indicator of the depths of evidentiary argumentation and the interrelation of evidentiary elements as characteristic of English procedure is the elaboration in case law on the implications of a shifted burden of proof on the required standards of proof in relation to *single* pieces of information in assessment, prior to their classification according to Lord Brooke.[112]

---

[111] See *Sivakumaran, supra* at 64; *Karanakaran, supra* at 34, and as an example from within the AIT *IN, supra* at 102.

[112] *AA (Iran), supra* at 64, paras 22 ff.

5. *Conclusions*

English appellate asylum procedure offers a framework for evidentiary solutions based on the adversarial tradition. Partly as a result of this and partly as a result of the development of procedure, evidentiary practices and solutions form a central and deeply integrated part of RSD in general and appellate procedure in particular. Evidentiary issues are to a certain degree the backbone of the procedure in relation both to claims and procedural tactics and to assessment of claims and the decision.

The integrated nature of evidentiary issues in English appellate asylum procedure implies that evidentiary concerns are given an influential position in the procedure. Concerns regarding evidence and evidentiary standards constitute an innate part of the procedure in general, to the level that evidentiary assessment can be described as less systematic and more inclusive and intrinsic in its nature. Evidentiary issues are not assessed or seen in isolation at any time in the procedure but evidentiary concerns are raised throughout the assessment. This in turn ties the different evidentiary standards and concepts tightly together so that in English appellate asylum procedure they form a close cluster of tools for grasping realities.

Chapter VIII

Comparison of Evidentiary Standards

1. *Introduction*

Previous chapters outlined a structure in the European context for evidentiary assessment in national appellate asylum procedures as well as the realities of three national procedures, with four particular elements of evidentiary assessment in focus. In this chapter the findings in national procedures are studied comparatively. Further, the chapter will explore the signs of influences from the international and European in the national procedures as well as the influences from national legal systems on the solutions in other legal systems.

2. *Burden of Proof*

The burden of proof is a basic element of asylum procedures, in relation to which basic standpoints are taken. The burden of proof determines the outset for the procedure, implying either an obligation for the state to show that *non-refoulement* is not violated, or an obligation for the individual to show eligibility for benefits. Further, the burden of proof may be amended and construed in the particular national environment to allow for procedural help or robustness.

The pragmatic placing of the burden of proof in the national appellate asylum procedures studied is not surprising. In all the procedures included in the study, the formal burden of proof is placed with the appellant. Thus, the starting point for these procedures is that the appellant is not a refugee and that any prior, negative decision that is now appealed, is correct. Only if this assumption is overthrown will the appeal be successful. It is the appellant that suffers the negative consequences of the procedure not being able to prove the theme of proof up to a sufficient standard of proof.[1]

---

[1] Chapter IV 3. above deals with burden of proof as a theoretical element of the evidentiary field.

Placing the formal burden of proof with the appellant is in conformity with in both international and European law, even if these legal systems also leave the door open for other solutions. All procedures studied view asylum procedure as a procedure in which the individual is granted a benefit from the state in the first instance. Disregarding that the independence, institutional character and level of attachment to other actors of society of the appellate body may vary, the question is still about granting a benefit: Through the appeal, the appellant claims to fulfil legally predetermined criteria for a benefit, in this instance asylum. Clearly placing the formal burden of proof with the appellant also has support in the logic of the procedural setting of the national procedures. As the appellant is the initiator of the procedure, it is natural that the appellant would also carry the formal burden of proof in the procedure.

However, interpretation of the contents of the burden of proof, aside from the abstract notion of suffering negative consequences, varies between the national procedures studied. It is clear that the notion of material burden of proof is not used either abstractly or concretely in all procedures. Rather, the elements here interpreted as parts of this material burden of proof are in many instances connected with other duties and burdens in appellate asylum procedure.[2]

Finnish appellate asylum procedure recognises placement of the burden of proof with the appellant. When studying the implications of this burden and its contents, it becomes evident that relatively much weight is placed with the grounds for the claims presented. The grounds and claims, regardless of any evidence presented in their support, are to an extent disconnected from the procedural framework. For discharging the burden of proof, the appellate court namely requires that correct and sufficient grounds for claims are presented. However, there is no direct requirement either in practice or in legislation for presentation of evidence in general, or certain forms thereof, in order for the burden of proof to be discharged. Whereas the connection between presenting evidence and the burden of proof in Finnish appellate asylum procedure is rather weak due to the important role of the court's investigatory responsibility, in contrast the connection between claims and burden of proof is thus strong. This is also evident from the minor role played by the oral hearing in Finnish appellate asylum procedure.[3]

---

[2] An example of such a relationship is that between the requirements of the QD Art 4 (3), which provides a list of elements to be taken into account in any asylum procedure, and the facultative formal burden of proof as indicated in Art 4(1).

[3] Oral hearings in Finland are not frequent in any form of administrative justice, which may indicate that the strong link between the claims, the burden of proof and the role of the courts' investigatory powers are trademarks not only of asylum procedure, but of administrative judicial procedures more generally. See Mäenpää (2007 a) 423, who concludes that out of 23 000 matters handled by the administrative courts in 2006 oral hearings were arranged in 477 cases.

While German appellate asylum procedure also recognises that the applicant suffers negative consequences if the theme of proof is not proven, this solution has by no means been self-evident in this particular procedure. The fundamental rights character of the right to asylum combined with an institutionalised acceptance of formally shifted burdens of proof indicates that the position of the formal burden of proof as an obligation of the appellant is rather weak. Thus, German appellate asylum procedure seemingly awards the applicant 'procedural assistance' through particular features of the burden of proof.

Again, the material burden of proof in German procedure emphasises the link between production of evidence, especially oral evidence, and the burden of proof. Here, the claims or the grounds presented are not themselves seen as crucial, as the evidence produced constitutes the association between the appellant and the procedure.

Lastly in terms of the formal burden of proof, English appellate asylum procedure is sceptical towards any attempt to shift the burden of proof even slightly away from the appellant. As English procedure allocates 'procedural help' awarded the appellant to the assessment stage where the standard of proof is determined, the burden of proof is rigidly attached to the appellant. Clearly, the adversarial environment also impacts on the contents of the burden of proof, as production of evidence is more clearly allocated to the parties to the procedure. However, the strong position of the formal burden of proof also influences understanding of the appellant's possibilities to discharge this burden as practice shows that an obligation to present evidence, aside from oral evidence presented at hearings, is connected to the burden of proof. Further, a connection between claims and the evidence can be established, as the obligation of the appellant to present grounds for claims also plays a distinct procedural role in English appellate asylum procedure.

We have seen that the QD includes a list of elements in Article 4 (2) that Member States may require the applicant to present.[4] This list may, according to the logic of this study, be interpreted as presenting elements of the material burden of proof and as an indicator of the duty to present evidence for the

---

[4] QD Art 4 (2) refers to elements such as "the applicant's statements and all documentation at the applicant's disposal regarding the applicant's age, background, including that of relevant relatives, identity, nationality(ies), country(ies) and place(s) of previous residence, previous asylum applications, travel routes, identity and travel documents and the reasons for applying for international protection".

appellant.[5] Nevertheless, the content of this list is not directly reflected in the practice of any of the national appellate asylum procedures studied here. Rather, these elements are, as we will see, in the civil law countries included connected to the requirements of robustness of standards and responsibility for fact-finding. In English procedure, it is unclear whether the QD's list is reflected at all in appellate asylum procedure: Observed hearings indeed included questions regarding further information in line with the list of elements presented by the QD made by the judge but due to the common law nature of the proceedings these do not have the same function as requests for additional information in civil law proceedings in the name of responsibility for establishing facts.

As we have also seen, Article 4 (4) of the Qualification Directive includes an indication of shifted burden of proof. This shifted burden of proof stems from the requirement imposed by international law to take into account earlier persecution as an indicator of refugee status.[6] However, the direct reference to shifted burden of proof with implications for use of the standard of proof, as presented by the text of the directive, is a transplant from German asylum practice.[7] Thus, German appellate procedure is familiar with use of this particular shifted burden of proof and indeed puts it to use.[8] The norm, albeit also being of importance in international refugee law, is brought to the European legal order from the German legal system and in a form encouraging the 'German interpretation' of the norm. This particular instrument of evidentiary assessment is hence more at home in German asylum procedure than in any other European asylum procedure. In order for other courts to fully understand the implications of the article, references to German doctrine and practice would have to be made. However, such references are extremely

---

[5] Noll (2005 c) 7–8 explains the implications of the list of elements as limiting the requirements that MS can impose upon the applicant regarding presentation of evidence but not as limiting the scope of investigation and assessment for the decision-maker.

[6] UNHCR (1992) para 45, states "It may be assumed that a person has a well-founded fear of being persecuted if he has already been the victim of persecution for one of the reasons enumerated in the 1951 Convention."

[7] Also, it becomes clear that MS role in ensuring safe return is also emphasised procedurally from a textual comparison of the wording of the UNHCR Handbook's soft law guidance, and the wording of the QD, which reads "The fact that an applicant has already been subject to persecution or serious harm or to direct threats of such persecution or such harm, is a serious indication of the applicant's well-founded fear of persecution or real risk of suffering serious harm, unless there are good reasons to consider that such persecution or serious harm will not be repeated".

[8] In BverfG (2.7.1980) 54, 341 (361) at 11 the German Constitutional Court clearly endorsed the practice of shifted burden of proof.

rare.[9] As European asylum procedures emerge and conform, this Article will surely be put to the test.

Especially in German asylum procedure, the fundamental nature of the right to asylum has traditionally softened the concept of burden of proof in favour of shared responsibility, where the court has formally been given means to lighten the burden on the applicant either by using shifted burdens of proof or by the duty to investigate. The logic behind this practice is that state responsibility towards correct application of the right to asylum is accentuated due to the nature of the right and that the fundamental status of the right brings the right to asylum closer to being a claim-right than a mere service-right. So far German procedure is the only national asylum procedure in Europe to have experience with asylum as a fundamental right and it is clear that this notion has also impacted on evidentiary standards in the procedure, not least on the burden of proof. Nevertheless, the Charter of Fundamental Rights, which gained legal force with the Lisbon Treaty, includes direct reference to the right of asylum in Article 18.[10]

The link between the European fundamental rights status of asylum and the CEAS cannot as such be compared to the link in a national asylum procedure.[11] However, it is clear that if the EU also chooses to advocate the fundamental status of the right to asylum in procedural terms, all national procedures must re-consider the position of the state and responsibilities towards asylum seekers. Quite clearly, this could also have an impact on emerging practices in terms of burden of proof.

The impact of the competences of the decision-maker, the court or the tribunal, is not clear in relation to the burden of proof. One link of interest may be seen in the fact that Finnish courts, handling low numbers of asylum seekers and some possibilities for own investigations, seem to place more weight on claims and the grounds for these, in other words on the duty of the asylum seeker-appellant to lead the court on, than on particular production of evidence. In Germany, where numbers of cases are higher and the possibilities

---

[9] In Helene Lambert, "Transnational Judicial Dialogue, Harmonisation and the Common European Asylum System" (2009/3) *International and Comparative Law Quarterly*, 519–544, the author analyses the current lack of transnational use of national court decisions in the asylum field in the European setting. The report ECRE, *The Impact of the EU Qualification Directive on International Protection* (London 2008) 12–13 refers to the use of Article 4 (4) in UK asylum procedure only by stating that assessment in accordance with the Article has traditionally been carried out in UK asylum procedure

[10] Charter of Fundamental Rights of the European Union, OJ 7.12.2000 (C364) Art 18.

[11] This could, perhaps, change if a European asylum procedure were to be established, for instance with the help of the European Asylum Support Office. However, there are no indications so far in this respect.

of the courts to investigate are more limited, the link is also visible but not as strong. Finally, in English procedure, where the court does not itself engage in investigations *per se*, weight is placed on production of proof. Thus, the inquisitorial maxime and *de facto* possibilities for the court to carry out its duties in respect of this seemingly also affects the burden of proof and its content. The more the court is actually able to do in terms of evidentiary production, the less it expects the appellant or any other party to carry out these tasks.[12]

3. *Evidentiary Robustness*

Requirements on evidentiary robustness have been defined as elements of evidentiary assessment that refer on the one hand to practical responsibility for sufficiency of the basis for decisions and on the other to standards of quantitative and qualitative robustness in the procedure. Requirements on robustness are thus rather practical elements of evidentiary assessment in comparison for instance to the burden or standard of proof.[13]

Formal rules for requirements on robustness in national appellate asylum procedures in Europe are primarily found in general rules regarding the responsibilities of the court or tribunal towards the investigation. However, these rules are vague and general in nature and do not generally reflect any particular standards except for that of 'sufficiency'. Any particular references either in written norms or practice to more established requirements on robustness in relation to the division between quantitative and qualitative robustness were not witnessed in any of the asylum procedures studied. However, the EU has included norms regarding a minimum standard of robustness in RSD, in QD Art 4 (2) and (3).[14] Moreover, the case-law of the

---

[12] In terms of methods for evidentiary assessment this is evidence that courts apply methods emphasising robustness at least to some degree. Heuman (2005) 161–163.

[13] It could also be argued that the requirements on robustness, through the possibilities for altering the material basis for the decision that lies with the investigatory powers, constitute an important element of an extended understanding of the discretion entrusted to decision-makers. Roy Sainsbury, "Administrative Justice: Discretion and Procedure in Social Security Decision-Making", in *The Uses of Discretion*, ed. Keith Hawkins (Oxford 1992) 295–329, argues that especially in relation to administrative justice an expanded understanding of the concept of discretion may be useful.

[14] Council directive on minimum standards for the qualification and status of third country nationals or stateless persons as refugees or as persons who otherwise need international protection and the content of the protection granted. Council directive 2004/83, OJ 29.4.2004 (L 304) 12 and Proposal for a Directive of the European Parliament and of the Council on minimum standards for the qualification and status of third country nationals or stateless persons as beneficiaries of international protection and the content of the protection granted COM (2009) 551. See Noll (2005c) 8–9 for comments.

European Court of Human Rights takes a stand on robustness in matters concerning international protection.[15]

Not surprisingly, the differences between common and civil law procedures in Europe become crystal clear in relation to robustness, as possibilities for actively safeguarding the requirements on robustness standards on the court's or tribunal's part are understood in divergent manners in these traditions.[16]

All procedures studied recognise in one way or another that the role of the court or tribunal is emphasised in ensuring the material basis of knowledge for a decision in appellate asylum procedure.[17] Depending on the procedural possibilities within each system to increase the responsibilities of the decision-maker towards investigations, solutions are then found as follows: In Finnish procedure the court actively and as a first means uses its possibility to request additional information from the parties. This is possible as a result of the inquisitorial maxim. The court also makes use of internal fact-finding. German courts, on the other hand, often make additional investigations themselves by filing questions with expert bodies or by conducting investigations of their own. In English procedure the adversarial nature of the proceedings implies that the emphasised role of the judge is not evident in activism towards the material basis as such. Nevertheless, in this procedure, too, the tribunal is active in its own right – the active role of the judge in cross-examining those giving oral evidence and when establishing the claims of the parties, the extensive use of tacit knowledge and, to a certain degree, requests for material from the parties.[18] It must also be acknowledged that the role of the judge in this respect can be seen as emphasised through the role of the judge in communicating and structuring the evidence.[19]

---

[15] In *Salah Sheekh v. the Netherlands*, Appl. No. 1948/04, Council of Europe: European Court of Human Rights, 11 January 2007, the European Court of Human Rights states that robustness, both quantitatively and qualitatively, is central to considerations under Art 3.

[16] This goes hand in hand with divergences in the understanding of the role of administrative review in different countries. See Eliantionio (2009) 203–206.

[17] In order to say something about the absolute character of activism, a study would be needed on investigatory standards of other procedures in the same setting. Nevertheless, the conclusion analysing only asylum procedure must be that decision-makers have a structure for their activism and are accustomed to using this.

[18] Eliantionio (2009) 203–209, describes the English judge as reluctant to actively use powers of fact-finding and disclosure in administrative justice procedures. In this respect, judges involved in asylum procedure seem somewhat more inclined to participate actively.

[19] The judge will lead so called case management hearings where the prime purpose is to structure the proceedings and evidence. See Section 44 of the Asylum and Immigration Tribunal

So why do all procedures studied in practice include courts that are comparably active in relation to the requirements on robustness? The weighty interests in the procedure that lie with both parties, the implications of these interests on evidentiary assessment and interpretation of these implications as requiring a strong, independent and objective court, play a role in the equation. Activism in all procedures studied seems to be based on practical concerns rather than formal. No reference to for instance lists of required elements of investigations or the like are made despite the explicit reference to certain elements in QD Article 4 (3). Also, activism takes on an institutional character as courts and tribunals are well accustomed to activism and have structured channels for their activism in asylum procedure.

An interesting difference in how activism is carried out can be found between Finland and Germany: Finnish judges rely more often than their German colleagues on the parties to the procedure to bring about more information, whereas German judges seem to be more inclined towards fact-finding of their own. This is the case even though the Finnish competent court is a quasi-expert court with at least some additional resources for fact-finding, whereas German courts are general administrative courts without much in the way of specific means for investigations in asylum procedure.

One possible explanation lies in the established role of the independence of the judiciary in the German setting. German judges at all instances place weight on their independence from on the one hand the state and on the other hand from the parties to the procedure.[20] Through internal fact-finding the court isolates itself from the interests of the parties, even in relation to requirements for robustness, thus emphasising its independence. However, this explanation is not fully satisfactory as we will see that the means of enquiry in

---

(Procedure) Rules 2005. The Asylum and Immigration Tribunal (Procedure) Rules 2005 are also in force in relation to the FTT by virtue of Statutory Instrument 2010 No.21 Tribunals and Inquiries: The Transfer of Functions of the Asylum and Immigration Tribunal Order 2010, in force 15.2.2010.

[20] It is perhaps possible to argue that the emphasis placed on independence in German procedure may also have some institutional sources, such as the nature of service as a judge as a life-time commitment. See also Gordon P. Foxall, "What Judges Maximise: Toward an economic psychology of the judicial utility function" (2004/3) *Liverpool Law Review*, 177–194, where the author puts forward some elements on the nature of service as a judge that can impact on decision-making. Also in the asylum setting the incentives for legal activities may vary depending on personal circumstances among judges and others involved.

German procedure, as well as in the Finnish, are questionable in the light of the independence of the judiciary.

Further, it is clear that use of the very particular procedural instrument of the *Beweisantrag* adds to the picture in the German setting. Through use of a special instrument that allows the parties to request the court to conduct additional research, the responsibility for investigations is in fact completely turned over to the court in relation to certain questions. However, it must be remembered that the *Beweisantrag* is by no means special to asylum procedure and must be seen as a complement to rather than the reason for activism.

Another feature of importance to quantitative robustness is the oral hearing of the appellant. Both English and German procedure use oral hearings of all appellants as a central means of investigation in appellate asylum procedure. Finland, the country with the least applicants in terms of numbers and with a quasi-specialised court, is reluctant to arrange oral hearings. As oral hearing is often the norm in asylum procedures and is also taken as a starting point in doctrine due to the particular evidentiary situation, the question must be asked why Finnish procedure is reluctant towards oral hearings. What is it in the culture of administrative justice in Finland, particularly in asylum matters, that renders the procedure averse to oral hearings?

One salient feature is, without a doubt, questions of procedural economy and perceptions of efficiency.[21] As the Finnish competent court also deals with numerous other matters, oral hearings are seen as impediments for effective procedures and reasons for clogs in the efficiency of the court. However, this concern could also be valid in German procedure where the courts are also competent in issues other than asylum and is therefore not completely satisfactory as an explanation. Another reason may be found in the relationship between the investigations of the first instance decision-maker and the appellate decision-maker, allowing the court to thoroughly rely on the records of the first interview. Such a relationship is also evident in heavy reliance on the first instance research department in Finnish appellate procedure.

The division into common and civil law procedures is clear when looking at the formal responsibilities of the court or tribunal towards robustness. However, there is also a link in relation to qualitative robustness and source

---

[21] Sainsbury 1992 also refers to promptness, which can be interpreted as a feature of procedural economics, as an element of decision-making creating expectations both from outside and inside decision-making. See also Helene Oosterom-Staples, "Effective Rights for Third-Country Nationals?", in *A Right to Inclusion and Exclusion? Normative fault lines of the EU's area of freedom, security and justice*, ed. H. Lindahl (Oxford 2009) 65–92.

criticism in appellate asylum procedures. In English procedure it is not possible for the judge to 'choose' the sources of information to any degree, even if some pre-determination of sources does indeed exist through the influence of the first instance Home Office decision and its background material on the procedure. Also, English procedure includes a comparably high amount of expert evidence both in oral and documentary form. And the judge in the English asylum procedure must, as a result of passivity in relation to choice of sources of information, be highly aware of the need for source criticism. The empirical research conducted also makes it quite clear that English judges are accustomed and willing to apply source criticism and scepticism towards the background of experts, for instance.[22]

In Finnish and German procedure, judges will to a certain degree themselves select the sources of importance for the material basis for decision. In Finland, reliance on the Immigration Service research department is strong. Comparably, in German procedure the role of the *Auswärtigesamt* is enhanced. Thus, both in Finnish and German procedures the decision-maker relies to a high degree on evidence presented by state agents, thus linked to one of the parties in the procedure.

Both 'big procedures' studied, England and Germany are well acquainted with expert evidence in appellate asylum procedure, despite their differences in procedural tradition.[23] This is not the case in Finnish procedure. Again, one could suspect that Finnish procedure would be more inclined towards incorporating expert evidence in the procedure due to its limited amount of appeals and the rather flexible procedural structure but this is not the case. One can perhaps link use of experts to the large numbers of cases involved and the fact that due to case volume experts are indeed to be used.[24] Also, both Germany and England have long traditions in creating particular case-law for asylum matters, which is fairly distant from Finnish procedure.

A central element relating to quality of evidence presented that is somewhat troublesome, but at the same time recognised in all three procedures, is the need for hearing the parties and communication of the evidence.[25] In English

---

[22] Good (2007) 129–151 discusses use of expert witnesses in UK asylum courts.

[23] On differences in procedural framework to allow for expert evidence in Germany and the UK see Eliantonio (2009) 221–222 for a comparative overview of the competences of European administrative justice procedures towards evidence.

[24] The opposite would be valid for Finland, a country with a small foreign population and a small asylum procedure, where even finding interpreters is sometimes challenging.

[25] In Holm (1968) 382 ff and particularly 391, the author considered communication in administrative procedure in the light of the *Offizialmaxime*, albeit from a Danish point of view, and suggests that communication is indeed of importance for the quality of evidentiary assessment.

procedure, the evidence is thoroughly communicated through the trial bundles. However, tacit knowledge of judges, which can be significant, is not always ventilated with the parties. German procedure for its part acknowledges the importance of communication of the evidence produced by the court. However, the means of communication are often lacking as only lists of sources or the like are handed out. Lastly, Finnish procedure makes an effort to communicate evidence presented by the parties but often leaves out evidence acquired *ex officio* from any form of communication.

It would thus seem that the hearing itself as a procedural obligation and as a means of increasing the quality of evidence is indeed recognised in the appellate asylum procedures studied, regardless of their differences in procedural nature and tradition. However, national procedures struggle with the practical task and are more reluctant to communicate evidence produced or obtained by decision-makers than evidence by the parties. Again, procedural economy may play a role in choices made as exchange of sometimes large amounts of information must be seen as challenging.[26] Nevertheless, the special reluctance to share information obtained *ex officio* and tacit knowledge can perhaps be connected to reluctance by the decision-maker to reveal the means of decision-making and through this to an emphasised self-perception of the independence of the decision-maker.[27]

The Asylum Procedures Directive presents provisions regarding legal representation to asylum seekers in Europe. The ground rule laid down in Article 15 is that a negative decision at first instance will allow the applicant the right to free legal aid. However, the APD places a number of restraints on this right by stating for instance that legal aid can be limited only to cases where the appeal is likely to succeed.[28]

---

[26] However, draft amendments to the APD presented in October 2009 suggest some improvements in the rules regarding communication. Council directive 2005/85, OJ 1.12.2005, (L 326) 13 on Minimum Standards on Procedures in Member States for Granting and Withdrawing Refugee Status and Proposal for a Directive of the European Parliament and of the Council on minimum standards of procedures in Member States for the granting and withdrawing of international protection COM (2009) 554/4 and Amended proposal for a Directive of the European Parliament and of the Council on common procedures for granting and withdrawing international protection status (Recast), COM(2011) 319 final.

[27] See also Gilboy (1988) presenting the self-understanding of judges in immigration adjudication as independent and 'servants of justice'. These conclusions connect well with the desire of judges to keep some of the evidentiary assessment outside the public realm.

[28] The particular reference to possibilities of success as a criterion for granting legal aid was abolished in the October 2009 draft amended APD, but reintroduced in the 2011 recast. *Supra* at 26. The UK will, however, most likely opt out from the amendments.

Both English and German asylum procedures use this limitation, thus limiting the grant of legal aid in asylum appeals only to cases where the appeal is likely to succeed.[29] The grant of legal aid is a decision made by the tribunal or court in conjunction with the main decision, so that the legal representative will not know in advance if legal aid will be available. This limits the possibilities for asylum seekers wishing to appeal a negative decision to find a willing legal representative.

Looking more closely at the role of the legal representative in the appellate asylum procedures in question, it is apparent that the implications for robustness are vast. For instance, a legal representative will most surely help the appellant prepare for the oral hearing and may also be more acquainted with which forms of documentary evidence must be presented. At all events, the presence of a legal representative serves to increase the evidentiary robustness of the procedure. However, this is more important in one procedure than the other: In English appellate asylum procedure, equality in procedural power between the parties to the procedure is of vital importance for the procedure in general, as for instance evidentiary solutions presuppose equal power and a clear cut two-party procedure to function optimally. As the adversarial procedure restricts the powers of the tribunal towards evidentiary issues, the procedure is based on a scenario with two equal parties creating an optimal evidentiary base for decisions through competition and a form of battle of knowledge. Thus, restricting access to legal representatives in this procedure has far-reaching effects on all evidentiary solutions as it distorts one of the cornerstones of the background framework for asylum procedure. In the inquisitorial environment of Finland or Germany, equality in arms is not of the same importance for evidentiary solutions as the main responsibility for evidentiary standards rests with the decision-maker.

By imposing the limitations included in APD Art 15 and therefore effectively decreasing the possibilities for appellants to use legal representatives in procedures, the discrepancies in qualitative and quantitative robustness between the common law systems and civil law systems of appeal in Europe are enhanced.

---

[29] The frameworks for granting legal aid in the UK and Germany are, however, somewhat different. In Germany, the decision is made post procedure by the judge. In the UK the decision is pre procedure and carried out according to a funding scheme within the Community Legal Aid Programme. The merits test in UK asylum procedure is set out in paras 13.3 to 13.5 of the Funding Code Criteria http://www.legalservices.gov.uk/docs/civil_contracting/Funding _code_criteria_Jul07.pdf (visited 23.11.2011).

4. *Methods of Evidentiary Assessment*

4.1. *Methods of Evidentiary Assessment*

Methods used for evidentiary assessment are abstract notions of how evidence has been weighed and assessed in order to reach a conclusion on the theme of proof. Guidance from the supranational level is provided primarily by EU, which in its APD states that decision-making in asylum matters must be undertaken individually, objectively and impartially.[30] As became apparent in the study of national appellate asylum procedures, discovering the methods used in procedures through analysis of written decisions requires that decisions are well-argued, motivated and reflect the strategies used for assessment, either expressly or implicitly. Whereas German and English appellate asylum procedures displayed decisions with clear structures and information about the means of reaching the end result, the decisions included in analysis of Finnish appellate asylum procedure provided less information about methods of evidentiary assessment.

Similarly to the lack of communication and hearing in relation to *ex officio* evidence in Finnish procedure, lack of references to evidentiary assessment in the decisions studied signalled at least partly reluctance to official deliberation by the court.[31] In contrast, the English and German decisions included in the study frequently weighed and assessed evidence openly. Debates pro and con in terms of either prognosis or the factual basis for the decision are commonplace and the judges are not afraid to admit to difficulties in decision-making at times.

However, using the information from English and German procedures from decisions as well as other sources, and from Finnish procedure the scarce information available in decisions and interviews, it is clear that the procedures studied show common features as well as divergences in terms of evidentiary assessment.

Considerations relating to efficiency in gathering of knowledge and to the special circumstances regarding acquisition of evidence in the asylum environment influence all studied procedures. Moreover, in evidentiary assessment all procedures included pay particular attention to the at times difficult evidentiary situation and to the difficulties involved in obtaining

---

[30] APD, Article 8 (2) (a).
[31] Partly, reluctance to reveal information about decision-making through decisions or communication of evidence can be seen as either an intentional or unintentional creation of a gap between the court and the parties, and society in general. Gilboy (1988).

reliable information, thus emphasising the need for attention to evidentiary robustness and effective implementation of the law.[32] This also shows that the procedures are aware of uncertainties and the space that must be awarded the unknown in evidentiary assessment.

Also, none of the procedures studied show signs of particularly clear use of theories of probability or methods emphasising statistical or mathematical assessment of evidence. On the contrary, all procedures included show similar approaches to evidentiary assessment in that they use utterly pragmatic reasoning through use of non-abstract points of reference in deliberations on the implications of certain information. Undoubtedly, the procedure most inclined to formal categorisation using structured and abstract references is English procedure. That is, English appellate asylum procedure applies a system, particular for the asylum setting, structuring evidence into categories of different 'values' of credibility as a first step in evidentiary assessment.[33] The purpose of this exercise is to distinguish between which evidence is included in the assessment and which is not. Despite the fact that the rest of the evidentiary assessment is indeed carried out without further reference to structured models using probabilities or the like as points of reference, use of the first step model is a clear sign of a minor formal configuration of evidentiary assessment in English appellate asylum procedure.

4.2. *Practical Assessment of Evidence*

However, whereas general ideas regarding evidentiary assessment such as the attention paid to the particularities of evidentiary material in the procedure and application of pragmatic reasoning to assessment show similarities between the procedures studied, the actual road-map from claim to decision displays vast differences between countries. Perhaps the most crucial difference is that between the inclusive, all-embracing, method of assessment used in English procedure and the clear-cut two-stage assessment of German procedure.[34] Moreover, German decisions, doctrine and interviewees are

---

[32] Also the European legislator calls for effectiveness. Oosterom-Staples (2009) 75.

[33] *Karanakaran v. Secretary of State for the Home Department*, [2000] EWCA Civ. 11, Court of Appeal (England and Wales), 25 January 2000.

[34] As it is difficult to retrieve information about evidentiary assessment in Finnish appellate asylum procedure it is also difficult to place the procedure on the European map in this respect. However, a tentative estimate about the nature of evidentiary assessment in Finnish appellate asylum procedure places the procedure in the sphere of two-pronged assessments, though without clear doctrine or advice in this respect.

clear that assessing whether the appellant is entitled to asylum starts with gathering evidence. The assessment then firstly applies common administrative standards of evidentiary assessment to establish which facts to include in general risk assessment. Thus, the first step is a separate establishment of facts based on evidentiary assessment using standards of proof not particularly designed for asylum procedure. Secondly, the established facts are then used to make a prognostic conclusion regarding well-founded fear of persecution. In this second step particular standards of proof applicable only to the asylum environment are then used. Thus, in this procedure the lowered standard of proof only becomes important in relation to calculation of probability.

Again, English procedure is directly opposed to any division between establishing facts and making a prognosis on well-founded fear of persecution.[35] It is clear that initially the structure of evidentiary assessment is similar, as English procedure is also interested in the legality of the prior decision and for this purpose re-evaluates the refugee status of the appellant. However, the means of establishing the possible refugee status of the appellant are different. The English judge is encouraged to use lower standards to allow evidence for assessment and to assess "well-founded risk of persecution" inclusively so that historical facts and prognosis are assessed 'in the round'. It is possible to say that English procedure also applies a two-pronged approach, as there is indeed a differentiation between inclusion of evidence in evidentiary assessment and the assessment itself – evidence which the judge is convinced is not credible is left out. Nevertheless, the approach is still inclusive in terms of evidentiary assessment as the same requirements are applied to all stages of the procedure and as the decision-maker is required not to separate past from future in drawing conclusions. The particular asylum-oriented standard of proof is here applicable to all steps in assessment, also to establishing facts.

This difference cannot be directly attributed to the division between inquisitorial and adversarial procedures in a technical manner, as the method of assessment is largely independent of the role of the judge. Moreover, it cannot be directly attributed to an understanding of the English procedure studied as more prone to review than reconsideration, which would then be the leading function of German procedure.[36] In the English, the standards and the direct reference to 'one assessment' directly refer to all decision-making where a

---

[35] *Supra* at 33.
[36] Eliantonio (2009) 203, singles out UK administrative justice procedures as mostly concerned with supervision rather than revision.

stand has to be taken in relation to the refugee status of the applicant regardless of the level of decision-making.[37]

Rather, it must be appreciated that divergent approaches to evidentiary assessment come from a divergence of traditions and also a divergence in terms of discussion partners. English procedure has been prone to discussion on correct implementation of asylum and refugee law with partners from the common law tradition. Doctrine and references for decision-making have been created in debates in which representatives from the civil law tradition have taken little part.[38] However, at the same time very little discussion on the application of refugee law in national procedure has taken place on a level above the national among countries from the civil law tradition. A result has been that international standards regarding refugee law have also been shaped by common law debates, not only regarding evidence but in relation to this field of law in all its essence.[39]

Thus, the common law English has long participated in discussions recognising the particularities of the asylum field and making recommendations for solutions in international law – one of these solutions being a lowered standard of proof. At the same time, these international recommendations are also imposed on German and Finnish procedures without the same background framework. Hence, implementation of particular standards in the asylum environment in German procedure is placed within and on top of regular administrative decision-making to a greater extent than in English procedure. In contrast, English procedure is more prone to inherent solutions and procedural solutions valid for the procedure in its entirety, also because of apparent lack of separate administrative classifications of matters.

---

[37] The divergent understanding of the division of evidentiary assessment can be transferred to a divergent understanding RSD. In Jean-Yves Carlier, "The Geneva refugee definition and the 'theory of the three scales'", in *Refugee Rights and Realities Evolving International Concepts and Regimes*, eds. Frances Nicholson & Patrick Twomey (Cambridge 1999) 37–54, the author states that he advocates a low level or risk but a higher level of proof to be used in RSD. When analysing the model presented by Carlier, It becomes evident that with standard of proof he refers to establishing facts in the assessment and thus sees establishing risk as something done outside evidentiary assessment. In the understanding of English procedure, and also more widely, risk assessment is a part of evidentiary assessment, to which the lowered standard of proof applies.

[38] An example is negotiations, creation and publishing of the so called Michigan Guidelines relating to certain topics of international protection. The Guidelines were prepared within the framework of the Refugee Law Colloquium held at the Program in Refugee Law at Michigan Law School, and today include guidelines on Protection Elsewhere, Well-Founded Fear, Nexus-grounds and the Internal Protection Alternative, all available at http://refugeecaselaw .org/MichiganGeneralGuidelines.aspx (visited 23.11.2011).

[39] See for instance influential works by Hathaway (1991) and Goodwin-Gill (*et al.*) (2007).

5. *Standard of Proof*

Even if the standard of proof is an utterly abstract part of the evidentiary framework, it is also an element that is given vast attention by doctrine, practice and the national procedures included in this study. All national procedures studied in one way or another use the standard of proof as a device to adapt this particular procedure of administrative justice to the requirements of the asylum environment.

A reason for the attention paid to the particular element of standard of proof may be that alterations in the standard are relatively easily applied as pragmatic solutions for situations where the evidentiary playing field must be adapted to a special environment. It may so to speak be easier to alter applicable standards of proof than to require special methods of evidentiary assessment or investigatory standards to be used in national procedure. The standard of proof is also relatively free from ties to institutional or other external factors and is hence a module that can be consistently applied throughout the entirety of a procedure of justice.[40]

It is evident from all national appellate asylum procedures studied that the standard of proof is used sensitively to the asylum environment. All procedures studied in one way or another apply a standard of proof that is particularly adapted to asylum procedure – commonly by lowering the required threshold in relation to other administrative procedures. Moreover, all procedures consider the standard of proof to be an important part of decision-making not only in that it deserves adaptation to the particular environment but also with regard to separate reasoning and motivations in decisions.

England as we have seen favours an inclusive approach to evidentiary assessment where the standard of proof is applied to all considerations at a level of "reasonable likelihood". The standard used, "reasonable likelihood", is derived from national case law and from considerations regarding the applicable standard of proof in international refugee law doctrine. This standard is particular for the asylum ˋenvironment and also differs from the standards used in other forms of immigration proceedings.[41]

---

[40] The standard of proof for a certain procedure is always given in relation to the type of procedure, not in relation to the level of procedure. See Lappalainen (*et al.*) (2007) 588 and 591, where the author examines the concept of standard of proof.

[41] The particularity and "isolation" of standard of proof can easily be seen in UK asylum proceedings, where judges are very careful to use particular standards when assessing asylum claims as opposed to other immigration claims, even if this is done under the same oral hearing.

The German approach is that of divided assessment, using two different standards of proof for firstly establishing facts and secondly for constructing a prognosis on the basis of established facts in the case. The threshold for establishing historical facts is that of *Überzeugungsgewissheit*, implying a standard beyond reasonable doubt where the judge is convinced. This standard is derived from general administrative practice. On the other hand, a standard at the level of *beachtlicher Wahrscheinlichkeit* is applicable for making a prognosis based on the historical facts. This standard is interpreted as being close to that of "reasonable likelihood" and thus represents a lowering of the threshold.

Due to unclear elaborations on evidentiary assessment in Finnish procedure it is not possible to establish with certainty whether two standards of proof or one apply. Short elaborations also make it difficult to interpret the material meaning of the standard of proof expressed. Decisions themselves refer to one standard at the level of *todennäköistä* or 'probable'. Semantically the standard used at least to the prognostic part of the decision is at the level of probability higher than the internationally advocated 'reasonable likelihood'. We have seen that tracing the semantic expression used in the Finnish asylum appellate asylum procedure back to a Nordic evidentiary context, the standard would be placed at a higher level than the balance of probabilities. At the same time, it is possible that the standard is still lower than the standard used for administrative justice procedures in general.[42] In the country report we also saw that the substantial content of the standard of proof may vary, and that the semantic expression used may in substance reflect different probabilities. However, as courts indeed do use evidentiary language and concepts to motivate their decisions, the interpretation of semantic expressions cannot be made in contrary of their dogmatic context, and the starting point must hence be, that the semantic expression of probable is not the same as reasonable likelihood.

Hence, traces of international doctrine in standards of proof applied can indeed be seen in European appellate asylum procedures. However, as international doctrine is heavily influenced by common law, including English case law, the impact may not only have gone one way and it is quite clear that recommendations from international legal doctrine partly build on English practice. The standard of proof in Finnish procedure nevertheless does not follow either international doctrine, other European standards or general

---

[42] In order to reach conclusions on the standard used in asylum matters as opposed to other administrative matters requires a separate and comparative study of administrative decision-making in different fields.

administrative standards of proof but represents a lowered standard of proof applicable exclusively to the asylum environment without, however, reaching standards advocated internationally.[43]

Similar in all procedures studied is the rather formalistic and standardised manner in which the standard of proof is referred to, in contrast to the opinions of stakeholders in the procedures, which seemingly indicates that the standard may indicate different thresholds despite a clear and consistent semantic use in practice. Different judges may simply understand the threshold differently. Opinions of stakeholders were also similar in the sense that they voice concern that the factual standards applied may at times be higher than the standard set in practice. No stakeholder indicated that the standards used could be lower than semantically indicated.

Further, procedures seem to be unified in a pragmatic approach to understanding the standard of proof, even if Finnish procedure as mentioned is difficult to analyse in this respect. In the English context, stakeholders refer to the test as being one of plausibility – a threshold built on pragmatic considerations as to the reasonability of the theme of proof.[44] However, in the particular environment of English procedure pragmatism in terms of the standard of proof is also closely connected to the role of credibility in evidentiary assessment. German procedure also includes emphasis on pragmatic understandings of the standard of proof through the connection to the need for the 'judge's conviction' about the historical facts. However, this is not by any means specific to the asylum context.

Lastly, German interpretation of the principle set out in Article 4 (4) of the QD is more closely connected to the standard of proof than in other procedures.[45] This perhaps indicates an emphasis on formalistic interpretation of the article. Nevertheless, German interpretation of the Article emphasises the role of standards of proof, clearly recognising that two different standards of proof are included: One for establishing prior persecution and one for the possibility to rebut the presumption of future persecution as a result of

---

[43] The examples used in Chapter IV uses elements of this argumentation.

[44] This view was expressed both by legal representatives and representatives of the decision-maker.

[45] Art 4 (4) of the Qualification Directive states that "The fact that an applicant has already been subject to persecution or serious harm or to direct threats of such persecution or such harm, is a serious indication of the applicant's well-founded fear of persecution or real risk of suffering serious harm, unless there are good reasons to consider that such persecution or serious harm will not be repeated". The Article in thus pre-supposing prior persecution enacts a standard of proof at the level of "good reasons" for the shifted burden of proof. See also Noll (2005c) at 13, recognising that the European rule requires representatives of the state to show good reasons for believing that no future persecution will occur.

established prior persecution. This interpretation does not fit neatly into the understanding of the Article as expressed by, as an example, the UK rapporteur in the ECRE study on implementation of the QD, where 'inclusive assessment' is also applied in relation to Article 4 (4) and where the requirements of this Article are perceived as distinct from particular requirements on the burden or standard of proof and more as a general indicator that prior persecution must be taken into account in decision-making.[46] It could also be said that the English understanding of the mechanism is closer to that expressed by international law through the UNHCR Handbook, for instance.[47]

6. *The Role of International Refugee Law in Forming National Evidentiary Standards*

In order to be able to say something about the effects and implications of international law on European appellate asylum procedures, it is necessary to define what is meant by international refugee law. For the purposes of this study, this concept has been defined positively as including doctrine, case-law from international organs, guidelines and positions presented by international institutions and organisations with authority in the field.[48]

For the purpose of this study and in the definition of the keys of comparison we have seen that international law does not in written legal sources, conventions or likewise provide norms for evidentiary solutions in national asylum procedures as the procedural aspects of RSD by international legal sources have been left for the national legislator to decide on. However, practice, doctrine and commentaries provide guidance for how national asylum procedures shall tackle evidentiary questions.

International law has, thus, through above mentioned sources played a role in the creation of binding European standards of protection and procedure.[49] The implications of international law can either be seen as direct effects on national procedures established before or independent of the European legal

---

[46] ECRE (October 2008) 12–13. Unfortunately, the most comprehensive comparative study on the QD to date, the UNHCR study (2007), does not include data on implementation of Art 4.

[47] UNHCR (1992) para 45.

[48] On the role of soft law in creating a structure for international refugee law in particular see also Ulrike Brandl, "Soft law as a source of international and European refugee law", in *European and Refugees: A Challenge?*, eds. Jean-Yves Carlier & Dirk Vanheule (The Netherlands 1997) 203–226.

[49] Clear examples of the impact of the international refugee on European standards are the definitions and criteria for eligibility included in the Qualification Directive, Art 2 (c) and (e).

framework of international protection or as indirect effects through inclusion of international standards in binding European norms on national asylum procedures. Both forms of impact will here be taken into account even if the indirect implications must also be included in considerations regarding European influences on national procedures.

It is not difficult to identify international law influences in the European national appellate asylum procedures studied. However, it is not easy to establish to what degree the impact is that of international law on the national system or that of the national system on international law. Doctrine in international immigration law, and particularly in the fields of asylum and forced migration, tend to be inspired by ideas and developments in the common law sphere.[50] Doctrine has also an enhanced position in the influences from the international field, due to the lack of detailed procedural normative guidance. Thus to a certain extent English legal practice is also reflected in recommendations and positions at the international level so that when then considering the implications of international law on national European procedures this special relationship must be taken into account. That is, inevitably the impact of international law on specific European procedures partly depends on the practical possibilities for and readiness of national procedures to embrace legal transplants coming from the European or international level. It goes without saying that for procedures which themselves have been actively involved in creation of standards that need to be implemented, transposition and adoption may be less troublesome than for procedures for which the standards are completely foreign.[51]

In adapting national asylum procedures to the requirements of international law, the opinions expressed by international law only present one source of demands placed on national procedures, whereas requirements from other sources such as EU law or national administrative law may pose divergent or competing requirements. Navigating between these demands and requirements is at least partly steered by economic considerations: At the macro-level in relation to implementation costs but also at the micro-level in terms of considerations of procedural economy.[52]

---

[50] A further example can be taken from the training in RSD currently carried out by the UNHCR in Europe under the name of the "Quality Initiative", which has its roots in training carried out by and for UK RSD and Border agency personnel.

[51] As mentioned, European legislation also partly relies on international law. Hence, effective costs of implementing the rules will be different for European countries depending on their legal system and framework. In Nuno Garoupa & Anthony Ogus, "A Strategic Interpretation of Legal Transplants" (2006/2) *The Journal of Legal Studies*, 339–363, the authors' presentation of a theory of economic explanations of how and why adaptations to legal transplants fail could also be used to study approximation of the asylum field in Europe.

[52] *Ibid.*

There are several individual indicators of the impact of international law on European national asylum procedures. Perhaps the brightest examples are to be found outside the scope of this research in areas such as the definition of eligibility for asylum.[53] However, the domain of procedural asylum law and the evidentiary standards herein also show that adapting to the standards of international law has indeed taken place:

The standard of proof in appellate asylum procedures is a clear example of the impact of international law. International legal commentaries and guide-lines point out the necessity of adapting the standard of proof to a level spe-cific for the asylum environment.[54] This recommendation is adhered to by all national appellate asylum procedures included in the study. However, interna-tional legal practice and doctrine in this respect goes as far as recommending a standard to be used at the level of "reasonable likelihood".[55] Both English and German procedure makes use of this particular standard, albeit in somewhat different structures, and explicitly refer to the requirements of international law in applying this standard. Thus, in these procedures the standard of proof is an example of clear influence from international law. Finnish procedure, however, seems to be content with observing only the general requirement for a lowering of standards and in practice ignores the precise requirement for a standard at the level of "reasonable likelihood". Thus, Finnish procedure shows some adaptation to the opinions expressed in the international field but not to the extent evident in the other procedures studied.

We have also seen that international law presents requirements as to the role of prior persecution in evidentiary assessment in asylum procedure. The UNHCR Handbook explicitly refers to situations of prior persecution by stat-ing that "It may be assumed that a person has a well-founded fear of being persecuted if he has already been the victim of persecution".[56] This provision has been adopted by the EU legislator in the QD.[57] However, even before this standard was included in European frameworks and hence independent of EU frameworks, national procedures in Europe recognised the importance of prior persecution as an indicator of future persecution in their national legal orders. In England, prior persecution is included in the requirement for inclusive evidentiary assessment as presented in *Karanakaran*, requiring all

---

[53] These are directly derived from international refugee law. However, as Battjes (2006) 274–275 concludes, not all elements of definitions and eligibility criteria in EU legislation are, when put under the microscope, in conformity with the requirements of international law.

[54] See also UNHCR (1998).

[55] See for an overview of the roots of this standard Gorlick (2003) 366–370.

[56] UNHCR (1992) para 45.

[57] QD, Art 4 (4)

elements of relevance to the definition to be taken into account in evidentiary assessment – thus also prior persecution.[58] The similarities between the English approach and the expressions used for describing the requirement at the international level are clear as both approaches use a rather general approach pointing to the importance of prior persecution as an indicator of the seriousness of claims so that a connection can thus be made. In Germany, on the other hand, inclusion of the requirement from international law in national legislation took on a structurally different form, imposing a clear structure and method for inclusion of prior persecution in the assessment and defining more closely the meaning of presumption of future persecution. The German approach has favoured a distinct shift in the burden of proof and particular standards of proof to be applied to the particular case of prior persecution, as well as a two-pronged approach to evidentiary assessment, with rigid requirements for inclusion of considerations regarding prior persecution in evidentiary assessment. This approach is again evident in the European rules on the matter, where the wording of Article 4 (4) implies the use of particular standards of proof, divided assessment of evidence and a shifted burden of proof.[59]

Further, the requirements of international law regarding methods of evidentiary assessment are reflected in all three national procedures studied. The UNHCR Handbook expresses the requirements of international doctrine on evidentiary assessment by stating that "Firstly, it is necessary to ascertain the relevant facts of the case. Secondly, the definitions in the 1951 Convention and the 1967 Protocol have to be applied to the facts thus ascertained".[60] As we have seen, the expression used by UNHCR does not endorse the clear separation between historical facts and prognosis, but separates the stages of drawing conclusions from the facts of the case and of subsuming conclusions under international norms.

Evidentiary assessment is undertaken in various manners in the countries studied. Whereas English procedure uses an inclusive approach and also lowers the barriers for establishing facts, German procedure separates two stages of establishing historical facts and making a prognosis in terms of standards of proof. Not many facts are on the table regarding Finnish

---

[58] In the UK reflection of the norm in ECRE (October 2008) 12–13, the author explicitly states that no need arose to amend UK practice as a result of the EU requirement, as the principle was fully recognised as practice stood.

[59] See Noll (2005c) 13, recognising that the European rule requires representatives of the state to show good reasons for believing that no future persecution will occur.

[60] UNHCR (1992) para 29.

practice but a tentative conclusion would be that this procedure also at least partly uses a two-phased model of assessment on the lines of German procedure. The expressions used by UNHCR in this respect do not as it stands seem to endorse the clear separation between historical facts and prognosis. In this respect, it would seem that German and Finnish procedure alike practice a model of evidentiary assessment other than the one endorsed by international recommendations on the matter, whereas the English approach is more likely to be in line with the opinions expressed in the Handbook.

Finally, something can be said also in relation to the burden of proof in European appellate asylum procedures. International law does not *per se* provide guidance as to the correct placement of the burden of proof, even if international doctrine and commentaries commonly place the burden with the applicant. We have seen that all countries included in this study view the asylum procedure as a procedure for the granting of the benefit of asylum and where the asylum-seeker and appellant hence is obliged to show that he or she is a refugee. The alternative point of view, to perceive the asylum procedure as a means for the state to ensure *non-refoulement* thus placing the burden of proof with the state is not embraced, even if also European law leaves the door open for this possibility.

Let us return briefly to consideration of costs of implementation. From the above, it would appear that England has the appellate asylum procedure most in line with evidentiary requirements presented by international law, whereas Germany, and especially Finland, fall behind in this respect. In the light of the links between international refugee law and common law asylum procedures this is not surprising if considering the divergent cost-effects for the countries.

7. *The Role of EU Law in Forming National Evidentiary Standards*

As well the EU Charter of Fundamental Rights and general principles of EU law include guarantees for an effective remedy and fair trial also in asylum matters. The procedural implications of these guarantees are explicated by secondary legislation.

The EU Asylum Procedures Directive and the Qualification Directive are central parts of secondary European Union legislation that impacts on evidentiary standards of Member State national appellate asylum procedures. It is true that both directives primarily target first instance proceedings and that the EU has focused on front-loading. Nevertheless, the directives are of relevance to the appellate level of decision-making, either directly or indirectly: Some rules are applicable to all forms of decision-making, regardless of level, regarding definitions and eligibility as well as procedural issues linked to evidentiary requirements and the burden of proof. Of imperative importance especially for issues linked to evidentiary standards are the requirements presented in the QD Article 4, which spells out detailed provisions regarding use of information and the role of the applicant versus the decision-maker in asylum procedure. Also, especially if taking into account the changes to the directives as proposed in June 2011 and following the inclusion of the Charter of Fundamental Rights in binding primary legislation, certain procedural rules directly target appellate institutions.[61] These include, for instance, rules regarding communication and the suspensive effect of appeals.[62]

EU rules on evidentiary standards in asylum procedure are at least partly derived from rules at international level. For instance, rules regarding the role of prior persecution, the importance placed on representation and also the use of the benefit of the doubt are examples of European norms with direct reference to requirements presented by international refugee law.[63] However, this does not by any means imply that requirements at international level would be implemented as such at European level.[64] Often, the requirements are amended to fit the agenda of the EU.

QD Article 4 (1) and (2) enable Member States to consider it the duty of the asylum applicant to substantiate all claims for international protection with statements and documentation regarding the age, background and identity of the applicant. Article 4 (5) sets out the requirements for granting the benefit of the doubt. In essence, these norms thus indicate the burden of proof and its contents.

We have seen that German and Finnish procedures included in the study employ a shared burden of proof in appellate asylum procedure. While the formal burden of proof rests rather rigidly with the appellant, the material burden of proof is used flexibly in order to recognise some of the particularities of asylum procedure and the evidentiary handicap of the appellant.

---

[61] *Supras* at 14 and 26. At the time of writing, it nevertheless seems likely that the UK will opt out of amendments to both directives.

[62] See also Ida Staffans, "Judicial Protection and the Future Common European Asylum System" (2010/3) *European Journal of Migration and Law*, 273–297, where the author argues that the effectiveness of national appellate asylum procedures depends on the means of harmonisation.

[63] In Brandl (1997) lines are drawn between the European framework for international protection and international legal requirements, while international soft law is presented as a source of European standards. Also McAdam (2005) points to the importance of international law for standards of protection in Europe.

[64] Battjes (2006) 274–275.

However, in practice none of the appellate procedures studied have formal requirements for the appellant to deliver information about the precise elements referred to in Article 4 (2) in order to see the burden of proof discharged. Rather, the procedures studied use a highly case-sensitive assessment of when the burden is discharged. Thus, whereas the requirements of the directive indeed in practice may be met in the appellate setting, any formal conditions in this respect are not presented in national law.

Article 4 (3) of the QD poses a list of elements which must be taken into account in assessing any claim for international protection, regardless of the level of decision-making. These include "all relevant facts as they relate to the country of origin", "the relevant statements and documentation presented by the applicant" and "the individual position and personal circumstances of the applicant", amongst others. The norm thus spells out criteria for the robustness of investigations in asylum procedure.

In the same manner as with the material burden of proof, the appellate asylum procedures studied tend to favour a flexible approach to the requirements mentioned in Article 4 (3) as opposed to rigid lists of elements. The elements listed in the Article all refer to relatively 'basic' information, which is included in any quantitatively and qualitatively defendable investigation. It is also noteworthy that the elements as mentioned in the Article are not connected with any responsibility of the parties in the procedure but rather with the investigatory responsibility placed with the decision-maker. However, in appellate procedures this connection precisely makes the requirements imposed by the Article a challenge:

Whereas it is natural to require first level authorities to conduct fact-finding and thus to carry responsibility over robustness of investigations, in reference to QD Article 4 (3) the possibilities to formally place similar requirements with an appellate body are limited, depending on the legal system surrounding the procedure. In a civil law country such as Germany or Finland where appellate administrative courts would also function in an inquisitorial manner, the appellate institution's responsibility for evidentiary robustness is inherent. By contrast, in common law procedure where the court or tribunal adheres to adversarial principles, the possibilities for the decision-maker to fact-find and to take practical responsibility over robustness are limited. However, as English asylum procedure shows, there are indeed procedural devices in adversarial procedure that to a certain degree aid the situation, such as the clear cut two-party structure to the proceedings. Still, in situations where one or more of the requirements as presented in Article 4 (3) are missing, it is unclear how an adversarial tribunal would tackle the problem.

The fact that the appellate instance is concerned with the refugee status of the applicant only via the claims and the grounds for these does not make the issue regarding responsibility over robustness less challenging.[65] Whereas appellate courts indeed have the possibility not to take a direct stand on the subject matter themselves and merely refer the decision back to the first level authority, assessment at appellate instance is still subject to the legislator's requirements of robustness as well as general administrative requirements in the matter.[66] Moreover, it is imperative for the review on facts and law of the first instance decision that the appellate organ can draw its own conclusions as to the refugee status of the appellant. Thus, robustness poses a valid challenge to appellate systems in Europe, especially in connection with the individual requirements placed in QD 4(3).

Lastly, in reference to Article 4 of the QD, Article 4 (4) concerns the role of prior persecution in assessing claims for protection. The norm states that prior persecution "is a serious indication of the applicant's well-founded fear of persecution [...], unless there are good grounds to consider that such persecution [...] will not be repeated".

Much was said about the implications of this rule already in connection with the international appearance of this principle, and it was established that the EU norm differs partly from the international principle in its references to particular standards of proof, divided evidentiary assessment and the shifted burden of proof. The QD rule is seemingly inspired by German practice in the matter. This is also evident from how the QD Article 4 (4) is implemented in national procedures, where German practice is the most similar to that prescribed by the QD and English practice follows a more flexible and 'inclusive' approach as referred to in the requirements of international law. Finnish procedure stands tentatively in the middle.

It should be noted that no changes to the existing rules in Article 4 have been proposed in the October 2009 proposal for amendments to the QD.[67]

Further, there is the question of legal representation and legal aid at appellate instances. This is also a matter of vast impact in terms of evidentiary standards, as the possibilities for the appellant to fully make use of the procedural possibilities without a representative are limited due for instance to cultural and linguistic barriers. Legal aid is of imperative importance, as asylum

---

[65] In Eliantonio (2009) 203 ff the author studies the framework of administrative justice in England from a comparative perspective, juxtaposing the competences of procedures in different countries and arriving at a dichotomy between supervision and revision.

[66] If the appellate body does not decide on the substantive matter but decides to refer the matter back to the first level authority, it still has come to a conclusion regarding the required standards of proof, albeit for the first instance level.

[67] *Supra* at 14.

seekers are commonly not in a financial position that would allow for hiring legal representatives without state funding.

Rules regarding the right to legal representation and legal aid can be found in APD Article 15. Article 15 (1) states that legal representation is allowed in matters of international protection and Article 15 (2) and (3) goes on to list requirements for free legal assistance in the first appellate instances of national asylum procedures. As the rules stand today, Member States are allowed to restrict access to legal aid only to those who lack sufficient resources and only to cases where the appeal is likely to succeed.[68] Additionally, the rules enable Member States to allow for legal aid to be granted only to advisers specifically designated by national law to carry out work in asylum procedure.

The October 2009 and June 2011 recast versions of the APD include far-reaching changes to many relevant articles. Partly, the changes suggested are due to the impact of the Charter of Fundamental Rights, which extends the fundamental procedural rights also to the asylum environment.[69] The amendments concern, amongst others, access to information for legal representatives, suspensive effect of appeal and the obligation for Member States to provide for legal aid, legal representation and information for asylum seekers. At the time of writing, the negotiations on the recast APD give little hope for all proposed amendments to be adopted.

As of the time of writing, German and English asylum procedure use a merits test aside from the means test to determine access to free legal assistance at the first appellate level. In order to be granted legal aid, appellants are required to show, apart from financial eligibility, that their claims have a certain possibility of succeeding. In Finland, no such requirement is imposed and the grant of legal aid depends entirely on the income level of the appellant.

It was mentioned earlier that one of the central features that helps ensure evidentiary robustness in the adversarial English procedure is the clear cut two-party structure. This, however, requires that the parties are at least close to equal in procedural power. If the asylum seeker is not represented by a legal representative, the positions of the parties will be utterly unequal – a governmental body against an alien to the system. In German procedure, on the other hand, representation is important but perhaps lacks the central position in terms of evidentiary robustness as the court is responsible for robustness of investigations as a result of the investigatory maxim.

---

[68] Reference is thus made to tests of both means and merits. The merits test is in EU legislation referred to with the wording "likely to succeed". APD Art 15 (3) (d).

[69] ECRE (2010) 25–27.

The use of the merits test in England and Germany can be seen to be moti-vated as much by a desire to deter asylum seekers from appealing as by a desire to streamline and speed up proceedings at the first appellate level. The Finnish solution can be seen as motivated by a general striving towards incorporating as much of the asylum procedure as possible in the general frameworks of administrative justice by means of avoiding special solutions. However, the Finnish position in terms of legal representatives must also be seen in the light of the rare arrangements for oral hearings. In a written procedure, access to a legal representative cannot be sidestepped, especially taking into account the requirements of the Act on Administrative Judicial Procedures in terms of the procedure being conducted only in Finnish or Swedish.[70]

In relation to the amendments presented to the APD concerning rights of representation and the like, it should be noted that the UK has opted out of amendments both to the APD and to the QD. The decision was made as a result of a general assessment but it is nevertheless interesting to note that at least for the UK national traditions and national practices have in this sense taken the lead over harmonisation.

Finally, the APD also refers to hearing requirements in asylum procedure. Article 16 states that legal advisors, with some exceptions referring e.g. to national security, shall have access to information in the "applicant's file as is liable to be examined by the authorities referred to in Chapter V" (referring to appellate authorities). This rule concerns information of importance to the first instance decision which will be reviewed by the appellate instance. However, there are no rules regarding communication of evidence in the appellate instance itself. Nevertheless, in the amendments proposed to the APD in June 2011, a revised Article 21 (1) b states: "Member States shall make access to the information or sources in question available to the authorities referred to in Chapter V" (appellate authorities). Thus, the revised APD would indeed include a general right to communication of information, though without detailed rules regarding the manner, timeliness or other procedural factors in connection with communication.

Hearing the parties is in general a matter that presents itself as rather trou-blesome to all appellate asylum procedures studied, especially German and Finnish. English asylum procedure uses trial bundles as means of communi-cation, requiring the parties to inform each other about the information being used. Nevertheless, outside the scope of communication lies information including tacit knowledge that judges may use without having the information

---

[70] The Finnish Constitution (731/1999) section 17 states that the languages of the court system in Finland are Finnish and Swedish.

presented by the parties. German appellate procedure recognises the need for communication of all evidence but undertakes this obligation only with reference to lists of sources available. These sources do not distinguish between sources actually being used and sources merely available but are only lists of documentation. Finnish appellate procedure is thorough in the communication of party produced evidence but lacks practice for communication of evidence based on fact-finding by the court. As oral hearings in Finnish procedure are seldom arranged, these cannot be used as a possibility for informing the parties of the evidence used.

It is nevertheless clear that communication is a central requirement for an effective procedure, which is also recognised in the amendments to the APD as presented by the Commission.[71] It is of importance for national practice that rules on the obligation to communicate are imposed on Member State asylum procedures, including at the appellate level. However, as especially the examples from England and Germany show, the understanding varies between countries as to what information to communicate and how to go about the task in cases of communication. A general obligation to communicate without detailed requirements as to which evidence must be communicated and how this should be done may not be optimal if the goal is to produce quality-enhancing results.

One issue that is still not referred to in EU legislation on appellate asylum procedures is the right to oral hearings at the appellate stage, despite the proposed amendments to the APD and the QD.[72] We have seen that oral testimony in general is important in the asylum context both as a result of lack of other evidence and the crucial importance of credibility in the procedure. Furthermore, oral hearings are also imperative in the sense that they give the decision-maker the opportunity to overcome cultural and linguistic borders and to be direct in communication to the asylum seeker. Further, the oral hearing is of importance to the appellant in terms of communication of evidence, as referred to above.

---

[71] The Commission states that the amendments to the rules on communication are direct results of the need to adapt European asylum procedures to the requirements for effective remedies imposed by both the ECJ and the European Court of Human Rights. Proposal for a Directive of the European Parliament and of the Council on minimum standards of procedures in Member States for the granting and withdrawing of international protection COM (2009) 554/4, Annex: *Detailed Explanation of the Proposal*, 10–11.

[72] The right to an interview at first level decision-making is, in EU legislation, seen as central. Both "old" legislation and proposed legislation require a personal interview to be arranged at the first stage of the procedure. The Charter of Fundamental Rights requirement for a fair trial, in Art 47 further emphasises the requirement for an oral hearing at the appellate stage. *Supra* at 10.

Of the asylum procedures studied, Germany and England have realised the importance of the oral hearing and structured an appellate system which allows for at least one compulsory oral hearing. This does not mean that 100% of all matters are heard orally, as there may also be reasons from the appellant's side to decline the offer of an oral interview. However, in Finnish appellate asylum procedure oral hearings were only offered to a limited number of appellants. The appellate court states that on the one hand it would like to organise more hearings but says on the other hand that oral hearings are not crucial to decision-making even if the credibility of the appellant is at stake.

8. *The Role of National Traditions in Forming National Evidentiary Standards*

Evidentiary practices at the appellate level of asylum decision-making differ between the national asylum procedures included in this study, despite guidance from international and EU law. The last factors of impact to be studied as an explanation of the standards used stem from the national environment and stem from legal practices and traditions in the Member States, linked either to practices or to the institutions, actors or stakeholders in asylum procedure.

We have seen that the national procedures studied all display a need for emphasising certain elements of appellate decision-making, certain links between decision-making and the legal framework in general and also certain institutional factors. However, the points of emphasis are not similar in all countries studied and national appellate asylum procedure is bound to find its own solutions depending on background, framework, legal tradition and the general setting of asylum procedure.

It is clear that the general legal tradition of the national legal system is of importance to the solutions found in terms of evidence in asylum procedure. Firstly, there is the dichotomy between civil and common law traditions that impacts on the European field of asylum law. Secondly, there is also the more precise dichotomy between adversarial procedures and inquisitorial procedures.[73]

---

[73] Most often these two dichotomies go hand in hand: common law implies adversarial procedures, whereas civil law tradition implies inquisitorial procedures. However, this is not always the case and variation between and within national procedural frameworks is also great. Swedish asylum procedure, for instance, is an inherently inquisitorial procedure in which adversarial measures have been introduced during the past decade. Also Jacobini (1991) 125 ff.

For the purpose of this study, the important framework is that of either inquisitorial or adversarial administrative justice procedures and it is clear that the dichotomy here in question can be fairly directly referred back to that between common and civil law traditions.[74] However, the administrative setting and also the special refugee law-induced procedural requirements that affect asylum procedure, to a certain extent diminish and tone down the impact of the dichotomy between common and civil law traditions. As we will see, civil law systems like Germany or Finland also display patterns of adversarial justice in asylum procedure, whereas English procedure steps outside the most rigid forms of understanding of the requirements posed by adversarial justice.[75] Nevertheless, procedural principles, the competences of the decision-maker and the role of the parties to the procedure are all issues of importance to the evidentiary setting directly dependent on the procedure belonging to either the common or the civil law framework.

England presents an asylum procedure that in its appellate stages as a starting point is adversarial in nature in accordance with the common law tradition prevailing in the country. However, the institutional setting of the first instance proceedings to a particular tribunal and the impact of international refugee law render alterations to the most rigid understanding of adversarial justice. Partly, these alterations can be seen in the procedural rules for appellate procedure and partly they are evident from the practice of the Chamber. In the rules, opening up the procedure to evidence that according to general common law and adversarial rules of evidence would not be allowed in a judicial proceeding is a clear departure from the general rules that could be expected to apply as a result of the common law setting.[76] In the practice of the tribunal, the comparably active role of the judge in the proceedings before the tribunal can be seen as specific to the asylum environment. By and large, however, English procedure follows the general understanding of adversarial justice and will thus also interpret the rules imposed by international and European law according to the paradigm of adversarial justice.

---

[74] Jacobini (1991) 75–98 and 99–124.

[75] An example of this is the rule in UK appellate asylum procedure allowing for the First-Tier and Upper Tribunal to circumvent "normal" rules of evidence. The Asylum and Immigration Tribunal (Procedure) Rules, Section 51 (1). The Asylum and Immigration Tribunal (Procedure) Rules 2005 are also in force in relation to the FTT by virtue of Statutory Instrument 2010 No.21 Tribunals and Inquiries: The Transfer of Functions of the Asylum and Immigration Tribunal Order 2010, in force 15.2.2010.

[76] *Ibid.*

As we have seen, a central feature in the adversarial setting of particular importance to appellate asylum procedure is access to and use of legal representatives. As the judge will not actively engage in fact-finding and as procedural strength between the parties is unequally distributed, a clear need exists for action to strengthen the position of the appellant in the name of evidentiary robustness. Legal representation and access to legal aid are typical such actions.[77] Thus, in making rules and guidelines at regional level it is imperative that the central position of legal representation in adversarial settings is taken into account.

In Germany and Finland, appellate asylum procedure is a part of the inquisitorial proceedings of administrative justice, as apparent from the civil law setting of those countries. A vast number of elements to the evidentiary setting of the procedure are clearly characteristic of the inquisitorial environment. The procedure is not a clear cut two-party procedure as the role of the first instance authority in appellate proceedings is often small.[78] The judges are also active in relation to fact-finding. The oral hearing is not as important as in the common law procedure. However, in the asylum context the inquisitorial setting is not completely 'pure', as for instance oral hearings may at times be conducted using adversarial methods of examination.[79]

The framework of national asylum procedure often also determines the links between the particular procedure and frameworks outside the national setting. The importance of such communication is noted in influences on national procedure as such as well as in terms of contributions by national procedure to international refugee law doctrine, for instance. We have seen that English procedure has undertaken a discourse on refugee law with other countries from the common law sphere. This 'group' has proved to be leading in the development of international law standards on international protection. Finland has a tradition of close Nordic cooperation, encompassing countries with the same structure of civil law decision-making as Finland itself.[80] Additionally, asylum procedure is to a certain extent a product of comparisons between fellow Nordic states. In the discourse, the role of human rights and the European framework have always been important, something also reflected in, for instance, early standards on subsidiary protection incorporated in Finnish legislation. Also, very pragmatically, the Nordic

---

[77] In Staffans (2006b) the author discusses the role of legal representation in asylum procedures from an inquisitorial point of view.

[78] The first instance authority in Germany very seldom participates in oral hearings. In Finnish procedure, which is mostly written, the impact of the first instance authority is usually also only that of repeating the grounds for a previous decision.

[79] This was especially noticed in the oral hearing observed in Finnish asylum procedure. Annex I.

[80] See Nykänen *(et al.)* (2010) 15–17, where the impact of the Nordic community on Finland's immigration policy is analyzed.

framework becomes apparent in the use of sources in appellate asylum procedure.

German procedure in this context is outstanding. German appellate procedure is as we have seen inherently inquisitorial and to a certain extent isolated as to its nature. Germany has also succeeded in transposing some of its national norms on procedural asylum law at the European level.[81] However, a characteristic element of German asylum procedure is its confinement to the national environment and a of discourse at international or transnational level.[82] In appellate asylum procedure in Germany, solutions in terms of evidence are based on national considerations. The reasoning of the procedure is formed, not by the standards set by international or regional courts, but by the *Bundesverwaltungsgericht* and the *Bundesverfassungsgericht* and thus has its boundaries within the German sphere. It should also be noted that the supreme courts in their guiding decisions tend to favour an inherently national reasoning as opposed to inclusion of international or regional argumentation.[83] Further, from a more pragmatic point of view, national confinement can also be seen in the fact that very few international sources are used as evidence in German asylum procedure and that national sources are favoured.

Several reasons exist for national confinement in Germany. Pragmatic reasoning regarding the language skills of those involved in appellate asylum procedure and the apparent availability of high standard information within Germany can be taken as an explanation.[84] On the other hand, more abstract views as to the background of the immigration debate in Germany and the role of the Basic law are clearly also of importance.

---

[81]   Of which the QD Art 4 (4) is an example.

[82]   Tiedemann (2010) 78 ff, refers to a "widespread ignorance of foreign jurisprudence by the German administrative judiciary". He continues by stating that "the average German administrative judge does not directly engage with the Refugee Convention" and that "the absence of interest in foreign case law could be attributed to a fixation by domestic administrative courts with national law". In his article Tiedemann points to the fact that even if the highest courts do engage with international sources at time, lower instances as a rule set aside any reflections of international law.

[83]   The same tendencies, but on a different level, can also be found in the general positions of supreme German courts towards the framework of the European Union, clearly displayed in the Solange III /Lisbon decision, BVerfG (30.6.2009) 2 BvE 2/08. See also Jacques Ziller, Solange III (or the Bundesverfassungsgericht's "Europefriendlyness"). On the decision of the German Federal Constitutional Court over ratification of the Treaty of Lisbon, translation of "Solange III, ovvero la *Europarechtsfreundlichkeit* del *Bundesverfassungsgericht*. A proposito della sentenza della Corte Costituzionale Federale Tedesca sulla ratifica del trattato di Lisbona", in (2009/5) *Rivista Italiana di Diritto Pubblico Comunitario* 2009, 973–995.

[84]   Tiedemann (2010) 78–80 argues that difficulties in language is an important reason for the lack of impact of foreign jurisprudence in German asylum procedure.

National confinement impacts on how regional law is received in Germany. It also functions as an impetus for transposing national law to the regional setting where possible. In terms of reception, it is clear that the 'double' theme of proof in German asylum procedure and lack of integrated practice taking into account sources outside the domestic level may lead to structurally rather rigid and technical implementations of regional rules.[85] On the other hand, we have seen that lifting German practice to the EU level may cause divergent understandings of the rules in other Member States.[86]

Partly connected to the setting of national procedures are also elements concerning the institutional structure of first instance appellate asylum procedure. The institutions used for this level of decision-making are in themselves products of the national setting of administrative justice combined with concerns about the optimal way for the particular procedure to organise itself. The English solution implies a form of administrative streamlining of asylum procedure with inclusion of the asylum field under the competences of the First-Tier and Upper Tribunal. In Germany, the procedure is set in the general administrative framework making use of all administrative courts. Finland has chosen a semi-specialised solution with only one district administrative court competent to review decisions on asylum.

These institutional solutions also have effects on the evidentiary standards of procedures. Concrete effects of this kind are linked for instance to the resources available for special fact-finding in matters relating to RSD, specialisation of judges in terms of refugee law and also tacit knowledge on COI and other issues and possibilities for the parties to the procedure to actively take part. Again, there are also abstract implications of the institutional setting: The position of considerations regarding independence in decision-making does seem to depend on the actual institutional possibilities to make such demands. Such decisions tend to be made in institutional settings where the decision-maker has the option in terms of resources and practical possibilities to deny linkages to direct state power. Instead of using databanks provided by the Government, German judges at times conduct their own research. Finnish judges fact-find using their own resources as far as possible but rely on the Research Department of Immigration Services for information that is difficult to find. In England, the comparably vast use of external experts in the procedure is a manifestation of striving towards independence in the procedure.[87] The striving and importance of manifestations

---

[85] UNHCR (2007) and (2010).
[86] Again, divergent interpretations of the practical implications of QD Art 4 (4) serve as a good example.
[87] Cpr Good (2007) 34–37, where anthropological evidence in court trials is described in the light of American social anthropology.

and arguments of independence thus seem to be common to all procedures studied. This can indeed be seen as a reaction against the politicisation of immigration matters in general.

It is interesting to note that all courts seem keen on using the powers vested in them for the benefit of the procedure. All procedures studied show clear signs of a practice which indicates that the more power is given to the court in terms of production of evidence and responsibility for investigations, the less is required of the appellant to the procedure. Further, all procedures show that courts make use of possibilities given them in terms of fact-finding and questioning. Also evidentiary assessment as undertaken in the various countries suggests that national decision-makers are ready to use the knowledge they possess of refugee issues, COI and the like. In both Germany and England, decisions in themselves signal a sense of pride in the thorough work of the courts and tribunal in terms of vast reasoning and attention to detail.

Lastly, there is the issue of streamlining asylum procedure and the impact of this on evidentiary standards. Streamlining here refers to the practice of advocating inclusion of appellate asylum procedure within the framework of other administrative justice procedures. Whereas England has traditionally seen asylum procedure as a rather distinct form of decision-making, inclusion of appellate procedure under the First-Tier and Upper Tribunal clearly implies a shift towards a more streamline-friendly approach.[88] In Germany, both institutional and procedural factors are clear indicators of streamlining, as no specialisation of the courts that handle asylum matters has been institutionally enacted. Another indication of streamlining is the relatively far-reaching embracing of evidentiary standards from the general administrative context in German procedure and imposing particular refugee law-induced standards only in special situations.[89]

---

[88] The move from the AIT to the First-Tier and Upper Tribunal was motivated by reasons of efficiency, procedural economy and fast-tracking the procedure. However, these are all reasons with a result that will inevitably move asylum procedure closer to other procedures handled by the First-Tier and Upper Tribunal. See Tribunal Service: *The Tribunal Procedure (Upper Tribunal) Rules 2008 – consultation on rule amendments for Asylum and Immigration Upper Tribunal Chamber*, available at http://www.tribunals.gov.uk/Tribunals/Documents/Releases/combined_PDF_AIT_consultation2.pdf (visited 23.11.2011).

[89] Evidentiary assessment, where the general administrative framework is used to establish the facts, whereas the special refugee law standard is used only for prognosis, functions as an indicator of the role of general administrative procedures in asylum procedures.

9. Conclusions

National, EU and international law impose requirements on evidentiary standards applicable in appellate asylum procedures. These requirements are most clearly related to particular evidentiary elements in the frameworks presented by national and international law. European law certainly includes rules on evidence but is less clear on the relationship between norms and elements of evidentiary assessment, so that the European rules are thus more material than evidentiary formal in nature. This is also evident when analysing their impact on national procedures.

In the analysis of impacts on national procedures, it is important to see the impact on evidentiary standards by different frameworks outside the national environment as a two-way process. While it is clear that standards imposed on a European or international level influence national procedures, it is equally clear that national procedures influence the requirements imposed by international and EU law. The manner and extent of this influence nevertheless very much depends on traditional and cultural connections between national judicial procedure and the frameworks outside this. Thus, divergences between evidentiary solutions in national procedures and differences between national procedures in complying with and accepting standards from EU or international law at least partly depend on the possibilities for or the willingness of national procedure to influence the requirements imposed. In the end national frameworks hence constitute both the beginning and the end of communication between different frameworks.

As analysis of national procedures shows, any regional rule imposed that sets duties or rights for the decision-maker will have divergent effects in Member States, not only because of the different understandings of the role of the judiciary but also because of divergent practical and institutional possibilities. In order to reach common standards in terms of these issues, there are thus two possibilities: Either the rules take into consideration divergences in institutional and practical frameworks that exist in Member States, or rules imposing common practical outsets are enacted.

Chapter IX

Harmonisation of Procedures in the Common European Asylum System

1. *Outsets*

This chapter concerns the role of EU in the advancing of procedural and evidentiary approximation of Member States' appellate asylum procedures. It asks how EU has influenced national procedures, evaluates the influence and also explores future possibilities.

1.1. *Aims and Competence*

The goal for the EU in work towards commonality in the sphere of asylum as a particular status of immigration is still to create a Common European Asylum System, including a common procedure and uniform status.[1] The Union has gone far along this road and the work has been fairly consistent. However, as the Stockholm programme sums up "There are still significant differences between national provisions and their application".[2] Regardless of whether this statement is understood as implying differences between different national frameworks or between norms and their application, it also goes to the core of challenges for creation of the CEAS in terms of evidence. Harmonised procedural standards are still not the reality of European asylum procedures.[3]

---

[1] The Stockholm programme endorses work towards the CEAS and shifts the focus from legal approximation to practical cooperation and joint ventures in the area of asylum and immigration. Communication from the Commission to the European Parliament and Council: An Area of Freedom, Security and Justice Serving the Citizen, COM(2009)262/4.

[2] *Ibid* at 29. Also the Stockholm programme action plan envisages further steps towards harmonisation only in some years' time, which must be seen as an indicator that much remains to be done to reach present goals.

[3] Joanne van Selm asks whether, to support the harmonised procedure, there can be said to exist a common asylum policy in Europe and suggests that national policies indeed still prevail over European ones. Joanne van Selm, "The Europeanisation of Refugee Policy", in *New Regionalism and Asylum Seekers Challenges Ahead*, eds. Susan Kneebone & Felicity Rawlings-Sanaei, Studies in Forced Migration Vol 20 (New York – Oxford 2007) 79–107 at 85 ff.

On the one hand, it can be questioned whether the minimum standard norms and flexible approaches used in harmonising legislation would imply a high enough degree of commonality to actually form a common procedure even with optimal implementation and application. On the other hand, clearly implementation and application has not been optimal and Member States have struggled to keep up with even the most basic minimum standards.[4] The recent infringement procedure initiated against Greece, where compatibility of Greek asylum procedure with EU minimum standards is questioned, is evidence of poor quality of implementation.[5]

Issues relating to evidence have not been at the forefront in approximation of national asylum procedures nor have procedures at appellate level been given much attention. Indeed, rules and norms are found about both subjects but only to a limited degree. Norms with direct reference to evidentiary issues primarily included in the QD are vague and have not been fully explained by the EU. Thus, implementation has as we have seen been colourful. It is only in the amended APD from October 2009 and June 2011 that appellate level is given broader attention, with additional rules suggested for instance on access to information for legal representatives and the like.[6]

Nevertheless, if the goal is a common procedure, evidentiary issues will inevitably have to be addressed. As this study has shown, divergent norms and practices in the field of evidence do indeed have an impact on the outcomes of procedures either through differently defining the roles of the participants in the procedure, through enforcing different degrees of robustness or through using different thresholds for granting refugee status, resulting in differences in the personal scope of protection. Thus, aside from substantive norms guiding interpretation of criteria for eligibility and access, procedural norms defining how a decision is to be reached must be enforced. Also, the role of the

---

[4] The UNHCR has undertaken a vast study of implementation of the APD in a number of Member States. The results of the study clearly point towards difficulties in interpreting common norms and the prevalence of national traditions and customs in understanding and implementing common norms. UNHCR (2007) and (2010).

[5] Dutch Council for Refugees, Pro Asyl, Finnish Refugee Advice Centre and Refugee and Migrant Justice: Complaint to the Commission of the European Communities concerning failure to comply with community law 10.11.2009 (Failing Member State: Greece).

[6] Council directive 2005/85, OJ 1.12.2005, (L 326) 13 on Minimum Standards on Procedures in Member States for Granting and Withdrawing Refugee Status and Proposal for a Directive of the European Parliament and of the Council on minimum standards of procedures in Member States for the granting and withdrawing of international protection COM (2009) 554/4 and Amended proposal for a Directive of the European Parliament and of the Council on common procedures for granting and withdrawing international protection status (Recast), COM(2011) 319 final, Arts 18 and 19.

appellate level of decision-making as both a court and as a guide for practice in Member States must be taken seriously.[7] The importance of appellate asylum bodies in Europe today stems from their dependence on the legal order in which they function, their important roles as guides of practice and issuers of precedents, and from the fact that strictly in terms of numbers they effectively deliver the final decision in a vast number of asylum matters.[8] Thus the role of appellate bodies as independent decision-makers cannot be neglected.

Evidentiary issues can be focused on either directly or indirectly. We have seen that direct focus paid to evidence in the norms so far implemented has not delivered harmonised practices.[9] Rather, the emphasis has been on the need to recognise the importance of norms with indirect effects on the evidentiary field and use of other measures of convergence than traditional legislative harmonisation.[10] Judges, too, have realised that the EU framework is a patchwork of national legislative practices spiced with interpretations of international law and regional requirements and that uniform implementation of this requires transnational cooperation and work at a much lower level than legislative.[11]

Even if it is clear that evidentiary frameworks must be targeted if the object is to harmonise, the question still remains of Union competence to do so. Article 78 of the TFEU states clearly the goal to reach 'common procedures' as a central focus point in work in the immigration sector.[12] The Union is competent to adopt measures in order to reach the goal of the CEAS, including common procedures. Rather evidently, this has been interpreted as also giving

---

[7] Staffans 2010 examines the position of the appellate organ in the European asylum procedure. Oosterom-Staples (2009) 65–92, argues that the MS obligation to ensure effective remedies for asylum seekers follows inherently from construction of the area of freedom, security and justice, and that also third country nationals are entitled to an effective judicial remedy in order to enforce their individual rights.

[8] On the role of the appellate instance see J Fischman, *Appellate Supervision of Lower Court Decision-Making: Evidence from Asylum Adjudication* (Paper presented at the annual meeting of The Law and Society Association, Hilton Bonaventure, Montreal, Quebec, Canada 27.5.2009).

[9] An example of such direct attention is QD Art 4, which goes directly to issues of evidence.

[10] Also the EU itself has endorsed the idea of new, more practical approaches to harmonisation. The Stockholm programme, *supra* at 1, as well as the 2007 Green Paper on the Future of the Common European Asylum System presented by the Commission 6.6.2007, COM(2007) 301 Final, both focus on possibilities to establish functioning structures for cooperation, common training-schemes and the like.

[11] Member of the Swedish Migration Court in Stockholm Anna Bengtsson in her speech at the conference The Common European Asylum System: Future challenges and opportunities organised by the UNHCR and the Swedish Red Cross, 4.11.2009.

[12] Art 78 TFEU.

the Union the competence to legislate regarding evidentiary matters as long as these are considered to be necessary parts of the common procedure. The rules of evidence included in the rules have at least so far been devised as rules connected to substantive decision-making and thus applicable to all forms of decision-making, regardless of instance or order. However, it is clear that the evidentiary environment is different in the different instances of decision-making and that procedural issues, including evidentiary issues, are given a lift in the transfer from first to appellate instance of decision-making. Thus solutions that are optimal for decision-making at the first level in asylum procedures may not work equally well at appellate level.[13]

However, with regard to the possibilities for procedural legislation over appellate procedures the Union has so far been rather careful.[14] As mentioned, it was only in the negotiations during the autumn of 2009 that more attention was paid to asylum procedures from the standpoint of procedural law.[15] On the one hand, questions of competence and procedural autonomy of Member States are not easily solved in this regard. On the other hand, interference with national judicial procedures is also politically charged and the boundary between state sovereignty and EU competence is here frail.

Lastly, when considering the implications of the results of this study in the light of future developments, the implications of the Treaty of Lisbon must also be taken into account.[16] The Treaty, in force since 1.12.2009, does not imply changes to the procedural environments of asylum procedures or to striving towards commonality in procedures *per se*. However, the Treaty of Lisbon has brought about a number of novelties that clearly will have an impact on the possibilities for the Union to go about harmonisation in the field of evidentiary standards at the appellate level of refugee status determination:

---

[13] Evidentiary rules specifically targeting appellate organs have to a limited extent also been included in the new proposals for the APD, which include rules regarding access to information available to the appellate instance. See Art 41 of the Proposed amendments to the Asylum Procedures Directive, *supra* at 5.

[14] Oosterom-Staples (2009) at 75 ff, argues that the EU so far has refrained from interactivity with national procedures of justice in the form of procedural harmonisation in the name of procedural autonomy, and that the only requirements for procedures from the EU are imposed in the form of general requirements for equivalence and effectiveness. Both values are easily detectable in the limited norms on procedural matters included in the legislation relevant for the asylum field.

[15] In the future asylum procedure, perhaps depending on the vague nature of the procedure as judicial in some Member States, may prove interesting grounds for competition between the EU urge to harmonise and the procedural autonomy of the MS. *Ibid.*

[16] Treaty of Lisbon amending the Treaty on the European Union and the Treaty Establishing the European Community, signed at Lisbon 13 December 2007 (EUT 306 17.12.2007).

Firstly, there is increased access to the ECJ. That is, with the Treaty of Lisbon the ECJ has gained full competence over matters of asylum.[17] Prior to the Treaty, competence was restricted to matters referred to the ECJ by the final national court instance in the matter, which imposed imminent restrictions on access for national courts.[18] It can thus in the future be expected that more guidance and leading interpretations regarding relevant norms will be given by the ECJ. However, it must be remembered that the ECJ in itself is a 'harmonised organ' – a court where judges and decision-makers as persons represent the same diversity which we have seen can lead to difficulties in interpretation of evidentiary standards in refugee status determination.

Secondly, there is the impact of the Charter of Fundamental Rights (CFR).[19] Article 18 of the CFR confirms the right to asylum and the link to the 1951 Convention.[20] However, what is meant by the "right to asylum" is not self-evident, nor is it clear whether the implications of the 1951 Convention with the CFR will receive a different position that that previously enforced by Article 78 TFEU. Thus, the added value of Article 18 is yet to be seen. Aside from Article 18 it is also clear that Article 47 invoking the right to a fair trial for everyone "whose rights and freedoms have been guaranteed by the law of the Union are violated" will also have an impact on the require-ments imposed for appellate procedures in asylum matters. The impact can already be seen in the enhanced procedural appellate rights included in the recast APD. As the Article includes rights similar to the rights included

---

[17] On the implications of the Lisbon Treaty for asylum matters in terms of ECJ competence see Lehte Roots, *The Impact of the Lisbon Treaty on the development of EU immigration legislation* (Conference paper Dubrovnik 21.5.2009). Also Maria Fletcher, "Schengen, the European Court of Justice and Flexibility Under the Lisbon Treaty: Balancing the United Kingdom's 'Ins' and 'Outs'" (2009/1) *European Constitutional Law Review*, 71–98, for consideration of the general implications of the Lisbon Treaty on areas of community legislation where the UK has been able to opt in or out, such as asylum and immigration matters.

[18] See Frances Nicholson, "Challenges to Forging a Common European Asylum System in Line with International Obligations", in *EU Immigration and Asylum Law*, eds. Peers & Rogers (Nijmegen 2006) 505–537 at 516–518.

[19] Charter of Fundamental Rights of the European Union, OJ 7.12.2000 (C364). See Maria-Teresa Gil-Bazo, "The Charter of Fundamental Rights of the European Union and the Right to Be Granted Asylum in the Union's Law" (2008/3) *Refugee Survey Quarterly*, 33–52, for comments on the relationship between the material right to asylum and the CFR.

[20] For comments see EU Network of Independent Experts on Fundamental Rights, *Commentary of the Charter of Fundamental Rights of the European Union* (2006) 170–177. See also Dominick McGoldrick, "The Charter and UN Human Rights Treaties", in *The EU Charter of Fundamental Rights*, eds. Steve Peers & Angela Ward (Oxford and Portland Oregon 2004) 113–114.

in both articles 6 and 13 of the European Convention on Human Rights, the CFR may in fact notably further the procedural rights of asylum seekers, depending on the future interpretation of the article.[21] Inevitably, the ECJ will play a key role in interpreting and determining the scope of rights under the CFR, as also the right to asylum and its relation to the requirement for a fair trial.[22]

Thirdly, and perhaps most importantly, with the Lisbon Treaty the goal for the work of the EU in the field of asylum has shifted from creating *minimum* standards to establishing *common* standards. In the Amsterdam-age the TEC Art 79 stated that the Council was to adopt measures on minimum standards of procedures for RSD. With the Lisbon Treaty the wording has changed to require the Union to adopt measures to reach common procedures in RSD.[23] This shift in terminology clearly opens up the competence of the EU in relation to asylum procedures to measures directly targeted at increasing commonality of procedures. This may entail possibilities for the Union to include more specific, targeted and tailor-made solutions in work towards a common European asylum procedure.

---

[21] European Convention on Human Rights, *supra* at 73. McGoldrick (2004) 116–117 and Dinah Shelton, "Remedies and the Charter of Fundamental Rights of the European Union" in Peers (*et al.*) (2004) 355–359 and EU Independent Experts (2006) 359–371. See also Alfred de Zayas, "The United Nations and the Guarantees of a Fair Trial in the International Covenant on Civil and Political Rights and the Convention Against Torture and Other Cruel, Inhuman or Degrading Treatment or Punishment", in *The Right to a Fair Trial*, eds. David Weissbrodt & Rüdiger Wolfrum (Berlin – Heidelberg – New York 1997) 669–696. See also ECRE (2010) 45–47, where the impact of Article 47 on appellate asylum procedures is assessed.

[22] The CFR may become an interesting bridge between international human rights norms and EU legislation. Allan Rosas, "The European Court of Justice and Public International Law", in *The Europeanisation of International Law The Status of International law in the EU and its Member States*, eds. Jan Wouters, André Nollkaemper & Erika de Wet (Cambridge 2008a) 71–85, describes the role of the ECJ in this respect as the role of both a supreme court and a constitutional court determining amongst others the position of international law as a legal source in the EU legal order. Also Allan Rosas, "International Human Rights Instruments in the Case-Law of the European Court of Justice", in *Teisė besikeičiančioje Europoje / Law in the changing Europe / Le droit dans Une Europe en changement*, Liber Amicorum Pranas Kūris (Vilnius 2008b) 363–382, for consideration of the role of international human rights instruments, as well as refugee law oriented instruments such as the 1951 Convention, in the practice of the European Court of Justice.

[23] Treaty of Lisbon, *supra* at 16, Art 78 (1) states: "The Union shall develop a common policy on asylum, subsidiary protection and temporary protection with a view to offering appropriate status to any third-country national requiring international protection and ensuring compliance with the principle of *non-refoulement.*"

1.2. *From Here...*

The results of harmonising measures in the field of asylum purporting to achieve the CEAP have so far not been satisfactory.[24] There is today no common European asylum procedure and Member States do not comply even with the minimum standards presented in relevant directives.[25] Additionally, the EU itself as external stakeholder representative of Member States has repeatedly stated that the position today is not pleasing. However, steps towards commonality have been taken: Member States have embraced the idea of the CEAS and are actively working towards commonality. Drastic divergences between national procedures in terms of eligibility and categories have been done away with and common ground to build on has been created.[26] Lastly, Member States have grown accustomed to the thought of a common procedure and the CEAS has been embraced nationally.

Several elements are specific to the field of asylum as an object for harmonisation that influence the outcomes of measures taken. In this study of national procedures, the impact of harmonisation on national structures and the challenges observed in existing differences, these elements present themselves as the structures and frameworks posing challenges for the national implementer and often leading to divergent understandings of optimal implementation in Member States.

As has repeatedly been stated, asylum is a procedure of an administrative character. Member States go about administrative conduct and procedures differently, depending on their judicial traditions. A result of divergences in the field is that very few common norms for this sector have been issued by the EU even if general norms and principles regarding for instance effective remedies are valid.[27] Nevertheless, impact on issues within the sector of administrative law has been reached through harmonisation in substantive fields of law and with highly concrete and practical measures. This is also true of harmonisation undertaken in relation to asylum, which remains characterised by relatively

---

[24] Pieter Boeles, Maarten den Heijer, Gerrie Lodder & Kees Wouters, *European Migration Law*, Ius Communitatis III (Leiden 2009) 359, describe the level of harmonisation in the particular field of asylum as "modest".

[25] UNHCR (2007) and (2010). The ECJ will have to take a stand on the difficulties of implementation in the matter brought before the court in relation to infringement of EU rules in Greece, *supra* at 759. Further, as the UK opt-out to amendments to the APD and the QD shows, the will among Member States to create something common may be lacking.

[26] Boeles (*et al.*) (2009) 359, presents creation of EU-wide subsidiary protection status as a clear positive reinforcement to international protection. Cpr McAdam (2005) who does not share the praise.

[27] Oosterom-Staples (2009) 75 ff.

isolated approaches without support in general administrative rules, even if harmonisation certainly does not take place in a vacuum.

The impact of the absence of general guidance for administrative procedures at EU level for national asylum procedures has been further emphasised by the lack of bodies with competence to create such guidelines. It is certain that introduction of a new organ, the EASO, and the increased jurisdiction of the ECJ will have an impact in this respect.

The main impact of harmonising legislation and also the field where the most positive outcomes for harmonisation have been seen are thus in concrete and non-abstract norms such as those regarding eligibility and contents of protection.[28] Relatively far-reaching discussions have been undertaken in the name of harmonisation in relation to the precise meaning of 'serious harm' or other essentially basic questions of substantive asylum law.[29] Abstract rules such as rules on evidence have been greeted with less interest by the European legislator and national implementers.[30]

Many evidentiary issues have not been addressed at all by the European legislator, even if taking into account measures affecting evidentiary issues both directly and indirectly. Article 4 of the QD, the 'main' article concerning evidentiary issues, focuses mainly on robustness and the obligations of the applicant. Standards of proof, the precise contents of the burden of proof, methods of evidentiary assessment are just examples of evidentiary issues that are either left completely outside the picture of Union legislation or are included only as 'side-tracks' to other issues. Also, when analysing the impact of EU legislation on evidentiary standards in national asylum procedures, it becomes apparent that norms outside the articles directly aiming at evidentiary issues may also have disharmonising indirect effects on evidentiary standards. Further, as Article 4 (4) of the QD shows, the EU legislator has not in all instances been sensitive to or aware of the particular and very detailed rules and implications for evidentiary standards practices advocated by the harmonising directives.

---

[28] Central are the Qualification Directive and the Asylum Procedures Directive, Boeles (*et al.*) (2009) 336–357.

[29] *Elgafaji v. Staatssecretaris van Justitie*, C-465/07, 17.2.2009.

[30] Jane McAdam, *The Standard of Proof in Complementary Protection Cases: Comparative Approaches in North America and Europe*. Critical Issues in International Refugee Law Research Workshop at York University, Toronto, May 1–2, 2008 UNSW Law Research Paper No. 2008–50 (2008) presents an analysis of the standard of proof in complementary protection in Europe. In this analysis, it is argued that the main source for evidentiary standards is not EU legislation, but rather international law and human rights law.

The EU legislator has clearly not set aside attention particularly for evidentiary issues and has thus neglected to create a coherent structure for evidentiary standards that could also function outside the first level of decision-making in the procedurally more demanding region of appellate procedures.

However, even when standards are imposed by the European legislator, according to the results of this study national asylum procedures find it difficult to interpret and implement these abstract norms in a way that would enhance commonality between national procedures. This is rather natural since evidentiary standards are interlinked and are also linked to other parts of the procedural framework for appellate procedure, as we have seen in the analysis of national procedures. A change in the burden of proof or in indirect matters such as the right to representation may also have far-reaching consequences outside the evidentiary sphere.[31]

1.3. ... To There

Also the impact of EU harmonising measures on national evidentiary practices can be studied with the aid of the outline of national evidentiary solutions and the framework created for the keys of comparison. Whereas measures towards optimal standards clearly cannot be taken in isolation and the whole of the CEAS needs to move forward in order for the evidentiary field to be furthered, it is still possible to present some basic points of reference for achievements in relation to the individual keys of comparison so far and progress yet to be desired.

1.3.1. Burden of Proof

In terms of the material burden of proof the EU has indeed created a list in Article 4(2) QD, including elements considered to be part of the material burden of proof that can be placed with the appellant. At the same time, the EU, through Article 4 (3) QD listing elements that must be included in evidentiary assessment, has emphasised division of the material burden of proof. These rules apply to the appellate level of decision-making, both indirectly through the formal requirements placed with first instance decisions and directly by also imposing requirements for decision-making at appellate level.

---

[31] Abstract norms, such as those relating to evidentiary issues, are possibly also the norms that suffer most from what Tobias Billström, Swedish minister of Migration at a conference on the CEAS in Stockholm 3-4.11.2009, described as "legislative fatigue in the area of asylum law". Member States are required to deal with a great amount of EU legislation, and it is natural that concrete norms on easily "measurable" issues like eligibility and definitions are the first to benefit from implementing efforts. Abstract norms, such as those regarding evidence, may come in second place and even then may not receive the same attention as the firstly implemented norms.

Differences in understanding the exact contents and implications of the material burden of proof at national level stem from divergences in procedural framework, institutional character and administrative traditions. However, all procedures studied follow common general standards so that differences between national solutions are not dramatic. Alterations of requirements at European level in terms of burden of proof would thus be motivated rather by pure desire to harmonise rather than desire to improve evidentiary standards of national procedures. Nevertheless, it is clear that possible alterations to other elements of the evidentiary framework, such as requirements for robustness or the standard of proof, may require attention to be paid to the implications of such alterations in terms of burden of proof.

1.3.2. *Evidentiary Robustness*
The European Union has taken measures in relation to requirements on evidentiary robustness mainly in the form of lists included in QD Article 4 (2) and (3). In relation to requirements on robustness at first instance proceedings the requirements for a personal interview and calls for representation are also central.

It is clear that the lists include elements regarded as of crucial importance to decision-making. It is also clear that the EU ultimately sees the decision-maker as responsible for inclusion of the elements listed in Article 4 (3) in the evidentiary basis of decisions. Nevertheless, the implications of this requirement on the appellate level remain somewhat unclear, as the institutional competences of the appellate body to interfere with production of evidence in Member States are varied. In terms of desired robustness and minimum requirements placed with evidentiary standards at the appellate level, the current rule is thus not sufficient.

Further in relation to robustness, Member State opinions differ about the need for oral hearings at the appellate stages of asylum procedure. Whereas some states see oral hearings as an inevitable and indispensible part of the proceedings, some view these as rather unnecessary.[32] We have seen that oral hearings *per se* constitute a means for improving robustness of investigations and the evidentiary basis for decisions both qualitatively and quantitatively. Thus, within the reasoning of this study, omission of oral hearings is a clear

---

[32] However, as noted, proposed amendments to the APD suggest that the EU itself views oral hearings at the appellate stage as a self-evident part of the proceedings. Proposal for a Directive of the European Parliament and of the Council on minimum standards of procedures in Member States for the granting and withdrawing of international protection, *supra* at 7, Art 18 (2) (b).

disadvantage to investigatory standards in Member States where these are not conducted. Additionally, there do not seem to exist direct institutional or structural hindrances for increased requirements on the role of oral evidence at appellate level. The reluctance of the EU to interfere in this matter must hence be seen as either a result of intentional or unintentional omission of the importance of oral testimony at the appellate stages of procedure or as an expression of reluctance to interfere in procedural matters in Member States. Disregarding the possible reasons for not imposing requirements to this end, in the eyes of this study EU rules on oral hearings at appellate instances would be a clear advantage and a means of directly increasing quantitative and qualitative standards of robustness in asylum procedures in Europe.

Furthermore, in relation to evidentiary robustness we have seen that communication of evidence is a key to enhancing qualitative standards and that communication can also further quantitative robustness. Communication is seen as an important part of evidentiary work, as evident from the analysis of national appellate asylum procedures, but practical solutions in terms of how to go about communication are not optimal. Additionally, the Commission has signalled that they are aware of the need for coherent practice in this field as new rules on appellate communication have been introduced to the amended APD presented in October 2009 and June 2011.[33] However, the Commission does not go as far as to suggest how communication should be handled or to impose minimum qualitative requirements on the duty to communicate. As Member States today already seem largely to have reached a common understanding that communication is indeed important and as the main hindrance for effective quality enhancement in the form of communication is found in dysfunctional practical outsets, the EU could be making an even higher contribution to evidentiary robustness by being more specific in its requirements.

Last on the list of practical measures enhancing evidentiary robustness of appellate asylum procedures in Europe stands the role and position of legal representatives and legal aid in procedures. Legal representation and availability of legal aid are factors that clearly impact on robustness in any asylum procedure as this study has already shown. We have seen that the adversarial procedure is more dependent on these than inquisitorial procedures. Regardless of the form of procedure, it is thus clear that access to and availability of legal aid are crucial factors if purporting to actually enhance the possibilities of the appellant in asylum procedure to participate in fact-finding and production of evidence. It goes without saying that there is also a strong

---

[33] *Ibid* at Art 19 (1) (b).

linkage to the availability of oral hearings in the procedure. Standards of robustness in general directly depend on possibilities to enhance the procedural power of the appellant. The European Union has indeed recognised the need for legal representation and legal aid and has included articles on the matter in the APD. These, however, are not sufficient to guarantee optimal robustness as the standards imposed allow for exceptions from the main rule on access to legal aid. Furthermore, and even more alarming, is that the rules as they stand today actively enforce disharmonisation in terms of robustness. The restrictions imposed are sensitive to the legal system surrounding asylum procedure and we have seen that restrictions on legal aid weaken the position of the appellant much more in the adversarial procedure than in the inquisitorial.

It is clear that future institutional developments within the EU's field of asylum will also impact heavily on standards of robustness in national appellate asylum procedures. On the one hand, the EASO will clearly also impact on the relevant standards of robustness: qualitatively, through ensuring that data and evidence collected by the office for the purpose of serving national asylum procedures is of a high standard; quantitatively, through ensuring that sufficient information is made available for national decision-makers. On the other hand, the ECJ will also to a higher degree be able to take a stand in matters relating to formal requirements on effective remedies in asylum matters.

1.3.3. *Methods of Evidentiary Assessment*
The EU has not integrated into its norms on asylum or asylum procedures any norms regarding particularly methods or forms of evidentiary assessment, aside of general requirements for individuality, impartiality and objectivity. However, as we have seen, differences in national frameworks in this respect may have far-reaching consequences for harmonisation: differences in methods of assessment and the understanding of the evidentiary playing field today clearly lead to divergences in the basis for decisions and hence to divergences in decision-making outcomes.

Whereas national appellate procedures seem to embrace principles like effectiveness and robustness in evidentiary assessment, a fundamental difference exists in the understanding of the practical means for assessing evidence – the roadmap itself is created differently in different countries, sometimes favouring an 'integrated' and all-encompassing approach to assessment and sometimes favouring a more formalistic and divided approach.

As evidentiary assessment, abstract as it may be, is a momentum of evidentiary work streaming through all other elements, perceptions and uses of evidentiary assessment will inevitably influence the understanding of any other element on the evidentiary map. Is lowering the standard of proof in relation to 'normal' administrative matters relevant for establishing historical factors and risk of future persecution? Can the burden of proof be discharged only with relevance to historical events or must a contribution to the prognosis also be made?

1.3.4. *Standard of Proof*

The standard of proof is a central element to the evidentiary area of asylum law. It is thus somewhat surprising that neither the QD nor the APD take particular notice of the applicable standard of proof in RSD outside the requirement in the definition of a refugee referring to a "well-founded fear" of persecution.[34] We have seen that international law advocates lowering the standard compared to the standard regularly used in civil or administrative procedures. A possible standard of proof could, as seen in Chapter IV, be placed at a slightly higher level though still clearly below general standards for administrative or civil judicial procedures.

Indeed, all procedures studied recognise the need for and possibility to lower the evidentiary threshold in appellate asylum procedure. Nevertheless, the applicable standard is not common for all countries and further the precise use of the standard is divergent in the countries studied. It goes without saying that shifts in the applicable threshold will lead to shifts in decision-making and that harmonisation will not lead to common results if the applicable evidentiary thresholds diverge.

A common indicator of the applicable standard of proof in matters of asylum could certainly be beneficial for harmonisation in the field. It would imply that Member States would be required not only to adjust standards but also and perhaps more importantly that Member States would be required to reflect on the standards used in their procedures. Nevertheless, as this study has repeatedly shown, a common standard does not imply that the standard will be applied coherently. Thus also in relation to the applicable standard of proof, the Union will need to take into account the effects for instance of divergent approaches to evidentiary assessment.

---

[34] In comparison, the QD is explicit when it comes to the standard of proof for subsidiary protection, as in Art 2 (e) it states that a person eligible for subsidiary protection is a "third country national or a stateless person who does not qualify as a refugee but in respect of whom *substantial grounds* have been shown for believing that the person concerned, if returned to his or her country of origin, or in the case of a stateless person, to his or her country of former habitual residence, would face a real risk of suffering serious harm as defined in Article 15, and to whom Arts 17(1) and (2) do not apply, and is unable, or, owing to such risk, unwilling to avail himself or herself of the protection of that country" (emphasis added). See also McAdam (2005) 470 ff, for a study of the standard as prescribed in the Directive in the light of international refugee law.

Finally, the Union must be aware of the standards already imposed. Perhaps the only reference to the standard of proof that the Union has made, in Article 4 (4) of the QD, represents a rule that has been utterly divergently understood by Member States. Sufficient information about the precise requirements of the rule and its relation to requirements presented in international law has not been given to the implementing parties.

2. Working Towards Commonality

2.1. The Limits of Legal Approximation

So far approximation of rules concerning eligibility, definitions and procedures has been the main strategy used by the EU to achieve CEAP. The norms used are both of facultative and binding character and the directives enacted impose both directly applicable rules and minimum standard norms. Whereas the QD, with its emphasis on eligibility and definitions, to a higher degree encompass binding norms, the APD with its focus on procedures in Member States uses the possibilities of flexibility to a higher degree.

The EU has chosen this flexible approach to harmonisation as a first step in a gradual approximation of Member State asylum systems. By establishing at least some common ground, a platform to build on has been created and the Commission itself has expressed that rather than being concerned with detailed matters of quality, the focus in the work so far has been directed towards actually establishing a base, and at times quantity has indeed surpassed quality.[35] Nevertheless, it should be remembered that many of the rules and norms that are flexible have been given this character in the stages of negotiation in the Council and not necessarily in the legislative work of the Commission. Thus, the intention of the Commission has been to establish a stronger base for the work forward than the result of Council negotiations and implementation of directives in the end has produced.

Divergent approaches to asylum, differences in ambitions and goals combined with the flexibility of the rules imposed by the Union have led to Member States being able to pick and choose within the framework of the CEAP. The same rules are not applicable in all appellate asylum procedures and even in instances where the rules are common between some countries their 'standard of rights' – minimum or beyond – may diverge. The legal framework established at European level has thus not yet fully been transposed to national level.

---

[35] Georgia Georgiadu, representative of the Commission of the European Union, Statement at the Nordic Refugee Seminar 6.2.2009.

Further, even in those instances where common norms have been adopted, their application and interpretation vary. Norms do not function in isolation but depend on the frameworks surrounding them even in terms of procedural and institutional environments. Hence, if the EU achieves a network of commonly regulated appellate asylum procedures, there will also be deviations and divergences between procedures. The limit of purely normative approximation is then reached so that other measures must be applied in support of furthering common applications, understandings and interpretations.

Considering the challenges posed to all these national factors that impact on the position of European standards in national procedures, and keeping in mind the goal of the CEAS, it is clear that legal approximation can only be used as a base for developments and that the road ahead must also be built with other bricks than mere substantive harmonisation.

However, it is also imperative to realise that some elements of the external frameworks affecting the functions of EU norms in national appellate asylum procedures are of such a basic nature that these cannot and should not be amended by imposed common European standards. Even if norms can be interpreted and applied and even if application and interpretation can be given guidelines, the history, the administrative system or the jurisprudential legacy of a country will not bend for the CEAS.[36] Achieving a common legal base where the operation, performance and meaning of a norm is more important than the strict wording of the norm may require 'divergences in commonalities' – alternatives to common rules or at times perhaps individualised solutions for the states involved.

Thus, flexibility as a start and end to the CEAP is of utmost importance and must be used carefully within approximation of the legislative base in Member States for the Union in practice to achieve the commonality to which it aspires. Aside from the optimal common base, measures outside normative approximation and possible individualised solutions are nevertheless of vital importance in order to push the base towards the common procedure in practice as well.

2.2. *Means of Convergence*

There are means outside the framework of pure approximation of legal rules that can be used in creating the CEAP and that thus can also impact on the evolution of evidentiary standards of appellate national asylum procedures.[37]

---

[36] However, one can ask whether it is possible that national traditions and jurisprudential legacies may, in time, bend for the EU as such.

[37] Staffans (2010) gives an account of a number of strategies for convergence and their respective implications for judicial protection in asylum matters within the CEAS.

The impact nevertheless can be of either direct effect through particular targeting of issues relating to evidence in this particular procedure or of indirect effect through the targeting of measures and procedural elements indirectly affecting evidentiary standards.

As has been established, normative approximation requires support primarily in the areas of interpretation and application. Aside from this, tailor-made normative solutions may become necessary in order to reach the goals of a common procedure and uniform status.

Of imperative importance in relation to interpretative support is guidance by the ECJ. So far, the ECJ has only had the opportunity to decide on a handful of asylum-related matters due to the restrictions imposed pre-Lisbon on the competence of the court. However, interest from the legal community in these judgments has been notable, especially perhaps from stakeholders in national appellate procedures, so that it can be expected that the judgments indeed have an effect on interpretation of EC law in the field concerned. As an example, reception of the ECJ judgment in *Elgafaji v. Staatssechretaris van Justitie* was somewhat divided.[38] Nevertheless, the judgment produced vast discussion and offered an incentive for stakeholders in the Member States to exchange views and form common opinions. The decision thus must be said to have had effects at national level.

Also the interest shown towards the decisions by the ECJ in cases C-357/09 and in combined cases C-57/09 and C-101/09 is a clear indicator of the importance of ECJ guidance.[39] In the first mentioned matter, the referring court, the *Administrativec sad Sofia-grad* (Bulgaria), quite clearly phrased the questions posed to the ECJ in order to receive as far-reaching harmonising guidance as possible, even relating to interpretation of norms outside the scope of this particular ruling. The second mentioned matters relate to the scope of exclusion from status according to the QD.

Additionally, judges and other stakeholders in national appellate asylum procedures have expressed the urgent need for enactment of measures in order to facilitate transnational dialogue between decision-makers in Member States.[40] Transnational dialogue could support harmonisation of substantive

---

[38] *Supra* at 29.

[39] *Saïd Shamilovich Kadzoev v. Direktsia 'Migratsia' pri Ministerstvo na vatreshnite raboti*, Case C-357/09, European Union: European Court of Justice, 30.11.2009 *and Bundesrepublik Deutschland v. B (C-57/09) and D (C-101/09)*, combined cases C-57/09 and C-101/09, European Union: European Court of Justice, 9.11.2010.

[40] This view was communicated, amongst others, at the conference The Common European Asylum System: Future challenges and opportunities, organised by the UNHCR and the Swedish Red Cross, 5.11.2009.

rules and interpretation of the procedural requirements imposed by EU law, including matters linked to evidentiary assessment. Empirical studies have shown that very little cross-border dialogue today is undertaken within the appellate asylum procedures of Europe and that that dialogue between national procedures today is carried out mainly via international or regional bodies such as the ECJ.[41] Stakeholders call for active support for direct communication between national appellate asylum procedures in order to facilitate dialogue, argumentation and the understanding of the common.[42]

In order to enable dialogue between national procedures, means and facilitators need to be created. The obstacles are, as it seems, not on the side of enthusiasm but rather of a practical nature and there are two sides to the story: On the one hand, access to national practice should be provided. On the other hand, dialogue and communication between national procedures should be facilitated.

Measures facilitating access to national appellate asylum practice should necessarily include measures relating to translation of relevant practice, anonymisation of decisions and creation of a common database. In particular, translation is seen by many commentators as a key factor in advancing transnational communication.[43] Further, facilitation of dialogue should be advanced institutionally in a flexible manner. Communication at present takes place primarily through informal networks of judges and through various professional organisations and bodies.[44] Structures should also be provided within the EU for exchange of practices and views among key stakeholders in national appellate asylum procedures. The future European Asylum Support Office (EASO) could perhaps form a platform for such communication.

Further, common training of stakeholders involved in RSD should be undertaken, including appellate asylum procedure. Such training would in itself function as a part of the measures above-described advancing communication and dialogue. Today, some initiatives towards this end have

---

[41] Lambert (2009) 519–543. See also Mitchel De S.-O.-l'E. Lasser, *Judicial Transformations The rights revolution in the courts of Europe* (Oxford 2009) 226–232, for a consideration of how europeanism is created in courts.

[42] There are also examples of grassroots level attempts to facilitate such dialogue. See for instance www.qualificationdirective.eu/ (visted 23.11.2011).

[43] Translation is of key importance also when it comes to harmonisation of evidentiary standards, as evidentiary issues are often disclosed only through a very careful reading of decisions. In interviews with stakeholders both in Germany and the UK language barriers were often pointed to as hindrance in using decisions from other Member States.

[44] The most prominent of these societies today are the International Association of Refugee Law Judges, and the Immigration Law Practitioners' Association, even if the latter concentrates on UK matters.

indeed been made, as the General Directors' Immigration Services Conference (GDISC) has implemented the European Asylum Curriculum (EAC) – a training instrument aimed at training personnel at first instances of decision-making.[45]

However, in order for training to have optimal results in terms of harmonisation, attention must be paid to the method of training. Presupposing that the aim is also that training is European and 'shared', OMC-related methods such as peer review and exchange of practices must be seen as an imperative part of any advancements. Also the training could, so to speak, build on bottom-up frameworks. On the other hand, training must be shaped with a particular sensitivity to the European field and the legal traditions represented within the CEAS. It must be ensured that training is either all-inclusive or tailor-made to fit the particular procedure and that unnecessarily imposing foreign reasoning on national procedures is avoided.[46] This also includes considerations as to organs and bodies involved.

Aside from ECJ competence, transnational dialogue and appropriate training, it is important to recognise the role of the European Asylum Support Office in European developments.[47] A support office with adequate funding and independent resources will be able to facilitate most of the above measures. Nevertheless, the feasibility of creating support mechanisms within a political structure such as the EASO must be analysed and it must be established that stakeholders will be able and willing to make use of the services of the Office. Without such readiness the possibility arises that investments in harmonisation through the EASO will be obsolete before they begin.

Indeed, the question that must be asked in relation to any measure of convergence undertaken in the CEAS is whether the measure as a matter of fact furthers the goal or if the measure of harmonisation is taken for other reasons. We have seen that flexibility is a must, and that differentiated solutions may also become necessary in order to reach an optimal level of harmonisation especially in the field of evidentiary standards. This reasoning is very much applicable also to any form of supportive harmonising measure since excessive, unreasonable or superfluous harmonising measures can prove to

---

[45] The EAC will, in line with developments at European level, be transferred under the competence of EASO.

[46] The EAC is vastly inspired by the UNHCR-promoted Quality Initiative I, carried out in the UK, which by its nature is firmly focused on common law asylum procedure. This inevitably also affects the EAC, rendering it more sensitive to common law procedures than civil law procedures.

[47] Staffans (2010).

be directly harmful, besides unnecessary. The aim must be to reach optimal common standards and the means for doing so must be adapted to this goal – not the other way around.

3. *Conclusions*

The competence of the EU to interfere with procedural matters in national appellate asylum procedures of Member States derives from competence in material harmonisation within the framework of the creation of the CEAS. Thus, harmonisation in relation to procedural rules and thence evidentiary rules is material to its outset and not formal. Work towards commonality also relies much on traditional means of harmonisation with added support from the ECJ, the Charter of Fundamental Rights and a resolute target to reach commonality in the procedural aspects of RSD.

However, as we have seen the resolution to create common procedures especially at appellate level may in fact imply that other strategies than harmonisation and pan-European rules must be applied. As connections between national procedures and the European level are divergent and as procedural traditions imply divergent understandings of common norms, differentiated approaches could most surely be of use.

Moreover, with reference to what became apparent in analysis of the impact of European, international and national influences on national appellate asylum procedures, it is also important to pay adequate attention to the origins and thus the natural and inherent framework for European norms imposed. National norms lifted to European level must be seen against the background of their origins and their function in this procedure. This, perhaps, is not as much a question of interpretation and understanding, as a question of legislative quality.

Chapter X

Evidence in European Appellate Asylum Procedure

1. *The Goal of Commonality*

Fuelled by the Lisbon agreement and also including developments concerning matters of evidence, the goal of developments in the field of immigration and asylum in the EU is harmonisation of national asylum procedures, including national appellate asylum procedures. The aim is to create a common procedure and uniform status, implying that throughout Europe the same persons are granted the same forms of protection including the same rights and obligations. Creation of common procedures and statuses is seen by the EU as a means of reducing the costs of immigration by diminishing the need for secondary movements and for enforcing the European dimension in policies on immigration and asylum.

Stakeholders, spectators and commentators on developments at European level have often asked whether harmonisation is a feasible means for reaching these overarching goals. Harmonisation is not easily undertaken and harmonising measures may at times do more harm than good – with a view to standards of protection, cost effectiveness and approximation. Further, enforcement of harmonising measures at national level can constitute a momentum for decreased standards of international protection. We have nevertheless seen that the incentive for harmonisation has created a sense of commonality in the European debate on asylum, regardless of the challenges. Elements have been introduced to national asylum procedures that unquestionably raise the bar for acceptable standards of protection in many countries and steps have been taken towards facilitating increased European involvement not only in legislative matters but also in matters of implementation, application and interpretation. Moreover, asylum and immigration as matters of judicial procedure have been lifted to the common agenda and discussion board for states in Europe. The European legislator has also as this study has shown taken a step towards introducing procedural harmonising measures to nationally developed and created asylum procedures.

2. *Evidence in the National Framework*

This study has focused on evidentiary solutions in national appellate asylum procedures in Europe. The study has, in short, concluded that the solutions found and requirements imposed in terms of evidence in national appellate asylum procedures are indeed strictly national. They can on the one hand be influenced by national, regional and international law. On the other hand, national customs and traditions, legal contexts and practices in the field of administrative and asylum law impose limits to inclusion of concerns arising from regional or international sources. Thus, the end results are always national.

Finnish, German and English asylum procedures agree on the importance of evidentiary issues in asylum matters. To a certain extent all these countries also seem to share basic understandings of the most optimal evidentiary structures of asylum procedure. Nevertheless, based on divergences in frameworks and settings, practical solutions for these optimal solutions vary greatly between countries. Additionally, to a varied degree the countries reach their goals of optimality. Further, national asylum procedures differ in their relation to sources of evidentiary standards outside the national environment. In terms of influence at regional or international level and in the national tradition of recognising the importance of such sources, procedures are divergently equipped. Thus, national legal cultures and legal traditions and what these bring along in terms of institutional and procedural solutions do indeed influence creation of the CEAS.

Hence, in relation to pragmatic evidentiary solutions found in national procedures it is clear that the national environment vastly influences choices made. Firstly, the understanding and perception of evidentiary issues in relation to other matters of the procedure diverge depending on the extent to which evidentiary issues can be viewed in isolation through national lenses. Whereas German and Finnish procedure on the one hand provide possibilities for isolation and separation of evidentiary issues from other formal and material concerns in the procedure, and thus creation of evidentiary solutions in isolation, English procedure on the other hand presents a more inherent and intrinsic view of the relationship and provides evidentiary issues with a more native and built-in character. Secondly, this argument and difference can also be applied to the nature of individual elements of national evidentiary assessment. While these in all procedures are separate and can separately be identified, their ties and their inherent functions in the evidentiary system vary. English procedure presents a more all-inclusive, encompassing approach, whereas German and the Finnish procedures apply more isolated evidentiary features.

Divergences in nature do not necessarily affect the meaning or contents of evidentiary elements. However, divergences in nature to a high degree affect the manner in which changes to the system can be made, and also the effects of changes to the system.

3. *Evidence in Common European Asylum Procedure*

The objects for this study are the foundations for and developments in the field of substantive procedural harmonisation of European asylum procedures. It has striven to analyse the basis construed of national procedures and some of the challenges and the tensions inherent in work towards commonality within the particular framework of evidence.

Procedural harmonisation is relatively new, abstract and also difficult to implement, especially in the field of administrative procedures. Procedural harmonisation is, however, also of vital importance for a functioning European sphere of asylum – substantively harmonised rules on standards of protection only become relevant if it can be guaranteed that firstly those benefiting from harmonised standards of international protection are the same persons in all countries and secondly that those benefiting from these standards are those who are indeed in need of international protection and thirdly that all who are in need of international protection according to norms binding on Member States do indeed benefit from substantive standards of protection.[1] The personal scope of protection is determined on the one hand by substantive rules on eligibility. On the other hand, procedural rules on interpretation and assessment, including evidentiary assessment, are key components in determining the boundaries of protection. If these give rise to divergences in practice, the ratio behind approximation and harmonisation is lost.

As this study has shown, the position of evidentiary standards is central to procedural harmonisation. Evidentiary issues must be acknowledged as impacting on the scope of protection and thus on the level of harmonisation but also directly on the standard and quality of asylum procedures in the EU both at the first and appellate levels. Nevertheless, this study has shown that evidentiary issues lie close to the deepest structures of asylum procedure made up of the legal system and the legal tradition surrounding any judicial

---

[1] Further, focus on procedural issues at the European level has effects for development of procedural administrative law on a broader scale. Giacinto della Cananea, "Beyond the State: the Europeanisation and Globalisation of Procedural Administrative Law" (2003/4) *European Public Law*, 563–578.

procedure. With a view precisely to ties to legal traditions and systems, it has been established that common measures do not necessarily entail common effects in the European setting. We have furthermore seen that evidentiary issues are of key importance in comparison of European procedures with the requirements and preconditions for Member States stipulated by binding obligations arising from international law.

The role of appellate procedure is important both due to the large number of cases actually decided at this level and because of the steering effect of the higher procedure on the conduct of administrative authorities in the field. In a broader context, the procedural implications of harmonisation in asylum matters are important lessons for the Union, as it may be expected that harmonisation in the procedural field will be extended to other forms of administrative procedures and frameworks in future integration. The combination of evidentiary issues and appellate procedures is challenging since as we have seen this is a point in asylum procedure where loose frameworks and vast influence of legal practice and traditions are allowed to influence and affect the procedure and the solutions found.

Member States are highly aware of their international obligations, and national practice and traditions have for many years been formed to facilitate these obligations – it is not only a question of Member States being willing to uphold higher standards than the minimum standard imposed by the Union, but also a question of understandings, interpretations (also of EU law) and rooted practices, which cannot be the target for regional harmonisation, being created with reference to obligations arising from international law. Further, as we have seen, these understandings and rooted practices are in themselves to a certain degree sources of international law. Hence, harmonisation in the field of evidentiary standards of appellate asylum procedures cannot be seen as a means either purely for the purpose of harmonising or purely for implementation of optimal evidentiary standards, but must be seen as a combination of these two factors. Only through a harmonised environment of not only defendable but optimal and high evidentiary standards can the goal of a common procedure be reached. In order to reach this goal, it has been established that flexibility and the support of the legislator are vital.

And on the journey towards the goal it is important to remember that commonality is not only found in legal premises of measures taken, nor purely in goals established or perceptions of the position of regional measures. Commonality is also present in will and effort, and it is indeed, in the words of Zenon Bankowski, the 'European journey' itself, and the openness and fluctuations of our legal environment that this journey entails, that provide us with the greatest possibilities.[2] For evidentiary practices, where much is determined by pragmatic concerns, the access to ground for trial and error, to interaction by and among stakeholders and to shared possibilities of learning are crucial elements on the way ahead.

---

[2] Zenon Bankowski, "Europe In and Out", in *European in Search of "Meaning and Purpose"*, ed. Kimmo Nuotio (Helsinki 2004) 21–50.

Annex I

Sources Germany

Interviews

Interviews have been conducted 24.10.2007–6.12.2007 with ten representatives of academia, judges and providers of legal services.

Observations of Hearings

Verwaltungsgericht Karlsruhe 14.10.2007
Verwaltungsgericht Freiburg 6.12.2007

Sources Finland

Interviews

Interviews have been conducted 24.5.2008–9.12.2008 with four judges and providers of legal services.

Observation of Oral Hearing

Helsinki District Administrative Court 7.5.2008

Sources England

Interviews

Interviews have been conducted 25.4.2007–11.5.2007 with six representatives of academia, judges and providers of legal services.

Observations of Hearings

AIT Field House 18.4–16.5.2007

Bibliography

Literature

A. Aarnio, *The Rational as Reasonable. A treatise on Legal Justification* (Dordrecht 1987).

A. Aarnio, *Laintulkinnan teoria* (Juva 1988).

J. Aer, *Oikeussuojan ulottuvuus hallinnossa: hallintolainkäytön antaman oikeussuojan merkitys viranomaistoiminnan auktoriteetin kannalta* (Helsinki 2000).

J. Aer, "Maassa oleskelu ja maasta poistaminen EY-oikeuden välissä" (2001/5) *Defensor Legis*, 879–888.

F. Alink, "Reforming Germany's Constitutional Right to Asylum: A Shifting Paradigm", in *Reform in Europe Breaking the Barriers in Government*, eds. L. Heyse, S. Resodihardjo, T. Lantink & B. Lettinga (Cornwall 2008), 73–87.

M. Appelqvist, "Refugee Law and Case Lawyering: A Swedish Study of the Legal Profession" (2000/1) *International Journal of Refugee Law*, 71–89.

M. E. Badar, "Asylum Seekers and the European Union: Past, Present and Future" (2004/ 8) *International Journal of Human Rights*, 159–174.

R. Bank, "Transposition of the Qualification Directive in Germany", in *The Qualification Directive: Central Themes, Problem Issues, and Implementation in Selected Member States*, ed. K. Zwaan (Nijmegen 2007), 109–126.

Z. Bankowski, "Europe In and Out", in *European in Search of "Meaning and Purpose"*, ed. K. Nuotio (Helsinki 2004), 21–50.

H. Battjes, *European Asylum Law and International Law* (Leiden 2006).

R. J. Beck, "Britain and the 1933 Refugee Convention: National or State Sovereignty" (1999/4) *International Journal of Refugee Law* 4, 597–624.

M. Beckmann, *Europäische Harmonisierung des Asylrechts* (Münster 2001).

J. Bell, "Administrative Law in a Comparative Perspective", in *Comparative Law A Handbook*, eds. E. Öröcö & D. Nelken (Oxford Portland 2007), 287–311.

W. Berg, *Die verwaltungsrechtliche Entscheidung bei ungewissem Sachverhalt* (Berlin 1980).

D. von Beseler, Barbara Jacobs, *Law Dictionary* (Berlin 1971).

P. Birkinshaw, *European Public Law* (Beccles – London 2003).

M. K. Block, J. S. Parker, O. Vyborna & L. Dusek, "An Experimental Comparison of Adversarial versus Inquisitorial Procedural Regimes" (2000/1) *American Law and Economics Review*, 170–173.

P. Boeles, M. den Heijer, G. Lodder & K. Wouters, *European Migration Law*, Ius Communitatis III (Leiden 2009).

P. O. Bolding, *Bevisbörda och beviskrav* Skrifter utgivna av Juridiska Föreningen i Lund Nr 61 (Lund 1983).

P. O. Bolding, *Går det att bevisa?* (Stockholm 1989).

U. Brandl, "Soft law as a source of international and European refugee law", in *European and Refugees: A Challenge?*, eds. J.-Y. Carlier & D. Vanheule (The Netherlands 1997), 203–226.

G. Brinkmann, "The Immigration and Asylum Agenda" (2004/2) *European Law Journal*, 182–199.

E. Brouwer, "Effective Remedies in EU Migration Law", in *Whose Freedom, Security and Justice? EU Immigration and Asylum Law and Policy*, eds. A. Baldaccini, E. Guild & H. Toner (Cornwall 2007), 57–84.

J. Bunker, "Burden Sharing or Burden Shifting? Asylum and Expansion in the European Union" (2006/2) *Georgetown Immigration Law Journal*, 293–322.

N. Burrows & R. Greaves, *The Advocate General and EC Law* (Oxford 2007).

R. Byrne, G. Noll & J. Vedsted-Hansen (eds.), *New Asylum Countries? Migration Control and Refugee Protection in an Enlarged European Union* (The Netherlands 2002).

R. Byrne, G. Noll & J. Vedsted-Hansen, "Understanding Refugee Law in an Enlarged European Union" (2004/2) *European Journal of International Law*, 355–379.

R. Byrne, "Credibility in Changing Contexts: International Justice and International Protection", in *Proof, Evidentiary Assessment and Credibility in Asylum Procedures*, ed. G. Noll (Leiden 2005), 179–194.

G. della Cananea, "Beyond the State: the Europeanization and Globalization of Procedural Administrative Law" (2003/4) *European Public Law*, 563–578.

J.-Y. Carlier, D. Vanheule, K. Hullman & C. Peña Galiano (eds.): *Who is a Refugee? A Comparative Case Law Study* (Leiden 1997).

J.-Y. Carlier, "The Geneva refugee definition and the 'theory of the three scales'", in *Refugee Rights and Realities Evolving International Concepts and Regimes*, eds. F. Nicholson & P. Twomey (Cambridge 1999), 37–54.

J. Cohen, "Of Credibility: Omissions, Discrepancies and Errors of Recall in the Testimony of Asylum Seekers" (2001/3) 13 *International Journal of Refugee Law*, 293–309.

R. Cotterell, "The Concept of Legal Culture", in *Comparing Legal Cultures*, ed. D. Nelken (Dartmouth 1997), 13–31.

P. Craig & G. de Búrca, *EU Law Text, Cases and Materials* (Oxford 2008).

S. Da Lomba, *The Right to Seek Refugee Status in the European Union* (Leiden 2004).

T. von Danwitz, *Europäisches Verwaltungsrecht* (Heidelberg 2008).

I. H. Dennis, *The Law of Evidence* (London 2007).

C. Diesen, *Utevarohandläggning och bevisprövning i brottmål* (Stockholm 1993).

C. Diesen, "Grunderna för bevisvärdering", in *Bevis. Värdering av erkännande, konfrontationer, DNA och andra enstaka bevis*, eds. C. Diesen, J. Björkman, F. Forsman & P. Jonsson (Stockholm 1997), 13–81.

C. Diesen & J.Björkman, *Prövning av flyktingärenden* (Stockholm 1998).

C. Diesen & A. Lagerqvist Veloza Roca, *Bevisprövning i förvaltningsmål* (Stockholm 2003).

N. Doornbos, "On Being Heard in Asylum Cases – Evidentiary Assessment through Asylum Interviews", in *Proof, Evidentiary Assessment and Credibility in Asylum Procedures*, ed. G. Noll (Leiden 2005), 103–122.

M. Duchstein, *Das Internationale Benchmarkingverfahren and seine Bedeutung für den gewerbliche Rechtsschutz* (Heidelberg 2010).

A. Duffy, "Expulsion to Face Torture? *Non-refoulement* in International Law" (2008/3) *International Journal of Refugee Law*, 373–390.

J. Dürig, *Beweismass und Beweislast im Asylrecht* (München 1990).

T. Einarsen, *Retten til vern som flykting I* (Bergen 1998).

P. O. Ekelöf, H. Edelstam & L. Heuman, *Rättegång – fjärde häftet* (Stockholm 2009).

M. Eliantonio, *Europeanisation of Administrative Justice? The Influence of the Ecj's Case Law in Italy, Germany and England* (The Netherlands 2009).

L. Ellison, *The Adversarial Process and the Vulnerable Witness* (Oxford 2001).

A. Favell & R. Hansen, "Markets Against Politics: Migration, EU Enlargement and the Idea of Europe" (2002/4) *Journal of Ethnic and Migration Studies*, 581–601.

C. Filzwieser & B. Liebminger, *Dublin II Verordnung das Europäische Asylzuständigkeitssystem* (Vienna 2006).

M. Fletcher, "Schengen, the European Court of Justice and Flexibility Under the Lisbon Treaty: Balancing the United Kingdom's 'Ins' and 'Outs'" (2009/1) *European Constitutional Law Review*, 71–98.

M.-C. Foblets, "Migration and Integration of Third-Country Nationals in Europe: The Need for the Development of an Efficient and Legitimate System of Governance", in *Rules of Law and Laws of Ruling On the Governance of Law*, eds. F. von Benda-Beckmann, K. von Benda-Beckmann & J. Eckert (Cornwall 2009), 191–216.

G. P. Foxall, "What Judges Maximize: Toward an economic psychology of the judicial utility function" (2004/3) *Liverpool Law Review*, 177–194.

D. Frände, *Finsk straffprocessrätt I* (Helsinki 1999).

D. Frände, *Finsk straffprocessrätt* (Helsinki 2009).

S. Galera, "European legal tradition and the EU legal system: understandings and premises about the rule of law's requirements", in *Judicial review A comparative analysis inside the European legal system*, ed. S. Galera (Council of Europe 2010), 277–299.

N. Garoupa & A. Ogus, "A Strategic Interpretation of Legal Transplants" (2006/2) *The Journal of Legal Studies*, 339–363.

M.-T. Gil-Bazo, "The Charter of Fundamental Rights of the European Union and the Right to Be Granted Asylum in the Union's Law" (2008/3) *Refugee Survey Quarterly*, 33–52.

G. Gilbert, "Exclusion and Evidentiary Assessment", in *Proof, Evidentiary Assessment and Credibility in Asylum Procedures*, ed. G. Noll (Leiden 2005), 161–170.

J. A. Gilboy, "Administrative Review in a System of Conflicting Values" (1988/3) *Law and Social Inquiry*, 515–579.

H. P. Glenn, "Com-Paring", in *Comparative Law A Handbook*, eds. E. Öröcö & D. Nelken (Oxford Portland 2007), 91–108.

A. Good, "'Undoubtedly an Expert?' Anthropologists in UK Asylum Courts" (2004a) *Journal of the Royal Anthropological Institute*, 113–133.

A. Good, "Expert evidence in Asylum and Human Rights Appeals: an Expert's View" (2004b) *International Journal of Refugee Law*, 358–380.

A. Good, *Anthropology and Expertise in the Asylum Court* (Oxford 2007).

G. S. Goodwin-Gill & J. McAdam, *The Refugee in International Law* (Oxford 2007).

G. S. Goodwin-Gill & Héléne Lambert (eds.), *The Limits of Transnational Law* (Cambridge 2010).

B. Gorlick, "Who needs and deserves protection?" (1997/4) *The Indian Journal of International Law*, 677–689.

B. Gorlick, "Common Burdens and Standards: Legal Elements in Assessing Claims to Refugee Status" (2003/3) *International Journal of Refugee Law*, 357–376.

A. Grahl-Madsen, *The Status of Refugees in International Law Vol I* (Leiden 1966).

A. Grahl-Madsen, *The Status of Refugees in International Law Vol II* (Leiden 1972).

K. Groenendijk, "The Long-Term Residents Directive, Denizenship and Integration", in Baldaccini *(et al)* (2007), 429–450.

X. Groussot, *General Principles of Community Law* (Groningen 2006).

E. Guild, "International Terrorism and EU Immigration, Asylum and Borders Policy: The Unexpected Victims of 11 September 2001" (2003/3) *European Foreign Affairs Review*, 331–346.

E. Guild, "Seeking Asylum–Storm Clouds Between International Commitments and EU Legislative Measures" (2004/2) *European Law Review*, 198–218.

M. Haapaniemi, *Virallisperiaate tuloverotuksessa ja tuloveroprosessissa* (Helsinki 2001).

J. Haapasalo, K. Kiesiläinen & J. Niemi-Kiesiläinen, *Todistajanpsykologia ja todistajankuulustelu* (Helsinki 2000).

K. Hailbronner, *A Study on the Asylum Single Procedure ("One Stop Shop") Against the Background of the Common European Asylum System and the Goal of a Common European Asylum Procedure* (European Commission 2002).

K. Hailbronner, "One Single Procedure", in *The Emergence of a European Asylum Policy*, eds. P. de Bruycker & C. D. U. De Sousa (Brussels 2004).

K. Hailbronner, *Ausländerrecht Losblatkommentar* (Heidelberg 2007).

K. Hailbronner, *Asyl- und Ausländerrecht* (Stuttgart 2008).

L. Halila, *Hallintolainkäyttömenettelyn oikeusturvatakeista* (Helsinki 2000).

P. Hallberg, P. Ignatius & H. Kanninen, *Hallintolainkäyttölaki* (Helsinki 1997).

P. Hallberg, *Oikeudenmukainen oikeudenkäynti 2000-luvulla* (Helsinki 2001).

C. Harlow, "Proceduralism in English Administrative Law", in *The Europeanisation of Administrative Law – Transforming national decision-making procedures*, ed. K.-H. Ladeur (Ashgate Darmouth 2002), 46–67.

A. S. Hartkamp, E. H. Hondius & R. Zimmermann, *Towards a European Civil Code* (Nijmegen 2004).

R. Hassemer, W. Hamm & J. Pauly, *Beweisantragsrecht* (Heidelberg 2007).

J. C. Hathaway, "The Evolution of Refugee Status in International Law: 1920–1950" (1984/2) *The International and Comparative Law Quarterly*, 348–380.

J. C. Hathaway, *The Law of Refugee Status* (Toronto 1991).

J. C. Hathway, *The Rights of Refugees under International Law* (Cambridge 2005).

J. C. Hathaway & W. S. Hicks, "Is there a Subjective element in the Refugee Convention's Requirement of 'Well-Founded Fear'?" (2005/2) *Michigan Journal of International Law*, 505–562.

H. Heinhold, *Legal Handbook for Refugees – A Practical Guide Through German Asylum and Alien Law* (Karlsruhe 2000).

M. Henderson, *Best Practice Guide to Asylum and Human Rights Appeals* (ILPA Refugee Legal Group 2003).

B. A. Hepple, "Immigration Appeals Act 1969" (1969/3) *Modern Law Review*, 668–672.

J. Herlihy, P. Scragg & S. Turner, "Discrepancies in autobiographical memories – implications for the assessment of asylum seekers: Repeated interview study" (2002) *British Medical Journal*, 324–327.

J. Herlihy, "Evidentiary Assessment and Psychological Difficulties", in *Proof, Evidentiary Assessment and Credibility in Asylum Procedures,* ed. G. Noll (Leiden 2005), 123–137.

L. Heuman, *Bevisbörda och beviskrav i tvistemål* (Stockholm 2005).

K. Heuru, *Hyvä hallinto* (Helsinki 2003).

N. E. Holm, *Det kontradiktoriske Princip i Forvaltningsprocessen* (Copenhagen 1968).

T. Hupli, *Täytäntöönpanointressi yrityssaneerauksessa* (Helsinki 2004).

A. Hurwitz, "The 1990 Dublin Convention: A Comprehensive Assessment" (1999/4) *International Journal of Refugee Law*, 646–677.

J. Husa, *Julkisoikeudellinen tutkimus* Acta Universitatis Lapponensis N:o 4 (Jyväskylä 1995).

J. Husa, *Johdatus oikeusvartailuun* (Helsinki 1998).

J. Husa, "Valkoista yksisarvista pyydystämässä vai mörköä paossa – 'oikeaa oikeusvertailua'" (2010/5) *Lakimies*, 700–718.

H.B. Jacobini, *An Introduction to Comparative Administrative Law* (New York – London – Rome 1991).

C. Jarvis, "The Judge as Juror Re-visited" (winter 2003) *Immigration Law Digest.*

J. Jonkka, *Todistusharkinnasta* (Helsinki 1993).

S. S. Juss, *International Migration and Global Justice* (Cornwall 2006).

A. Jyränki, "'In fremden Spiegel' – Tankar om jämförande rättsforskning", in *Jämförande juridik: Vad, varför, hur?,* ed. M. Suksi (Turku 1996), 9–24.

M. Kagan, "Is Truth in the Eye of the Beholder?" (2003/3) *Georgetown Immigration Law Journal,* 367–415.

D. K. Kagehiro & W. C. Stanton, "Legal vs. Quantified Definitions of Standards of Proof" (1985/2) *Law and Human Behavior*, 159–178.

A. Keane, *The Modern Law of Evidence* (Oxford 2006).

M. Kenny, "Standing Surety in Europe: Common Core or Tower of Babel?" (2007/2) *Modern Law Review*, 175–196.

A. Kiralfy, *The Burden of Proof* (Abingdon 1987).

P. Kirchhof, "Europäische Integration", in *Handbuch des Staatsrechts,* eds. J. Isensee & P. Kirchhof (Heidelberg 1992), 857–873.

J. van der Klaauw, "Towads a Common Asylum Procedure", in *Implementing Amsterdam: Immigration and Asylum Rights in EC Law,* eds. E. Guild & C. Harlow (Oxford 2001), 165–193.

H. T. Klami, *Empirical Studies on Finnish Evaluation of Evidence* A research plan (Turku 1986).

H. T. Klami, M. Rahikainen & J. Sorvettula, *Todistusharkinta ja todistustaakka* (Helsinki 1987).

H. T. Klami, "Kommentarer till diskussionen om bevisvärde och bevisbörda", in *Rätt och sanning,* ed. H. T. Klami (Uppsala 1990), 67–70.

H. T. Klami, *Todistusratkaisu* (Helsinki 2000a).

H. T. Klami, *Oikeusvertailun erityiskysymyksiä* (Publications of the Institute for Jurisprudene Helsinki 2000b).

H. T. Klami, M. Gräns &J. Sorvettula, *Law and Truth: A theory of evidence* (Helsinki 2000).

M. Knuts, "Lectio" (2010/3) *Tidskrift utgiven av Juridiska Föreningen i Finland,* 285–292.

M. Knuts, *Kursmanipulation på värdepappersmarknaden* (Helsinki 2010).

J. Kokott, *Beweislastverteilung und Prognoseentscheidungen bei der Inanspruchnahme von Grundrechten und internationalen Menschenrechten,* Beiträge zum ausländischen öffentlichen Recht und Völkerrecht (Berlin – Heidelberg – New York 1993).

F. O. Kopp & W.-R. Schenke, *Verwaltungsgerichtsordnung Kommentar* (München 2007).

Korkein Hallinto-oikeus/Högsta förvaltningsdomstolen, *Päätösten perustelemisen kehittäminen/Utvecklande av beslutens motivering* (Helsinki 1996).

P. Kourula, *Broadening the Edges: Refugee definition and international protection revisited* (The Hague 1997).

P. J. van Krieken (ed.), *The Asylum Acquis Handbook The Foundations for a Common European Asylum Policy* (Leiden 2000).

H. Kulla, *Hallintolainkäyttö ja hallinto* (Helsinki 1980).

H. Kulla, "Oikeusvertailu ja eurooppalainen hallinto-oikeus", in *Jämförande juridik: Vad, varför, hur?*, ed. M. Suksi (Turku 1996), 39–51.

H. Kulla, *Hallintomenettelyn perusteet* (Helsinki 2008).

K. H. Kunert, "Some Observations on the Origin and Structure of Evidence Rules Under the Common Law System and the Civil Law System of 'Free Proof' in the German Code of Criminal Procedure" (1966/1) *Buffalo Law Review*, 122–164.

T. Kuosma, *Legal Conditions of Refugees in Finland* (Helsinki 1993).

T. Kuosma, *Ulkomaalainen, pakolainen, turvapaikanhakija* (Helsinki 1999).

H. Lambert, "Transnational Judicial Dialogue, Harmonization and the Common European Asylum System" (2009/3) *International and Comparative Law Quarterly*, 519–544.

H. Lambert & G. S. Goodwin-Gill (eds.), *The Limits of Transnational Law: Refugee Law, Policy Harmonization and Judicial Dialogue in the European Union* (Cambridge 2010).

H. Lambert & R. Husain, "British Judiciary's Search for Reciprocal Relations" in *The Limits of Transnational Law: Refugee Law, Policy Harmonization and Judicial Dialogue in the European Union*, eds. Hélène Lambert & Guy S. Goodwin-Gill (Cambridge 2010), 127–131.

J. Lappalainen, *Siviilioikeus II* (Helsinki 2001).

J. Lappalainen, D. Frände, E. Havansi, R. Koulu, J. Niemi-Kiesiläinen, A. Nylund, J. Rautio, J. Sihto & J. Virolainen, *Prosessioikeus* (Helsinki 2007).

J. Lawis, *Immigration and Asylum Law Bench Book* Court of Appeal Civil Division (London 2007).

M. De S.-O.-l'E. Lasser, *Judicial Transformations The rights revolution in the courts of Europe* (Oxford 2009).

A. Leggatt, *Tribunals for Users One System* (London 2001).

P. Legrand, "European legal systems are not converging" (1996/1) *International and Comparative Law Quarterly*, 52–81.

P. Legrand, "The impossibility of legal transplants" (1997/4) *Maastricht Journal of European and Comparative Law*.

P. Legrand, "Uniformity, Legal Tradition, and Law's Limits" (1996–1997/2) *Juridisk Tidskrift*, 307–322.

A. Leitzinger, *Ulkomaalaiset Suomessa 1812–1972* (Helsinki 2008a).

A. Leitzinger, *Ulkomaalaispolitiikka Suomessa 1812–1972* (Helsinki 2008b).

J. Lewis, *Immigration and Asylum Law Bench Book* (Court of Appeal Civil Division 2007).

X. Lewis, "The Europeanisation of the Common Law", in *Transfrontier Mobility of Law*, eds. R. W. Jagtenberg, E. Örükü & A. J. de Roo (The Hague 1995), 47–61.

B. Lindell, *Sakfrågor och rättsfrågor* (Uppsala 1987).

B. Lindell, *Civilprocessen* (Uppsala 1998).

B. Lindell, *Civil Procedure in Sweden* (Uppsala 2004).

U. Liukkonen, "Oikeuden yhdentäminen ja kansallinen diversitetti – näkökulma eurooppalaiseen kansainväliseen yksityisoikeuteen ja oikeusvertailuun" (2010/5) *Lakimies*, 739–755.

P. L. Martin, "Germany: Reluctant Land of Immigration", in *Controlling Immigration A Global Perspective*, eds. W. A. Cornelius, P. L. Martin & J. F. Hollifield (Stanford 1994), 189–215.

R. Marx, *Aufenthalts-, Asyl- und Flüchtlingsrecht* (Frankfurt a M 2005a).

R. Marx, *Handbuch zur Flüchtlingsanerkennung – Erläuterlungen zur Richtlinie 2004/83/EG* (Frankfurt a M 2005b).

R. Marx, *Aufenthalts-, Asyl- und Flüchtlingsrecht in der anwaltlichen Praxis* (Frankfurt a M 2007).

J. McAdam, "The European Union Qualification Directive and the Creation of a Subsidiary Protection Regime" (2005/3) *International Journal of Refugee Law*, 461–516.

I. A. Macdonald & F. Webber, *Immigration Law and Practice in the United Kingdom* (London 2005).

D. McGoldrick, "The Charter and UN Human Rights Treaties" in *The EU Charter of Fundamental Rights*, eds. S. Peers & A. Ward (Oxford Portland Oregon 2004), 83–122.

A. Meyerstein, "Returning the Harmonization EU Asylum Law: Exploring the Need for an EU Asylum Appellate Court" (2005/5) *California Law Review*, 1509–1555.

S. Mineur, "Förhör i flyktingärenden", in *Prövning av flyktingärenden*, eds C. Diesen & J.Björkman (Stockholm 1998), 267–296.

N. Mole, *Asylum and the European Convention on Human Rights* (Council of Europe 2008).

M.-A. Monnier, "The Hidden Part of Asylum Seekers' Interviews in Geneva, Switzerland: Some observations about the socio-political construction of interviews between gatekeepers and the powerless" (1995/3) *Journal of Refugee Studies*, 305–325.

O. Mårsäter, *Folkrättsligt skydd av rätten till domstolsprövning* (Uppsala 2005).

O. Mäenpää, *Hallinto-oikeus* (Helsinki 2003).

O. Mäenpää, *Hallintoprosessioikeus* (Helsinki 2007a).

O. Mäenpää, *Oikeudenkäynnin julkisuus hallintotuomioistuimissa* (Helsinki 2007b).

O. Mäenpää, *Hallintolaki ja hyvän hallinnon takeet* (Helsinki 2008a).

O. Mäenpää: *Julkisuusperiaate* (Helsinki 2008b).

O. Mäenpää: *Julkisuuslaki* (Helsinki 2008c).

D. Nassimpian, "National legal tradition – United Kingdom", in *Judicial review A comparative analysis inside the European legal system*, ed. S. Galera (Council of Europe 2010), 157–172.

D. Nelken, "Comparatist and Transferability", in *Comparative Legal Studies: Traditions and transitions*, eds. P. Legrand & R. Munday (Cambridge 2003), 437–466.

D. Nelken, "Defining and Using the Concept of Legal Culture", in *Comparative Law A Handbook*, eds. E. Öröcö & D. Nelken (Oxford Portland 2007), 109–132.

F. Nicholson, "Challenges to Forging a Common European Asylum System in Line with International Obligations", in *EU Immigration and Asylum Law*, eds. Peers & Rogers (Nijmegen 2006), 505–537.

J. Niemi-Kiesiläinen, *Pakolaisoikeus* (Helsinki 1989).

M. Niemivuoto & M. Keravuori, *Hallintolaki* (Helsinki 2003).

M. Nierhaus, "Administrative Law", in *Introduction to German Law*, eds. W. F. Ebke & M. W. Finkin (Leiden 1996), 96–100.

G. Noll, *Negotiating Asylum. The EU Acquis, Extraterritorial Protection and the Common Market of Deflection* (Dordrecht 2000).

G. Noll, "Formalism vs. Empiricism: Some Reflections on the Dublin Convention on the Occasion of Recent European Case Law" (2001/1–2) *Nordic Journal of International Law*, 161–182.

G. Noll, "Risky games? A Theoretical Approach to Burden-Sharing in the Asylum Field" (2003/3) *Journal of Refugee Studies*, 236–252.

G. Noll (ed), *Proof, evidentiary assessment and credibility in asylum procedures* (Leiden 2005a)

G. Noll, "Salvation by the Grace of State? Explaining Credibility Assessment in the Asylum Procedure", in *Proof, Evidentiary Assessment and Credibility in Asylum Procedures*, ed. G. Noll (Leiden 2005b), 197–214.

G. Noll, *Evidentiary assessment and the EU qualification directive* New Issues in Refugee Research UNHCR Working Paper No. 117 (Geneva 2005c).

G. Noll, "Evidentiary Assessment Under the Refugee Convention: Risk, Pain and the Intersubjectivity of Fear" in *Proof, Evidentiary Assessment and Credibility in Asylum Procedures*, ed. G. Noll (Leiden 2005d), 141–157.

G. Noll, "Asylum Claims and the Translation of Culture into Politics" (2006/3) *Texas International Law Journal*, 491–501.

E. Nykänen, E. Pirjatanniemi, I. Staffans & O. Sorainen, *International Encyclopeadia of Migration Law Finland* (The Netherlands 2010).

E. Nykänen, *Fragmented State Power and Forced Migration: Study on Non-State Actors in Refugee Law* (Turku forthcoming 2011).

A. Nylund, *Tillgången till den andra instansen i tvistemål* (Helsinki 2006).

C. Ovey & R.C.A White, *European Convention on Human Rights*, (Oxford 2006).

H. Oosterom-Staples, "Effective Rights for Third-Country Nationals?", in *A Right to Inclusion and Exclusion? Normative fault lines of the EU's area of freedom, security and justice*, ed. H. Lindahl (Oxford 2009), 65–92.

A. Peczenik, *Vad är rätt? Om demokrati, rättsskerhet, etik och juridisk argumentation* (Gothenburg 1995).

S. Peers, "EU Immigration and Asylum Law: Internal Market Model or Human Rights Model?", in *European Union Law for the 21st Century: Rethinking the New Legal Order*, ed. T. Tidimas (Oxford 2004).

S. Peers & N. Rogers (eds.), *EU Immigration and Asylum Law* (Leiden 2006).

M. Pellonpää, *Turvapaikkaoikeiden myöntäminen* (Helsinki 1974).

M. Pellonpää, *Alueellisen turvapaikkaoikeuden myöntäminen* (Helsinki 1976).

A. Popovic, "Evidentiary Assessment and Non-Refoulement: Insights from Criminal Procedure" in *Proof, Evidentiary Assessment and Credibility in Asylum Procedures*, ed. G. Noll (Leiden 2005) 27–56.

D. Prawitz, "Några filosofiska synpunkter på rationell argumentation i juridiken", in *Rationalitet och empiri i rättsvetenskapen* Juridiska Fakulteten i Stockholm skriftserien nr 6, eds. A. Peczenik, D. Praqitz, T. Eckhoff, L. Lindahl & J. Hellner (Stockholm1985).

P. Pölönen, *Henkilötodistelu rikosprosessissa* (Helsinki 2003).

H. Quaritsch, *Recht auf Asyl* (Berlin 1984).

J. C. Reitz, "How to Do Comparative Law" (1998/4) *American Journal of Comparative Law*, 617–636.

P. Roberts & A. Zuckerman, *Criminal Evidence* (Oxford 2010).

A. Rosas, "The European Court of Justice and Public International Law" in *the Europeanisation of International Law The Status of International law in the EU and its Member States*, eds. J. Wouters, A. Nollkaemper & E. de Wet (Cambridge 2008a), 71–85.

A. Rosas, "International Human Rights Instruments in the Case-Law of the European Court of Justice", in *Teisė besikeičiančioje Europoje / Law in the changing Europe / Le droit dans Une Europe en changement*, Liber Amicorum Pranas Kūris (Vilnius 2008b), 363–382.

C. Rousseau, F. Crépeau, P. Foxem & F. Houle, "The Complexity of Determining Refugeehood: A Multidisclipinary Analysis of the Decision-making Process of the Canadian Immigration and Refugee Board" (2002/1) *Journal of Refugee Studies*, 43–70.

A. S. Rudolph, "Sakkunniga som bevismedel i flyktingärenden", in C. Diesen & J.Björkman, *Prövning av flyktingärenden* (Stockholm 1998), 299–245.

O. Ryynänen, *Bevisning i inkomstbeskattningen* (Helsinki 2000a).

O. Ryynänen, *Proof in income tax assessment and litigation* (Helsinki 2000b).

M. Saarelainen, *Perusteltu pelko* (Helsinki 1996).

R. Sainsbury, "Administrative Justice: Discretion and Procedure in Social Security Decision-Making", in *The Uses of Discretion*, ed. K. Hawkins (Oxford 1992), 295–329.

T. Saranpää, *Näyttöenemmyysperiaate riita-asioissa* (Helsinki 2010).

L. Schelin, *Bevisvärdering av utsagor i brottmål* (Stockholm 2006).

J. van Selm, "The Europeanlization of Refugee Policy", in *New Regionalism and Asylum Seekers Challenges Ahead*, eds. S. Kneebone & F. Rawlings-Sanaei (New York – Oxford 2007), 79–107.

D. Shelton, "Remedies and the Charter of Fundamental Rights of the European Union", in *The EU Charter of Fundamental Rights*, eds. S. Peers & A. Ward (Oxford Portland Oregon 2004), 355–359.

H. G. Sicakkan, "Political Asylum and Sovereignty-Sharing in Europe" (2008/2) *Government and Opposition*, 206–229.

O. F. Sidorenko, *The Common European Asylum System* (The Hague 2007).

R. Siltala, *Oikeustieteen tieteenteoria* (Helsinki 2003).

E. Smith, "Bevisoptagekse og bevisvurdering", in *Asyl i Norden*, Dansk Flyktinghjälp (Copenhagen 1990), 89–101.

I. Staffans, "The Appellate Organ in the Asylum Procedure" (2006a/4) *Nordic Journal of International Law*, 89–119.

I. Staffans, "Biträdet i asylärenden – utsikter för en omorganisering" (2006b/3) *Defensor Legis*, 483–493.

I. Staffans, "Convergence and Mutual Recognition in European Asylum Law" in *The Internationalization of Law and Legal Education*, eds. J. Klabbers & M. Sellers (The Hague 2008), 149–168.

I. Staffans, "Judicial Protection and the Future Common European Asylum System" (2010/3) *European Journal of Migration and Law*, 273–297.

A. J. Stedman & B. Hawkin, *A practical guide to presenting asylum and human rights claims* (UK 2003).

A. Stening, "Konflikt mellan två bevismodeller" (1979/4) *Svensk Juristtidning*, 283–296.

D. Stevens, *UK Asylum Law and Policy: Historical and Contemporary Perspectives* (London 2003).

O. Suviranta: *Virkamiesten ratkaisutoiminta ja Euroopan yhteisön oikeus* Suomalaisen lakimiesyhdistyksen julkaisuja A-sarja N:o 207 (Helsinki 1996).

J. A. Sweeney, "Credibility, Proof and Refugee Law" (2009/4) *International Journal of Refugee Law*, 700–926.

M. Symes & P. Jorros, *Asylum Law and Practice* (Wiltshire 2010).

V. Tarukannel & H. Jukarainen, *Oikeudenkäynti hallintotuomioistuimessa* (Helsinki 1999).

G. Teubner, "Legal Irritants: Good Faith in British Law or How Unifying Law Ends Up in New Divergences" (1998/1) *Modern Law Review*, 11– 32.

E. R. Thielemann, "Between Interests and Norms: Explaining Burden-Sharing in the European Union" (2003/3) *Journal of Refugee Studies*, 253–273.

R. Thomas, "Asylum Appeals Overhauled Again" (2003) *Public Law*, 260–271.

R. Thomas, "Evaluating tribunal adjudication: administrative justice and asylum appeals" (2005/3) *Legal Studies*, 462–498.

R. Thomas, "After the Ouster: review and reconsideration in a single tier tribunal" (2006/4) *Public Law*, 674–686.

R. Thomas, "Risk Legitimacy and Asylum Adjudication" (2007/1) *Northern Ireland Legal Quarterly*, 49–77.

R. Thomas, "Consistency in Asylum Adjudication: Country Guidance and the Asylum Process in the United Kingdom" (2008/4) *International Journal of Refugee Law*, 489–532.

R. Thomas, "Administrative Justice and Asylum Appeals A Study of Tribunal Adjudication" (Cornwall 2011).

P. Tiedemann, "Foreign Asylum Jurisprudence in German Courts", in *The Limits of Transnational Law*, eds. G. S. Goodwin-Gill & H. Lambert (Cambridge 2010), 57–84.

H. Tolonen, *Oikeuslähdeoppi* (Helsinki 2003).

W. Treiber, "Politische Verfolgung im Kontext eines Bürgerkrieges: Anmerkungen zur deutschen Entscheidungspraxis", in *Aktuelle asylrechtliche Probleme der gerichtlichen Entscheidungspraxis in Deutschland, Österreich und der Schweiz*, eds. K. Barwig & A. Brill (Baden-Baden 1996), 33–60.

A. Triandafyllidou, *Immigrants and National Identity in Europe* (London 2001), 55–76.

K. Tuori, *Critical Legal Positivism* (Cornwall 2002).

K. Tuori, *Sosiaalioikeus* (Helsinki 2004).

A. Tähti, *Periaatteet Suomen hallinto-oikeudessa* Suomalaisen Lakimiesyhdistyksen Julkaisuja No 205 (Helsinki 1995).

K. Törnudd, *Finland and the International Norms of Human Rights* (Leiden 1986).

E. M. Ucarer, Managing Asylum and European Integration: Expanding Spheres of Exclusion" (2001/2) *International Studies Perspectives*, 288–304.

C. Varga, "Common Law and Civil Law: Encounters", in *Comparative Legal Cultures*, ed. C. Varga (Dartmouth 1992), 101–172.

J. Vedsted-Hansen, "Common EU Standards on Asylum – Optional Harmonization and Exclusive Procedures?" (2005/4) *European Journal of Migration and Law*, 369–376.

V. Vevstad, *Refugee Protection A European Challenge* (Oslo 1998).

V. Vevstad, *Utvikling av et felles europeisk asylsystem* (Universitetsforlaget Oslo 2006).

H. Vihriälä, "Diesenin metodin soveltamisesta tuomioistuimen ratkaisutoiminnassa talousrikoksissa", in *Rikostuomion perusteleminen*, eds. M. Huovila, R. Lahti & T. Ojala (Helsinki 2005), 281–300.

H. Wagenaar, "'Knowing' the Rules: Administrative Work as Practice" (2004/6) *Public Administration Review*, 643–656.

N. Walker, "In Search of the Area of Freedom, Security and Justice: A Constitutional Odyssey", in *Europe's Area of Freedom, Justice and Security*, ed. Neil Walker (Oxford 2004), 3–37.

S. Weidlich, "First Instance Asylum Procedures in Europe: Do Bona Fide Refugees Find Protection" (2000/3) *Georgetown Immigration Law Journal*, 643–672.

T. Wilhelmsson, *Critical Studies in Private Law* (Dordrecht 1992).

R.E. Wraith & P.G. Hutchesson, *Administrative Tribunals* (London 1974).

H. Zahle, "Competing Patterns for Evidentiary Assessments", in *Proof, Evidentiary Assessment and Credibility in Asylum Procedures*, ed. G. Noll (Leiden 2005), 13–26.

A. de Zayas, "The United Nations and the Guarantees of a Fair Trial in the International Covenant on Civil and Political Rights and the Convention Against Torture and Other Cruel, Inhuman or Degrading Treatment or Punishment", in *The Right to a Fair Trial*, eds. D. Weissbrodt & R. Wolfrum (Berlin – Heidelberg – New York 1997), 669–696.

J.Ziller, *Solange III (or the Bundesverfassungsgericht's "Europefriendlyness")*. On the decision of the German Federal Constitutional Court over ratification of the Treaty of Lisbon, translation of "Solange III, ovvero la *Europarechtsfreundlichkeit* del *Bundesverfassungsgericht*. A proposito della sentenza della Corte Costituzionale Federale Tedesca sulla ratifica del trattato di Lisbona", in (2009/5) *Rivista Italiana di Diritto Pubblico Comunitario* 2009, 973–995.

A. Zimmermann, *Das neue Grundrecht auf Asyl* (Berlin – Heidelberg 1994).

R. Zimmermann, "Roman law and the harmonization of private law in Europe", in *Towards a European Civil Code*, eds. A.S. Hartkamp & Martijn Hesslink (Nijmegen 2004), 21–42.

K. Zwaan (ed.), *The Procedures Directive: Central Themes, Problem Issues and Implementation in Selected Member* States (Nijmegen 2008).

K. Zweigert & H. Kötz, *An Introduction to Comparative Law* (Amsterdam – New York 1977).

K. Zweigert & H. Kötz, *Einführung in die Rechtsvergleichung* (Tübingen 1996).

International Organizations

Council of Europe, *Asylum Seekers and Irregular Migrants in Turkey*, Report by the Committee on Refugees, Migration and Population, Doc. 10445 (Geneva 2005).

Dutch Council for Refugees, Pro Asyl, Finnish Refugee Advice Centre and Refugee and Migrant Justice: Complaint to the Commission of the European Communities concerning the failure to comply with community law 10.11.2009 (Failing Member State: Greece).

ECRE, *Analysis of the Treaty of Amsterdam in so far as it relates to asylum policy* (London 1997) 5–6.

ECRE, *ECRE Information Note on the Council Directive 2004/83/EC of 29 April 2004* (London 2004).

ECRE, *Memorandum to SCIFA – Improving the Functioning of the Dublin System* ECRE document AD7/8/2006/EXT/CW/RN (London 2006).

ECRE, *The Impact of the EU Qualification Directive on International Protection* (London 2008).

ECRE, *The EU must stop slamming door at refugees* (press release 28.10.2009)

ECRE, *Comments from the European Council on Refugees and Exiles on the European Commission Proposal to recast the Asylum Procedures Directive* (2010).

EU Network of Independent Experts on Fundamental Rights: *Commentary of the Charter of Fundamental Rights of the European Union* (2006).

Red Cross, *Freedom, Security and Justice: What will be the Future? Consultation on priorities of the European Union for the next five years* Opinion of the National Red Cross Societies of the Member States of the European Union and the International Federation of Red Cross and Red Crescent Societies (2008).

Red Cross, *Proposal for a Directive on minimum standards for the qualification and status of third country nationals or stateless persons as beneficiaries of international protection and the content of the protection granted, Proposal for a Directive on minimum standards on procedures in Member States for granting and withdrawing international protection*. Opinion of the National Red Cross Societies of the Member States of the European Union and the International Federation of Red Cross and Red Crescent Societies (2010).

UNHCR, *Handbook on Procedures and Criteria for Determining Refugee Status under the 1951 Convention and the 1967 Protocol relating to the Status of Refugees* (Geneva 1992).
UNHCR, *Note on Burden and Standard of Proof in Refugee Claims* (Geneva 1998).
UNHCR, *Note on the Applicability of Article 1 D of the 1951 Convention relating to the Status of Refugees and Palestine Refugees* (Geneva 2002).
UNHCR, *Asylum in the European Union: A Study on the Implementation of the EC Qualification Directive* 7.11.2007 (Geneva 2007).
UNHCR, *Improving Asylum Procedures Comparative Analysis and Recommendations for Law and Practice* (Geneva 2010).
UNHCR, *The Implementation of the Asylum Procedures Directive* (Geneva 2010).

Papers, Speeches and Presentations

A. Bengtsson, The Common European Asylum System: Future Challenges and Opportunities, Red Cross and UNHCR seminar, Stockholm, 4.11.2009.
T. Billström (Swedish minister of Migration), *Legislative fatigue in the area of asylum law*, conference on the CEAS in Stockholm 3–4.11.2009.
J.-F. Durieux, *Salah Sheekh is a Refugee New insights into Primary and Subsidiary Forms of Protection* Refugee Studies Centre Working Paper Series No. 49 (Oxford 2008).
J. Fischman, *Appellate Supervision of Lower Court Decision-Making: Evidence from Asylum Adjudication* (Paper presented at the annual meeting of the The Law and Society Association, Hilton Bonaventure, Montreal, Quebec, Canada 27.5.2009).
G. Georgiadu (representative of the Commission of the European Union), Statement at the Nordic Refugee Seminar 6.2.2009.
E. Guild, *The Biopolitics of Refugee Law*, Paper presented at the Nordic Refugee Seminar, 5–6.2.2009.
P. Hallberg, *Perusoikeudet ja oikeusvaltion periaatteet*, speech given at the Seminar for Leading Prosecutors, Turku, 22.9.2000.
J. McAdam, The Standard of Proof in Complementary Protection Cases: Comparative Approaches in North America and Europe. *Critical Issues in International Refugee Law Research Workshop at York University, Toronto, May 1–2, 2008 UNSW Law Research Paper No. 2008–50.*
L. Roots, *The Impact of the Lisbon Treaty on the development of EU immigration legislation* (Conference paper Dyubrovnik 21.5.2009).
A. Rosas, *Justice in Haste, Justice Denied? The European Court of Justice and the Area of Freedom, Security and Justice*, The Mackenzie-Stuart Lecture, University of Cambridge, 6.11.2008.
D. Post & A. Niemann, *The Europeanisation of German asylum policy and the "Germanisation" of Europan asylum policy: The case of the "safe third country" concept* (Paper prepared for the conference of the European Union Studies Association EUSA Montreal May 2007).
V. O. Wiebe, *Maybe You Should, Yes You Must, No You can't. Shifting Standards and Practices for Assuring Document Reliability in Asylum Cases* University of St. Thomas School of Law Legal Studies Research Paper No. 06–18 (2006).

Case Law

European Court of Human Rights

Cruz Varas and Others v. Sweden, 46/1990/237/30, Council of Europe: European Court of Human Rights, 20 March 1991.

Vilvarajah and Others v. The United Kingdom, 45/1990/236/302–306, Council of Europe: European Court of Human Rights, 26 September 1991.

Chahal v. The United Kingdom, 70/1995/576/662, Council of Europe: European Court of Human Rights, 15 November 1996.

Potocka and Others v. Poland, Appl. No. 33776/96, Council of Europe: European Court of Human Rights 4 October 2001.

Salah Sheekh v. The Netherlands, Appl. No. 1948/04, Council of Europe: European Court of Human Rights, 11 January 2007.

Saadi v. Italy, Appl. No. 37201/06, Council of Europe: European Court of Human Rights, 28 February 2008.

European Court of Justice

C-357/09 *Saïd Shamilovich Kadzoev v. Direktsia 'Migratsia' pri Ministerstvo na vatreshnite raboti*, European Union: European Court of Justice, 30 November 2009.

C-57/09; C-101/09 *Bundesrepublik Deutschland v. B (C-57/09) and D (C-101/09)*, European Union: European Court of Justice, 9 November 2010.

C-465/07 *Elgafaji v. Staatssecretaris van Justitie*, European Union: European Court of Justice, 17 February 2009.

C-33/76 *Rewe-Zantralfinanz eG and Rewe-Zentral AG v. Landwirtschaftskammer für das Saarland* European Communities: European Court of Justice, 16 December 1976.

C-14/83 *Von Colson and Kamann v. Land Nordrhein-Westfalen*, European Communities: European Court of Justice, 10 April 1983.

C-213/89 *R. v. Secretary of State for Transport, ex parte Factortame Ltd. and Others*, European Communities: European Court of Justice, 19 June 1990.

C-430–431/93 *Van Schijndel & Van Veen V. Stichting Pensioenfonds voor Fysiotherapeuten*; European Communities: European Court of Justice, 14 December 1995.

C-70/95 *Sodemare SA, Anni Azzurri Holding SpA and Anni Azzurri Rezzato Srl v Regione Lombardia*. European Communities: European Court of Justice, 17 June 1997.

C-120/97 *Upjohn v. The Licensing Authority*, European Union: European Court of Justice, 21 January 1999.

C-228/98 *Dounias v. Ypourgio Oikonomikon*, European Union: European Court of Justice, 3 February 2000.

C-526/04 *Laboratoires Boiron SA v. URSSAF de Lyon*, European Union: European Court of Justice, 7 September 2006.

C-244/00 *van Doren + Q. GmbH v. lifestyle and sportswear Handelsgesellschaft mbH*. Opinion of Advocate General Stix-Hack. European Union: European Court of Justice, 18 June 2002.

German Courts

BVerfG (2.7.1980) 54, 341 (361) 1980.
BVerfG (26.11.1986), 74, 51 [64].
BVerfG (1.7.1987) 76, 143 f.
BVerfG (10.10.1989) 80, 315 f.
BVerfG (10.8.2000) 2 BvR 260/98 und 1353/98 – NVwZ 2000, 1165.
BVerfG (30.6.2009) 2 BvE 2/08.

BVerwG (22.1.1985) 9 C 52.83.
BVerwG (14.12.1993) 9 C 45.92.
BVerwG (20.2.2001) 9 C 20.00.
BVerwG (18.7.2006) 1 C 15.05.
BVerwG (24.6.2008) 10 C 43.07.
BVerwG (14.10.2008) 10 C 48.07.
BVerwG (21.4.2009) 10 C 11.08.
BVerwG (24.11.2009) 10 C 11.08.
BVerwG (27.4.2010) 10 C 5.09.
BVerwG (1.6.2011) 10 C 25.10.
BGH 14.6.2005 – 5 StR 129/05.
Bayerischer VGH 14.11.2007, 23 B 07.30496, 8.
VGH Baden-Württemberg 17.6.1998 A 14 S 1178/98.
VGH Baden-Württemberg 26.10.2006 13 S 1799/06.
VGH Baden-Württemberg 11.12.2008 A 5 S 1251/06.
VG Karlsruhe 22.4.2002 A8 K 12204/00.
VG Karlsruhe, 13.2.2007A 11 K 11438/05.
VG Karlsruhe 6.2.2009 A 1 K 2018/08.
OVG Nordheim-Westfalen 27.7.2007 13 A 2745/04.A.

Finnish Courts

KHO 2006:1872 (11.8.2006).
KHO 2007:47 (12.7.2007).
KHO 2008:21 (3.4.2008).
HO 03/0027/7 (20.1.2003).
HO 05/892/1 (21.6.2005).
HO 05/1924/1 (8.12.2005).
HO 05/1940/1 (13.12.2005).
HO 06/0076/1 (23.1.2006).
HO 06/0761/1 (30.5.2006).
HO 06/0884/1 (21.6.2006).
HO 06/1325/1 (21.9.2006).
HO 06/1451/1 (13.10.2006).
HO 06/1505/1 (25.10.2006).
HO 06/1689/1 (5.12.2006).
HO 07/0043/1 (24.1.2007).
HO 07/0106/1 (30.1.2007).
HO 07/0161/1 (13.2.2007).
HO 07/0163/1 (14.2.2007).
HO 07/0201/1 (27.2.2007).
HO 07/0253/1 (8.3.2007).
HO 07/0274/1 (14.3.2007).
HO 07/0401/3 (15.3.2007).
HO 07/0402/3 (15.3.2007).
HO 07/0474/1 (20.4.2007).
HO 07/0779/3 (23.5.2007).
HO 07/0700/1 (4.6.2007).
HO 07/0716/1 (5.6.2007).
HO 07/0826/1 (26.6.2007).
HO 07/1213/1 (28.9.2007).
HO 08/0274/1 (18.2.2008).

English Courts

R v. Governor of Pentonville Prison, Ex parte Azam; R v. Secretary of State for the Home Department, Ex parte Khera; R v. Secretary of State for the Home Department, Ex parte Sidhu, [1973] 2 All ER 741, [1973] 2 WLR 949.

R v. Secretary of State for the Home Department, Ex parte Sivakumaran and Conjoined Appeals (UN High Commissioner for Refugees Intervening), [1988] AC 958, [1988] 1 All ER 193, [1988] 2 WLR 92, [1988] Imm AR 147.

Abdi and another v. Secretary of State for the Home Department and another, [1996] 1 All ER 641, [1996] 1 WLR 298, [1996] Imm AR 288.

Ali Haddad v Secretary of State for the Home Department [2000] INLR 117 (IAT).

Kaja v Secretary of State for the Home Department [1995] Imm AR 1.

Kacaj (Unreported, IAT, Appeal No. *23044/2000,* 19 July 2001).

Karanakaran v. Secretary of State for the Home Department, [2000] EWCA Civ. 11.

MT (Algeria), RB (Algeria), U (Algeria) v. Secretary of State for the Home Department, [2007] EWCA Civ 808.

Sepet and Bulbul v Secretary of State for the Home Department (UN High Commissioner for Refugees intervening) [2001] Imm. A.R. 452 at 488.

Kajac v Secretary of State for the Home Department [2001] UKIAT 00018.

R v. Secretary of State for the Home Department, ex parte Thangarasa; R v. Secretary of State for the Home Department, ex parte Yogathas, [2002] UKHL 36.

Ahmed v. Secretary of State for the Home Department [2002] UKIAT 00439.

Klodiana Kacaj v. Secretary of State for the Home Department, [2002] EWCA Civ 314, United Kingdom: Court of Appeal (England and Wales).

SY (Kurd – No Political Profile) Syria v. Secretary of State for the Home Department, CG [2005] UKIAT 00039.

IN v Secretary of State for the Home Department [2005] UKIAT 00106.

Detamu v Secretary of State for the Home Department [2006] EWCA Civ 604.

AA (Iran) -v- Secretary of State for the Home Department [2006] EWCA Civ 1027.

International Legal Sources and Legislative Material

Arrangement with regard to the Issue of Certificates of Identity to Russian Refugees 13 LNTS 237 (1921).
Arrangement with regard to the Issue of Certificates of Identity to Russian and Armenian Refugees Supplementing and Amending the Previous Arrangements 89 LNTS 47 (1926).
Arrangement concerning the Legal Status of Russian and Armenian Refugees, 89 LNTS 53 (1928).
Convention relating to the International Status of Refugees 159 LNTS 199 (1933).
Convention Concerning the Status of Refugees coming from Germany 192 LNTS 59 (1938).
The Universal Declaration of Human Rights adopted and proclaimed by General Assembly resolution 217 A (III) of 10 December 1948.
General Assembly Resolution 319 A (IV) (1949).
General Assembly Resolution 428 (V) (1950).
Convention for the Protection of Human Rights and Fundamental Freedoms, 4.11.1950, ETS 005.
Convention relating to the Status of Refugees, Adopted on 28 July 1951 by the United Nations Conference of Plenipotentiaries on the Status of Refugees and Stateless Persons convened under General Assembly resolution 429 V) of 14 December 1950, 189 UNTS 150.
Protocol to the Convention Relating to the Status of Refugees, approved by the Economic and Social Council in Resolution 1186 (XLI) 18.11.1966 and UN General Assembly Resolution 2198 (XXI) 16.12.1966.
Convention against Torture and Other Cruel, Inhuman or Degrading Treatment or Punishment, 10.12.1984, UNTS 24841.
The Schengen Agreement, 14 June 1985.
Convention Determining the State Responsible for Examining Applications for Asylum Lodged in one of the Member States of the European Communities, OJ 5.6.1990 (C 254), 1.

European Union Legal Sources and Legislative Material

Treaty on the European Union, signed 7.2.1992, OJ 7.2.1992 (C 191).
Treaty of Amsterdam, signed 2.10.1997, OJ 2.10.1997 (C 340).
The Schengen acquis OJ 22.9.2000 (L 239), 0019–0062.
Charter of Fundamental Rights of the European Union, OJ 7.12.2000 (C364).
Treaty of Lisbon amending the Treaty on the European Union and the Treaty Establishing the European Community, signed 13 December 2007 (EUT 306 17.12.2007).
Council directive 2001/55, OJ 20.7.2001 (l 212) 12.
Council directive 2003/9, OJ 27.1.2003, (l 31) 18.
Council directive 2004/83, OJ 29.4.2004 (L 304) 12.
Council directive 2005/85, OJ 1.12.2005, (L 326) 13.
Council decision 2000/596, OJ 28.9.2000, (L 252) 12.
Council decision 2004/904, OJ 2.12.2004, (L 381) 52.
Council regulation 2757/2000, OJ 11.12.2000 (L 316) 1.
Council regulation 343/2003, OJ 18.2.2003 (L 50) 1.
Presidency Conclusions from the Council Meeting in Tampere 15 -16.10.1999.
The Hague-Programme, Strengthening freedom, security and justice 13.12.2004, 6054/04.
European Union, Council and Commission Action Plan implementing the Hague Programme on strengthening freedom, security and justice in the European Union, 12.8.2005, 2005/C 198/01.
Proposal for a Directive of the European Parliament and of the Council on common standards and procedures in Member States for returning illegally staying third country nationals, 1.9.2005, COM(2005) 391 final,

The Council and Commission Action Plan implementing the Hague Programme on strengthening freedom, security and justice in the European Union, 10.6.2005, COM(2005) 491.

Communication from the Commission to the Council and the European Parliament on Strengthened Practical Cooperation: New Structures, New Approaches: Improving the Quality of Decision Making in the Common European Asylum System, 17.2.2006, COM(2006) 67.

Green Paper on the Future of the Common European Asylum System presented by the Commission, 6.6.2007, COM(2007) 301 final.

Proposal for a Regulation of the European Parliament and of the Council establishing the criteria and mechanisms for determining the Member State responsible for examining an application for international protection lodged in one of the Member States by a third-country national or a stateless person, COM(2008) 820 final.

Court of Justice of the European Union, Information for the Press, *A New Procedure in the Area of Freedom, Security and Justice: the Urgent Preliminary Ruling Procedure* 3.3.2008.

Proposal for a Regulation of the European Parliament and of the Council establishing a European Asylum Support Office, COM(2009) 66 final.

Multiannual Programme for an area of Freedom, Security and Justice serving the citizen (Stockholm Programme), 16.10.2009, COM(2009) 262.

Communication from the Commission to the European Parliament and Council: An Area of Freedom, Security and Justice Serving the Citizen, COM(2009) 262/4.

Proposal for a Council Decision on requesting comparisons with EURODAC data by Member States' law enforcement authorities and Europol for law enforcement purposes, COM(2009) 342 final.

Proposal for a Directive of the European Parliament and of the Council on minimum standards for the qualification and status of third country nationals or stateless persons as beneficiaries of international protection and the content of the protection granted, COM(2009) 551.

European Commission Proposal for a Directive of the European Parliament and of the Council on minimum standards on procedures in Member States for granting and withdrawing international protection, COM(2009) 554/4.

Communication from the Commission to the European Parliament, the Council, the European Economic and Social Committee and the Committee of the Regions: Delivering an area of freedom, security and justice for Europe's citizens, COM(2010) 171 final.

Amended proposal for a Directive of the European Parliament and of the Council on common procedures for granting and withdrawing international protection status (Recast), COM(2011) 319 final.

National Legal Sources and Legislative Material

Germany

Strafprozessordnung (RGBl I 1877, S. 253).
Grundgesetz (BGBl I 1949, S. 1)
Asylverordnung (BGBk. 1. 1953, S. 3).
Ausländergesetz (BGBl. 1. 1965, S. 353).
Gerichtsverfassungsgesetz (BGBl. I 1975, S. 1077).
Asylverfahrensgesetz (BGBl 1978 I, s. 1107).
Beratungshilfegesetz (BGBL I 1980, 689).
Asylverfahrensgesetz (BGB1. I 1982, S. 946).
Grundgesetz (BGBl 1987 I, S 89).
Ausländergesetz (BGBl I 1990, 1354–1356).
Verwaltunggeritchtsordnung (BGBl. I 1991, S. 686).
Gesetz zur Änderung des Grundgesetzes (BGBl. I 1993, S. 1002).
Gesetz über das Bundesverfassungsgericht 11.11.1993 (BGBl. I S. 1473)

Beratungshilfegesetz (BGBl I 1999, S. 2400).
Aufenthaltsgesetz (BGBl I 2004, S. 1950).
Zuwanderungsgesetz (BGBl. 2004 I, S. 1950).
Zivilprozessordnung (BGBl. I S. 3202; 2006 I S. 431; 2007 I S. 1781)
Gesetz zur Umsetzung aufenthalts- und asylrechlicher Richtlinier der Europäischer Union (BGBl 2007 I, S 1970).

Finland

Government Bill for the Aliens Act 47/1990.
Government Bill proposing the Aliens Act 28/2003.
Government Bill 166/2007 amending the Aliens Act.
Government Bill 86/2008 amending the Aliens Act.
Code on Judicial Procedures (4/1734).
Aliens Decree (27/7.2.1930).
Aliens Decree (182/1958).
Aliens Decree (187/1958).
Aliens Act (400/1983).
Decree imposing Changes to the Ministry of the Interior (78/1989).
Aliens Act (378/1991).
Decree on the Asylum Board (448/1991).
Act on Administrative Judiciary Procedures (586/1996).
Act on Administrative Courts (430/1999).
Act on the Openness of Government Activities (621/1999).
The Constitution (731/1999).
Act on Legal Aid (257/2002).
Administrative Procedure Act (434/2003).
Aliens Act (301/2004).
Act on the Supreme Administrative Court (1265/2006).
Act on the Publicity of Administrative Court Proceedings (381/2007).
The Administrative Asylum Guidelines – Turvapaikkaohje SM 109/032/2008.
Ministry of Interior: *Näkökulmia turvapaikkapolitiikkaan* (2009).
Finnish Immigration Service: Annual Report 2008 (Helsinki 2009).

England

Immigration Appeals Act (1969).
The Asylum and Immigration Appeals Act (1993).
The Special Immigration Appeals Commission Act (1997).
Nationality, Immigration and Asylum Act (2002).
Guidance Note on Unrepresented Appellants Who Do Not Understand English (12.8.2004).
Asylum and Immigration (Treatment of Claimants, etc) Act (2005).
Asylum and Immigration Tribunal (Procedure) Rules 2005, Statutory Instrument 2005 No. 230.
Immigration Advisory Service, *Country Guideline cases: benign and practical?* (2005).
Immigration Advisory Service: *Submission to APCI: An Analysis of Home Office Country Reports* 2005.
Answers by Mr Justice Hodge in oral evidence before the House of Commons Home Affairs Committee's inquiry, *Immigration Control* (2005–2006 HC 775-iv) (2006).
Tribunal Service: *The Tribunal Procedure (Upper Tribunal) Rules 2008 – consultation on rule amendments for Asylum and Immigration Upper Tribunal Chamber* (2008).
Tribunal Procedure (Upper Tribunal) Rules 2008, Statutory Instrument 2008 No. 2698 (L 15).
Consultation, *Immigration Appeals Fair Decisions; Faster Justice* (2008).

The Tribunal Service: Transferring asylum and immigration appeals into the unified tribunal structure Q&A (2008).

Asylum policy instruction *Assessing credibility in asylum and human rights claims* (2009).

Legal Services Commission's Funding Code Criteria (2009)

Tribunals and Inquiries: The Transfer of Functions of the Asylum and Immigration Tribunal Order 2010, Statutory Instrument 2010 No.21.

Miscellaneous

Black's Law Dictionary, West Publishing, Centennial edition (1991).

Statskontoret, *En tydligare styrning av Migrationsverket* 2004:20.

The Michigan Guidelines on Well-Founded Fear as presented at the Third Colloquium on Challenges in International Refugee Law, University of Michigan Law School, 26-28.3.2004.

Immigration and Refugee Board of Canada: Interpretation of the Convention Refugee Definition in the Case Law (2005).

Sweden: Act on Administrative Procedure (1971/291).

Sweden: Aliens Act (2005/716).

Index